Unit Studies Made Easy

A Guide to Simplified Learning at Home

Valerie Bendt

Other books by Valerie Bendt:

(See pages 329-334 for more information)

Making the Most of the Preschool Years

The Frances Study Guide

Creating Books with Children

Successful Puppet Making

Reading Made Easy: A Guide to Teach Your Child to Read

Front cover and back cover artwork: original acrylic paintings by
Liz Ann Alvarez

ISBN: 1-885814-13-5

Bendt Family Ministries

333 W. Rio Vista Court

Tampa, FL 33604-6940

813-758-6793

www.ValerieBendt.com

Table of Contents

Dedication

I would like to dedicate this book to my loving husband who has encouraged and supported me in our homeschooling journey for these many, many years.

In the early 1980s — during the "olden days" in the modern history of homeschooling, even before the Christian textbook companies would sell to home educators — a small movement was afoot by parents using Living Books to teach their children.

The term Living Books, which was introduced to America through Susan Schaeffer Macaulay's book, *For the Children's Sake*, brought a new understanding of educational philosophy and books in particular.

For the Children's Sake highlighted the philosophy of Charlotte Mason, an educator who lived in Victorian England at the turn of the last century. Miss Mason treated children as real people who were created in the image of God. She believed that children needed to experience and observe creation, live full lives, and feed their minds and hearts on lofty ideas and Living Books, not twaddle.

Living Books are usually written by one author, whose love of his or her subject shines through, begging the book to be read again and again by people of all ages. In fact, C.S. Lewis defines Living Books as those that "capture the issues of life in such a way that they challenge the intellect, they inspire the emotions, and they arouse something noble in the heart of the reader." He also noted, "No book is really worth reading at the age of ten which is not equally (and often far more) worth reading at the age of fifty and beyond."

Reference and resource books are the second category of books. Even these can be Living Books. Just read a few definitions in *Noah Webster's American Dictionary of the English Language*, published in 1828. It is truly a Living Book!

Twaddle, however, is usually written by a committee of people. Though each person might love the subject being covered, that love doesn't shine through, but instead is dumbed down and uninteresting. Twaddle pretends to teach something meaningful, but does not deliver truth, purpose, or vitality to the reader's heart. Therefore, most children and adults have no desire to re-read textbooks.

As I reflect on the history of modern home education, another landmark event took place in the mid-1980s. Shortly after Macaulay's *For the Children's Sake* was published, American educator, Dr. Ruth Beechick, whose philosophy is similar to Charlotte Mason's in many respects, played a major role in the shaping of our philosophy.

Dr. Beechick's many books, especially *The Three Rs* and *You Can Teach Your Child Successfully*, lay a firm understanding for both *why* and *how* to teach reading, writing, and arithmetic in a very simple and straightforward manner, without the use of textbooks. Dr. Beechick's methods freed families to teach the basics and use Living Books for everything else.

At about the same time there was an awakening among Christian home educating couples to allow God to plan their families, and often they were blessed with more than the typical 1.5 children. So, homeschooling mothers stayed home with their children — allowing the family to discover, learn, and think together in the God-designed environment of the home.

This was the time that the friendship between the Bendt and

Farewell families was born. Because some of the Bendt children were a bit older than ours, Bruce and Valerie became our friends, but also our mentors and teachers. We spent many hours, yes, even days together, discussing educational philosophy, ideas, methods, books, religion, politics, the Constitution, health, and even midwifery.

In those early days we were often frustrated because we were unable to find excellent teaching materials designed for home-style learning rather than school-style learning. Another complication was teaching children of multiple ages. This frustration motivated many homeschool parents to give workshops, and design and publish excellent curriculum.

As Valerie Bendt presented workshops on the methods she used with her family, countless moms and dads were enamored with its simplicity. A feeling of "I can do this!" pervaded the rooms where she spoke. This led Valerie to write *How to Create Your Own Unit Study*, revolutionizing and simplifying existing methods of teaching, making the unit study concept simple and attainable for both small and large families. Her simple pattern allows families to study a subject together, teaching to the strength of each child and encouraging their individual interests and passions.

Valerie's methods dispel the myth of grade levels and curriculum, allowing instead the freedom of parents to obey the Holy Spirit in the education of their children. Her methods are a refreshing oasis in the desert of "You must study this for that grade level." When the whole family enjoys a subject together, unity and joy are more likely to reign instead of disjointedness and confusion.

Focusing on one major subject at a time is a natural way to learn. A unit study can last for a few minutes or for a lifetime and is for all ages — toddler through adult. For example, think about how many books you read when you were fifteen years old on the subject of pregnancy and labor. Probably very few, if any. But I'll bet you studied several books when you were pregnant with your first child. If you did this, you did a unit study: you learned in a natural way!

In 2004, mothers and fathers are asking the same questions they did in the early 1980s. They are searching for something special for their families. Perhaps they are unable to verbalize their questions, just as we couldn't back then, but when they hear the simple philosophy and methods explained, they know they've found the right answers.

The answers are simple, but thought provoking. Education within God's context of the home is part of the answer. The rest of the answer is experiencing God's Word, experiencing the life He gave us at this time in His story, and experiencing Living Books in the quest for faith, wisdom, and knowledge, building precept upon precept.

Allow Valerie and others who have walked before you to come alongside you and show you His glorious path!

Tina Farewell   March 3, 2004
Lifetime Books and Gifts
Lake Wales, Florida
www.LifetimeBooksandGifts.com

*I*n 1990 I published the first edition of ***How to Create Your Own Unit Study***. It began as a pamphlet to explain how my family conducts unit studies. I found I was spending lots of time on the phone and in person detailing our methods to interested homeschooling parents. I decided to write a pamphlet, as I told my husband, for I was sure it would save me lots of time in counseling with families. Well, this pamphlet grew into a book, and three other books focusing on unit studies soon followed. This decision to write our methods did not eliminate the time problem, as I found I was now being asked to speak to homeschool groups. However, the books did allow me to communicate our ideas with more individuals than in the past.

Over the last 14 years I have conducted workshops and have loved getting to know homeschooling families across the country. The internet has opened up yet another means of communicating with fellow homeschoolers all over the world. It is hard to believe there was ever a time when we had to strain to find another homeschooling family with which to fellowship. Walk into a curriculum fair display hall, and you will find it almost impossible to believe that it was once a struggle to find curriculum materials.

Now it is 2004, and I have more information to share about unit studies and how they have been a blessing to our family. Rather than rewrite my four unit study titles, I have decided to edit them somewhat and compile them in one easy-to-use volume.

In the next chapter, *Biblical Parenting or Schooling at Home?*, I detail our more recent educational pursuits, and then I move back in time to my first book, ***How to Create Your Own Unit Study***. After this I proceed to ***The Unit Study Idea Book***, followed by ***For the Love of Reading***, and ending with ***Success with Unit Studies***. I have deleted some references made to materials that are no longer available and added information about newer materials I feel are worthwhile; however, I have tried to keep the essence of these four books intact to preserve our family's educational experiences as they happened. You will also find some repetition from one "book" to the next. Hopefully you will not find this tedious, but you will look at it as a review of material that I feel is most significant.

It is my desire that you will find comfort, advice, and encouragement in these pages. It has been an honor, a privilege, and a blessing to be able to homeschool our six children. I would like to close this introduction with a poem I wrote that describes how I feel about my job as a homeschooling mother. I hope you share these feelings.

I am a Professional

I am a professional
And I hold a high degree,
My clients are but children
And they're very dear to me,
I work extended hours
And the pay is not too fair,
But the benefits are great –
No other job can compare,
So as I look around me
And see women at their jobs,
I gladly claim the title –
Full-time professional mom!

My husband, Bruce, and I have educated our six children at home all of their "school lives." We began this journey more than twenty years ago. Most people who begin homeschooling wonder, "Can I go the distance? Can I homeschool all the way through high school?" They ask, "Will my children learn to function in society? Will they be able to get a job? Will they be able to attend college? Will they be normal?"

The answer to these questions is *yes*. You can adequately prepare your children for life. The Lord has given your children to you — not to the school system, not to the state, not to your great aunt who taught school for 35 years, not to your neighbors, not to the other families in your church or homeschool support group, and not even to your parents — all of whom may question your ability and your authority to teach your children. The Lord will direct your path — be open to His leading — after all, He is the one who called you to train up your children. He is ultimately the One to whom you will have to answer.

I would like to share a little about each of our children — not to boast, but to be an encouragement to you. Our oldest daughter Michelle is married and has two children. She and her husband are educating their children at home. As I believe education begins at birth, they are actually homeschooling already even though their children are not "school aged."

Michelle was not interested in attending college. She began cake decorating at home when she was ten years old and later worked as a cake decorator for Publix supermarkets for seven years. In 2003, she entered a national cake decorating contest. She and her husband, Victor, traveled to Las Vegas for the competition, and Michelle took first place. She now operates her own custom cake business from home. Michelle has also illustrated several of my books, including **The Frances Study Guide** and **Successful Puppet Making**. She designed all the puppets in the puppet making book, which consists of 24 easy-to-make felt puppets. We are currently working together on a Bible story puppet book that we hope to publish in 2005. Floral arranging and interior decorating are additional areas where Michelle puts her artistic talents to use .

Our second daughter, Melissa, graduated Magna Cum Laude from the University of Tampa with a Major in English and a Minor in Art in December of 2003. Last summer she studied at Kent University in Canterbury, England. She is a member of the International English Honor Society and the National Honor Society. While in college she held a number of jobs, spending most of her time working in the technical department of a medical transcription company. Since she was a young teenager, Melissa has typed and edited manuscripts for a number of my books. She loves literature and dancing ballet and jazz. Melissa has been reading and dancing since she was three years old. She plans to continue her studies, perhaps pursuing a Masters Degree in English.

Biblical Parenting or Schooling at Home?

"Will my children learn to function in society? Will they be able to get a job? Will they be able to attend college? Will they be normal?"

The Lord will direct your path – be open to His leading – after all He is the one who called you to homeschool.

Our oldest son, Robert, participated in the dual enrollment program at our local community college during his last two years of studying at home. He received his AA degree and then joined the U.S. Marine Corps in December 2002. He is now stationed in Monterey, California, where he is studying to be a linguistic cryptologist. (It took me three weeks just to learn how to say that!) Robert is learning Arabic. He said, "Mom, it's just like a unit study. We study about the culture, language, history, and geography of the Arabic nations — 5 days a week, 6 ½ hours a day — for 14 months!"

Our next son, Raymond, completed the traditional high school requirements in the spring of 2003. He also participated in the dual enrollment program at our local community college. In the summer of 2004, he will complete the courses necessary to obtain his AA degree in Computer Engineering. Then he plans to transfer to the University of South Florida to complete his Bachelor's Degree in Engineering.

Both Robert and Raymond have worked extensively in the residential remodeling field with my husband, Bruce. I am thankful that they have had the opportunity to learn valuable skills and propitious lessons about life from their father. Raymond continues to work part time with Bruce while attending college.

We are currently educating our daughter, Mandy, who is 14 years old, and our son, Randall, who is 9 years old, at home. Mandy enjoys reading, writing, learning to play the bagpipes, sign language, doll making, and acting. As her brother Randall says — Mandy *lives* in books. Randall enjoys acting, dancing, photography, and Legos — including Lego Robotics. Each of our children has taken a different route. It is our prayer that the Lord will place people and events in our children's lives to help them become the individuals He wants them to be.

When teaching our children at home, we must ask ourselves, "Are we going to reconstruct school at home, or are we going to provide our children with a meaningful education?" When we began our homeschooling journey more than 20 years ago, I tried desperately to re-create school in our home. I soon realized that I could not do it, but more importantly I realized that I should not.

And so I want to encourage you not to try to re-create school in your home because you have access to a superior mode of instruction. I think it is important that we not view education as a 12 year prison sentence — that is basically how I viewed it growing up. When does the Lord admonish us to teach our children? From 9:00 a.m. to 3:00 p.m., 5 days a week, 180 days a year, for 12 years?

No, he tells us in Deuteronomy chapter 6 to instruct them when we sit in our house and when we walk by the way and when we lie down and when we rise up. Education is to be a lifestyle. I believe it is important

It is our prayer that the Lord will place people and events in our children's lives to help them become the individuals He wants them to be.

"Are we going to reconstruct school at home, or are we going to provide our children with a meaningful education?"

that whatever we teach our children, we teach them what we know — what we have a passion for — whether that is writing, cooking, sewing, painting, gardening, woodworking, baseball, or swimming.

Do you have a hobby that you enjoy? Can you devote as much time as you would like to this hobby? Years ago I wanted to learn about sign language. I did not have the time to pursue this on my own, so I studied this with my kids. Often when I want to learn about something or delve into a project, I include my kids and call it "school!" For that matter, whenever one of my children takes an interest in a topic, that topic becomes our unit of study. I want my children to know that their interests are worthy to be pursued.

I have to constantly remind myself that my husband and I are not preparing our children for a good job in the marketplace, but we are preparing them for a fulfilling life. This entails so much more than academic success. Academics are important, but living a full life is even more important. The most important lessons our children will learn are not about academics but rather are about relationships, and the best place to learn these lessons is in the surroundings of a loving home.

Most people equate schooling with a plethora of textbooks and workbooks. I want to encourage you to try some different educational approaches this year. Take on a project, go on a family field trip, do a unit study on something that interests you or your children. As we engage in projects, our children learn things they would never learn from textbooks. Most parents moan when the word "project" is mentioned, but I have never heard a child moan about participating in a project.

When submersed in textbooks and workbooks, children often groan, "I'll never use this – why do I have to learn this anyway?" When absorbed in a project, children see the necessity for using basic skills in order to complete the task. Projects bring basic skills to life.

I also want to encourage you to spend time relishing the classics and other great books. You will be amazed at how your children's vocabulary, composition skills, general knowledge, and thinking skills soar as you share great literature. There is more to education than is found between the pages of textbooks. I do not mean to totally discount the use of textbooks in our educational endeavors; however, do not allow textbooks to swallow up all of your time so that you have no time left for *real* books and *real* activities that will get your children excited about learning. Textbooks and workbooks are time robbers. They rob us of the time that can be spent engaging in real-life activities and projects, and in reading real literature.

Do you have young children who enjoy hearing a well-loved story again and again? Do you have independent readers who return to the same book again and again because it has become a household favorite? Do you

Often when I want to learn about something or delve into a project, I include my kids and call it "school!"

The most important lessons our children will learn are not about academics but rather are about relationships, and the best place to learn these lessons is in the surroundings of a loving home.

There is more to education than is found between the pages of textbooks.

have children who pull that textbook off the shelf and hide it under their pillow so they can stay up half the night relishing its pages? Real books inspire us the way textbooks never can. Most textbooks are written by committees – committees that want to tell us what and how to think – real books are written by individuals -- individuals who are bubbling with enthusiasm about their story or topic of interest.

Great literature nurtures creativity. As my young children play I am reminded of the positive influence of literature in their lives. Several years ago when my youngest daughter, Mandy, was 7 years old, she began taking piano lessons. This sparked an interest in the lives of the great composers, so we read more than twenty biographies. Some were the easy-reader-type, which she could read to me, while others were more lengthy books, which I read to her. I was amazed at how she kept the events of the different composers' lives so neatly sorted.

This enthusiasm flowed over into her playtime where she centered her activities on a composer's era. She managed to draw her little brother, Randall, into her pretend world.

I recall one day in particular when Mandy and Randall were totally absorbed in their play. I rushed into the bedroom because we were hurrying to leave for an appointment, and there they stood – coats on (in the heat of summer) and suitcases in hand. I abruptly commanded, "Hurry up! We are going to be late for the orthodontist. Take off these things, and get into the van."

The children took no notice of me. I repeated my orders. Then Mandy said in an emphatic tone, "He's Mozart (pointing to her little brother) and I'm his big sister, Nannarel. Mozart is performing at a concert tonight in Vienna. We cannot go with you. We must be off to Vienna at once!"

"I'm sorry," I said, "Mozart can have his concert when we come back home. We must go to the orthodontist NOW!"

My teenage son, Robert, was listening from the hallway. He burst into the bedroom exclaiming, "Nannarel, Mozart, we must hurry! The last coach leaves for Vienna in five minutes!" Without a word, the two little waifs ran outside and jumped into the van. I stood silently in the bedroom for a few moments until my son put his hand on my shoulder and said, "Mom, you just have to meet them in their world."

I encourage you to begin building great minds as you assist your children in creating worlds of their own. A great book is a gateway into such golden worlds. Many people ask, "But how do you find time to read all those books?" The answer is that we have the time because we are not slaves to the textbook-workbook task master. Real books stimulate us.

Educators who are honest with themselves know that real books are far more valuable to one's education than schoolbooks. When my daughter Melissa began college, she went to see the head of the English department because she had declared an English Major. The woman asked her why she had chosen English as a major.

Melissa went on to tell her about her favorite authors such as James Fennimore Cooper, Jane Austin, Shakespeare, Charles Dickens, Mark Twain, and so on. She said, "A Tale of Two Cities is my favorite book. I've read it 5 times, and I've read all of Cooper's works." She added, "And Jane Austin taught me how to write. And I've memorized several of Shakespeare's plays." The woman was astounded and asked Melissa where she went to high school. Melissa said, "Oh, I was homeschooled."

The professor said, "I knew it had to be something – you don't get an education like that in any school." Then she said, "I have two little girls that I want to homeschool. Tell me about homeschooling." After awhile Melissa asked the woman to check her class schedule to make sure she had signed up for the right classes. The woman briefly looked it over and said, "Oh, it's fine. Now tell me more about homeschooling." When Melissa returned home she told me about this encounter and said, "Now who was counseling whom?"

A good book draws my husband into our homeschooling in a positive way as I choose a book for him to read aloud at dinnertime that somehow relates to a topic we are studying. I was frustrated when he would come home from work and ask the kids, "What did you learn today?" And they would reply, "I don't know." As he reads aloud, the children are reminded of details from our study, and a hearty discussion ensues.

When we conducted a unit study on the Revolutionary War period, my husband read aloud a biography of Patrick Henry at the dinner table — one chapter per night. When he finished the book, I asked the children if they wanted me to read an excerpt about Patrick Henry from an American History textbook. (I happened to have bought this textbook at a used book sale.)

The children agreed, so I read them the entire paragraph about Patrick Henry that was included in the textbook. The children looked at me and said, "Is that it?" I said, "Yes, that's it." They were amazed that this American History textbook only contained one paragraph about this man. Then my son Raymond, who was 5 years old at the time said, "Mom, they left out the best part!" I asked, "What was that?" And he said, "That Patrick Henry didn't make his kids wear shoes until they were ten!" Then the other children went on to add what important elements they felt were missing.

A stimulating analytical literary exercise is to read a book aloud

A good book draws my husband into our homeschooling in a positive way as I choose a book for him to read aloud at dinnertime that somehow relates to a topic we are studying.

A stimulating analytical literary exercise is to read a book aloud with your children, and then watch a movie based on the book.

Oral narration is an effective means for a child to recount a book that he has read. Rather than have a child give a written book report, he can give an oral presentation.

with your children, and then watch a movie based on the book. This helps to stimulate a discussion whereby the children compare and contrast the book and movie. It encourages them to become detail oriented as they search for similarities and differences. They learn to express their opinions as to whether they liked the book or movie better and why.

I remember the first time I read **Caddie Woodlawn** with my four oldest children. After finishing the book, we watched the movie that Disney produced based on the book. The children were outraged to find out how many details — details they deemed important – were either changed or left out altogether. They were ready to write a letter to the Disney studios and include their list of grievances. This has become a favorite practice of ours — to read a book, and then watch a movie based on the book.

Oral narration is an effective means for a child to recount a book that he has read. Rather than have a child give a written book report, he can give an oral presentation. Dinnertime is a great place for this as your child has a captive audience. I remember one day when my daughter Michelle had just finished reading a book by Gary Paulsen entitled **Hatchet**. I knew it would be useless to get Michelle to write a composition about this book — she disliked writing. So at dinnertime, I asked her to tell us about the book. I wish I had taped this because it was priceless. She used excellent storytelling techniques to keep her siblings perched on the edges of their chairs.

Hatchet is about a twelve-year-old boy whose parents are divorced. His mother is driving him to an airport where he will fly in a small plane with only one pilot to the Canadian wilderness. There he will meet his father who has previously arrived and has been busy setting up camp. The boy really does not want to go on this camping trip, and to make matters worse, his mother gives him a gift of a hatchet with a carrying case. Reluctantly he secures the case and hatchet to his belt. He thinks the hatchet is a corny gift, and he wonders how much worse things can get.

Well, he finds out how much worse things can get very quickly. As the boy and pilot are flying over a lake in the Canadian wilderness, the pilot has a heart attack and dies. Michelle then used her best dramatic capabilities to describe what follows this perilous scene:

"The plane plummets downward and plunges into the lake. The plane's fuselage cracks from the impact. Down, down, down, it sinks to the bottom. Water rushes in as Brian struggles to climb through the broken windshield. He wrestles with the thick vegetation clinging to his body as he tries to escape the wreckage. His lungs are about to burst. Upward, upward he swims, with his hatchet still secured to his belt."

The children were spellbound as Michelle wove her tale. She

knew how to agitate her siblings by pausing at the most dramatic scenes. The kids would beg her to tell what happened next. If Michelle had written a composition about this book, she might have written a paragraph, and it would probably have been very dry. I timed her oral narration of this account and it was 55 minutes long. I recorded this in our school log as **Oral Narration** for Michelle and as **Listening Comprehension** for the other children.

Some of the most meaningful moments we have spent together as a family have been while sharing great literature. I encourage you to make this a part of your curriculum. Even as your children get older, it is important to read aloud to them. Maybe they will do part of the reading aloud. This helps to relieve your own vocal cords and helps to strengthen their oral reading skills. Also, as your children read aloud, you are made aware of words they find difficult to pronounce. I remember skipping over the words I did not know when I read silently as a child.

Some of the most meaningful moments we have spent together as a family have been while sharing great literature.

I recall reading aloud **Ben-Hur: A Tale of Christ** to my boys, Robert and Raymond, when they were teenagers. My son, Raymond, was on the telephone with a friend when I told him it was time for us to read from **Ben-Hur**. I heard him tell his friend, "Well, I have to go now because my mom's going to read to us." Then his friend must have made a reply because Raymond said, "Doesn't your mom read to you?" Finally Raymond responded, "Well, my mom still reads to us, so I have to go."

Once we finished this book of more than 600 pages, we watched the classic movie *Ben-Hur* starring Charlton Heston. We had seen the movie many times before, but the boys remarked how much more they enjoyed the movie as a result of gleaning significant background information from the book. We also learned about the author, General Lew Wallace, and why he wrote this epic tale.

I have to remind myself to include my children in real-life experiences. Our children should help us with our daily tasks. A young child especially wants to spend time with Mom or Dad doing laundry, helping in the kitchen, working in the yard, repairing the kitchen faucet, and so on. My husband has always been a good example to me in this area by including the children in whatever he is doing. Often my thoughts are — I can do it better and faster by myself!

I have to remind myself to include my children in real life experiences.

Often my thoughts are – I can do it better and faster by myself!

Our children learn from being with us and working alongside us. I know it helps me if I look at these often mundane tasks such as cooking, gardening, sewing, and cleaning, as part of our children's education. Books must make way for real learning experiences, or we may find our children have head knowledge but not knowledge of the hand and heart.

Books must make way for real learning experiences, or we may find our children have head knowledge but not knowledge of the hand and heart.

If you keep a journal or log of your educational activities, you can include these tasks under headings such as **Home Economics** for cooking, laundry and sewing; **Auto Maintenance** for changing the oil in the car or changing a flat tire; **Child Care Development** for caring for a younger sibling; **Botany** for helping with lawn and garden chores. It is really all in a name — naming these activities makes them an acceptable part of "school."

How many of you feel obligated to complete an entire textbook or workbook once you begin? What if your child already knows the material and he finds it repetitious? Rather than trudging through it for the sake of "completing the book" — put a check mark with the date at the top of the workbook page if he already knows the material. Or, if using a textbook, make an entry in your homeschool log stating that the material on pages 29- 39, for example, was covered. Oftentimes material can be covered quickly by allowing the child to complete it orally rather than in written form. Not every page of every workbook needs to be filled in.

Games are an excellent way to learn new concepts and facts. Try turning one school day a week, or one school day every other week, into game day. Include money for the purchasing of educational games in your homeschool budget. Educational games can also be made using books like: *Games for Learning, Games for Reading, Games with Books, Games for Math,* and *Games for Writing*. All of these books are written by Peggy Kaye. Peggy states, "Games put children in exactly the right frame of mind for learning difficult things. Children will throw themselves into playing games the way they would never throw themselves into filling out workbook pages." Peggy offers simple-to-make games for Kindergarten through 3rd grade; however, they can be adapted for both older and younger children.

Children who are older also love making board games to accompany a unit of study. What better way for a child to exhibit all that he has learned about a particular topic than through the developing of a game based on that topic? As he plays commercial games, he learns details about game construction and development. As with other projects, children cultivate numerous skills when creating games.

My youngest children, Mandy and Randall, and I made a board game to accompany a unit study we created based on C.S. Lewis and *The Chronicles of Narnia*. We read a biography of C.S. Lewis while reading all 7 books in The Chronicles of Narnia series. Mandy and Randall participated in our homeschool drama group's production of *The Lion the Witch and the Wardrobe*. We also attended a professional performance of *The Lion the Witch and the Wardrobe* at the Performing Arts Center in Tampa, Florida.

While reading C.S. Lewis' biography and the Narnia books, the children made up game questions at the conclusion of each chapter. They wrote the correct answer for each question, while also including three answers that sounded authentic. By making the questions multiple choice, friends who may not have read all of the books, could also play the game.

The children came up with such believable "false" answers to the questions, they often had me wondering which answer was really correct! They also made non-question cards to help move the game along — such as one which reads, "You see Reepicheep fall overboard. Jump overboard to save him, and as you are rescuing him lose a turn!" Some cards move the player ahead a certain number of spaces or give the player another turn.

Once we finished reading all the books, the children typed the questions on the computer and made them into game cards. They downloaded pictures from the Narnia website to be printed on the game board and the backs of the game cards. They learned how to put these pictures in the Paint computer program and touch them up by removing unwanted details or adding more details. Mandy and Randall made free-standing game pieces representing the different characters, and they even constructed a game board that folded in fourths. They created a game strategy and typed up the game directions. You can imagine how many skills were developed as they created this game!

Projects are an important part of learning and should not be something we crowd in from time to time. We have to be willing to put the textbooks aside in favor of real learning. While engaged in projects, children begin to see how phonics and mathematics are necessary in order to read and comprehend instructions and measure and compute numbers.

Book making has been another favorite family project over the years. During our homeschooling years, my children have made more than 60 books based on my book *Creating Books with Children*. (See page 331 for more information.) This is a six-week book-making unit study guide whereby children learn about authors and illustrators while constructing their own books. As children study about their favorite authors and illustrators, they are motivated to create their own publications.

History comes alive as we study about real people in real space and time. For example, suppose while making a book your family chooses to study about Margret and H.A. Rey. Can you think of the name of a famous children's book authored by this couple? That's right – Margret and H.A. Rey were the creators of *Curious George*. The Rey's were German Jews who sought refuge in Paris during World War II. It is fascinating to learn that the Reys fled Paris in June of 1940 only hours before the Nazis invaded France. H.A. Rey cobbled together two bicycles from spare parts, and he and Margret pedaled for four long days from France to Spain. All they took with them was a bit of food, their warm coats, and their manuscripts – including their *Curious George* manuscript.

The Reys sold their bicycles to the border guards and bought train

While engaged in projects, children begin to see how phonics and mathematics are necessary in order to read and comprehend instructions and measure and compute numbers.

History comes alive as we study about real people in real space and time.

tickets to Portugal. From there they secured passage by ship to America. Upon entering the New York harbor, they welcomed the sight of the Statue of Liberty. Within one week, they found a publisher for their *Curious George* story. Margret and H.A. Rey went on to write 6 more books about that lovable little monkey. This example offers us a unique historical perspective of World War II – far different from a traditional textbook perspective.

Many other skills are enhanced as children make books. They learn to be keen observers of books, noting how pictures and text are integrated. They learn about the structure of a book — about the copyright, summary, dedication, title pages, closing pages, and book flap copy. They learn how to include key elements in their books — such as the use of dialogue, action, description, and proper punctuation. They learn the basic structure of a story — beginning, middle, and ending. They learn that a story needs a conflict, problem, or mystery. They learn to include additional details about this conflict or problem. They learn to resolve the problem, thus wrapping up the story. The children learn about creating effective illustrations. They learn all of this and much more as they are active participants in the story creation process.

And best of all, they have a product they can be proud of when they are finished. Children are motivated to do their best as they know others – besides Mom and Dad – will be looking at what they have made. They know this is not just something Mom is going to stuff into a folder to be put in a file hidden away somewhere.

Relatives and friends who are skeptical of homeschooling will be impressed when they see hardback, hand-sewn, professional looking books made by your children. And to think that you – perhaps without any teaching credentials – could guide your children in creating such a wonderful book! "Well, maybe homeschooling isn't so bad after all," the skeptics remark.

Do you have preschoolers as well as school-aged children? Do you ever feel your preschoolers are "in the way" when you are trying to teach your older children? Do you include your preschoolers in your homeschooling? Did you know that educational psychologists claim that more than half of a child's learning occurs during his first few years?

These are important years when many life-long habits are formed. I encourage you to include your preschoolers in your educational endeavors. Little children are sponges and will pick up more than we realize. Just try saying something around them that you would rather not have them repeat! I find it helpful to set up play centers in our school room to keep my preschoolers entertained while I work with my older children. As they play close by, they absorb much of what I am teaching. My book, *Making the Most of the Preschool Years* contains 100 ideas for

Children are motivated to do their best as they know others – besides Mom and Dad – will be looking at what they have made. They know this isn't just something Mom is going to stuff into a folder to be put in a file hidden away somewhere.

Do you ever feel your preschoolers are "in the way" when you are trying to teach your older children?

Did you know that educational psychologists claim that more than half of a child's learning occurs during his first few years?

setting up such play centers. (See page 329 for more information.)

Although young children are very receptive to new ideas and concepts, do not try to push your little ones into workbooks. Hands-on learning is best for this age group. For example, a young child's creativity is stimulated through dramatic play. Have you watched a young child playing with stuffed toys or dolls when he did not know he had an audience? He uses different voices for each character and acts out stories all on his own.

Dramatic play helps a child build composition skills as he works at weaving his tale. His vocabulary is enhanced as he searches for the right words. Try making simple puppets with your young children, and encourage them to act out the stories that you read aloud to them. They will learn multiple skills as they help construct the puppets and as they work to retell a favorite story using dialogue and narration. It is through this play acting that children learn the basics of story construction.

Dramatic play helps a child build composition skills as he works at weaving his tale. His vocabulary is enhanced as he searches for the right words.

Older kids will beg to make puppets and put on plays as well. If you need help creating simple felt puppets, my daughter, Michelle, and I wrote **Successful Puppet Making** — which includes patterns and diagrams to create 24 easy-to-make felt puppets featuring: Animals on the Farm, Animals in the Woods, and Animals in the Jungle. The book also includes a poem for each animal, a factual description of each animal, and a list of library picture books highlighting each animal, so you and your children can act out the stories with the puppets. Visit my website to find a free pattern and directions for making a cow puppet. (www.valeriebendt.com/puppet.asp). (See page 332 for more information regarding this book.)

I have talked about three types of projects to help stimulate creativity and encourage learning. They are game making, book making, and puppet making. Be on the look out for other ways to include hands-on-learning in your homeschooling. Your children will be glad you did, and you will be amazed at how much your children will learn from these real-life projects.

Be on the look out for other ways to include hands-on-learning in your homeschooling.

What about testing? Are you intimidated by standardized tests? I think it is unwise to subject children, especially young children, to standardized written achievement tests. Not only is it stressful for the child, but it is stressful for the parent. It can effect *what* and *how* you teach. This is known as "teaching to the test." Would you breathe a sigh of relief if you could forgo end-of-the-year testing altogether?

Would you breathe a sigh of relief if you could forgo end-of-the-year testing altogether?

Our own children did not take written standardized achievement tests until they were in their junior year of high school. The only written standardized test our oldest sons ever took during their homeschooling years was the SAT to get into college. There is no limit on the number of times a student can take the SAT. The first time or two that our children took the SAT, it was for practice. I told them not to worry about their scores because I expected them to take the test again. They each said this made the test taking experience less stressful. It is a myth that children need to spend X number of years practicing test taking. The fact that the public schools place such a heavy emphasis on test taking and test results should be a clear indication that we should steer clear of this enterprise.

I would like to offer a quote from a book by Karl Reed entitled, **The Bible, Homeschooling, and the Law.**

> A very important point in the education of the child is that God makes every child special with his own special bent toward his own special calling in life, for the purpose of fulfilling a place in the community. That calling will normally generate into an interest, which leads to equipping him to fulfill his station in life. For that reason, if no other, it is extremely foolish to try and standardize children by standardizing their education. Herein also lies one of the dangers of the alleged "nationally normed standardized achievement tests." It is foolish to invent artificial measurements to determine whether one child is educated and another is not. All children are gifted and each child is to be guided by the Creator at some point in his education to travel his own avenue in his pursuit of knowledge, in order to develop his own special gift or calling for the purpose of meeting his mission in life.

I feel that maintaining a portfolio is far more valuable than test taking. In many states, if you have chosen to register with your county school system, this portfolio can be assessed by a certified teacher in order to satisfy the evaluation requirement. A portfolio offers a better representation of what a child knows — what he has accomplished. It is more of a scrapbook detailing his or her educational pursuits for a given school year. We talked about doing projects. Although it is hard to slip most projects into a portfolio, you can easily include photos of completed projects. You can add photos of field trips, plays, and other productions in which your children participate.

If you visit a museum or other point of interest, grab brochures and put them in your children's portfolios — being sure to obtain one for each child. Anything that documents your educational activities can be included in their portfolios. You only need to enclose a sampling of your children's work – not every page from every workbook! Portfolios are something your children will come to treasure rather than something they will come to dread – like the end-of-the-year achievement tests!

As you teach your children, remember the Lord gave these children to you. You know and love your children better than anyone else. Therefore, you are your children's best curriculum specialists. Pray that the Lord will guide you and reveal the proper course for your family. Have fun with your children and remember that learning lasts a lifetime!

It is foolish to invent artificial measurements to determine whether one child is educated and another is not. —Karl Reed

I feel that maintaining a portfolio is far more valuable than test taking.

Portfolios are something your children will come to treasure rather than something they will come to dread – like the end of the year achievement tests!

How to Create
Your Own
Unit Study

Valerie Bendt

Contents

*I*f you are interested in this book, you have probably already spent time analyzing what is truly valuable in education. You have asked yourself, "What is really important, and how can I give my child the best?" After all, is it not for their good that we have taken on this responsibility?

The key to finding direction in all of life is knowing our God-given responsibilities. In regard to children, we are told to "train up a child in the way he should go." Truth, therefore, becomes the major emphasis, with academics taking on a lesser role.

If we are going to successfully bake a loaf of bread, we need the right proportion of ingredients: flour being the major foundation, with other necessary ingredients in smaller portions. Likewise, without giving our children a foundation of truth on which to build other learning, their education is not a success no matter how high the test scores.

Our society is trying to function with the belief that education in academics is the solution for all ills. Teaching academics only for success is like trying to make bread using only yeast. It can not be done.

Why is it we can readily recognize proportion and order in other areas of life, but somehow we have been deceived in the area of education?

One of the most difficult tasks in homeschooling is breaking away from the idea that we must teach just like the schools. This belief puts great pressure and guilt on us when we search for a more sensible approach to teaching.

In this book, Valerie has developed a framework for us to break away from school and get involved in life-training using academics to assist us in building that foundation of truth.

Kathleen Ann Albert

1990

All Scripture is inspired by God and profitable for teaching, for reproof, for correction, for training in righteousness; that the man of God may be adequate, equipped for every good work.

2 Timothy 3:16 (NASV)

Introduction

*T*his book was written to encourage you to create studies to strengthen your family. You are your family's best curriculum specialist. You can devise studies superior to any curriculum on the market.

I urge you to put away the tedious texts and delve into real, living books. Sharing good books with your family is rewarding. Involve your children in real-life experiences, providing them with a multitude of pertinent educational encounters. Train them to become self-taught individuals, ensuring a life-long love for acquiring knowledge.

In the margins I have included quotes from the Bible, key educators, and various classics. Each quote is pertinent to the section in which it is contained. It is my hope that these will spark your interest and cause you to read further. Excerpts from selected classics have been included, as reading good literature is a significant part of our studies.

The wide margins allow you to make notes beside significant passages. An outline is provided to afford you quick reference to desired information.

My children's names and ages at the time of publication (1990) are as follows: Michelle, 11 years old; Melissa, 9 years old; Robert, 7 years old; Raymond, 5 years old; and Mandy, 1 year old.

I. Defining Our Goal

A. Definition of education taken from the ***American Dictionary of the English Language, Noah Webster, 1828,*** contrasted with more current definitions

B. The purpose of education

C. Thoughts pertaining to education, by Susan Schaeffer Macaulay

II. Evaluating Curriculums

A. Most curriculums foster a multiple choice mentality

B. Texts offer bits and pieces of predigested material

C. Children are not encouraged to think or reason due to the influence of inferior curriculums

D. Textbook and workbook approaches stifle creativity

III. Unit Study Approach

A. Major subjects integrated into a particular topic, theme, or historical time period

B. Studies can be approached biblically

C. Lesson plans simplified as all ages study one topic

D. Family unity strengthened

E. Skills strengthened as each child works at his own level

IV. Some Educational Philosophies

A. Charlotte Mason: 1842-1923

   1. Wrote, among other books, ***Home Education***

   2. Chose living books covering a vast range of topics rather than textbooks

   3. Use time saved in not drilling facts to read good books

   4. Use narration — simply having children retell what has been read

B. Ruth Beechick

   1. A present-day educator

   2. Uses real books rather than textbooks

   3. Uses dictation and copying to strengthen skills

   4. Wrote several excellent books including, ***You Can Teach Your Child Successfully***, and her "little books" on Reading, Arithmetic, and Language.

V. Phonics and Math

A. ***Reading Made Easy***

   1. No need for workbooks

   2. No need for phonetic readers; use the library or have the children dictate their own stories and use them for readers

B. ***Math***

   1. It is not always convenient to integrate math into your unit study

   2. Use lots of hands-on manipulatives with the younger children

   3. Use a good math text, like ***Saxon***, for grades 4 and up

VI. Schedules and Routines

A. Maintain a schedule while remaining flexible

B. Children perform best when they have a set routine

C. Tone for the day is set as Dad spends time with the children before work

    D. Using the same unit for each child simplifies matters, but use a method that works best for your family

    E. Break teaching time into manageable segments, giving each child some individualized attention

    F. Devise a schedule for yearly studies, i.e., a two-weeks-off, ten-weeks-on plan

VII. Getting Started

    A. Use various books to help you determine what needs to be studied at each level – *Teaching Children* by Diane Lopez and *The Christian Home Educators' Curriculum Manuals* by Cathy Duffy

    B. Unit study method is effective for teaching high school students as well

       1. Teaches them how to research information on their own

       2. Older children can lead the rest of the family in a unit study

    C. How to determine what topics your high school student should cover

       1. School textbooks

       2. Scope and sequence charts

       3. *Christian Home Educators' Curriculum Manual* for Junior and Senior High by Cathy Duffy

    D. Read biographies to your children

    E. Develop a timeline, making figures to represent people you study

    F. Unit studies can be used to enhance regular textbook studies

    G. If using a published unit study, tailor it to your family's needs and desires

VIII. Using the Library

    A. Biographies

    B. Reference books

       1. *Index to Collective Biographies for Young Readers*

       2. *People in Books*

    C. Subject card catalogue

    D. Library materials checklist

    E. How to categorize and use the books you have chosen

IX. Using Games and Teaching Aids

    A. Games are non-consumable

    B. Games are beneficial for reviewing previously covered material

    C. Aristoplay games

    D. Create your own games to accompany a specific unit study

X. Using Dictation and Copying

    A. Strengthens spelling, punctuation, and grammar skills

    B. Uses good composition models

    C. Allows children to learn about a topic of study while strengthening basic skills; time is not wasted on irrelevant workbook material

XI. The Importance of Writing

    A. Makes a lasting, good impression

    B. Can be used to effectively convey the message of our Lord

    C. Children's writing is influenced by the material that they hear and read

XII. Projects: Friend or Foe
    A. Published unit study curriculums place a heavy emphasis on projects
    B. Use projects to your advantage; do not allow them to dictate your schedule
    C. Ease up on academics while engaged in a project to reduce tension

XIII. Choosing Your Units of Study
    A. Organize units to encompass a wide variety of subject matter during the year
    B. Units may be studied together as a family, or capable children may conduct their own unit studies

XIV. Reading Good Literature
    A. Read books of a high literary value on a daily basis
    B. Use literature to stretch vocabulary and increase knowledge
    C. Provides a springboard for various writing activities
    D. Have children narrate what you have read to them
    E. Reading to your children strengthens their listening comprehension skills

XV. Fine Arts
    A. Often overlooked in favor of more academic endeavors
    B. Use music, art, and poetry to enhance your units
    C. Have children draw, paint, perform musically, and write poetry

XVI. Nature Studies
    A. Children need to be acquainted with nature
    B. Nature walks
    C. Sketch samples collected from nature
    D. Use nature guides to identify specimens

XVII. Using the Bible
    A. Many published unit study curriculums integrate Scripture into the study
    B. Use a concordance and a topical Bible to locate passages relating to studies
    C. Bible verses make excellent typing exercises

XVIII. Record-Keeping
    A. Daily Log
        1. Enter material covered as you progress through your day
        2. Make a basic outline, leaving room for flexibility
        3. Use a spiral notebook or other record-keeping book
        4. Write the dates in your log book and list the unit studies; keep this for future reference
        5. Record life skills as well as academics
    B. Have children keep their own log or journal
        1. Record-keeping teaches children responsibility
        2. Record-keeping also teaches children to organize their thoughts

XIX. Reflecting on Unit Studies

The following definitions were taken from the *American Dictionary of the English Language, Noah Webster, 1828.*

EDUCATION: n. The bringing up, as of a child; instruction and discipline which is intended to enlighten the understanding, correct the temper, and form the manners and habits of youth, and fit them for usefulness in their future stations. *To give children a good education in manners, arts and science, is important; to give them religious education is indispensable; and an immense responsibility rests on parents and guardians who neglect these duties. [1]

EDUCATE: vt. To bring up, as a child; to instruct; to inform and enlighten the understanding; to instill into the mind principles of arts, science, morals, religion and behavior. *To educate children well is one of the most important duties of parents and guardians. [2]

The following is a definition taken from the *Webster's Encyclopedia of Dictionaries* – 1978:

EDUCATE: vt. To cultivate and discipline the mind and other faculties by teaching; send to school. [3]

and *Webster's New World Dictionary* – 1988:

EDUCATE: vt. To train or develop the knowledge, skill, mind, or character of, esp. by formal schooling or study; teach; instruct. [4]

There is a tremendous difference between the definition or concept of education in the 1828 Webster's Dictionary and the definitions we have today. In 1828, education was clearly the responsibility of the parents, and now that responsibility has been given over to the schools. Once parents allowed the schools to take control of the education of their children, it was not long before the schools demanded that they have total control. Parents were no longer qualified to oversee their children's education.

You will also notice another sharp contrast between the 1828 definition and the modern definitions of education. In the 1828 version, academics were secondary. A religious education and the child's behavior were deemed most important. Today, the Bible is not even allowed in the public schools. Can character be taught without a basis for truth?

When teaching our children at home, we must ask ourselves, "Are we going to reconstruct school at home, or are we going to provide our children with a real education?" In her book, *For the Children's Sake*, Susan Schaeffer Macaulay states:

Education extends to all life. The truly educated person has

Defining Our Goal

It is significant that there is no reference in the Scriptures to the school as a separate institution established by God. In spite of the great importance of the teaching ministry, God has not seen fit to ordain schools as such. Even the implications of the cultural mandate and the Noahic covenant, with the establishment of the institution of human government, do not suggest a parallel establishment of schools as instruments of such human governments. As far as the Bible is concerned, the function of transmitting truth and educating the young belongs to the home and church.
— *Henry Morris Christian Education for the Real World, Master Books*

only had many doors of interest opened. He knows that life will not be long enough to follow everything through fully. [5]

It is our job as parents to introduce our children to a wide variety of interesting topics. We must teach them how to learn so they may further explore areas to which they are drawn.

The child is not made for education, but education is to serve the child, serve his personality, his life, his needs.

– Susan Schaeffer Macaulay [6]

As we teach our children, we should ask ourselves, "Is what I am teaching really serving my children's needs? Am I filling their minds with tedious, nebulous facts, or am I feeding their minds with the good, the wonderful, the excellent?" Enjoy learning and exploring with your children. Learning lasts a lifetime. Scripture gives us that ultimate ruler by which to measure all things.

Finally brethren, whatsoever things are honest, whatsoever things are just, whatsoever things are pure, whatsoever things are lovely, whatsoever things are of good report; if there be any virtue, if there be any praise, think on these things.

Philippians 4:8 (NASV) [7]

Much of the curriculum written for children today fosters the multiple choice or fill-in-the-blank mentality. The children are not introduced to something as a whole but in bits and pieces of predigested material which they are to regurgitate at the appropriate time. In trying to complete their work, they are looking for the right answers rather than being given the opportunity to grasp a whole concept or idea. Curriculum-driven textbooks and workbooks most often stifle learning and creativity. The use of real or living books allows the children to interact with some very creative and interesting people. These are real authors, not curriculum specialists. Real authors write because they feel they have something valuable to share. Of course, we must still cautiously apply our measuring stick found in Philippians 4:8. There may be parts of books we do not agree with, but we can filter these out or use them to show our children that other people think or act differently than we do. The key here is not to dwell on evil. Our children should know that evil exists, but let us not give them any how-to lessons.

Good books stimulate discussion. If your children can enter into a discussion with you about a book you have read aloud together, then you know they comprehend. This also helps them to retain a good deal of the material covered. Do not feel you have to process the ideas covered and break them down for the children. Let them try to understand for themselves. This is especially true when reading classics or other great literary works, as it will help to stretch their minds. Do not worry about them comprehending every bit of it, but let them take in what is appropriate for them at the time.

I find this a helpful thing to consider as I am teaching four of my five children together. The younger ones pick up certain things while the older ones pick up more. I try to get them to grasp a whole picture of what is being studied as opposed to isolated facts here and there. These isolated facts have no meaning if there is not a larger framework upon which to build. Sometimes I do find it best in certain areas of study, however, to choose simple books that explain things without throwing in a lot of difficult facts. This is true in the area of science.

We studied the human body, and I wanted my children to get a feel for the way the body systems work together as a whole before I bombarded them with facts about cells, neurons, and protoplasm. They needed to be able to grasp the whole and be acquainted with it before breaking it down into minute parts.

You will find that in technical areas such as science, the simpler books provide the child with an adequate overview of the particular subject being tackled. Few school children are able to recall all the tedious facts drilled into them by their teachers. They get so wrapped up in memorizing these difficult facts that when all is said and done, they do

Evaluating Curriculums

True Christian education, as set forth in the Bible, embraces all truth, whether "secular" or "spiritual." It is not narrow and restricted education, as some might assume, but extremely comprehensive — in fact universal — in its scope. Nothing is to be excluded except false knowledge and harmful philosophy, but, unfortunately, these constitute a large component of modern educational curricula. They must be removed from a Christian curriculum, but there is far more than enough genuine and valuable truth to incorporate in their stead.
— *Henry Morris* Christian Education for the Real World, *Master Books*

How to Create Your Own Unit Study

Balboa set off to climb the hill, with Leoncico as his only companion. The journey took him two hours, for he was desperately tired. As he drew near the rocky summit, he realized that he might be approaching the greatest moment of his life. If nothing was visible except more mountains, then his first attempt to find the Southern Sea would have failed. The men were too exhausted to travel much farther without rest and proper food. But if the sea was visible, then he Vasco Nunez de Balboa would be the man who had found it. He would be the first European to see the new ocean.

Balboa reached the summit. Eagerly he gazed westward. Far away in the distance lay the Pacific Ocean! Sunshine was sparkling on an expanse of blue water that matched the brightness of the morning sky.

Balboa raised his arm to salute the splendid sight. Now, whatever happened, his name would be remembered in centuries to come. He fell on his knees and began to pray. Far away at the bottom of the hill, seventy Spaniards looked at one another and grinned.
— Balboa, Finder of the Pacific *by Ronald Syme, William Morrow and Co.*

not even have a clear overview of what was being studied. Keeping with the simpler books in such cases provides the children with enough knowledge to have an understanding of the subject without being overwhelmed and, therefore, totally confused.

We tackled a unit on world geography, but I did not have the children learn all the countries of the world until they were able to have an understanding of what we mean by "world," "country," and so on. We began with simple library books and branched out from there.

Children can often be introduced to such concepts through literature. Read a story that takes place in a different country, and they begin to get a feel for that country. They realize that it is both similar to and different from their own. Such books can be read on a level above that of your children's reading or comprehension level; this will serve the purpose of stretching their minds while not confusing them with tedious facts to be memorized. They will be introduced to new vocabulary, which they will comprehend as the story unfolds. Children can understand many difficult words when used in the context of a story. This is not to be confused with reading them a book with a lot of technical information on which they have no basis to hang this knowledge. There is a big difference between pleasurable reading and technical reading. Technical reading has its proper place after sufficient ground work has been laid.

Biographies are an excellent introduction to different people, ideas, places, and times. While studying our unit on world geography, we read biographies about explorers and missionaries and studied the geographical terms we encountered. Geography came alive through these books.

Let us not recreate the school in the home when we can utilize a superior method of instruction. We do not need to rely on textbooks and workbooks designed to accommodate 30 or 40 children in a classroom. We can use real books, living books that spark our children's interests. You can study history, science, art, music, literature or a host of other subjects by reading biographies about real people in real places in real space and time. Children prefer this to dry textbooks.

We read twenty biographies in one year. A textbook would possibly have donated one or two paragraphs about each of the people we studied. We read entire biographies about these people and in turn received a taste of the cultural, economical, political, and geographical climates in which they lived. We were able to experience them as real people, not merely as paragraphs in a textbook. While studying particular units, we were able to see how the lives of certain people overlapped. We made figures of each of the people and placed them on our timeline. We chose a specific item to go with each person to enable us to better remember them.

Quoting from Charlotte Mason's book entitled **Home Education:**

The children should have the joy of living in far lands, in other persons, in other times – a delightful double existence; and this joy they will find, for the most part, in their story-books. Their lessons, too, history and geography, should cultivate their conceptive powers. If the child does not live in the times of his history lesson, be not at home in the climes his geography book describes, why, these lessons will fail of their purpose. [8]

You must be wondering, how do I know which books are best, and where do I find them? How do I know I am teaching all that I should and that there will not be any gaps in my child's education?

Well, this life does not afford us enough time to fill in all the possible gaps. The only gap to be concerned with is a void in your child's life that can only be filled by the Holy Spirit. Remember, academics are not everything.

Expose your children to the best in music, art, history, science, and literature. This can be done through the use of living books, real artwork, games, tapes, and so on. Put away the tedious workbooks that inhibit your child from experiencing real life. Through literature we form intimate relationships with people, historical events, and places. As Susan Schaeffer Macaulay states in her book, **For the Children's Sake**, "In literature, perhaps more than through any other art form, we are able to get into the other man's shoes." [9]

These relationships are formed as you share books with your children. A good deal of your school time should be spent reading together. To have time to accomplish this, you must eliminate the unnecessary busy work. It is difficult because we equate learning with filling in countless workbook pages or answering questions at the end of tedious textbook chapters. In order to partake of the excellent, we must throw out what the curriculum specialists have deemed as good.

Suppose I had a room full of parents and I divided it down the middle. Then I informed those on my right that they must complete five workbook pages dealing with reading comprehension, involving isolated paragraphs and answering teacher contrived questions. Meanwhile, those on my left would listen to me read several chapters from an excellent book about an interesting person, whom we would afterwards discuss. Before we engaging in these activities, I would allow anyone to change sides of the room. How many do you think would choose the workbook side? The discussion side? Which side do you think your children would choose? More importantly, which situation is more conducive to learning? Which lesson would be more cost efficient; the one involving a consumable workbook or the one involving a library book or a book of

In my experience, God's direction is much more evident when we design our own unit studies than when we use formal curriculum. As we choose topics and activities we are more open to God's leading than when we work with curriculum that has already been designed by someone else.
— Cathy Duffy
Christian Home Educators' Curriculum Manual, Elementary Grades, *1990 edition, Grove Publishing*

Unit Study Approach

Some Educational Philosophies

your own which can be used again and again? Let us not have the children equate education with being bored!

Susan Schaeffer Macaulay's book, ***For the Children's Sake***, has two companion volumes, which I find to be a tremendous aid in formulating my own curriculum: ***Teaching Children: A Curriculum Guide to What Children Need to Know at Each Level Through Sixth Grade***; and ***Books Children Love: A Guide to the Best Children's Literature***. These books are categorized by subject and grade level, which makes them very easy to use. Two additional guides that I highly recommend are Cathy Duffy's ***The Christian Home Educators' Curriculum Manual*** for the elementary grades and ***The Christian Home Educators' Curriculum Manual*** for junior and senior high school. Be flexible when using any book as a guide. Remember, your children are unique and you understand them better than anyone. Follow your instincts.

Next, we will define the term *unit study* and see why it is a more simple and effective way to teach. Along with the unit study approach, I combine the educational practices of both Charlotte Mason and Ruth Beechick.

Basic school subjects are studied in light of a particular topic, theme, or historical time period instead of studying eight or more isolated subjects.

Children are able to grasp the wholeness of truth as they see how these subjects relate to one another. Studies are approached from a biblical philosophy of education. Lesson planning is simplified because all ages study a topic together. Families are strengthened through this unity. Field trips, projects, and games all center on a particular unit.

Basic skills are taught in an informal manner while engaged in the study of a particular unit. Previously learned skills are strengthened as the children work at their own levels.

Let me introduce Charlotte Mason. She lived from 1842 to 1923 and was a teacher, author, and lecturer in England. Her own writings have recently been reprinted; her book, ***Home Education***, has a wealth of knowledge for us as parents. She believed in respecting children as whole persons. She believed children should be involved in real-life situations, learn self-discipline, and be given ample time for free play.

Studies were limited to the morning hours with the afternoons free for creativity and play. The evening hours were to be spent enjoying a good book with the family. She chose to use living books covering a wide range of topics instead of textbooks. She utilized the time saved in drilling facts in a textbook to read good books. Charlotte Mason did not believe in pressuring a child into a specific grade level. She stated that this would diminish his assurance of his self-worth. She allowed the child to progress at his own rate while exposing him to the best. I quote Miss Mason:

> This horse-in-a-mill round of geography and French, history and sums, was no more than playing at education; for who remembers the scraps of knowledge he labored over as a child? And would not the application of a few hours in later life effect more than a year's drudgery at any one subject in childhood? [10]

She believed in giving the child a liberal education, introducing him to good books and protecting him from "twaddle." Twaddle was her own word for the worthless, inferior material published for children. She saw that it underrated the child's intelligence. Miss Mason had her students narrate books that had been read aloud. Later, as they matured, this narration would develop into a written composition. This is reading comprehension fully exercised.

A child who learns early on to narrate orally will be less apt when he is older to encounter the typical problems often associated with written compositions. Narration is simply a retelling of what has been read. You know a child comprehends the material and his retention of that material will be greater when he can express himself through oral narration.

Ruth Beechick, a truly great author and educator of our present day, has also seen the value in using real books rather than textbooks. In her three "little books," she instructs parents how to use a natural method in teaching preschool through third grade. One book deals with arithmetic, one with language, and one with reading. She dispenses with complicated teaching methods in favor of simpler and more practical methods. She has also written a number of other books including an excellent volume entitled, *You Can Teach Your Child Successfully*. In this book she gives helpful instruction on how to teach using real books instead of texts or workbooks.

Quoting from her book, *You Can Teach Your Child Successfully*:

Some educators question whether textbooks, even at their best, could ever do the job. "The very nature of textbooks is to present information that is predigested, pre-thought, pre-analyzed, and pre-synthesized," says a school learning specialist. A steady diet of such books deprives children of the joy of original thought. It turns them off to learning. [11]

In saying that EDUCATION IS A LIFE, the need of intellectual and moral as well as of physical sustenance is implied. The mind feeds on ideas, and therefore children should have a generous curriculum.
— *Charlotte Mason,* Home Education, *Charlotte Mason Research and Supply*

To the memory of my mother: wise in counsel, tender in judgment and in all charity, strong in Christian faith and purpose, I dedicate, with reverence, this simple book.
— *Author's dedication to* The Five Little Peppers and How They Grew *by Margaret Sidney, Grosset and Dunlap, Inc.*

Ruth Beechick explains that although textbook series publishers boast about strengthening concepts, basic skills, and generalizations from one grade to the next, these things are not accomplished. The texts are a compilation of separate, disjointed topics.

She stresses the use of dictation as a significantly successful means of teaching. Copying selected passages is useful to younger children and can also be useful to children who find dictation too difficult. Lessons using copying or dictation integrate writing, grammar, spelling, punctuation, vocabulary, and comprehension skills for a well-balanced educational program.

Dictate a paragraph to your child, observe what he has trouble with and work on that. A grammar/composition handbook will prove to be a beneficial resource. **Writer's Express** is a good book to start with for the lower grades. For the middle grades and high school, I recommend **Write Source 2000** and **Writer's Inc.** All three handbooks are published by The Write Source. This company produces grammar/composition handbooks for each grade level, but as much of the material overlaps, you can use the titles I have recommended and adapt them to your children's levels. (I prefer to use only the student handbooks — not the teacher's guides or student workbooks.)

Common Sense Press publishes a series entitled, **Learning Language Arts through Literature**, which implements the copying and dictation learning approach set forth by Ruth Beechick. Each book in the series gives step-by-step instructions on how to get the full benefit of this method. The selections to be dictated or copied are chosen for you. This series will be helpful for those of you new to the dictation method of instruction.

As I use the unit study approach, I incorporate the dictation and copying methods whether we are conducting a literature unit, science unit, or other type of unit. Because all of our studies center on a particular topic, theme, or time period, the dictating and copying methods are a very easy way to integrate language arts into any study area. Charlotte Mason's narration method of study is also easily incorporated into a unit study.

There are many other experts in the homeschooling arena advocating a more practical approach to learning as opposed to a textbook-workbook oriented approach. I have read a number of the books by these people, but space does not permit me to comment on all of them. Raymond and Dorothy Moore have written numerous books expelling the myth that seeks to legitimize the effectiveness of the workbook approach. As a result of increased awareness, several publishers have produced materials based on the unit study method, some of which I have used or examined. Although superior to the basic workbook-oriented curriculums, I still felt in bondage when using them.

My family's particular needs and desires drive me to develop our own unit studies. It does take time and dedication, but so does trying to keep up with several children working at different levels, on different subjects, in different books. We are learning as a family. Our goals and priorities are based on our needs; they are not based on someone else's lesson plans — someone who is not familiar with my family.

Next, we will discuss how you can successfully create your own unit studies. Do not let the self-proclaimed experts intimidate you. What was accepted as educationally sound a few years ago is now regarded as incorrect. Why? Because the experts are realizing that their inferior teaching methods and materials do not work. The curriculum specialists plod away trying to come up with new and better methods and materials, and the textbook publishers happily print and sell new editions of texts and workbooks each year. Have you ever gone to a public school book depository and wondered why they were getting rid of so many books? If the public school does not want them, I certainly do not! Let us be cautious of some Christian textbook publishers who mimic the secular, but throw in a Bible verse here and there as a peace offering. This is an insult to true Christianity.

Quoting from Ruth Beechick's book, **You Can Teach Your Child Successfully**:

> For some children and for some time, certain books will happen to be just right. But if you find yourself struggling to mold your child to a book, try reversing priorities. It is the child you are teaching, not the book. Bend the book or find another; make the studies fit the child! [12]

Before we dive into the *how* of creating your own unit studies, I would like to review some simple and effective programs for teaching phonics and math to younger children. These are also helpful for those needing remedial work.

In recent years, I have developed a phonics program entitled **Reading Made Easy: A Guide to Teach Your Child to Read**. (See pages 333-334 for more information.) This program uses special "print clues" to help the child know what sounds the letters make in each word. For example, when the letter "a" makes a short vowel sound as in "cat," the letter "a" appears in a gray font. When the letter "a" makes the long vowel sound as in "cake," it appears in a bold black font. This simple, no-frills approach allows the child to begin reading stories right away without spending weeks and weeks on word drills.

Some phonics programs are so detailed that the student becomes

The first period — from colonial times to the 1840s — saw the dominance of the Calvinist ethic: God's omnipotent sovereignty was the central reality of man's existence. In the Calvinist scheme, the purpose of man's life was to glorify God, and the attainment of Biblical literacy was considered the overriding spiritual and moral function of education. Latin, Greek and Hebrew were studied because they were original languages of the Bible and of theological literature. Thus, this period in American education is characterized by a very high standard of literacy.
— Samuel Blumenfeld, "Who Killed Excellence?" Imprimis 1985

Phonics and Math

confused. Too many rules often complicates matters. Generally, most any phonics program will do, but you will do well to eliminate much of the workbook tedium. Here again, dictation and copying work well when teaching phonics, and I have incorporated this learning approach in my phonics program. You need only spend about 20 minutes each weekday to teach phonics.

Read often to your children. Point out letters or combinations of letters and the sounds they make as you read along. Keep this brief so as not to put a damper on story time. Read using your finger as you go along so your children will become accustomed to reading from left to right. Point out parts of books, such as the table of contents, index, glossary, copyright, author, and illustrator. Read the book jacket, which usually includes information about the author and illustrator. Books come alive as you become familiar with their features. The more you read to your children, the more they will want to read for themselves. Continue to read aloud to them even when they become proficient readers. Begin reading to your children when they are very young as this helps to build their attention spans.

It is not necessary to buy very controlled phonetic readers. I was using some with my son, Robert, who was almost six at the time. He was dutifully reading one when he remarked, "Mommy, people don't really talk like that!" I asked him if he would rather write his own books, and he agreed that would be much better. I brought out some large newsprint paper with big lines. I told him to dictate a story to me and I would write it down. He came up with many truly creative stories. Afterward, I would have him read the stories back to me. I was fearful that the vocabulary would be too difficult for him, but to my surprise I only had to help him occasionally. His familiarity with his own story enabled him to coast over the more difficult words. I continued to give him more phonics instruction for brief periods, and within six months he had progressed from reading on a kindergarten level to reading on the third grade level. His self-confidence was tremendously boosted and he became quite a good storyteller.

His younger brother, Raymond, did not want to be left out, and although he could only read a few short vowel words, he also wanted to dictate stories. I would read his stories back to him. He was so pleased with himself, and I often had to force him to end his stories as his imagination did not want to quit. Now when I ask my boys to write a story, they are not overwhelmed because they have had ample practice. This method also works well with older children who are reluctant writers.

I like to play games with my children to increase their reading ability. Sometimes I send them on a treasure hunt. First, I give them a note which leads them to another note I have hidden. They continue from note to note until they find the treasure, usually a cookie. I write them notes at night and leave them in their room for them to discover the next morning. You can make mail boxes for them to keep in their rooms for these special notes.

The library is loaded with easy readers and picture books. Mary Pride advocates the use of Dr. Seuss books as beginning readers. These are easily found even in the most meager of libraries. Let you children choose from several you select. Allow them plenty of time to read at an easy level so they become comfortable with books. Let them continue to choose some easy books even when they are beyond this level. This can be just for fun. Have them dictate stories to you, and if they are comfortable enough, they can write down short stories for themselves. Perhaps they may want to only write a sentence or two and dictate the rest to you or an older sibling. Do not worry about technicalities or spelling at first. Just give lots of encouragement.

If a child does not seem to be picking up the phonics, let it rest for awhile and continue to read excellent books to him. A child should never be deprived of the benefits of good literature because he cannot read well. Read to him. This is a must for older children as well, who may not read proficiently.

I normally use a math text during our unit study schedule for the older children and a math manual for the younger children. We also play a variety of math games. It is not always possible to integrate math into your unit studies enough to provide sufficient practice in the appropriate areas. I feel that the Saxon Publishing Company markets one of the best math curriculums for the upper grades, 4th through 12th.

I find that hands-on math is best for Kindergarten through 3rd grade. I use a large hundred-board with removable number tags. In recent years I have found that Learning Resources produces several hundred-board products. My favorites are the **Hundreds Pocket Chart** (LER 2208) and the **1-100 Combination Kit** (LER 0373). Learning Resources also produces **Cuisenaire Rods** (LER 7480), which I find extremely beneficial for teaching mathematical concepts. These rods can be used with a host of reusable workbooks designed for Kindergarten through high school level.

Using a manual or a text is desirable when studying math because it is important to follow a sequential order. But it is extremely important that we do not just teach our children how to do math; they need the concepts behind the figures. Share math with your children in your everyday affairs. Help them to see the importance of using math in real life. There are a number of adequate math curriculums available. You should find one that suits your needs.

Nat was still working on surveying when he got his first glimpse at an algebra book. That night, for the first time, he studied all night. The sky was paling in the east when he started another notebook: ALGEBRA AND MATHEMATICS: Nathaniel Bowditch His Book.

Every time he had a chance he borrowed the algebra book, to copy it into his notebook. Between times, he copied everything on mathematics he could find in the Cyclopedia. Then he studied everything he could find on astronomy over again. He was sixteen the summer he figured how to make an almanac.
— Carry On, Mr. Bowditch *by Jean Lee Latham, Houghton Mifflin Company*

Schedules and Routines

My method and schedule for conducting unit studies may not be suited to you and your family. I am trying to emphasize that you can devise a program that will be right for your family, which can be superior to anything else on the market because you know your children better than anyone. Earnestly pray that the Lord will give you the guidance you need.

Please, do not assume that other home educators have it all together and never experience failure. This is not true. Neither is it true for the classroom teacher. You will grow as a home educator only when you are willing to jump in with both feet. Experience will be your best teacher. What may work with some families might not work with yours. Dare to be different. Our Heavenly Father created us all with unique abilities and tastes. If we were all the same, we would find life very monotonous. You can gain a great deal from other home educators, but you must first temper it with biblical truth and then rely on your intuition. I cannot begin to tell you the number of plans and curriculums I have tried over the years. A fair amount of selection is trial and error, but if we can push aside the world's false view of education, we will be on the road to a happy home education experience.

Reading has helped open my eyes in the area of education. I may not agree with every point that every author brings forth, but I am now able to sort out what is good for my family from what is not. There is a fine balance to be had between structure and freedom. We should never get so far from the middle that we lose sight of either end. We need to be able to lean to one side or the other.

Just as our Heavenly Father has given us laws to govern our lives, He has also given us much freedom within those boundaries. Some people have gone too far one way, leading to legalism, while others have gone too far the other way, leading to licentiousness or a free-for-all lifestyle.

Homeschooling requires maintaining a schedule while remaining flexible. When we were immersed in our world geography unit, my children were writing about the countries in South America as I was dictating to them. I said to my girls, "Today I am going to dictate to you about Brazil." Then they both blurted out, "Oh, please let's do Chile today instead!" I was able to be flexible enough to agree to that, since it did not alter my ultimate goal. If they had asked to cancel school that day instead of taking dictation on Brazil, I am sure I would have responded quite differently!

We must learn to be patient with our children, not pushing them to the point of being stressed out, while encouraging them to do their best and not be lazy. As my father once commented, it takes a "quiet determination" to educate your children. Education is a discipline. We must set a good example for our children in this area.

Children perform best when they have a set routine. This is an area where fathers can help out. Although I do the majority of the teaching, my husband gets the children up at six o'clock each weekday morning, gets them breakfast, has a breakfast Bible study with them, and helps them get started on their chores before he leaves for work. All the while I am dragging myself out of bed, showering and dressing. Then I get something to eat, and by the time I am finished eating they are dressed and ready to begin their school work. School goes very smoothly when we begin and end early, and my husband can spend time with the children before he leaves for work. It is amazing how positive their attitudes are when we keep this schedule. My husband is the key factor for setting the tone for the day.

It is important for husbands and wives to sit down together and decide what sort of schedule should be arranged for their school day. They should decide what forms of discipline should be used for laziness, disobedience and so forth. Then, the children should be made aware of these rules and the consequences of not following them. If a child thinks he can wear down Mom and therefore not have to do his work, or at least not all of it, then he will do just that. Mom will be burned out in a very short time. As difficult as it may sometimes be, Mom must not give in to the manipulating child. Here Dad can relieve Mom of some of the mental stress of dealing with disruptive attitudes. Often these attitudes can be squelched if Dad spends only a few minutes with his children in the mornings before school. He can let them know that he wants to see what they have accomplished when he gets home from work. This does not necessarily have to be done in a negative way, but even so, it makes them accountable for their behavior and school work. Then the children will actually look forward to showing Dad all they have done during the day.

You have undoubtedly read about or come across mothers who teach all their children together at the same time. They may be teaching several children, all at the dining room table, all working out of different textbooks, all working on different subjects, all at the same time! Somehow they manage. But that is just it, they are managers and not necessarily teachers.

I find that using the same unit study for all my children works best. They each work at an appropriate level, while we still maintain a sense of oneness. Even while utilizing this study method, I find it best not to try to always work with all my children at the same time. The baby plays during the first part of our school time and naps during the second part. Generally, I begin by working with the four older children as a group, then I allow the two younger boys to go and play while I work with my two older girls. After I have finished studies with the girls, they read silently or attend to a project, thus enabling me to give more individualized attention to my boys. I find it helpful to pair them in this

This relation of habit to human life — as the rails on which it runs to a locomotive — is perhaps the most suggestive and helpful to the educator; for just as it is on the whole easier for the locomotive to pursue its way on the rails than to take a disastrous run off them, so it is easier for the child to follow lines of habit carefully laid down than to run off these lines at his peril. It follows that this business of laying down lines towards the unexplored country of the child's future is a very serious and responsible one for the parent.
— Charlotte Mason, Home Education, *Charlotte Mason Research and Supply Co.*

How to Create Your Own Unit Study

way. We actually accomplish more than if I tried to continuously work with them all. It makes for much less competition and confusion. However, because we are all studying the same unit, the synergy of the unit is preserved and my preparation time is shortened. You must experiment to see what works best for your family.

When approaching a unit, it is often helpful to do an overview initially. Then you can temporarily drop the unit and come back to it at a later date and focus on some of its finer details. When we studied our unit on world geography, for instance, there was no realistic way to study each and every country in depth. But because we learned many geographical terms and the locations of all the countries, we will be able to conduct a mini-unit pertaining to one or more countries at a future date. The main world geography unit gave the children an overview of the world, while the mini-unit zeroes in on a specific location in the world.

This holds true for our unit on the human body. We did an overview of the body and its systems and learned the names of the organs and bones. I chose to study the eye, the skeletal system, and the digestive system in more depth. We read two biographies, one of a scientist and one of a physician. Later we will go back and study the other systems in more depth. Now they have some general information about the body on which to hang the information they will be exposed to in the future.

How much time should be spent on each unit? This should be left to your discretion because you know your own family's needs and abilities. Many people ask this question, so I will share a plan with you that we use.

We begin by taking off two weeks, during which time I plan two units to be covered during the following ten-week period. This two-week break enables the children and me to sew, make crafts, bake, or work on other projects that get pushed aside. In the midst of this two-week break, I go to the library by myself so I can concentrate on the units to be studied. I break the ten-week period into two, five-week units to prevent me from going overboard. I plan my units so that the more complicated unit comes first. If I find I need additional time, I borrow it from the next five-week period. I select something light and enjoyable for the second five-week unit, particularly something that allows us to get out of doors. (You can read outside under the shade of a big tree, and the toddlers can play in the grass and still absorb much information.) This is also a good time to conduct a unit that is primarily project-oriented, affording the children more enjoyment because there is less academic emphasis.

By implementing this two-week-off and ten-week-on schedule, we complete four, ten-week periods and five, two-week periods. In the course of a year, a two-week period remains and can be inserted at any time into my schedule, such as holiday times or vacations. This routine allows me to teach for 200 days out of the year, while a typical school year consists of 180 days.

Taking off three months during the summer only complicates matters as you lose the discipline of your schedule, and afterwards you must review rusty skills. My children really look forward to their two-week vacations, and they plan ahead the projects they want to undertake. During these two-week periods there is none of the "Mommy, I'm bored," as a result of having too much free time on their hands. They know their time is limited so they make the best of it. Each family is different so you should find a plan that works for you.

We previously homeschooled all year round, and I never seemed to have any time for myself. I was always trying to squeeze my lesson plans into any available slot. Now, I am much more content. I also read an inspiring book on homeschooling to help give me fresh ideas.

Over the course of the months that I have taken to write this book, my own schedule has been altered to meet the needs of my family. It is wonderful how homeschooling allows us the flexibility we need to remain close.

(Note: Once I became familiar with putting together a unit study, I included my children in the research process.)

Getting Started

*B*eginning your unit study is as simple as picking a topic. You can choose any topic that interests you and your family. If you are worried about covering all the necessary material covered in a regular school curriculum, use **Teaching Children** by Diane Lopez or **The Christian Home Educators' Curriculum Manual** by Cathy Duffy as a basic framework for the elementary grades. As I mentioned before, I am not too worried about what others say we should be teaching our children or when they say we should be teaching these things. Remember, you are *teaching* your children, not *following* a textbook.

I am often asked about the effectiveness of using unit studies when teaching high-school students. I believe this is definitely the best method for instructing older children as well and provides you with an opportunity to guide them in meaningful research. You are actually teaching them how to learn. You have an opportunity to show them how you put together a unit of study, and you are giving them the tools to go on and learn for themselves. After you have given them sufficient instruction in putting together a unit study, they can choose a topic to research on their own, and they can lead the rest of the family through this unit study. This teaches them about a particular topic, while simultaneously learning research and teaching skills. After all, we want

Since there is no widespread agreement on what should be taught in each grade, you can be assured that you will do no damage to your own curriculums by making adjustments that fit your situation.
— *Ruth Beechick*
You Can Teach Your Child Successfully, *Arrow Press*

our children to go on to teach their children at home.

This unit study conducted by your high school students can be as brief or as elaborate as suits their abilities and needs. It also provides a good opportunity to research careers, and maybe even spur them on to start their own businesses. The possibilities are endless.

Many may be concerned about teaching all the subjects ordinarily taught in high school. There are several approaches. One is to use textbooks (which can be obtained free of charge at certain times during the year from the public school book depository) and use them as a general guide. Be cautious and only use the table of contents, chapter outlines, summaries and/or glossaries. You can get a general feel for what is being covered and at what time for each subject. Some curriculum publishers make scope and sequence charts available free of charge, which are useful as guides. (When a scope and sequence chart states that a particular topic is covered, it may mean that only an introduction to this topic is given. You may notice this particular topic is covered again the next year, as is often the case.)

Cathy Duffy's **Christian Home Educators' Curriculum Manual** for junior and senior high school is the most comprehensive resource I have found for devising high school studies. Cathy indicates the usual subject matter covered in each grade and has many reproducible charts for keeping records to benefit the college-bound student. With a minimal amount of research, you can plan the unit studies for your high school student for the year.

Some topics we have chosen for our unit studies have been: sculpture, four composers studied simultaneously, three American poets studied simultaneously, architecture, famous painters, the writing of the Unites States Constitution, the instruments of the orchestra, sound, the Tabernacle, world geography and explorers, the human body, and children's authors — along with writing our own books. We plan to study more poets, artists, composers, geometry and famous mathematicians, astronomy, early America, flowers, butterflies, insects, trees, and Florida history, just to name a few. Sometimes, while in the midst of one study, our interests are sparked on to another related topic. Some teachers might call this being side tracked; I call it opportunity.

You can make your unit study brief or in depth. You can even decide as you progress through a unit just how much material you want to cover. Children do better if they first get an overall, basic-level picture of what you are studying. You can then proceed to more closely cover the fine points. You should be striving for real learning, not just fact memorization. When choosing a topic, be sure to pick one that will enable you to locate sufficient materials from the library. If you pick a topic that is too highly specialized, you may not find many resources. On the other hand, if you pick a topic that is too general, you may find the study to be never-ending. You need some limitations. When we did our unit on world geography, I began to realize that we could go on forever. I then made a basic outline of the material I wanted to cover. I deviated from this basic outline somewhat as we progressed, but it prevented me from going to extremes. I realized we just could not cover everything, so we hit what I felt were the main points. We can explore the other areas in more detail by planning mini-units covering various countries or geographical land formations. The topics for units based on a geography study are endless.

Some encyclopedias have outlines accompanying their various articles that you can use as a basic guide for your particular unit study. Try to think of other areas of interest you can tie into your basic topic. For instance, when we studied world geography, we studied the lives of seven early explorers and one female missionary. We read complete biographies of each of these people.

For each unit study I locate biographies of those whose lives relate to our particular topic. My older children and I take turns daily reading aloud from these biographies while my younger children listen. This gives practice with oral reading as well as listening skills. A biography is an excellent tool enabling our children to experience the cultural, economical, geographical, and political climate of a time and place. This encompasses actual social studies. We are learning about real people in real times in real places, not abstract data.

Use maps frequently so you and your children will become familiar with the places people lived. You can discuss how they talked, what they ate, what they wore, what they believed in, what they did for entertainment, and so on. Children are far more interested in these things than in dry textbook data.

I commented previously that for each biography read, my children and I make a figure representing that person to go on our timeline. We discuss what particular things about that person stand out foremost in our minds. For instance, when we studied various American poets, we read a biography about Robert Frost, and my daughter drew him with blue eyes and tennis shoes, holding a piece of paper in his hand with the title of his well-loved poem, "Stopping by Woods on a Snowy Evening." Those things stuck in her mind. We cover these timeline figures with clear contact paper for durability. You may choose to laminate your figures.

Many people like the idea of using a timeline but do not have the wall space. I will offer another alternative. We decided to remove our timeline even though we have the wall space, because it did not seem very effective. A ladder was needed to reach the top! I did not feel my children were able to benefit from it as well as from something they could hold in their hands. Consequently, we have switched to a 14" x 17" binder with

For children, timelines are not for pulling together the scattered pieces of knowledge, as they do so well for adults; children haven't yet collected enough pieces to pull together. What timelines can do for children is to provide a framework into which they can put pieces of knowledge as they learn them.
— Ruth Beechick
You Can Teach Your Child Successfully, *Arrow Press*

plastic sleeves purchased from an art and drafting supply store. We cut poster board, on which we draw three lines horizontally, one half inch wide and four inches apart, representing our timelines. As the portfolio opens, the lines continue across the two pages and, for example, represent the 1700's. We use different pages to represent different time periods, and where necessary, several pages represent a particular time period. When few individuals from a time period are likely to be studied, several hundreds of years are represented on one or two pages.

We cut 3" x 5" index cards in half, and the children draw their historical figure on the card. The children then add distinguishing features indicative of their historical figure, including the individual's name and birth and death dates at the bottom of the card. Using a card of a specific size helps us to maintain uniformity in our portfolio, but the children are allowed to represent their figure in any fashion they choose on the card. The timeline-figure cards are inserted into pre-cut slits made on the portfolio pages. These slits are made like those in an old-fashioned photo album, allowing the corners of the cards to be tucked into the slits. Each portfolio page holds twelve cards — four across and three down.

Borders around the pages, illustrative of the time period, enhance the timeline portfolio. This is especially useful for the time periods where we have studied few individuals, enabling the children to grasp the flavor of that segment of history. The timeline pages are inserted into the plastic sleeves and easily removed for including additional figures.

A timeline portfolio makes a great hands-on teaching aid for children and still allows your family the flexibility to be creative. Some children want their own timelines, in which case you can use a regular or slightly larger notebook with plastic sleeves. These are available at most office supply stores. Please see page 109 where I have added a new section about how to make timelines entitled, **A Word about Timelines**.

I am sure there are many of you who feel uneasy about breaking away from textbooks. It is my belief this anxiety will be relieved as you become more and more frustrated with textbooks. You can experiment with the unit study approach while remaining safe within the pages of your textbooks. Allow me to suggest a simple plan.

Choose one of your children's textbooks, a history text for example. Peruse the textbook until you find a chapter that interests you. Note the key people, places, and events in this chapter and choose relative library books. Generally I suggest selecting one biography; one or two books pertaining to the place being studied; and one or two books relating to a specific event, discovery, or invention mentioned in the textbook chapter. (See the library check list in the next section for more information on selecting books.) Do not read the textbook chapter to your children, although you may want to read it yourself. Do not have them answer the questions at the end of the chapter. Have fun with this unit. Determine how much time you will spend on this study (perhaps two or three weeks), and when you have completed the unit study resume your regular textbooks studies. Try this approach later in the year, using a chapter from a science text, literature text, or other textbook. If you are teaching several children, use a history text from one grade level to conduct a unit and a science text from another grade level for your next unit. Do not use any textbooks other than a math text during your unit study as all other subjects will be integrated into your main topic. You may need to reduce some of your children's workbook or textbook written work during the year to afford you the necessary time to conduct these unit studies. This can be accomplished as you have the children do some of their work orally.

I want to encourage those of you using a published unit study to tailor the study to fit your family. Do not feel obligated to cover all the material in the manual. Use the manual as a resource guide, selecting units that appeal to you and your family. Use the information that will help you achieve the goals you have for your family. If a particular study spurs your interest in another area, feel free to explore that area on your own.

You may not always be certain which biographies of famous persons are appropriate for your study. We like to read biographies of several explorers while studying our geography units. I can recall only a few explorers, so I go to the reference section of the children's department of the public library and find several indexes to aid me in my search for materials for my unit study. One such book is the ***Index to Collective Biographies for Young Readers: Elementary and Jr. High Level***, compiled by Judith Silverman. I look up explorers and find literally pages of them under subheadings such as French Explorers, Spanish Explorers, etc… This is helpful as I want to choose explorers predominantly from the same time period.

Our studies are enhanced as we read these biographies and begin to see how the lives of these explorers overlap. We find some of them had sailed together or used the knowledge acquired by another's voyage to further their own expeditions. History comes alive as you see how the lives of people intertwine.

We also use that particular index to find the names of American poets. First, I look up poets, and then under that I find the subheading for American poets. This index is also useful for browsing through to find a subject you are interested in studying. Then under the particular subject you choose, you will find various lists or pertinent names of persons whose biographies you can read. The titles for all of these biographies are

Young children are very much interested in the world and people around them. If we begin reading biographies and enjoyable historical novels to our children before history has a chance to become a boring subject, we are more likely to create a positive lifelong attitude towards history.
— *Cathy Duffy*
Christian Home Educators' Curriculum Manual, Elementary Grades, *1990 edition, Grove Publishing*

Using the Library

listed elsewhere in the book and are located by using the book's cross-reference coding. There is another helpful reference book entitled ***People in Books***, by Margaret Nicholsen. This is easier to use than the ***Index to Collective Biographies for Young Readers***, because no cross-reference system is used to locate book titles. However, it is not as extensive.

It is not always necessary to use one of these indexes to find biographies, as most are easily found by locating the Junior Biography section of your library and looking under that particular person's last name. The books are shelved in alphabetical order. The indexes are extremely helpful for locating persons who somehow relate to your study. If you library does not have an appropriate biography, the ***Index to Collective Biographies for Young Readers***, or ***People in Books*** will be helpful. Look in these indexes to see if such a biography does exist about a person, or perhaps that person is included in a book that covers several different persons. If you discover an appropriate book, find out if your branch has it in its card catalogue, and if it does not, have the librarian check to see if another branch does. Usually it only takes a few days to transfer a book from another branch.

The **subject card catalogue** can also aid in your search for particular books pertaining to your topic, including biographies and other helpful books. (Since the first printing of this book, library card catalogues have been computerized, thereby making it much easier to search for materials. You can use the computer to search for materials by subject as well as by author, title, and series. You can also narrow your search to locate books or materials within a specified format such as Adult Fiction, Books on Cassette, Books on CD, DVD's, Juvenile Fiction, Juvenile Biography, Easy Picture Books, and so forth.) When studying geography, I use the subject card catalogue to find books on maps and countries. Finding books will be much simpler after you become acquainted with your library. Often you can go straight to a certain area to find the books you want because you have become familiar with the layout of the library.

During your unit study, it is good to use some books that are written on an easy level but that cover key points. Do not be afraid to use books which are on an advanced reading level, even books from the adult section of the library, as many of these books have excellent pictures. This is especially true of the fine art section. You may choose to read various selections from these books to your children or use them only for their illustrations.

Not every book we find will be in harmony with our beliefs. You can either skip undesirable sections of books or use them for discussing your beliefs and how others believe. You can explain to your children that not everything in print is accurate and therefore must be tempered with

Scripture.

You will find many helpful guides and reference manuals in the children's reference section of your public library; some of these we reviewed earlier. Many of the children's classics are also found in the reference section. These may not be checked out, but they often have copies which may be checked out on the regular book shelves. Browsing through these classics in the reference section will familiarize you with these timeless books. Other pertinent books are located in the reference sections and are usually worth investigating.

Be sure to utilize audio cassette tapes, video tapes and art work which can all be checked out and will enhance your unit study. Remember, however, to keep things simple at first.

The following check list may assist you in your search for materials to be obtained from the library. This list suggests major areas from which to choose materials, depending on the unit.

Biographies: Select biographies of those persons relating to your unit of study. (Remember, the reference section is helpful for this.)

Non-fiction: Choose factual books pertaining to your unit, i.e., books on the solar system, the Revolutionary War, famous inventions, etc…

Fiction: These include stories relating by topic or time period to your unit. There are many interesting historical novels, animal stories, and so on.

Easy Books: Find both easy readers, picture books, and simple books that accentuate key points.

Fine Art: Investigate the children's section and the adult section. For instance, if you are studying boats, look for books with reproductions of boats. The fine arts section has a subject catalogue that makes this an easy task. Many libraries have framed art reproductions that can be checked out. Biographies and works of artists are also available. You will discover books pertaining to architecture in this section to enhance the study of a particular place or time period.

Music: Locate audio cassette tapes, records and song books relating to your unit by style or topic. Also examine composers or artists of the time period you are studying.

Arts and Crafts: Select arts and crafts books representative of your topic or time period. There are several historically based craft books. (Example: ***Let's Be Early Settlers with Daniel Boone***.)

Literature and Poetry: Investigate famous poets and authors who lived in the same time period and location as your study or who wrote about the topic you are covering. Investigate poems and plays relating to

Let him on the contrary linger pleasantly over the history of a single man, a short period until he thinks the thoughts of that man, is at home in the ways of that period. Though he is reading and thinking of the lifetime of a single man, he is really getting intimately acquainted with the history of a whole nation for a whole age.
— *Charlotte Mason,* Home Education, *Charlotte Mason Research and Supply Co.*

your topic. Plays may be either read aloud or acted out in costume.

Home Economics: Cookbooks are great tools for studying particular historical time periods or the cultures of various countries. (Example: *The Little House Cookbook*.)

Clothing: There are several interesting books that depict the costumes of particular time periods and various countries or trades.

Videocassettes: Numerous videos are available that pertain to foreign countries, artists' lives and works, storytelling, science experiments, foreign languages, and sign language. Classic movies, plays, and ballets are also obtainable on videocassette.

Science: If you are engaged in a unit that is primarily a science based unit, you will of course find books in this area. However, science can come into play in historical units as you investigate inventions, inventors, and discoveries of the day. There are many science experiment books that can be integrated into your unit.

Some of the areas mentioned can be incorporated later and used to review material previously covered. This material can be viewed from a different perspective.

(Please refer to the Library Reference Guide on page 89 for information on the resources available in the children's reference section of your public library.)

Briefly review the library books you have chosen. Find one or two key books to serve as your basic "texts," preferably a suitable biography and/or a readable book that covers key points. Books that have an abundance of technical information may be helpful for reference purposes but will not qualify as an overall text. Your text should present a general overview of the material to be covered.

These key books will suffice as material for you to read aloud to your children. This will unite the family in the study while offering discussion topics, which stimulate reading comprehension. Each child will benefit as he absorbs that which he is able. Employ the capable children to read portions of these books aloud.

It is helpful to categorize the remaining books into groups by subject, which relate to music, art, science, fiction, non-fiction, literature, easy books, and so on. You may use some books only for their illustrations or photographs, others may serve for your children to read on their own, and some books may be beneficial for copy work or dictation. As a suggested activity, have your children read some of these books on their own, making a list of the words they do not understand. These words can be looked up in the dictionary. Occasionally, glossaries are included in factual books. Index cards are helpful as the children write the unknown word on the front and the definition on the back. The cards are useful for later review and can be shared with the other siblings.

You may find some books are repetitious, so choose only those that suit your needs. Allowing older children to read some of the simpler books to the younger children benefits the older as well as the younger. It reinforces what they have been learning, gives them practice reading aloud, helps to form strong bonds between siblings, and prepares for future roles as parent-teachers. (Not to mention, it frees you up a little.)

As you become more proficient at conducting unit studies, you learn to weed out books while at the library so you do not come home swamped. Remember, you can always devote more time to a unit at a later date. Do not feel you have to totally exhaust the library and put to use every book it contains on any given subject. (For instance, we conducted an American Revolution unit and viewed that era through the eyes of its painters. At a later date, we will focus on the music of the Revolution.)

I have found that games are a great way for children to learn about various subjects. They are non-consumable (may be used again and again), and they are good for reviewing previously covered material. Aristoplay makes excellent educational games. We use their game *Where in the World?* when conducting our geography units. My girls and I learn the names and locations of each country in the world and their major seacoasts. We also learn key facts about many of the countries. Even my younger boys benefit from this game. One writing exercise that my children enjoy was inspired by this game. The game has a deck-sized card for each country including that country's name, flag, literacy rate, monetary unit, major languages, major seacoast, major import, and major export. I have my children make up their own country and make a card for it which includes these same items. Then they make a map showing the location of their country, and they write a paragraph about the people of their make-believe country. You will quickly find that it is not difficult to invent writing assignments or come up with projects relating to your unit study. Let the children think up some assignments for themselves; most children can be very creative when given an opportunity.

Each Aristoplay game has directions for playing several different games on several different levels, increasing its effectiveness. I like to have an accompanying game for each unit we cover. This offers variety to our study and is a good tool for review. You can also make your own games to fit your study. This of course takes time, but it is also less expensive. My children have always enjoyed the games I have made. Your children can invent games to go along with your unit study; this will cause them to probe for questions and answers pertaining to your unit

Using Games and Teaching Aids

We need to change the way most of us think, so that we can see learning opportunities in many things around us. We need to change our "mind set" so that we can see other things than textbooks as curriculum material.
— *Cathy Duffy* Christian Home Educators' Curriculum Manual, *Elementary Grades, 1990 edition, Grove Publishing*

Using Dictation and Copying

study. They will use many valuable skills making up their own games and have fun in the process.

For some units, you may want to do a little extra and purchase a few additional items to enhance for study. For instance, our biggest unit we covered one past school year was our world geography unit. Not only did we purchase the **Where in the World?** game, but we bought a map-of-the-world shower curtain. This has proven beneficial to the entire family. I find myself brushing up on my countries while in the shower. To keep pace with the children, this is necessary!

We already had a globe. I bought two tapes from Audio-Memory Publishing Company entitled **Geography Songs** and **More Geography Songs**. We still listen to these tapes to keep ourselves up to date on our geography facts. My dad gave the children a terrific book put out by National Geographic called **Exploring Your World**. It is an alphabetized glossary of geographical terms with beautiful full-color pictures. I use this book to dictate geographical terms to my children. As we read the biographies of the various explorers, we encounter certain terms which we look up in **Exploring Your World**, and I dictate the definitions of these terms to the children.

I would like to talk more about the benefits of dictation. Many older children do well when passages of pertinent material are dictated to them; however, younger children can copy the selections you choose. When implementing the copying exercises, I neatly write out what I want them to copy so they have a model showing proper letter formation. Older children may be able to copy directly from a book. As you work with your children you will be able to discern exactly what form of copying or dictation they can do and how much. Start slowly and gradually increase the amount to be copied or taken from dictation. Do not overwhelm them.

As I dictate to my children, or as they copy a selection, I emphasize important points about spelling, punctuation, capitalization, vocabulary, and so forth. When I am dictating a passage with difficult punctuation, I read in the punctuation and explain the reasoning for its use. Sometimes, I may dictate a sentence and then tell them that there are three commas in that sentence and ask them to put them in. Then I check to see if they have placed them in their proper places. Or, sometimes I put in extra commas and ask them which commas should be removed. For younger children copying a selection, I sometimes omit punctuation in the passage they are to copy and inform them that they need to put in the punctuation. They learn considerably more from these methods of dictation and copying than they would from isolated worksheets dealing with spelling, punctuation, capitalization, vocabulary, etc… They are also working from a model that uses correct grammar and sentence structure. At the same time the children are learning these useful skills, they are learning about the topic we are studying. Valuable time is not wasted in the area of basic skills, but rather is integrated into real learning.

If a child is continuously exposed to well written material, whether by reading, copying, dictating, or listening, he will be influenced in a positive way — much more so than by filling in worksheet after worksheet. Studies indicate that those who learn to diagram sentences well do not automatically become good writers. Those who write well do so because they are exposed to good writing, and they themselves write often.

I have a friend who is an author and a former editor who plainly states she could not diagram a sentence if her life depended on it! If you go for a job interview, certainly on the application they will not ask you to diagram a sentence; but, they might very well ask for an essay. Sentence diagramming is an effective tool allowing us to see **how** the parts of a sentence interact. It does not show **why**. Dwelling on such tedium is unnecessary; however, an introduction to these interrelations is a beneficial exercise for your high school students. I suggest using the *Winston Grammar Kit*, as it uses a hands-on approach to sentence diagramming. *Easy Grammar* by Wanda Phillips is also a good choice for your older student.

Many famous authors used the copying method to train themselves to be proficient writers, just as skillful artists have for centuries copied the works of the great masters. Copying was the self-teaching method of Benjamin Franklin. You will find in any field of excellence that conscientious people seek out and copy those who are experts. It is actually so simple and works so well that it is difficult for us to believe that it produces sound writers.

We use this method of dictation and copying extensively since it is beneficial and yet simple. After choosing the topic for our unit study, we converge on the library and I select our books while the children busy themselves choosing books of their own interest. As mentioned earlier, I select a biography or several biographies of persons whose lives somehow relate to our unit of study. I also choose books directly relating to the subject matter at hand, choosing both easy and more difficult books.

Before beginning our lessons, I briefly skim these books and choose a selection to dictate to the children. Generally, I pick the most significant material, sometimes skipping sentences that are not crucial. However, even those sentences that are skipped are read, but not for the purpose of dictation. Truly undesirable portions are left out altogether.

Usually, I will dictate **pertinent information** from an entire book

Where then does grammar fit in? Not before the writing. Not as a way to learn to write. Reverse this order; have your children write as a way to learn grammar. They learned a great deal of grammar as they learned to talk. Now as they write and read, they continue learning grammar.

When you treat writing holistically, encouraging and helping your child to ever better writing, the grammar comes along too.
Ruth Beechick
You Can Teach Your Child Successfully, *published by Arrow Press*

to give continuity to our study. Of course, with some books, only certain sections or chapters may pertain to your study, and some books I use for pictures or diagrams only. I also choose simple books that I read to the younger children, and they use these for their copy work. My older children read these books on their own during quiet time; this helps to reinforce our study. Once we have read a biography aloud together, I use the summary of the book found in the front of the book jacket as a dictation or copying exercise for my children. This is an excellent way to encapsulate the book. They are being given a good example of a book summary which will aid them in learning to write their own summaries.

How much dictation or copy work should your children do? The answer to this question can only be found as you work with your children. For very young children, one key sentence may be enough. More experienced children may write a paragraph. My two girls have worked up to writing 1 to 2 pages, handwritten on notebook paper from dictation. My boys, who are younger, copy one or two pertinent sentences that I have written for them after having read a book or chapters from a book to them. I select these sentences from those books dealing with our unit of study. For the boys, I use the large, lined newsprint paper purchased from a school supply store. I write the selection to be copied at the top of the paper, paying close attention to letter formation and spacing. This provides the children a good model from which to copy.

Writing is certainly a medium for communication, as all art forms are. It gives the opportunity for direct communication, for verbalizing thoughts and attitudes, for speaking truth and putting content into expression.
— *Edith Schaeffer* Hidden Art, *Tyndale House Publishers*

The Importance of Writing

*I*t is crucial that our children learn to write well. An excellent book offering much inspiration for teaching children to write entitled **Write From the Start**, by Donald Graves and Virginia Stuart, is available at the public library. In this book, Mr. Graves makes an interesting statement.

A well-written piece can transcend the barriers within a society that demands diplomas and other certificates of achievement. [13]

The apostle Paul states in the Bible that he could more effectively communicate the Lord's Word through the written word than in person. Therefore, he was able to have an effective ministry even while in prison.

Being able to put thoughts into words and thereafter into the written word is a goal we and our children should strive toward. Dictation and copying serve as an effective means of achieving this goal.

Let your children see you reading and writing and, thereby, serving as an example; for children love to imitate. Later, I will discuss the usefulness of incorporating Scripture into dictation or copying exercises…more precisely as typing exercises.

Most published unit study curriculums are noted for their heavy emphasis on projects. Their contention is that children learn best by doing. While this is generally true, most mothers burn out trying to organize all these activities. These hands-on projects are nice once in a while and add a change of pace to your unit studies, but a steady diet can lead to frustration for Mom.

Do not feel guilty if you hear about other mothers who produce volcanic eruptions on their dining room tables or make relief maps of the world from papier-mâché...done to scale! Tailor your curriculum to fit your family's needs. Do not try to "keep up with the Joneses." One advantage of creating your own curriculum is that if you find a technique or a book does not work for you or your children, you have the freedom to alter it. And if you have not spent hundreds of dollars on a curriculum you are not pleased with, you feel less obligated to continue because of a monetary investment.

I find my children prefer to have access to plenty of paper, markers, paints, fabric scraps, glue, and milk cartons from which to make their own creations. Whether pertaining to our unit studies or not, they are using their creative imaginations; therefore, real learning is taking place. All learning does not have to be adult-contrived.

Children learn about the world around them as they play, observe nature, observe others at play or work, and as they have the freedom to explore and create. Of course, this does not mean they are totally unsupervised, but they are given immense freedom within certain boundaries. Some of the best projects we have done relating to our unit studies have been those devised by my children. If you ask your children to devise a project for a particular unit, you will be surprised how creative they can be. I find it helpful when engaged in a project to ease up a great deal on the more academic aspects of our unit and just concentrate on the project.

As I plan my units to be studied, I try to organize them in such a way as to encompass a variety of subjects within the year. One unit may deal predominantly with social studies, such as a unit on world geography, while the next might have its main thrust in science, such as a unit on the human body. A following unit's major theme might be literary, based on the study of children's authors. (During this unit, the children can write and illustrate their own books.) A subsequent unit might have its roots in mathematics and encompass a study of geometry and famous mathematicians of long ago. Afterward, we might study something lighter—like animals or insects—then perhaps music or art. By

Projects: Friend or Foe?

We older people, partly because of our maturer intellect, partly because of our defective education, get most of our knowledge through the medium of words. We set the child to learn in the same way, and find him dull and slow. Why? Because it is only with a few words in common use that he associates a definite meaning; all the rest are no more to him than the vocables of a foreign tongue. But set him face to face with a thing, and he is twenty times as quick as you are in knowing all about it; knowledge of things flies to the mind of a child as steel filings to a magnet.
— Charlotte Mason
Home Education ,
Charlotte Mason Research and Supply Co.

Choosing Your Units of Study

alternating basic subject studies, we add variety to our curriculum and achieve a well-rounded course of study.

I am often asked if it is necessary to conduct units as a family, especially if the children have varied interests. I personally enjoy conducting units together as a family because of the closeness it builds and the discipline it instills in my children. As we work together, they learn to respect one another, and they have many opportunities to learn patience. However, just having your children home all day allows for this type of interaction to a large degree. If your children are capable of conducting a unit on their own, with a certain amount of input from Mom and Dad, they can share this newfound information with the rest of the family. You might wish to set aside a certain day or evening for this purpose. This in itself would be a good opportunity for the children to improve their oral skills. We have also heard it said many times that the best way to remember something is to teach it to someone else.

It would be wise for each of us to allow our children to pursue individual units at some point to strengthen additional skills. This is definitely a desirable method for older children. We should also be teaching them to teach themselves and others also.

Reading Good Literature

*T*here are certain subjects I feel are important enough to be studied on a more regular basis, and have so altered my unit studies. I feel that books of high literary content should be read aloud to the children on a daily basis. These include timeless classics, Newbery Award Books, and books that have merited other awards. I try to read one chapter or a substantial bit of a chapter from such a book each day.

Often, we break from our unit of study and take some time out to concentrate on the particular book I am reading aloud. Generally, I have the children engaged in a writing activity centered on this book. I may have the older children write two pages about any part of the book. Sometimes, I have them create their own stories that in some way relate to the story we are reading. For instance, after reading **The Indian in the Cupboard** (a book about a plastic Indian that comes to life when placed in an old cupboard that is locked with a special key), I asked my girls to write a three-page story about a toy that comes to life. They wrote imaginative stories, each completely different even though they had both been inspired by the same book.

I have separate story times with my two older girls and my two younger boys. They like having a more individualized story time. Even so, I still read books of high literary value to the younger children. They have no trouble with vocabulary above their level or with following a complicated storyline. If they do not understand something, they ask about it, and we discuss it. They like the fact that I take the time to answer their questions. Children who have not had more difficult books read aloud to them in the past will in time grow accustomed to listening to these stories and even find them enjoyable. My baby also wants to be included in story time. Sometimes she nurses while I read to the other children, or she plays quietly. She has special books I read to her, and she has books she can freely look through. I know not all children have an attention span for this, but you can build that attention span in them. Even babies should have picture books read to them each day.

My younger children are too young to write down their thoughts about the books I read aloud to them. Sometimes they retell the story or a portion of it to me. Sometimes they copy one or two key sentences that I choose from the book. They often make an illustration to go along with the book.

Most fictional books contain passages with dialogue, which make excellent dictation selections for older children, providing practice with commas, quotation marks, and beginning a new line when a different character speaks. Some writing activities can be as simple as having your children make lists of various things, people, or places in the story. You can have them compare or contrast two characters in the story. If you are still in the midst of reading the book, you can have them write their own ending.

If you feel you need more ideas for writing assignments, there are many creative writing books on the market. One useful book is entitled, *If You're Trying to Teach Kids to Write, You've Gotta Have This Book*. This book emphasizes that not all writing has to be creative writing but can be writing pertaining to everyday life.

To add variety to our lessons, we take a portion of our study time and devote it to taking a closer look at a pleasurable book I am reading aloud to my children. You might say that we are maintaining a continuing literary unit.

Fictional books can be used to enhance your study. For example, a unit involving the study of animals is an easy one for locating fictional books about these animals. While engaged in our world geography unit, we read a fictional story that took place in Japan, and it did much to open our eyes to the customs and beliefs of that country. These kinds of books add a little flavor to your study. Authors of fictional novels generally have extensive knowledge of their subject and location of their story. E.B. White's fictional story, *The Trumpet of the Swan*, although about a swan who could perform human-like tasks, was very real in its depiction of the geographical locations of the swan's travels.

Integrating classics and historical novels into your unit studies is

Mason called such works "living books," and her own extensive experience as an educator had demonstrated conclusively that when a child has an ongoing relationship with such books, he or she is willingly participating in the most effective form of education.

With good reason, Charlotte Mason equated the use of "living books" with the spreading of a lavish feast, full of flavor and nourishment, before children.
— Elizabeth Wilson
Books Children Love, *Crossway Books*

The train was coming, louder. They stood by the satchels on the platform and saw it coming. Laura did not know how they could get the satchels on the train. Ma's hands were full, and Laura had to hold onto Mary.

The engine's round front window glared in the sunshine like a huge eye. The smokestack flared upward to a wide top, and black smoke rolled up from it. A sudden streak of white shot up through the smoke, then the whistle screamed a long wild scream. The roaring thing came rushing straight at them all, swelling bigger and bigger, enormous, shaking everything with noise.

Then the worst was over. It had not hit them; it was roaring by them on thick big wheels. Bumps and crashes ran along the freight cars and flat cars and they stopped moving. The train was there, and they had to get into it.

—By the Shores of Silver Lake *by Laura Ingalls Wilder,* HarperCollins Publishers

an effective teaching method; however, reverse this technique, allowing the classics or novels to be the main emphasis of your study. Choose a classic relating to a specific time period and/or place you wish to study. Skim through the book noting key people, places, events, discoveries, inventions, trades, and so on. This method is similar to the textbook-unit study method I earlier described in the section **Getting Started**.

A book such as Robert Louis Stevenson's ***Treasure Island*** lends itself to a study of pirates, the ocean, islands, ships, navigational terms, the author himself, and his other works such as ***A Child's Garden of Verses***. We spent a couple of months on this study, reading ***Treasure Island*** and making a video of an excerpt from the book. The children and I made all the costumes and scenery, and my oldest daughter filmed the performances. We employed two other home-educated boys as pirates. During this time, my children also wrote their own 16-page books as we studied literary styles. We read ***A Child's Garden of Verses***, spurring many creative writing assignments and art projects.

There are many excellent classics relating to early America. The ***Little House*** books, by Laura Ingalls Wilder, are a marvelous choice for a pioneer literary unit. As I read ***By the Shores of Silver Lake*** with my two boys, we made a brief study of the early trains in America. Laura, Mary, Carrie, Grace, and Ma experienced their first train ride as they crossed the prairie by rail to join Pa in the Dakota Territory. A study of the terrain and climate of the Midwest would be advantageous while reading these books. You might also study locusts, malaria, mosquitoes, flowers, grasses, westward expansion, circuit preachers, farming, fiddles, Old West towns, one-room schools, territories or statehood, muskrats, prairie hens, prairie dogs, wolves, log cabins, and the list continues.

Lois Lenski's books, such as ***Strawberry Girl***, ***Peanuts for Billy Ben***, ***To Be a Logger***, ***Shoo-fly Girl***, and several others, are excellent in their depiction of the people from specific regions and times in our country's past.

Heidi, ***Hans Brinker***, ***Swiss Family Robinson***, and ***The Cat Who Went to Heaven*** are a few classics whose stories are based in other countries. One friend of mine suggests that ***Swiss Family Robinson*** be used as a springboard for an interesting and intense science unit. This book describes numerous habitats, animals, plant life, and land formations. It depicts a strong love for our Creator; it places a heavy emphasis on character building, industry, creativity, and physical development. Not to mention its literary excellence surpasses most books written today. Even a simple task or event is described in an eloquent fashion.

While reading a classic you will find many and varied details, such as I have briefly mentioned, providing you with plenty of interesting material to study. I strongly encourage you to read the unabridged versions of these timeless books in order to benefit form their rich vocabulary and literary superiority.

The Foundation for American Christian Education publishes materials incorporating the notebook approach, emphasizing the study of *Key Classics on the Chain of Christianity*.

Books Children Love is a prime source for locating appealing classics to serve as a basis for your studies. Use your imagination and develop your own classic units. This will prove a rewarding experience as you share these books with your children. I have found the books are even more enthralling when we read them for a second time.

*T*he fine arts are another area I feel is important to study. All too often we overlook the fine arts in favor of more academic endeavors. Fine arts can be integrated into many units of study, or the study can center entirely on the life of a poet, artist, or composer.

As I mentioned earlier in the section on **Using the Library**, we conducted a study of the American Revolution and learned about the painters of that time. This allowed us to view that time period through the artistic eye. We enjoyed reading about the painters' lives and viewing their works from library books. The subject card catalogue in the fine arts section of your public library enables you to locate art work pertaining to your unit of study. During a study such as this, it is enjoyable for the children to try their hand at painting.

Poetry is a wonderful avenue to explore while engaged in almost any unit. You can locate poems about boats, trains, seasons, astronomy, the ocean, animals, and so forth. (The Library Reference Guide located on page 89 will aid you in your search for poems pertaining to your unit.)

A simple way to locate poems relating to your study is to select a large volume of poetry with a subject index. Look up words pertinent to your study. If you have difficulty locating volumes with a subject index, browse through the title index, for many first words of titles are indicative of their subject matter. This is also true of first lines of poems, and many poetry volumes also have indexes of first lines.

Music of a particular time period or geographical location can be integrated into your unit study. We plan to study the music of the Revolution. There are several songbooks relating to the Revolutionary period that include the music, words, and historical background of each song. Our library contains a videotape, *The Music of Williamsburg*.

Diana Waring offers tapes and songbooks, tracing United States

Fine Arts

There are things in the Christian world which cause us to be sad. One of these is that for many Christians classical music is a complete vacuum. This robs individual Christians and their children of one of the very rich areas of joy in this world. Incidentally, an ignorance of classical music also separates us from many people to whom we wish to speak, and this is a hindrance in our communication with them. But the central sadness of knowing little about classical music consist in the loss of the Christian experiences in one of the areas of the affirmation of life.
—Francis Schaeffer , *excerpted from the preface to* The Gift of Music, *Crossway Books.*

How to Create Your Own Unit Study

Nature Studies

history through song. The titles available are *History Alive through Music—America*, and *History Alive through Music—Westward Ho!*

While studying a particular country, you can examine the accomplishments of one of its composers of the past or present. There are many interesting children's biographies telling of the great composers' lives. Check out audio cassette tapes featuring works of a chosen composer, and have your children write a poem to accompany a particular musical selection. They might enjoy writing a song and even composing the music.

Fine art, music, and poetry add an enjoyable and refreshing aspect to our studies. This type of study also serves to activate the children's creativities.

Several published curriculums are available to enhance your fine art studies. The Cornerstone Curriculum Project offers *Music and Moments with the Masters* and *Adventures in Art*. Fine art prints of various sizes can be ordered form the National Gallery of Art in Washington, D.C. (You can also visit virtual art museums on the internet.)

*I*n Charlotte Mason's book entitled *Home Education*, she strongly emphasizes the need for children to become thoroughly acquainted with nature. She states:

> …she will point to some lovely flower or gracious tree, not only as a beautiful work, but a beautiful thought of God, in which we may believe He finds continual pleasure, and which He is pleased to see his human children rejoice in. [14]

Miss Mason advocates taking nature walks, collecting berries, sticks, wild flowers, leaves, and so forth. She makes an entire lesson of this in which the children then make drawings of the items collected. She also suggests identifying these specimens. (This can be done using paperback field guides. The guides are quite inexpensive and fairly easy to use.)

The first time we decided to undertake a nature mini-unit, my children and I went on a short walk down the alley behind our house and were amazed at how many interesting plants, mushrooms, leaves, and wild flowers we could find. We took our treasures home and drew the specimens we liked best. We also located these specimens in the field guides. Two hours later I informed my children that we had done enough for one day, but they all wanted to continue making more sketches. I had them date their drawings and put them in a folder designated for their nature mini-unit. I decided to incorporate this nature mini-unit into our course of study, whereby on the third Monday of each month this study is our main thrust.

We recently studied the Dutch artist Jan van Huysum. My son Raymond noticed right away how van Huysum had painted insects on his flowers, and this really fascinated Raymond. These insects were extremely small, and I hardly noticed them myself, but Raymond was very observant. As we were sketching the leaves and treasures that we had gathered on our walk, Raymond said he wanted to draw a bug on his leaf. Well, at that precise moment a bug walked onto his paper and posed for him; Raymond was very excited. Afterwards, we pressed the leaves and flowers. (Raymond pressed the bug too!)

I would like to spend a few minutes discussing the integration of the Bible into your unit studies. Another factor common to several published unit study curriculums is the integration of Scripture into the study. By using a concordance, I am able to find Scriptures that relate to my particular unit of study. For instance, when we were working on our world geography unit, I looked up words in my concordance like mountain, valley, sea, earth, and river. We studied the creation account in Genesis chapter one, and the older girls used this Scripture for typing practice.

I checked out a children's typing manual from the library and spent about two months on intense typing instruction. Now my girls maintain their typing skills by typing biblical excerpts pertaining to our particular unit of study. Some of these passages are used for memorizing. A large print Bible works well for the children's typing exercises. It is advantageous for your children to learn the typing basics. Keyboard experience will have lasting benefits.

Generally, a concordance will point you to key passages that deal with your unit, but this is not exhaustive. For example, when studying astronomy, a concordance can be used to look up related terms such as *star, constellation, sun, moon,* and *heavens*, since these specific words appear in biblical passages. A topical Bible will point you to many passages that would be missed by only utilizing a concordance. When using a topical Bible, such as **Nave's Topical Bible**, you can directly look up *astronomy* and it will lead you to related passages without requiring you to have prior knowledge of the subject matter.

If you are studying a particular painter, for instance, it may prove difficult to use a concordance to locate biblical material relating to your study. If you are reading the biography of this individual, you could ask yourself what character qualities this man or woman possessed. You would then be able to proceed to a topical Bible and look up these specific

The heavens are telling of the glory of God; And their expanse is declaring the work of his hands. Psalm 19:1 (NASV)

Using the Bible

Five principles for educating our children are revealed clearly in the fountainhead of all biblical texts on education, Deuteronomy 6: 4-9.

In this passage we find the purpose of education, the primary site of instruction, the specific curriculum, the designated faculty, and the most effective methods of instruction. By looking at these principles, we can see the biblical basis for home education.
— Gregg Harris "The Biblical Basis for Home Education," The Teaching Home *Aug/ Sept 1990*

How to Create Your Own Unit Study

qualities. This could be true of negative qualities as well, such as drunkenness or pride. You could investigate what the Bible has to say about such things. This helps your children to learn to discern character traits in others and evaluate their own growth.

Do not feel as if you have to try to spiritualize everything. Those things which are sinful are to be avoided, but all other things are a very real part of our Christian lives. Our Heavenly Father created the whole universe; therefore, any and all of His creation is worthy to be studied. In his book, *Addicted to Mediocrity*, Franky Schaeffer states:

> Things do not need spiritual or theological justification. They are what they are—as God made them. We are those who have been freed to truly see the world as it is and enjoy and revel in the diversity and beauty that God has made. Not everything needs to be justified in terms of tacking on a few Christian slogans at the end to somehow redeem it. Christ redeems what we do. We do not need to redeem it with slogans. There is no Christian world, no secular world, these are just words. There is only one world—the world God made. [15]

It is crucial that our children see how Scripture relates to all of life. Everything for an abundant life can be learned from these pages. Too often Christian curriculums do a tacky job of integrating Scripture into a lesson. We can show our children how Scripture is the basis for all of life. We can also teach our children how to use biblical study aids to find desired information. A concordance is fairly easy to use.

In our study on the human body, my children typed and memorized Psalm 139:13-16, the account of the infant in its mother's womb. They also used various other passages as typing assignments. We looked up words in the concordance such as *eye, body,* and *blood.* After reviewing several of the verses listed, I picked some appropriate for typing, dictation, or memorization assignments.

Record-Keeping

I use a daily log. I find it is convenient to enter the material covered daily as we go along. Planning ahead has it merits, but I find lesson plans cannot always be strictly followed. Too many things come up as we proceed through our study. It is advantageous to have your basic outline for the material you intend to cover; then enter the actual material covered in your log. If you have your log filled out neatly ahead of time, you will be less likely to deviate from it and thus lose those teachable moments. When your children ask a question pertaining to your study, you should have the flexibility to use that opportunity to teach something perhaps not on that day's lesson plan. If they ask something that you cannot answer yourself, then you have the flexibility to research that topic together. There are also times when you cannot cover all the material you have planned. Perhaps it will take longer than you anticipated. It is very frustrating if you have your plans neatly logged and then you cannot accomplish them all. At times you may feel the need to force your children to finish what you have written down previously, to avoid disrupting your log. Let your lesson plans work for you as a general guide, not against you like a task master.

I use a spiral notebook to record our progress because it is easy to write in, inexpensive compared to lesson planning books, easy to store, can be left open to the current page, and is flexible — not filled with graphs and charts that do not suit my purpose.

I print the beginning date on the cover of my daily logbook with a permanent marker. When the book is filled, I put the ending date on the cover as well and keep these log books for future reference. I designate one page for each day of the week; I combine Saturday and Sunday on one page to be used for logging books read or listened to and any other educational endeavors. In the top right-hand corner I write the date and day of the week. Even on days we do not do schoolwork, I date the page and enter anything pertinent such as field trips, games played, books read, projects accomplished, physical activities, and so forth.

I use one record-keeping book for my four children. I use two pages daily, writing the information for each child on one side of each page. You may wish to have a logbook for each of your children, as this may eliminate confusion in record-keeping for the purpose of presenting information to local officials if necessary.

I use a number of abbreviations for logging material, and as you proceed you will devise your own system. I write the full title and author of any books we use. This makes a handy reference guide for future studies. It prevents occurrences such as, "Now what was the name of that book we used when we studied geography? I remember it was such a good book." Do not think that you will be able to recall all this information. Write it down. Be sure to log your studies on a daily basis. Do not assume you can just go back and fill in the days. After awhile, one day seems to flow into another.

Keep your log simple. Be sure to include extra-curricular activities. **Physical Education** can be logged as anything from biking to basketball. I list cooking, sewing, or cleaning under **Home Economics**. If the child has done a special picture or project, I log it under **Art** or **Projects**. Remember, education does not end with school work. Many valuable lessons are learned throughout the day. Older children can also be taught to keep a log of their studies. This would be an excellent lesson

If we choose to work informally in some subjects, we find much overlapping of subject areas. This can be difficult to break down into subject headings to fill in a teacher's plan book. In this case, a journal of some kind, such as a spiral notebook, works well for writing down everything our child has done.
— *Cathy Duffy* Christian Home Educators' Curriculum Manual, Elementary Grades, *1990 edition, Grove Publishing*

In the evening, when our room was illuminated with wax candles, I wrote a journal of all the events which had occurred since our arrival in this foreign land. And, while the mother was busy with her needle and Ernest was making sketches of birds, beasts, and flowers with which he had met during the past months, Fritz and Jack taught little Franz to read.
— *Swiss Family Robinson, by Johann Wyss, Grosset and Dunlap, Inc.*

in itself. I am personally going to try this with my two older girls once I have filled up our current log book.

Sample Day from Log:

Date/Day

MICHELLE:

Bible: Dad read aloud from *Once a Carpenter*, by Bill Counts

Math: *Saxon 65* — test 16

Listning Comp: Mom read chapter 5 from *Mrs. Frisby and the Rats of NIHM*, by O'Brien

Silent Rdng: *Hatchet*, by Gary Paulsen

Home Ec: sewing — made doll clothes

P.E.: roller skating

Human Body Unit:

Dictation: "The Supportive System" from the book *Your Body and How it Works*, by Wong

Oral Rdng and Listning Comp: *The Skeleton Inside You*, by Philip Balestrino. (Michelle, Melissa and Mom took turns reading aloud and read entire book)

Experiment: "Can You Change Your Height Overnight?" – from *Your Body and How it Works*, by Wong

Typing: Psalm 139:13-16

Date/Day

MELISSA

Bible: Dad read from *Once a Carpenter*, by Counts

Math: *Addison-Wesley*, 4th grade, pp 27, 28

Listning Comp: Mom read aloud ch 5 from *Mrs. Frisby…*

Home Ec: baked cookies

P.E.: roller skating

Silent Rdng: two chapters from *Little House in the Big Woods*, by Laura Ingalls Wilder

Human Body Unit:

Dictation: "The Supportive System"/*Your Body and How it Works*

Oral Rdng and Listning Comp: *The Skeleton Inside You*, by Balestrino

Experiment: "Can You Change Your Height Overnight?"/*Yr Bdy and Hw it Wks*

Typing: Psalm 139:13-16

Date/Day

ROBERT:

Bible: Dad read aloud from *Once a Carpenter*

Piano Lessons

Phonics: "le" as in "bottle," "little," etc., also explained about double const. Robt wrote and spelled words himself, also reviewed "baby," "happy," etc.

Listning Comp: Mom read aloud from *The Trumpet of the Swan*, by E.B. White, chapter 2

Math: 100 Board Activities

Art Proj: painted a T-shirt

P.E.: roller skating

Human Body Unit:

Listning Comp: Mom read entire book, *The Skeleton Inside You*, by Balestrino

Copy Work: From above book, "Bones give you shape. Bones are hard."

Oral Rdng: Robt read these sentences aloud

Date/Day

RAYMOND:

Bible: Dad read from *Once a Carpenter*

Phonics Work: "ay," "sh," silent "e" in long vowel words

Listning Comp: Mom read ch 2 from *The Trumpet of the Swan*

Math: 100 Board Activities

Art Proj: painted a T-shirt

P.E.: roller skating

Human Body Unit:

Listning Comp: Mom read *The Skeleton Inside You*, by Balestrino

Copy Work: "Bones give you shape."

Oral Rdng: Raymond read sentence aloud

Generally, I use abbreviations more extensively. For sake of clarity, I kept these to a minimum in my sample log. As you can see from the sample log, a good portion of our school day is composed of reading. A lot of busy work is eliminated, thereby giving us valuable time for reading.

As I stated earlier, we conduct math studies in addition to our unit studies to get plenty of practice with the basic skills. We integrate the math into our studies whenever possible. Math skills are also integrated

A long time ago, the Dutch sailors used to figure how fast they were going by throwing a piece of wood — they called it a log — overboard. One man stood forward in the bow of the ship and threw the log into the water. Another man stood aft, in the stern of the ship, and kept track of how many seconds it took until the stern of the ship passed the log. They knew how many seconds it took for the ship to go that many feet, so they could figure out how many knots it was making. That was the way they measured their speed. They said they logged their speed because they figured it with a log. And that's why we call this pie-shaped piece of wood a log; because we use it to log the speed of the ship — you see?"

Nat squared his shoulder. "So now I know what it means to keep a log."

Sam bellowed, "No! That isn't keeping a log! Keeping a log is keeping the record of what happens in the voyage."

Nat said, "Then why don't they call it keeping a record?"

"Because one of the most important things in the record is the speed they have logged; so they call the whole record of what happens the log."
— Carry On Mr. Bowditch, by Jean Lee Latham, Houghton Mifflin Co.

Keep a daily journal of your activities. Both you and your students should do this. It not only gives a good picture of organization to others, but also helps both teacher and child to be systematic and learn how to write. Besides, it can be fun now and provide fond recollections later.
— Raymond and Dorothy Moore
Home Style Teaching, *Word Publishers*

into our daily lives. I also mentioned that I read aloud each day from a book noted for its literary value. This too is separate from our unit study and is listed under **Listening Comprehension**. They are listening to me read and they comprehend what is being read, at least to some degree. How do I know they comprehend? Because they want me to go on. They are excited about what we are reading. Generally, people are not too interested in material they cannot understand. It is also beneficial to discuss what you have read and occasionally have each child narrate all or a portion of what you have read. Narration was one of Charlotte Mason's favorite exercises for children. I usually read this good literature at naptime or bedtime. It is a pleasant way to end the day.

You will notice a section on my sample daily log marked **Oral Reading and Listening Comprehension**. This oral reading pertains to our unit study and is shared by my two girls and me. They benefit from reading aloud and listening to others. This reading is usually from a biography corresponding to our unit study. This is not always the case (as you can see in the sample daily log, we were reading a book about the skeleton).

My children do not type every day, nor do they write from dictation every day. They generally perform some writing activity on a daily basis though. I try to use a number of approaches to teach each unit so that the children receive the benefits of a variety of techniques. Hopefully, this section pertaining to the daily log will give you a basic format to create a system of recording that works best for you. You may choose to be more or less formal in your record-keeping as you find what suits your needs.

As we consider logging the academic accomplishments of our children, we should also consider their endeavors. Do you realize the importance of training your children not only in academics but in life skills? As home educators, we are often unjustly accused of sheltering our children from the real world, when in actuality we possess the greater potential for sharing the real world with our children. Is the real world six or seven hours a day with your peers studying isolated subjects that are seldom integrated and even less frequently related to the real world? I think not. (If the real world is obscenity, sexual perversion, disrespect for authority, and so on, then by all means I want to shelter my child from that! I want to shelter myself as well.)

We must ask ourselves, for what purpose are we training our children? Are we training them to become academic robots or self-sufficient individuals with abilities in many areas?

Our society has become so specialized that people concentrate solely on a specific field and are nearly ignorant in every other field. We are taught to leave most things to the professionals, and in doing so we have lost our abilities to do for ourselves.

What I am trying to say is that there is more to education than academics. Do our children need to learn how to cook, clean, sew, grocery shop, care for others, plan a household budget, pay bills, work on the car, make home repairs, garden, mow the lawn, teach, and so on? Or should they leave matters to the professionals?

I think because society has distorted the true meaning of education, we often overlook these crucial areas in favor of concentrating on more academic endeavors. I used to feel guilty if I took time from academics to teach my children some of these skills. I thought I was depriving them of a good education, but in reality a well-rounded education encompasses real-life skills. I was apprehensive about training them in these less-academic areas because I had nothing tangible, such as a written piece of work, to show that I was indeed instructing my child. If my child spent forty-five minutes on a math page, I then had "proof" that education was truly taking place. But if my child spent two hours planning and preparing a meal, there was nothing tangible to represent this as "education," although many skills are necessary to perform this task.

I realize that if I somehow document this educational experience, I will have the proof or record I desire to show that education is indeed taking place. Well, then comes the problem of documenting this kind of learning experience. I devise names for these various learning experiences, life-training skills, or other activities my children are involved in. Cooking can be listed under **Culinary Arts** or **Home Economics**, including a list of the dishes prepared. Gardening can be listed under **Agricultural Studies**, housework listed under **Domestic Engineering**, changing the oil in the car recorded under **Auto Maintenance**, and babysitting logged under **Child Care** or **Child Development**.

Have your older child plan the family meals for a week. You can record this as **Dietary Planning**. Do your children like to draw, make art projects, paper crafts, and so on? Log these as **Creative Expression** or **Art**. Do your children clip coupons and help you grocery shop? This is **Food Budget Analysis and Planning**. Do your children fold laundry, sweep floors, clean tables, dust, make beds, vacuum, clean bathrooms, practice an instrument, play ball, ride bikes, skate, invent games, play board games, play card games, collect stamps, cross-stitch, knit, whittle, sing, sew, paint, wash the car, or attend outside activities? If the answer is *yes* to any of these, then you can devise a category to log these educational experiences. What kinds of things do your children do all day? If they sit around and watch TV or play video games, then your logbook may be nearly blank, but if they are involved in real-life activities, even on a day when "schoolwork" is not implemented, you should be able to just about fill a page with the educational activities of each of your children.

Do you read the Bible daily? Record the passages read under **Bible Studies**. Do your children read silently? Record the title and author under **Silent Reading**. Do you read aloud to your children each day? Record the title, author, and chapters read under **Listening Comprehension.** Do your children read aloud to you or their siblings? Record the title, author, and chapters read under **Oral Reading**. These are daily occurrences in our home, along with chores.

Biking, swimming, skating, playing at a park, or making and using an obstacle course can be logged as **Physical Education**. If you meet regularly with other home-educating families at a park or central location for play and fellowship, this can be recorded as **Physical Education** and **Socialization Skills**.

Do you ever attend plays, visit the zoo, investigate museums, and explore nature? Log these activities as **Field Trips**. It is not necessary that these activities be done with a group to qualify as a field trip. Whenever possible we prefer to do these things as a family, with perhaps one other family joining us, because the children are able to absorb more information.

As you begin to keep a daily log of all of the different things your children do along with their more academic endeavors, you will begin to see what makes up a real, well-balanced curriculum. A friend of mine began using this method of log-keeping. One day one of her sons saw here entering information about what he had done that day for school and he exclaimed, "I did all that!" Even he was impressed when he was able to see it recorded on paper. Children can also be taught to keep a log of their activities. This is a great way of teaching them to organize their thoughts as well as providing them with practice in language arts skills.

We must realize that all learning is not adult contrived. Children will learn on their own, as it is their nature to explore. We should expose them to a variety of things, provide them with materials to be creative, and be available to help and answer questions. We also need to know when to leave well enough alone and allow them to explore and experience failure and success on their own.

It is difficult to achieve a well-rounded education when we are in bondage to textbooks or workbooks, because we feel this ever-present pressure to complete the book. This leaves little time for other endeavors such as learning how to hang wallpaper, make cookies, wash clothes, paint the house, plan a meal, and plant a garden. Or, perhaps you are Super Mom and can juggle the textbooks, piano lessons, little league, soccer practice, and real-life skills. I have tried playing that game before, and I am glad to say I gave it up for something better. I gave it up for peace of mind and a happy household.

If you are using workbooks, textbooks, or a curriculum, feel free to break away and spend some time teaching your children how to cook, garden, or sew. What would be the loss of finishing a text in twelve months instead of nine, if you were able to have a host of other real-life experiences? If this would cause a problem, then you should re-evaluate your educational program because anything that would place such restrictions on your family can only be detrimental to their education. If it is the system or a book that is imprisoning you, is it not time you are set free?

Perhaps keeping a log of all your children's activities will help you realize how much learning is really taking place each day. I know it has helped to set me free, enabling my children to get on with real life.

*F*or several years now, my family has been using the unit study approach to learning. My children's attitudes about schoolwork have changed. They are interested in our studies and eager to learn. We occasionally have problems but not nearly so often as when we used textbooks and workbooks.

My attitude has changed because I too am eager to learn. I see my attitude reflected in their eyes. We must set a good example for our children to follow. They know that much of the material we are learning is new to me also. We are learning together. They quiz me on material that we are trying to memorize. They see that it is a challenge for me, too. I have to look up words in the dictionary just as they do. I discuss my strong points and my weak points with them openly. They know I am a real person. They know I am still learning and growing. They know learning lasts a lifetime.

They are not bound by graded textbooks or by learning labels. They are free to learn at a rate that is appropriate for them. They are free of busywork and boring work. My children know that if they are interested in a particular topic that we will supply them with the necessary elements so the can pursue their interests. They are free to be different from anyone else and still feel loved and accepted and valuable. They are individuals with their own needs, talents, and desires. If you can tap into your children's interests and help them cultivate those interests, they will begin to learn and explore on their own.

As we have progressed through our unit studies and read numerous biographies of people from all walks of life, one common thread we have noticed amongst them is that they were not ordinary. Their

Reflecting on Unit Studies

Praise the Lord! Praise God in His sanctuary; Praise Him in His mighty expanse. Praise Him for His mighty deeds; Praise Him according to His excellent greatness. Praise Him with trumpet sound; praise Him with harp and lyre. Praise Him with timbrel and dancing; praise Him with stringed instrument and pipe. Praise Him with loud cymbals. Let everything that has breath praise the Lord. Praise the Lord!
—Psalm 150 (NASV)

education was very different from what we know today. They pursued their interests with zealousness.

For example, when conducting our studies on children's authors, we read a biography about Beatrix Potter, author of **The Tale of Peter Rabbit**. She was schooled at home by a governess. They took numerous nature walks and collected flowers, fungi, and small animals. From these specimens, Beatrix would make sketches and study them in great detail, learning all she could about them. Her governess noticed her interest and talent and encouraged her in further pursuit of this interest. Beatrix Potter spent a couple of hours each day at a wildlife museum. She was not bored to tears with textbooks. She was gently guided in the things she had an affinity toward. Her grandmother encouraged her to be bold and different. And, therefore, a great author and illustrator of children's books was nurtured to fruition.

While reading biographies of famous people, point out the ways in which these people were different from those around them and from those today. Realizing, of course, that you will not want to emulate all those you read about. However, certain traits they bore may be worthy of emulation. Help your children to appreciate that they too are different. This is important for their self-esteem, especially when schools today try to press the masses into the same mold. It seems that this pressure causes children to regret being different from others. Different is considered good only if your child is in the gifted program. But all children are special and deserve a specially tailored curriculum. Think just how special each child is to our Heavenly Father.

As we study art, music, math, science, history, and literature, we get a glimpse of the different lifestyles and personalities of real individuals. We begin to appreciate the beauty in these things and in the world around us. Open up new and previously unexplored areas for your children. You never know what might spark their interests.

Sandi Patti sings a song about the creation of the world that goes like this: "He could have made it black and white and we'd have never known." [16] Let's help our children lead a life full of color. It is very difficult to encourage the development of extraordinary individuals with an ordinary curriculum. Let us not re-establish the ordinary classroom in our homes. We have a much greater potential than this, for we were created in His image. Through this realization of the importance of each individual as fashioned in His image, we can influence our children in understanding the importance of service toward others; family first, and then those less fortunate than ourselves. We want to raise self-sacrificing individuals, not self-seeking persons.

Begin with a unit you can easily manage and progress to a more detailed topic. Do not exhaust yourself by taking on too much at first. Do not be intimidated by others who appear to have it all together. Use any helpful advice they may have to offer and do not worry about the rest. We are all constantly learning; for remember, learning lasts a lifetime. It is important that you hang in there and do not give up. You will reap the rewards of perseverance.

We read in James 1:5, "But if any of you lacks wisdom, let him ask God, who gives to all men generously and without reproach, and it will be given to him." (NASV) [17]

"I want to see my sons strong, both morally and physically," said I. *"That means, little Franz,"* as the large blue eyes looked inquiringly up at me, *"brave to do what is good and right, and to hate evil, and strong to work, hunt, and provide for themselves and others, and to fight if necessary."*
— Swiss Family Robinson, *by Johann Wyss, Grosset and Dunlap, Inc.*

Sample Units

On the next several pages, you will find some sample units. (Also included are two sample units conducted by others.) They are not intended to be used in a step-by-step fashion but are rather to be viewed as something that we did as a family. I would never expect anyone to try to follow my plan, just as it would be extremely difficult for me to follow someone else's plan. The key to a successful unit study is for you to pick an interesting topic, raid your library for books, tapes, and other materials, and see how you can fit these into your schedule. Perhaps you will only pick a few books for younger children, a few books for older children and one or two books to be read aloud. We happen to have a family that devours books, as it is evident from our sample units that follow. Remember, you can fit in a lot more good books when you eliminate the busywork. It is important to keep things as simple as possible, especially in the beginning.

Note: Some of the books listed were read aloud together, with the older children taking turns reading along with Mom. Some of the books were read silently by some of the children. Some of the books were read entirely aloud by Mom or Dad. And finally, some of the books were read aloud entirely by the children. This was all done according to needs and abilities. It is not necessary to read this many books to satisfactorily complete a unit. Even though it seems we read a lot of books, we really just brush the surface when it comes to the vast wealth of books written for children. Remember, in any unit you pursue you cannot possibly cover all the material available on that subject. Do not try to take on too much at first; you can always go back and cover a unit more thoroughly at a future date. Relax and enjoy your family.

Activities and Creative Writing Assignments: Went on vacation and collected postcards, brochures, etc.; the children made a scrapbook and entered in information about each place visited. Worked on map-reading skills while on our trip. "Create a Country" – made a card with important information on it about an imaginary country, made accompanying flag and a map, gave brief description of the people. Filled in names of countries on map for each continent. Made a list of geography terms to use for writing a poem, and then wrote poems. Wrote a story about a mouse on Columbus' ship. Drew North and South poles, equator, and lines of latitude on an orange. Wrote a story using geographical terms and made a map to go with the story. For each biography read, we made time-line figures. Collected stamps, which included stamps from countries all over the world. Measured distances on a map using a scale. Made a list of geography terms from A to Z. Made a list of countries from A to Z. Located points on the map of the world using degrees of longitude and latitude. Made maps of interior of house. Made maps of neighborhood.

Games and Puzzles: *Where in the World?*, *Map of the World Puzzle* jigsaw puzzle, and *Map of the World Puzzle* wooden Judy Puzzle.

Non-Fiction Books Read: *The Columbus Story*, by Alice Dalgliesh. *Balboa, Finder of the Pacific*, by Ronald Syme. *Francisco Pizzaro, Finder of Peru*, by Ronald Syme. *Magellan, First Around the World*, by Syme. *A World Explorer, Ponce de Leon*, by Wyatt Blassingame. *John Cabot and His Son Sebastian*, by Syme. *Vasco Da Gama*, by Syme. *Pop-up Atlas of the World*, by Theodore Rowland Entwistle. *Looking at Maps*, by Erich Fuchs. *Maps and Globes*, by Knowlton. *Marco Polo*, by Ceserani. *Nigerian Pioneer*, by Syme. *New World History and Geography*, published by A Beka (used to dictate from or read about selected countries in each region or continent studied). *African Journey*, by John Chiasson, and *Explorers in Africa*, by Richard Seymour Hall. (These books were used for their pictures.) *The Voyages of Captain Cook*, by Roger Hart. *Where in the World do You Live?*, by Al Hine and John Alcorn. *The Discoverers*, by Grant Neil. (Used portions of this book; good illustrations.) *Shaka, King of the Zulus*, by Diane Stanley.

Fiction Books Read: *Henry the Explorer, Henry Explores the Jungle, Henry and the Castaways*, and *Henry Explores the Mountains*, all by Mark Taylor. (These books were used as an introduction to exploring with my younger children.) *The Happy Orpheline*, and entire Orpheline series, by Natalie Savage Carlson. (This series of stories takes place in France.) *The Cat Who Went To Heaven*, by Elizabeth Coatsworth. (This story takes place in Japan and gives insight into Hinduism.) *Ananda, a story of Buddhism in Sri Lanka*, by Carol Barker.

Terms and Their Definitions Used for Dictation: (Source of

information, *Nat'l Geographic, Exploring Your World*): isthmus, country, ocean, the ocean floor, coral reef, peninsula, latitude, longitude, equator, maps and globes, navigation, desert, valley, mountain, volcano, sea, island, tides.

Videos: *India, Morocco, Egypt.*

Audio Cassettes: *Geography Songs* and *More Geography Songs.*

Bible Verses: The following passages were dictated over a period of time. *Genesis* Chapter 1. *Job* Chapter 38. *Isaiah* 40:3-8.

Other Publications: "God's World Newspapers," "The Tampa Tribune."

Field Trips: Museum of Science and Industry, viewed traveling *Spanish Explorer Exhibit.*

Memorization Work: Learned names and locations of all the countries, oceans, and major seas in the world. Memorized portions of *Genesis* Chapter 1.

Activities and Creative Writing Assignments: Viewed and discussed a wide variety of children's books, noting writing styles and illustrations. Wrote three stories, beginning with rough draft, then editing, and then final product. (These books were of varying types: wheel books, flap books, pop-up books, etc.) Some of the stories were typed once they were completely edited; some stories were originally typed on the computer and then edited. The younger children dictated their stories to Mom; the older children helped with typing them. The children made covers for their books and illustrations to go along with their stories. Painted a book jacket and then proceeded to write a story to go with it; the younger children dictated the story to Mom. Younger children drew pictures to accompany various books that Mom read to them.

The older children wrote about various accounts they enjoyed most in stories selected by Mom. The older children gave an oral narration to the family of a book they had read. The children participated in reading aloud each day from some of the books listed below. Some creative writing assignments included having the children write a story of their own that patterned one we read together. I gave the children story starters and had them complete the story. The children rewrote a story we had read aloud and changed the ending. The children each wrote and illustrated a book which we "published" ourselves. These books were made like professional books and required six weeks to complete. (See my book ***Creating Books with Children*** for step-by-step instructions as to how to do this. See page 331 for more information.) These are books we will treasure forever.

Games: *Authors Card Game, Children's Authors Card Game*.

Non-Fiction Books Read: *Nothing is Impossible, the Story of Beatrix Potter*, by Dorothy Aldis. *Who Said There's No Man in the Moon? A Story of Jules Verne*, by Robert Quackenbush. *Laura Ingalls Wilder: Growing up in the Little House*, by Patricia Reilly Griff. *Mark Twain, What Kind of a Name is That?*, by Robert Quackenbush. *The Last Four Years*, by Laura Ingalls Wilder. *To the Point, A Story of E.B. White*, by David R. Collins. *Invincible Louisa*, by Cornelia Meigs. *A Country Artist, A Story About Beatrix Potter*, by David R. Collins.

Fiction Books Read: *Little House in the Big Woods*, and others in this series, by Laura Ingalls Wilder. *The Five Little Peppers and How They Grew*, by Margaret Sidney. *Shoo-fly Girl*, by Lois Lenski. *Peanuts for Billy Ben*, by Lois Lenski. *Christmas Stories*, by Lois Lenski. *Black Star, Bright Dawn*, by Scott O'Dell. *To be a Logger*, by Lois Lenski. *There's Nothing to Do and We Hate Rain*, by James Stevens. *Bayou Suzette*, by Lois Lenski. *The Merry Adventures of Robin Hood*, by Howard Pyle. *The Biggest Bear*, by Lynd Ward. *Little Sioux Girl*, by Lois Lenski. *Eight Cousins*, by Louisa May Alcott. *Hop on Pop*, by Dr.

Seuss. *Heaven to Betsy*, by Maud Hart Lovelace. *Little Women* and *Jo's Boys*, by Louisa May Alcott. *Strawberry Girl*, by Lenski. *Betsy, Tacy and Tib*, and others in this series, by Lovelace. *Hatchet*, by Gary Paulsen. *The Berenstain Bears and the Week at Grandmas*, and others in this series, by Stan and Jan Berenstain. *Curious Missy*, by Virginia Sorensen. *Miracle on Maple Hill*, by Sorensen. *The Case of the Missing Kittens*, by Mark Taylor. *Stream to the River, River to the Sea*, by Scott O'Dell. *Ida Early Comes Over the Mountain*, by Robert Burch. *The Tale of Peter Rabbit*, and other tales, by Beatrix Potter. *The Plant Sitter*, by Gene Zion. *A Harold Adventure*, by Crockett Johnson, and others in the series. *Bridge to Terabithia*, by Katherine Paterson. *The Indian in the Cupboard, The Return of the Indian*, and *The Secret of the Indian*, by Lynne R. Banks. *Esther Wheelright, Indian Captive*, by Marguerite Vance. *The Box Car Children*, and others in this series, by Gertrude Chandler Warner. *Hattie the Backstage Bat*, and *Corduroy*, by Don Freeman. *Stuart Little, Charlotte's Web*, and *The Trumpet of the Swan*, by E.B. White.

Dictation: Various selections from some of the books we read, especially portions that included dialogue, were utilized for dictation purposes. The younger children did copy work from some of the stories read. I used several of the book jacket, front flap summaries from biographies we read as dictation exercises.

Videos: *Little Women, A Connecticut Yankee in King Arthur's Court, Robin Hood and His Merry Men, The Rats of NIMH, Tom Thumb, Charlotte's Web, 20,000 Leagues Under the Sea*, and *Huckleberry Finn.*

Audio Cassettes: *Grimm's Fairy Tales, Robin Hood, Peter Pan*, and cassettes of other various children's stories.

Bible: Discussed and memorized the Ten Commandments with Dad. Read Peter Spier's books, *Noah's Ark* and *Jonah and the Big Fish*, and compared them to the biblical accounts.

*T*his unit's primary focus is on oral presentation; therefore, more time is dedicated to the spoken word rather than the written word. It is important that our children learn to express themselves both through the written and the spoken word. Generally, because our society places such a high value on the written word, little emphasis is placed on the spoken word. Also, in a conventional school setting, time does not allow for sufficient oral expression experiences. It is for these reasons that I have chosen to conduct this unit. Much time is spent in oral exercises, which are documented in my daily log. Here again, we often feel that learning is not taking place if we do not have a concrete piece of evidence, such as a written piece of work, to document this learning. That is why I document these oral exercises in my daily log.

Initially, I was encouraged to begin this unit because the time was approaching for our county's annual Storytelling Festival. I wanted my children to participate, but I felt it would be too much to take on while in the course of studying another unit. So, I decided we would conduct a storytelling unit to help prepare for the festival. This would give us ample time to prepare and thus reduce the stress of too much work. It is nice to be able to plan our units around events in the community and family interests without feeling bound to textbooks.

Activities: I obtained the rules and regulations for the festival to enable me to select suitable materials. No props of any kind were to be used to tell the stories; they were to be strictly narratives. The children and I visited our public library and chose many books, about 75, that we thought might be appropriate for storytelling. The children spent several days reading the books that interested them; the older children and I also read many of these books aloud to the younger children. After becoming familiar with the stories, I helped the children each select an appropriate story to tell. I tried to explain why some books were suitable, and some were not. I explained that books that rely too much on illustrations to convey the story were not good choices for storytelling. I encouraged them to find a book with which they could somehow relate, as this would aid them in their retention of the story. The stories were not to be memorized, except for key phrases and the beginning and ending sentences. Stories should not be acted out, and seldom should you try to use your voice to convey characterization, but rather let the language tell the story.

These tips and other helpful information were obtained from library books. I checked out two books, **Handbook for Storytellers**, by Caroline Feller Bauer, and **A Storyteller's Choice**, by Eileen Colwell. Both of these books gave good suggestions as well as references for stories to be read aloud.

Once the children had selected their stories, we read them over and over again, both silently and aloud, to become genuinely familiar with them. Michelle chose *The Quiet Mother and the Noisy Little Boy*, by Charlotte Zolotow. Melissa chose *All in One Piece*, by Jill Murphy. Robert selected *The Plant Sitter*, by Gene Zion. And Raymond chose *Henry Explores the Jungle*, by Mark Taylor. Then each child decided which portions of their books should be memorized word-for-word. We had many practice sessions in which the children would perform in front of each other. Praise and advice were lovingly offered.

We also used reference books while at the library to gather information about the author for each book chosen. We utilized *Children's Literature Review*, by Block, Riley, and Senick, and *The Who's Who of Children's Literature*, edited by Brian Doyle.

We taped the children reading their stories aloud and let them listen to themselves. Then we taped them giving their story presentation in their own words. This allowed them to hear themselves as others would hear them. This was beneficial; however, they still needed to be able to view themselves as others would view them. So we borrowed a video camera and videotaped the children giving their presentations.

Typing Exercises: The older children typed the entire text of their stories. They also typed parables from the Bible, and we discussed how our Lord used parables, or stories, to teach the people. These passages were from the Gospel of Mark. These parables were read aloud to the younger children.

Dictation: I dictated selected passages from the books the children chose for storytelling. This helped with story familiarization, spelling, and punctuation skills. I also dictated the passages from the front inside book jackets of each of their books, as these encapsulated the contents of each book. Portions from the book, *A Storyteller's Choice*, explaining the history of storytelling were also dictated to the children. The younger children did copy work relating to their books at levels appropriate for each of them.

Videos: *Storytelling Volume 3* and *Storytelling Volume 4*. (These videos were checked out at the public library; they were presentations done by professional storytellers.)

Live Performances: Attended the *Young People's Arts Festival* at Ruth Eckerd Hall to view the presentation of "Peter Rabbit and Other Tales," by Beatrix Potter. Attended and participated in the *Hillsborough County Storytelling Festival*.

Arts and Crafts: Each of the children made a poster advertising his story. Their posters were illustrated with their favorite scenes from the story.

*T*he following unit was created and conducted by Cameron Albert, Jr., a 15-year-old, home-educated student.

Books Read or Utilized for Reference:

Kings, Bishops, Knights, and Pawns, by Ralph Arnold.

Castles, by Richard Humble.

Simple Heraldry, by Iain Moncreiffe.

Medieval Days and Ways, by Gertrude Hartman.

Men in Armor, by Richard Suskind.

The Knights, by Michael Gibson

The Medieval Knight, by Martin Windrow.

A Complete Guide to Heraldry, by A.C. Fox-Davies.

The Institutions, Laws, and Ceremonies of the Most Noble Order of the Garter, by Elias Ashmore.

A Guide to Heraldry, by Ottfried Neubecker.

Heraldry of the Royal Families of Europe, by Jiri Louda and Michael Maclagan.

An Encyclopedic Dictionary of Heraldry, by Julian Franklin and John Tanner.

Design Your Own Coat of Arms, by Rosemary Chorzempa.

Mottoes, by George Earlie Shankle.

The Castle in the Attic, by Elizabeth Winthrop.

Heraldry, by Julian Franklin.

A Dictionary of Heraldry and Related Subjects, by Colonel A.G. Puttock.

Heraldry, by Walter Buehr.

Knights in Armor, by Shirley Glubok.

The First Book of Medieval Man, by D. Sobol.

The Story of Knights and Armor, by Ernest E. Tucker.

Knights and Castles, by John Rutland.

Knights of the Crusades, by Jay Williams.

The Knight of the Golden Plain, by Mollie Hunter

Activities:

Made a full suit of armor out of sheet metal.

Made two surcoats—stitched on a sewing machine.

Made a sword with a wooden handle and metal blade.

Made a wooden shield and painted it.

Designed and made a coat of arms.

Studied insignia and medals of U.S. Armed Forces.

Studied insignia and medals of Boy Scouts.

Prepared for Royal Ranger's Pow Wow consisting of a medieval theme.

Hosted a medieval tournament for boys.

Cam is currently writing and editing a medieval newsletter for boys ages 5 to 8 entitled, *The Crusader*, which is published monthly. The newsletter consists of the following:

Explanations for Code of Chivalry

Various activities; i.e., draw a picture and send it in to newsletter

History lesson based on medieval theme

Continuing story

Advancements and awards, i.e., badges in Boy Scouts

Certificate for each child's accomplishments

Scripture memory

Question-and-answer section

(This newsletter was published in 1990.)

*I*t takes time to prepare for our unit studies. We often find the house deteriorating about us. How can we find the time to effectively clean our homes and plan our units? First things first, let us get organized.

It is very difficult for me to teach school if my house looks as if it needs to be thoroughly raked out. Reading all those books on organizing your housework is great, but who has the time to implement all those terrific time-saving ideas, teach the children, and prepare a decent evening meal? Getting your youngsters to help is definitely the answer, but just how do you set up this routine and teach?

One possibility is to integrate your housework into a unit study. You may already own some of those wonderful how-to-clean-your-house books. But if you do not, have no fear for the library is near. Investigate the children's section as well as the adult section. Choose a plan that works for you, whether it be charts, graphs, calendars, or index cards to help you organize your work. Let each capable child make cards or a notebook with a list of his or her chores. Your charts or graphs can be as detailed as necessary, stating when each job is to be undertaken.

Some jobs require attention less frequently and are, therefore, often neglected entirely. Send your children on a house-cleaning hunt and have them make a list of all the tasks they can envision. Then categorize them according to how often they should be tackled, and determine the length of time needed to complete each job. Perhaps you may also want to rate each job as difficult, moderate or easy, and place age levels by each one.

Office supply stores have large, desktop calendars at very reasonable prices, which are excellent for logging specific chores, especially those undertaken less frequently. A smaller calendar may be purchased or designed and then photocopied for each child, thus enabling them to record their own jobs and any to be jointly tackled. Then as each chore is completed, they can mark it off their calendars. Younger children can use rubber stamps, magazine pictures, or their own drawings to represent chores on their calendars. You can choose to fill out an entire year or just a few months at a time.

You will be teaching your children valuable life skills, not only in how to clean but in how to organize their lives. Just think how much your children will learn about calendars by using this method. Also, many disputes over who is to do what are squelched in advance since all the information is recorded ahead of time. If the children want to trade jobs occasionally, housework coupons can be issued and exchanged.

How about doing a massive clean-out and hold a garage sale. The money earned can be used to buy household cleaning tools. It is difficult to get enthused about cleaning the house when the mop head leaves sponge crumbs all over the floor, and the vacuum blows out more dust than it takes in. Have your children clip coupons for cleaning products and check ads for the best prices. This helps them to be good stewards of the family's money.

It is necessary to train your children in effective cleaning methods, but it is also beneficial for the older children to train the younger in specific tasks that the older children have already mastered. Character qualities come into play here as the older must be patient with the younger. We also want our children to cheerfully do their work.

Besides making lists of jobs and filling in charts, calendars, or graphs, many other writing skills can be developed. For example, your children can write poems about cleaning. The book **Precious Moments Through the Year Stories** has several clever poems about housework. These can be used as typing exercises. Easily enough, several short stories can be written about housework. Detective or mystery stories seem good choices, i.e., **The Case of the Missing Sock**. Check your library for fictional books pertaining to housework.

Investigate the Bible to see what you can find about neatness and cleanliness. What character qualities should we stress when caring for our homes? Ask your children what they think. Are they thoughtful, considerate, patient, diligent, and trustworthy? What are the fruits of the Spirit? Housework may seem like a lowly job, but as our Messiah humbled Himself and became a servant, He set an example for us to follow.

Once you have developed a house-cleaning routine, you might want to take one day a week and devote your school time to housework. We have found this very effective since everyone knows his job and how to execute it well. This also allows time to train the children in additional jobs once others have been mastered. A house-cleaning unit is a great way to break the ice and cultivate lifelong cleaning habits.

*F*requently, a mother will remark that she finds it difficult to teach her children and prepare dinner. This is something that I struggle with, too. I feel the solution to this problem is to devise a unit study. This unit study involves cooking and can easily be a springboard for many other related studies. For instance, prepare cuisine from different countries and engage in a brief study about these countries at the same time. For an artistic project, create table decorations representing these countries. Math skills are sharpened as you measure and often double recipes. This is a excellent time to learn about cups, pints, quarts, gallons, teaspoons, tablespoons, and other units of measure. Even little ones will have fun using rice or water to fill measuring cups and containers.

Check out various recipe books from the library, both adult's and children's books, and let each child select one that interests him. Discuss nutrition, calories, fat, carbohydrates, and so on. Explore the Bible for insights into health and nutrition. Study the biblical dietary laws and discover how current books on nutrition support them. One helpful book is entitled *God's Key to Health and Happiness*, by Elmer Josephson.

Supply each of your children with an index card box or recipe box filled with plenty of cards. Have each child write or type tested recipes on their cards, being sure to include the golden oldies, but also include new recipes which you have prepared. Each child may be responsible for recording certain recipes, and they can exchange recipes by photocopying them and then gluing them to cards. Encourage your children to write letters to those friends and relatives they choose and ask for their favorite recipes. Recipes can be collected from magazines and newspapers, too. Have your children then categorize them according to kinds of foods.

One method of recipe-card-keeping shared with me by a friend requires a card listing the ingredients needed to make a complete meal. Instructions for preparing the meal are given on a separate card. When planning the meals for a week, remove the "ingredient cards" and make a grocery list for the necessary items.

Have your older children plan the meals for a week and then help prepare them. Also have them do the grocery shopping, clipping coupons, and checking ads ahead of time. Help them learn to stay within the grocery budget. Select a system for your meal planning, such as scheduling two weeks of evening meals in which no two meals are the same. This schedule can be repeated substituting optional meals that add variety and allow for experimentation.

Younger children can help plan and prepare a meal. Teach proper care of utensils and safety precautions. Remind them that cleaning up is part of the job.

As an additional writing exercise, have your children create a menu listing and illustrating their favorite foods. They can also make up silly recipes or poems about food. To make their recipe files elaborate, they can photograph various dishes they have prepared. Writing a family cookbook will be a rewarding project to share with relatives and friends.

Integrate science in the kitchen by conducting various experiments with different food substances. Jane Hoffman's **Backyard Scientist** books have many pertinent experiments.

Your children can add to their recipe file as they try new dishes. When they have their own homes, they will already be well prepared for managing meals. Even the boys will find this helpful as their wives are presented with tried and true recipes, and their wives will be pleasantly surprised to find their husbands are capable cooks.

Encourage your children to continue assisting you with the family meal planning and preparation. If you plan it just right, you may only have to spend a few days in the kitchen each week, while the children handle the meals for the remainder of the time. For an exciting unit finale, dine at a restaurant serving foreign cuisine, possibly dressing in foreign attire for the occasion.

*T*he following unit was submitted to me by Cathy Duffy, author of the *Christian Home Educators' Curriculum Manuals*.

I will list the books she feels are most worthwhile. She states that her children read much more than she did, although some books were used by them as a group. Even though some of these books may be out of print and difficult to obtain, she comments that the value of such a list probably is in suggesting types of books to look for.

The Wonderful World of Mathematics, by Lancelot Hogeben; Doubleday and Co., Inc., NY; 1955. Traces the history of mathematics in colorfully illustrated format through major cultures. Extremely interesting.

Archimedes, by Martin Gardner; The Macmillan Co., NY; 1965. Biography of the important Greek mathematician.

Alexander the Great, by John Gunther; Random House, NY; 1953. Well-written biography.

See Inside: An Ancient Greek Town, R.J. Unstead; A Grisewood and Dempsey Ltd., London; 1986. Helps with cultural understanding. Well illustrated. It looks like many of the Usborne books, but a little less cluttered.

The Adventures of Odysseus and The Tale of Troy, (Homer) adapted by Padraic Colum; The Macmillan Co., NY; 1918. Fairly easy-to-read version. Excellent for an overview of how gods and goddesses were perceived by the Greeks.

See Inside: A Roman Town, by R.J. Unstead, ed.; Kingfisher Books Ltd., Elsley Court, London; 1986. Furthers cultural understanding. Well illustrated. It looks like many of the Usborne books, but a little less cluttered.

The Everyday Life of a Roman Soldier, by Giovanni Caselli; Peter Bedrick Books (Distributed by Harper and Row), NY; 1999. Heavily and colorfully illustrated. Elementary grades.

Cultural Atlas for Young People: Ancient Rome, by Mike Corbishley; Facts on File, NY; 1989. History, geography, culture, and more is covered in depth with lots of illustrations.

How Should We Then Live?: The Rise and Decline of Western Thought and Culture, by Francis A. Schaeffer; Crossway Books, IL; 1976. The first chapter is specifically about ancient Rome, but the entire book is an excellent study of the interaction of philosophy, religion, art, literature, government, economics, and other major influences in all cultures.

Roman Mythology, by Stewart Perowne; The Hamlyn Publishing Group Ltd., London, England; 1969. Heavily illustrated with photographs of statues, reliefs, mosaics, and paintings of gods and goddesses. It correlates Greek and Roman deities and tells the story of each one.

History of Art, by H.W. Janson; Prentice-Hall, Inc., NJ, and N. Abrams, Inc., NY; 1965. Much history is incorporated into the teaching about art. It puts everything in context in a way that works nicely with Schaeffer's **How Should We Then Live** concept.

Julius Caesar, Shakespeare. We read some of this also.

In *How to Create Your Own Unit Study*, I rather briefly described some of the useful books that can be found in the children's reference section of the public library. There are a vast number of books in this section which would be beneficial in aiding you in the search for materials pertaining to your unit of study. Therefore, I have further researched this section of the library and have compiled a guide naming and describing some of the more useful books. Hopefully, this guide will acquaint you with the reference section and allow you to choose some helpful books without having to monotonously wade through them all.

Since these books cannot be checked out, you must use them while at the library, thus valuable time would be wasted if you had to first search for a particular book to suit your needs and then draw information from it. Naturally, we cannot expect all the libraries to have the exact same books in their reference sections, but enough books are listed in the guide that you will most likely find some in your library to suit your needs.

I have listed the call numbers for the reference books to enable you to more easily locate them. Some books I came across in my research I have omitted from this guide. For example, reference guides for books dealing in values clarification.

I have found that a small number of the books found in the children's reference section are also available on the regular shelves and may be checked out. Here again, the call numbers will help you to locate these books. The reference section is basically made up of four kinds of books: general reference books such as dictionaries, atlases, and encyclopedias; books deemed to be of high educational value, such as Newbery Medal Books, Caldecott Medal Books, history books, fairy tales, books on art, and books on music; handbooks for teaching various skills; and guides for locating specific books in the library.

When using the children's reference section of your public library, you will be more successful if you visit the main branch in your library system, as they will have the widest selection of books from which to choose. Remember also to investigate the adult reference section of your library. You may want to find some more challenging books for older students in this section. In smaller libraries, the adult and children's reference sections are combined. I feel this makes it more difficult to use, but having the call numbers from the reference guide will be helpful.

There are also many good biographies in the adult section that can be read aloud to the older as well as younger children. And of course, there is the fine arts section with its own guides and card catalogue to help you in selecting books to enhance your unit. I use many of the books from the fine arts section as they are useful for their excellent pictures. The quality of the art reproductions found in these books generally surpasses those found in the books in the children's section.

As I began to compile this guide for the reference section of the children's department, I realized it would be impossible for me to review every book. Many of the books are similar in content and it would prove repetitious for me to comment on each one; however, I have tried to include enough so that you many be able to find a sufficient number of them in your library. My main intention for this guide is to expose you to the kinds of resources available that will aid you in developing your unit study. Conducting this research has helped me a great deal to uncover the treasures that are buried in the library.

The library can be a tremendous source for materials if we can only learn how to tap into it. Unfortunately, many Christians feel that the public library is full of secular books, and they want their children to only read "Christian books," thus they miss out on some of the best books ever written. In the first half of this century, many books were written that exemplified Christian principles. And even today there are good books being written that uphold biblical, moral principles, but we often have to search to uncover these gems. This guide will serve its purpose if it acts as an instrument with which to unveil these treasures.

THE RANDOM HOUSE DICTIONARY OF THE ENGLISH LANGUAGE: JR423.

MACMILLAN PICTURE DICTIONARY FOR CHILDREN: JR423.

THE LINCOLN WRITING DICTIONARY FOR CHILDREN: JR423. Harcourt, Brace, and Jovanovich

DOUBLEDAY CHILDREN'S THESAURUS: JR423.1. Very helpful for allowing the children to find an alternative to overused words. Look for this book on the regular shelves under the same catalogue number.

THE COMPLETE RHYMING DICTIONARY: JR427. Edited by Clement Wood. Beneficial for enabling your children to become fine poets. Once again, check the regular shelves for this book.

MOTHER GOOSE BOOKS: You will find a large selection of Mother Goose-type books and other nursery rhyme books. Some of these are catalogued under ER, for easy reader, and are arranged alphabetically according to the author's last name. Others are catalogued under JR398. However, in the reference section, these are all located on the same shelves. This enables you to view these nursery-rhyme-type books at a glance. Most should be available on the regular shelves.

CALDECOTT MEDAL BOOKS: A large selection of these award books is located here and can usually be found on the regular shelves, but they are consolidated in the reference section to always be available for in-library use. This enables you to become familiar with these books at a glance. These are catalogued under the author's last name. The Caldecott Medal is awarded each year for the children's book with the most outstanding illustrations.

NEWBERY MEDAL BOOKS: Once again, a large selection of these books is available here for you to examine. Generally, these books are of a high literary quality and make very good read-aloud books. Next time you are looking for a good book to read to your children, try browsing through these. The Newbery Medal is awarded each year for the book published in that year making the greatest contribution to children's literature. Another excellent book is a biography of John Newbery, for whom the Newbery Award is named. It is entitled *Songs for Sixpence*, by Elizabeth Blackstock, and is located in the junior biography section.

CHILDREN'S BOOKS IN PRINT VOL. 1: SUBJECT GUIDE: JR028.52. R.R. Bowker Company. This enables you to find titles of books that pertain to a particular subject. Each subject is listed alphabetically.

CHILDREN'S BOOKS IN PRINT VOL. 2: AUTHORS, TITLES, AND ILLUSTRATORS: JR028.52. R.R. Bowker Company. This is useful for locating other books by an author you are interested in. Remember that just looking in the card catalogue under a particular author will not help you to locate books by that author that may not be in your library. Perhaps another library in the system would have a book you need. You could have the librarian check this in the computer. Or perhaps you like a particular illustrator and you want to find out what other books he or she has illustrated. You may know of a title of a book for which you do not know the author and cannot find this specific book in the card catalogue. This book would be helpful in both cases. This volume also includes children's book awards for 1980-1990.

AUTHORS: BOOKS IN PRINT: JR015. R.R. Bowker Company. This includes all books, not just children's books.

TITLES: BOOKS IN PRINT: JR015. R.R. Bowker Company. See above.

PUBLISHERS: BOOKS IN PRINT: JR015. R.R. Bowker Company. This will enable you to locate books by a particular publisher you may favor.

O.P., O.S.I., OUT OF PRINT, OUT OF STOCK INDEFINITELY: JR015. R.R. Bowker Company. This will aid you in locating pertinent information about a book you may be interested in but which is out of print. Many times libraries will own copies of out-of-print books, or specialty used book stores may be able to track them down for you.

ENCYCLOPEDIAS: All the basic encyclopedia sets are catalogued under JR031. Libraries will vary in their selection of encyclopedias. Looking these volumes over may help you decide which set of encyclopedias you might wish to purchase. You can pick up used sets at yard sales and used book stores. Those located in the public library we frequent are: ***Children's Britannica, Merit Student's Encyclopedia, World Book, The New Book of Knowledge*** and ***Compton's Encyclopedia.***

JR. HIGH SCHOOL LIBRARY CATALOG: JRO11. Edited by Juliette Yaakov. This edition includes 3,219 titles accompanied by descriptions, page numbers, date published, and Dewey Decimal Classification for grades seven through nine. An author, title, subject, and analytical index makes this easy to use.

HOW TO USE REFERENCE MATERIALS: JRO11.02. By Bernice MacDonald.

CHILDREN'S FILMS AND VIDEOS, FILMSTRIPS, AND RECORDINGS, 1973-1986: JRO11.37 Assoc. for Library Services to Children.

REFERENCE BOOKS FOR YOUNG READERS AUTHORITATIVE EVALUATIONS OF ENCYCLOPEDIAS, ATLASES, AND DICTIONARIES: JRO11.02. By Marion Sader. Buying guide series. This would be useful to look through before purchasing any reference materials.

BEYOND PICTURE BOOKS, A GUIDE TO FIRST READERS: JRO11.62. By Barbara Barstow and Judith Riggle.

BILINGUAL BOOKS IN SPANISH AND ENGLISH FOR CHILDREN: JRO11.62. By Doris C. Dale.

CHOICES: A CORE COLLECTION FOR YOUNG RELUCTANT READERS: JRO11.62. By Burke. I spent some time looking this one over and think it would be useful. The author says in the introduction that as she visited the schools, she found that the reluctant reader is the rule rather than the exception, and so she compiled this collection of titles and descriptions of readers for those children. These are books of high interest on an easy level.

THE ELEMENTARY SCHOOL PAPERBACK COLLECTION: JRO11.62. By John T. Gillespie. This volume includes brief descriptions. Some children prefer reading paperback books. Now many of the classics are printed in paperback form.

DEVELOPING LEARNING SKILLS THROUGH CHILDREN'S LITERATURE: AN IDEA BOOK FOR K-5 CLASSROOMS AND LIBRARIES: JRO11.62. By Mildred Knight Laughlin and Letty S. Watt. This book lists objectives, recommended reading, and activities for each topic. It includes *Winnie the Pooh*, Laura Ingalls Wilder, Hans Christian Andersen, and many more that look interesting.

MAGAZINES FOR SCHOOL LIBRARIES: JRO11.62. By Bill Katz. This includes elementary, junior high, and high school libraries. All magazines are arranged by subjects, including art, birds, comics, education, health, medicine, military, music and dance, geography, and more. This book informs you of magazines specifically related to certain topics. The addresses are listed as well so you can order particular magazines that would correspond with a unit you are doing. The library also carries magazines on various subjects, including back issues.

OPENING DOORS FOR PRESCHOOL CHILDREN AND THEIR PARENTS: JRO11.62. By the American Library Association. Includes books, films, filmstrips, recordings and toys, and regalia.

NEWBERY AND CALDECOTT MEDAL AND HONOR BOOKS AND ANNOTATED BIBLIOGRAPHY: JRO11.62. By Peterson and Solt. Lists Newbery Award Books beginning with the first in 1922 through today, and lists Caldecott Medal Books beginning with 1938 through today. One book is chosen for each award for the year it is published. This book provides descriptions of each book listed.

MASTER INDEX TO SUMMARIES OF CHILDREN'S BOOKS: JR011.62. By Eloise S. Pettus. Volume I: A-Z, Volume II: title and subject indexes. These volumes are to be used together; for example, look up *sewing* in the subject index in Volume II, and cross reference to volume I for titles, authors, and a description of books concerning sewing.

POETRY ANTHOLOGIES FOR CHILDREN AND YOUNG PEOPLE: JRO11.62. By Olexer. Includes author, title, and subject indexes. Descriptions of poems are given along with appropriate grade levels. If you are studying a particular topic, this book can be used to locate poems relating to that topic. For example, if you are studying the middle ages and are taking a close look at armor, you would look up "armor" in this book and find a reference for Longfellow's poem, an entire book, entitled *The Skeleton in Armor*.

INTRODUCING BOOK PLOTS 3: A BOOK TALK GUIDE FOR USE WITH READERS AGES 8-12: JRO11.62. By Diane L. Spirt. Contains summaries of various books falling into specific categories, such as: Getting Along in the Family, Making Friends, Developing Values, Forming a View of the World, Respecting Living Creatures, etc. Not only will this book introduce you to books for various ages and of various themes, but it will inform you as to how to introduce these books to your children to cause them to want to read them. It also lists related books and materials such as filmstrips and recordings. This book contains a subject index, helpful for locating books pertaining to your unit of study or to your child's particular interests.

PRIMARY PLOTS: A BOOK TALK GUIDE FOR USE WITH READERS AGES 4-8: JRO11.62. By Rebecca L. Thomas. Similar in content to the book listed previously but for use with younger children.

BOOKS FOR CHILDREN TO READ ALONE: A GUIDE FOR PARENTS AND LIBRARIANS, PRE-K THROUGH GRADE 3: JRO11.62. By George Wilson and Joyce Moss. This book is very helpful in that it breaks the books into categories such as: (1) Books for the Beginning Reader: Wordless or Nearly Wordless Books, (2) Books for the First Half of Grade One, and (3) Books for the Second Half of Grade One. This continues through grade 3. This book also has a subject index, readability index (i.e., indexed under grade levels such as 1.0 to 1.4 and 1.5 to 1.9), author index, and title index. Each grade level also has further categories such as Easy, Average, and Challenging. By using this book, you can easily put together your own beginning reader series, all from the library. Descriptions are included for many of the books listed.

DOORS TO MORE MATURE READING: DETAILED NOTES ON ADULT BOOKS FOR USE WITH YOUNG PEOPLE: JROI6. By Elinor Walker. This book helps familiarize the parent with adult books suitable for use by a teenager. It also lists persons to whom each book will appeal. Unfortunately, this book does not have a subject index, but it does have a title index. A big plus is that most of the books reviewed were written before 1950.

ENCYCLOPEDIA BUYING GUIDE: JROI6.03. By Kenneth Kister. This book reviews all general English language encyclopedias.

INDEX TO FAIRY TALES: JR0l6.398. **INDEX TO FAIRY TALE SUPPLEMENT:** JR0l6.398. **INDEX TO FAIRY TALES SECOND SUPPLEMENT:** JR0l6.398. The volumes listed above will prove helpful for locating fairy tales relating to your unit study. For instance, you can look under "A" for "ants" to find an entire page of ant tale listings. You can also use this guide to find fairy tales written by a specific author.

MATHEMATICS LIBRARY: ELEMENTARY AND JUNIOR HIGH SCHOOL: JR0l6.51. By Clarence E. Hardgrove and Herbert Miller. This slim volume includes books to enrich your math program with brief descriptions of each book.

SUBJECT INDEX GUIDE TO CHILDREN'S PLAYS: JR0l6.8. American Library Association, Elizabeth D. Briggs, Chairman. "Each entry gives the name of the play, indicates by code number the book in which the play is found, and includes a page reference to the play's location, the grades for which it is suited, the number of characters required, and the number of acts or scenes, or both." Plays are listed alphabetically according to subject, title, and author. Also included are listings of dramatizations from authors' works such as Hans Christian Andersen, and Ingri and Edgar D' Aulaire.

HISTORY IN CHILDREN'S BOOKS: AN ANNOTATED BIBLIOGRAPHY FOR SCHOOLS AND LIBRARIES: JR016.909. By Zena Sutherland. This book is divided into chapters: Primitive and Ancient Times, Africa, Asia, Pacific Regions, Polar and Far North, Europe, Latin America, Canada, Explorers of the New World and the United States, which itself is subdivided into time periods, peoples, and places. It includes biographies, as well as historical fiction and easy readers. You will find a brief description and approximate grade level for each book listed.

AMERICAN HISTORY IN JUVENILE BOOKS: A CHRONOLOGICAL GUIDE: JR016.973. By Seymour Metzner. This book lists biographies, fiction, nonfiction, and approximate grade levels; however, it does not give a description of the books listed.

THE PICTURE FILE: A MANUAL AND CURRICULUM-RELATED SUBJECT HEADING LIST: JR025.34. By Donna Hill. Tells how to create and use a picture file to enhance a curriculum. Gives ideas on how to locate free-of-charge pictures from various sources. It appears this book can be used for a family project to create a picture file for a specific unit.

BOOK SHARING: 101 PROGRAMS TO USE WITH PRESCHOOLERS: JR027.62. By Margaret MacDonald. Includes books, songs, and activities all centered on a particular theme.

MUSICAL STORY HOURS: USING MUSIC WITH STORYTELLING AND PUPPETRY: JR027.62. By William M. Painter. Suggests books to read aloud with music and activities to go with the stories. Many of the records and books can be found in larger libraries.

THE FLANNEL BOARD STORYTELLING BOOK: JR027.6251. By Judy Sierra. Includes entire story text, poems, songs, and over 250 accompanying reproducible patterns.

JUNIOR PLOTS: JR028.1. By Gillespie and Lembo. Lists books with their descriptions for young adults.

SUBJECT AND TITLE INDEX TO SHORT STORIES FOR CHILDREN: JR028.5. Compiled by the American Library Association, chairman Julia Carter. Lists books by subject and title but does not include descriptions of books.

BOOKS FOR CHILDREN: JR028.5. Compiled by the American Library Association. Lists books under various categories: Art, History, Geography, Science, Biographies, etc. Also gives descriptions of books.

CHILDREN'S LITERATURE REVIEW: JR028.5. Compiled by Block, Riley, and Senick. This set contains many volumes consisting of general commentaries about individual authors and many of their books. These volumes would prove beneficial for a study of a particular author and his or her works. Each volume is alphabetically arranged according to the author's last name. Each volume contains a listing of authors from A-Z; therefore, Volume I may not contain Lewis Carroll, but he is included in Volume II. Indexes are included so that you may quickly locate the volume needed for a particular author. These volumes allow you to get a feel for an author and some of his books at a glance. My library has 21 volumes.

CHILDREN'S BOOKS: AWARDS AND PRIZES: JR028.5. By the Children's Book Council, Inc. Prizes and awards for young adult books are also included in this book. It is divided into the following categories: U.S. Awards Selected by Adults, U.S. Awards Selected by Young Readers, British Commonwealth Awards, and International and Multinational Awards. Over 100 separate book awards and their recipients through 1985 are contained in this book. A description of each award is also given.

THE WHO'S WHO OF CHILDREN'S LITERATURE: JR028.5. Compiled and edited by Brian Doyle. Contains over 400 names with biographical, bibliographical, and background details covering a selection of British, Continental European, and American authors from 1800 to the present day. Very good for studying particular authors.

PICTURE BOOKS FOR CHILDREN: JR028.5. By Patricia J. Cianciolo. A guide to children's picture books with descriptions of books included.

THE BOOK FINDER: JR028.5. By Sharon S. Dreyer. "Helps you match books to the needs and problems of children and young people." You will find volumes with selections of books published from different years. Books are categorized according to theme, for example: Accidents, Adoption, Anger, Bedtime, Belonging, etc. Some categories are undesirable, but others are very useful.

TREASURE FOR THE TAKING: A BOOK LIST FOR BOYS AND GIRLS: JR028.5. By Anne T. Eaton. Includes categories such as Talking Beasts and Other Creatures, Trees and Flowers, Ships and the Sea, Legends and Hero Tales, Stories with Historical Background, What to Do, and How to Do It. Descriptions are included for each book.

BEST BOOKS FOR CHILDREN: PRESCHOOL THROUGH GRADE SIX: JR028.5. By John Gillespie and Corinne Nade. Major subjects are arranged alphabetically. Contains descriptions of each book listed and has a subject/grade-level index.

SPORTS BOOKS FOR CHILDREN: JR028.5. By Barbara Harrah. Includes book descriptions and books are arranged alphabetically by sport subjects.

STORY STRETCHERS: JR028.5. By Shirley Raines and Robert Canady. "Activities to expand children's favorite books." Probably for preschool through third grade.

BASIC COLLECTION OF CHILDREN'S BOOKS IN SPANISH: JR028.5. By Isabel Schon. Contains a subject and title index.

A TO ZOO: SUBJECT ACCESS TO CHILDREN'S PICTURE BOOKS: JR028.5. By Carolyn W. Lima. Alphabetically arranged according to topic. Contains descriptions of books.

CALDECOTT MEDAL BOOKS, 1938-1957: JR028.5. Edited by B.M.

Miller. Contains artists' acceptance papers, their biographies, and a critical analysis by Esther Averill: "What is a picture book?"

NEWBERY MEDAL BOOKS, 1922-1955: JR028.5. Edited by B.M. Miller and E.W. Field. Contains authors' acceptance papers, biographies of award winners, and appraisals of winning books.

NEWBERY AND CALDECOTT MEDAL BOOKS, 1966-1975: JR028.5079. Edited by Kingman. Same format as previously listed books.

NEWBERY AND CALDECOTT MEDAL BOOKS, 1976-1985: JRO28.0579. Edited by Kingman. Same format as above. (Note: There are probably other books for the years omitted. Also note the listing I made earlier for the *Newbery and Caldecott Medal and Honor Books, an Annotated Bibliography* by Solt. This covers all the years but does not include all the same information as these books listed above.)

ADVENTURING WITH BOOKS: A BOOKLIST FOR PRE K-GRADE 6: JRO28.5. Edited by Diane Monson. Includes categories such as Books for Young Children, Traditional Literature, Modern Fantasy, Historical Fiction, Contemporary Realistic Fiction, Poetry, Language, Social Studies, Biography, Sciences, Fine Arts, Crafts and Hobbies, etc. Each category is further divided. Each book listed includes appropriate grade levels, number of pages, and a description.

CHOOSING BOOKS FOR KIDS: CHOOSING THE RIGHT BOOK FOR THE RIGHT CHILD AT THE RIGHT TIME, OVER 1500 BOOK REVIEWS: JRO28.5. Edited by William Hooks. Includes divisions such as books for Babies, Toddlers, Three- and Four-Year-Olds, Books for Fives, Books for Sixes and Sevens, Books for Eights and Nines, and Books for Ten- to-Twelve-Year-Olds.

CELEBRATING WITH BOOKS: JRO28.5. By Polette and Hamlin. A review of books dealing with holiday themes.

BOOKS FOR BOYS AND GIRLS: A STANDARD WORK OF REFERENCE FOR LIBRARIANS: JRO28.5. Edited by Mary Bagshaw. "Each book is fully annotated and the list is arranged by subject according to the child's reading interests. Books chosen include only those considered to be of permanent interest to boys and girls."

TWENTIETH CENTURY CHILDREN'S WRITERS: JRO28.5. Edited by Daniel Kirkpatrick. Contains biographies, bibliographies, and critical essays detailing each writer's influences.

WORLD HISTORY IN JUVENILE BOOKS: JRO28.52. By Metzner. Books are categorized by country. Each division includes biographies, fiction, and nonfiction. The title, author, number of pages, and grade level are given, but descriptions are not included.

EUROPEAN HISTORICAL FICTION AND BIOGRAPHIES FOR CHILDREN AND YOUNG PEOPLE: JRO28.52. By Jeanette Hotchkiss. Categorized by country and then further divisions such as General History, Myths and Legends, and specific centuries are included. Contains descriptions of each book.

AMERICAN HISTORICAL FICTION AND BIOGRAPHIES FOR CHILDREN AND YOUNG PEOPLE: JRO28.52. By Jeanette

Hotchkiss. Divided into time periods such as Early Explorations, Colonial Period, Revolutionary Period, etc. Also categorized according to subject such as The Arts, Folklore, Industry and Technology, Science, etc. Includes description of each book.

AUTHORS OF BOOKS FOR YOUNG PEOPLE: JR028.5. By Ward and Marquardt. Includes biographical information on children's authors.

THE ELEMENTARY SCHOOL LIBRARY COLLECTION: A GUIDE TO BOOKS AND OTHER MEDIA: JR028.52. The Brodart Company. Contains a subject guide and lists authors, titles and descriptions of books. Includes fiction, non-fiction, and easy.

YANKEE DOODLE'S LITERARY SAMPLER OF PROSE, POETRY, AND PICTURES: JR028.52. By V. Haviland and M. Coughlan. "Being an Anthology of Diverse Works Published for the Edification and/or Entertainment of Young Readers in America before 1900." You can use this to give your children a glimpse of the past. This book is not a guide to other books, but rather is a sampling of books of long ago.

YOUNG PEOPLE'S LITERATURE IN SERIES: FICTION, NON-FICTION, AND PUBLISHER SERIES: JR028.52. By Rosenburg. Includes lists of authors and their works included in a series. Gives an overview of the content of the series and lists appropriate grade levels. Many young children are encouraged to continue reading if they are exposed to books within a series.

CHILDHOOD IN POETRY: JR028.52. By John Mackay Shaw. A multi-volume set consisting of a catalogue with biographical and critical annotations of the books of English and American poets. This is categorized according to the author's last name, but also includes indexes composed of the author's last name and subject headings. Therefore, you can find poems relating to a specific topic or other poems by a particular author. Also included are typical passages from the poems. I have found that these books tend to be difficult to use because many of the poems listed are not easily found in the library. If you do not have much success with this set, select a large poetry volume with a subject index and locate poems dealing with your topic. An author index will probably be included in this poetry volume as well for locating poems by a particular author.

CREATIVE ENCOUNTERS: ACTIVITIES TO EXPAND CHILDREN'S RESPONSES TO LITERATURE: JR028.55. By A. Polkingham and C. Toohey. Includes activities to be utilized with various books for young children. Some of the books selected are: *If the Dinosaurs Came Back, The Princess and the Pea, Harold and the Purple Crayon, Corduroy, A Pocket for Corduroy,* and *A Color of His Own.*

PROGRAMMING FOR SCHOOL AGE CHILD CARE: A CHILDREN'S LITERATURE BASED GUIDE: JR028.5. By Melba Hawkins. Contains ideas for integrating children's literature with creative art activities, creative dramatics, creative music activities, cooking experiences, and special days of the year. Book reviews are given along with suggested activities. Although the title indicates that this book is for child care, the book looks very interesting.

THIS WAY TO BOOKS: JRO28.55. By Caroline Bauer. Contains hundreds of ideas and programs designed to get children and books together. The methods described here include the use of toys, puppets, crafts, music, costumes, and banners as devices to unite children and books. The ideas are very interesting and creative.

THE INFORMATION PLEASE ALMANAC: JRO31 Houghton Mifflin Company. Contains information on business and economy, taxes, first aid, nutrition and health, geography and an atlas, and much more. There are also several other almanacs, including almanacs for children.

A FIRST DICTIONARY OF CULTURAL LITERACY: WHAT OUR CHILDREN NEED TO KNOW: JRO31.02. By E.D. Hirsch, Jr. Written in response to the outcry that our children today are suffering educationally. This book is interesting to browse through; however, it contains only snippets of information.

THE MACMILLAN BOOK OF GREEK GODS AND HEROES: JR292. By Alice Low, illustrated by Arvis Stewart. Includes popular myths and legends. Written in a simplified style and beautifully illustrated.

D'AULAIRES' BOOK OF GREEK MYTHS: JR292. By Ingri and Edgar Parin d' Aulaire. The D' Aulaires are known for their many wonderfully illustrated biographies which are considered children's classics. As Caldecott Award-winning artists, they have written and illustrated one of the most captivating books on Greek myths.

The reference section includes other exquisitely illustrated books on GREEK, ROMAN, CELTIC, RUSSIAN, INDIAN, and VIKING MYTHOLOGY and LEGENDS.

THE GOLDEN BIBLE ATLAS WITH RELIEF MAPS IN FULL COLOR: JR220.9. By Samuel Terrien. This book makes an historical and pictorial progression through the Bible written in a style that is understandable for young and old.

BIBLE ENCYCLOPEDIA FOR CHILDREN: JR220.3. By Denis Wrigley. This easy-to-read, fully illustrated text describes the people, main events, places, and leading ideas of the Bible.

THE JUNIOR JEWISH ENCYCLOPEDIA: JR296.03. Edited by Naomi Ben-Asher and Hayim Leaf. An illustrated reference guide covering Jewish life and culture from ancient times to the present.

BLACK STUDIES: A BIBLIOGRAPHY: JR301.45196. By Leonard Irwin. Includes: The History of the Black Experience in America, Biography, Memoirs, Autobiography, Essays, Anthologies, Literature, Music and Arts, and African Background and History. Gives brief reviews of each book listed.

CAREER DISCOVERY ENCYCLOPEDIA: JR331.702. Ferguson Publishing Company. A multi-volume set. "The Career Discovery Encyclopedia is written especially for younger readers. It is designed to enable them and to encourage them to begin learning and thinking about the kinds of jobs and careers that will be available to them as adults." It contains information about more than 500 different kinds of jobs, presented in the form of short articles, no longer than two pages. Each article explains different aspects of the job: what it is like, what kind of education and training are required, what the salary and future prospects for the job are like, and how to get more information.

ACCEPT ME AS I AM: BEST BOOKS OF JUVENILE NONFICTION ON IMPAIRMENTS AND DISABILITIES: JR362.4016. By Friedberg, Mullins, Sukiennik. Categorizes books according to: Physical Problems, Sensory Problems, Cognitive and Behavior Problems, Multiple/Severe and Various Disabilities. This book also includes a subject index. Each book listed receives a half-page to full-page review.

BASIC MEDIA SKILLS THROUGH GAMES: JR371.3078. By Irene Wood Bell and Jeanne E. Wieckert. This book is to familiarize students with the skills necessary to effectively use instructional materials. Although intended for use in a school library, many of these games could be adapted for home use in learning to locate information by using dictionaries, encyclopedias, atlases, tables of contents, and indexes. You can also create your own library at home and make author, title, and subject cards for library books you have checked out. Have the children alphabetize their cards and shelve the library books according to their call numbers. Many library skills can be learned at home. My children love playing library and even put slips of paper in the backs of the books and stamp them.

FELT BOARD FUN: FOR EVERYDAY AND HOLIDAYS: JR371.33. By Liz and Dick Wilmes. Includes units describing a variety of activities. Patterns for each unit are included and can be photocopied right at the library. You can let your children cut out the patterns you copy, color them and put them together while engaging in an activity described in the book. There's a good possibility that you will find this book on the regular shelves.

ACTIVE LEARNING: GAMES TO ENHANCE ACADEMIC ABILITIES: JR371.332. By Bryant Cratty. Includes activities for these categories: Calming Down and Tuning Up, Geometric Figures, Remembering Things, Numbers and Counting, Mathematics, Letters, Letter Sounds and Spelling, Reading, and Improving Coordination. The appropriate age is listed for each activity, and some activities are for children up to twelve years old.

MUD PIES TO MAGNETS: A PRESCHOOL SCIENCE CURRICULUM: JR372.35. By R. Williams, R. Rockwell and E. Sherwood. A collection of science activities involving: Construction and Measurement, Scientific Art, Health and Nutrition, Outdoor Science, Creativity and Movement, and more. This would be appropriate for the early grades as well. You could copy a few activities you are interested in. There are several other books for science activities. It is good to check in the reference section as many of these activity books are not found on the regular shelves.

MORE WINDOWS TO THE WORLD: A GOOD APPLE ACTIVITY BOOK FOR GRADES 2-8: JR372.83. By Nancy

Everix. This book allows your children to take a trip around the world through hands-on activities. Also includes addresses for the international tourist offices of many countries, enabling you to write for free or inexpensive materials. Here again, desired activities can be photocopied.

Other useful books that I may not have included are handbooks on: STORYTELLING, PUPPETRY, COSTUMES from around the world and from various historical periods, FESTIVALS and ANNUAL EVENTS, FOLKLORE, FAIRY TALES, FABLES, LEGENDS, and FOLKTALES. I have included some specific books, however, that fall into some of these categories. Also you will find BOY SCOUT, CUB SCOUT, BROWNIE, and GIRL SCOUT HANDBOOKS. These books are catalogued between JR369 and JR398.

ONCE UPON A TIME: A STORYTELLING HANDBOOK: JR372.64. By Lucille and Bren Breneman. "A study of the techniques of storytelling as an art form useful to teachers, librarians, entertainers, speakers, and those in the helping professions."

STORYTELLING: PROCESS AND PRACTICE: JR372.64. By Norma Liro and Sandra Rietz.

THE COMPLETE ANDERSEN: JR398. Translated and edited by Jean Hersholt. "All of the stories of Hans Christian Andersen collected into one volume for the first time. Some never before translated into English and some never before published."

THE STANDARD DICTIONARY OF FOLKLORE: JR398. Funk and Wagnalls. Comprising two volumes that exhibit a major overall survey of world folklore, mythology, and legend.

GRIMM'S TALES FOR YOUNG AND OLD: THE COMPLETE STORIES: JR398. Newly translated by Ralph Manheim.

THE OXFORD DICTIONARY OF NURSERY RHYMES: JR398. Edited by Iona and Peter Opie. Contains more than 500 rhymes and songs and the studies of their individual histories.

THE FABLES OF AESOP: JR398.2. Rand McNally. Illustrated by Frank Baber.

THE NEW ENCYCLOPEDIA OF SCIENCE: JR500. Raintree Publishers.

NATURE ATLAS OF AMERICA: JR500. By Roland Clement.

ILLUSTRATED LIBRARY OF NATURE: JR500.9. H.S. Stuttman Co., Inc., Pub.

THE MUSEUM OF SCIENCE AND INDUSTRY: BASIC LIST OF CHILDREN'S SCIENCE BOOKS: JR501.6. American Library Association. Includes reviews of books arranged alphabetically according to subject.

THE BEST SCIENCE BOOKS FOR CHILDREN: JR501.6. Edited by Wolff, Fritsche, Gross, and Todd. Includes a subject index and reviews of each book listed.

COMPTON'S DICTIONARY OF NATURAL SCIENCE: JR503.

COMPTON'S ILLUSTRATED SCIENCE DICTIONARY: JR503.

GROWING UP WITH SCIENCE: JR503. H.S. Stuttman Pub. An illustrated encyclopedia of science comprising twenty-five volumes.

RAND MCNALLY MATHEMATICS ENCYCLOPEDIA: JR51O.3.

THE INTERNATIONAL WILDLIFE ENCYCLOPEDIA: JR51O.3.
Marshall Cavendish Corporation. Twenty volumes.

THE BIRDS OF AMERICA: JR598.2. By John James Audubon.

You will find many other ENCYCLOPEDIAS pertaining to ANIMALS, PLANTS, and the SEA. You will find books on HORSES, DOGS, CATS, and other PETS catalogued under JR636.

GARDENER'S ART THROUGH THE AGES: JR709. By de la Croix Tansey.

THE GOLDEN ENCYCLOPEDIA OF ART: JR709. By Eleanor C. Munro.

THE PANTHEON STORY OF ART FOR YOUNG PEOPLE: JR709. By Batterberry. Well written and contains excellent photos of artwork.

THE ART OF BEATRIX POTTER: JR741.6. With notes by Enid and Leslie Linder.

THE RANDOLPH CALDECOTT TREASURY: JR741.6. Edited by Elizabeth Billington.

Other books on FAMOUS ILLUSTRATORS can be found in this section also.

A PICTORIAL HISTORY OF MUSIC: JR780.9. By Paul Henry and Otto Bettmann. "The Pageant of Music History presented with more than 600 pictures and an authoritative text."

Other books pertaining to MUSIC are catalogued from JR780 to JR784.

Books relating to SPORTS and GAMES are catalogued under JR793.

PRESENTING READER'S THEATER: PLAYS AND POEMS TO READ ALOUD: JR792.0226. By C.F. Bauer.

WRITING WITH PICTURES: HOW TO WRITE AND ILLUSTRATE CHILDREN'S BOOKS: JR808.068. By Uri Shulevitz.

SUBJECT INDEX TO POETRY FOR CHILDREN AND YOUNG PEOPLE: JR808.8. American Library Association. Allows you to locate poems pertaining to a particular topic and uses a cross-reference system to enable you to find the title of a book that a specific poem is published in.

INDEX TO CHILDREN'S POETRY: JR808.8. By John and Sara Brewton. The poems listed are classified by subject. A cross-reference system is used to locate books in which these poems appear. The front of this index, and the one listed above, explain how each of these books is to be used. Only a few minutes are needed to familiarize you with these books.

THE SCOTT FORESMAN ANTHOLOGY OF CHILDREN'S LITERATURE: JR808.89. By Zena Sutherland and Mira Livingston. This anthology of children's literature introduces the work of fine authors, new and old, as well as introducing the broad spectrum of contemporary and traditional literature. The material in this book has been divided into three main parts: An Invitation to Poetry, An Invitation to Folklore and Fantasy, and An Invitation to Fiction and Fact. Great as a read-aloud book as it encompasses many variations of children's literature for all ages. This book is often found on the regular shelves of the library as well.

There are many books in the reference section to be found pertaining to CHILDREN'S POETRY.

VALUES IN SELECTED CHILDREN'S BOOKS OF FICTION AND FANTASY: JR809.39. By C. Field and J. Weiss. "Here are over 700 annotations of books for children from the preschool level to the eighth grade, categorized by ten values they represent or reinforce. The books are culled from titles likely to be in school and public libraries and published in the United States between 1930 and 1984." The titles are divided by age level. Categories of values include: Cooperation, Courage, Friendship and Love of Animals, Friendship and Love of People, Humaneness, Ingenuity, Loyalty, Maturity, Responsibility, and Self-Respect. I recognize many of the titles listed and I am pleased overall with the book.

NAME THAT BOOK: JR809.8928. By Janet Greeson and Karen Taha. For primary through junior high. Includes titles, authors, and descriptions of books along with pertinent questions for each book. Apparently, this book has been used by librarians and teachers to play a game called "Battle of Books," which has been played in schools and libraries since 1940. You could use this book and locate books in it you have already read, or choose books listed that you would like to read, and have your own "Battle of Books" game at home. It sounds like great fun. You could even integrate a new aspect and call it "Name that Author."

YESTERDAY'S AUTHORS OF BOOKS FOR CHILDREN: JR809.89. Edited by Anne Commire. Two volumes containing facts and pictures about authors and illustrators of books for young people from early times to 1960.

PRIZE-WINNING BOOKS FOR CHILDREN: JR813.009. By Jacqueline Weiss. "It is the only known review of children's literature based exclusively on prizewinners, a logical source for those who want to read what has been judged as the best." Arranged under various themes, inclusive of descriptions and appropriate age categories. Contains author and title index.

THE FLORIDA HANDBOOK: FLORIDA'S PEOPLE AND THEIR GOVERNMENT: JR917.59. By Allen Morris.

Several other books are included in this section pertaining to FLORIDA. (Each library will have books representative of its state.) Also there are books on LANDS AND PEOPLES, EARLY AMERICAN LIFE, and a variety of ATLASES. These books are catalogued under the numbers 910 to 917.

THE LOOK-IT-UP BOOK OF PRESIDENTS: JR920. By Wyatt Blassingame.

Other books on the PRESIDENTS are in this same area.

FOURTH BOOK OF JUNIOR AUTHORS AND ILLUSTRATORS: JR920. Edited by Montreville and Crawford. Also *The Junior Book of Authors, More Junior Authors,* and *The 3rd Book of Junior Authors.* These books include biographical sketches of various authors, while the fourth book also includes illustrators.

ILLUSTRATORS OF CHILDREN'S BOOKS: JR920. Published by Horn Book Incorporated. Includes biographical sketches of various illustrators.

CHILDREN'S AUTHORS AND ILLUSTRATORS: JR920. Edited by Adele Sarkissian. An index to biographical dictionaries. "Provides quick and easy access to biographical information on approximately 20,000 persons found in more than 275 reference books." Useful for a study of children's literature.

INDEX TO COLLECTIVE BIOGRAPHIES FOR YOUNG READERS: ELEMENTARY AND JUNIOR HIGH LEVEL: JR920. By Judith Silverman. This book is divided into two sections, Alphabetical Listings of Biographies and Subject Listings of Biographies. The Alphabetical Listings of Biographies includes brief descriptions of each biographee, for example, baseball player, evangelist, dancer, and so on. The most helpful section of this book, however, is the Subject Listing of Biographies. By using this part of the book, you can locate persons relating to your particular topic or theme. For instance, if you are studying composers, you will find listings for composers under headings such as American, Austrian, Czech, English, French, Italian, and so on. The birth and death dates are listed for each composer, enabling you to focus on a particular time period as well as on a particular nationality. You will find lists of persons under authors, engineers, explorers, mathematicians, pianists, and many more. This index enables you to locate a biography on persons relating to most any topic. A cross-reference system is used to locate the books in which each person is depicted.

PEOPLE IN BOOKS: JR920.02. By Margaret Nicholsen. "A Selective Guide to Biographical Literature Arranged by Vocations and Other Fields of Reader Interest." I believe this book is easier to use than *Collective Biographies for Young Readers* in that no cross-reference system is needed to find book titles. You locate a particular topic such as abolitionists, authors, lawyers, physicists, or taxidermists, and the biographees' names are listed along with the titles of their biographies. The names of the authors, publishers, years published, and birth and death dates of the biographees are also included. After finding a person who fits your studies, it is advisable to check the adult section of your library for a biography of that person. I have sometimes found more interesting biographies in the adult section.

INDEX TO SHORT BIOGRAPHIES FOR ELEMENTARY AND JUNIOR HIGH GRADES: JR920.0016. Compiled by Ellen J. Stanius. This book contains a straight alphabetical listing of biographies. It does not include a subject index, detracting from its usefulness. It is helpful to use once you have located the name of a person whom you wish to study, perhaps through consulting *Index to Collective Biographies for Young Readers* or *People in Books*, but possibly you would like a simpler biography about that person. This *Index to Short Biographies* enables you to locate that particular person and thus a short biography title. If you find that your library does not have any of the titles you are looking for, have the librarian check to see if another branch owns one. Also, once you have located the name of a person related to your study, you can often find a book written about that person in the junior biography section of your library; these books are alphabetized according to the biographee's last name.

The reference section also includes books on AMERICAN INDIANS, FRONTIER LIVING, FLORIDA, and UNITED STATES HISTORY; these are catalogued from 970 to 975.

THE RAINBOW BOOK OF AMERICAN HISTORY: JR973. By Earl S. Miers and illustrated by James Daugherty. Contains superb illustrations and an easy-to-follow text written in a story-type fashion. This book is usually found on the regular bookshelves as well, and is one of my favorites.

It is my hope this brief reference guide will have sparked your interest enough to encourage you to take a closer look at what your library has to offer. Make it known to your librarians that you home educate your children and that the library is a valuable resource to your family. If there are books listed in this guide that you believe would benefit your studies but are not owned by your library system, inform your librarian. Find out, too, if you can have a voice in the purchasing of books for your county. I have found most librarians more than willing to help home educators. It is important, as well, that we teach our children how to use the reference section and also help them recognize the other services provided by the public library. You will do well to check out a book explaining the various services and systems the library makes available and utilizes.

The next section comprises an overview of the Dewey Decimal Classification System that divides all non-fiction books into ten groups and further divides each group. Fiction books are arranged alphabetically by the author's last name and appear in a separate section of the library. The children's section of the library is arranged like the adult section; only a "J" for "Juvenile" precedes the call number. An "easy reading" section of books is also available for beginning readers and picture books are available for younger children. Both these sections are arranged by author.

Dewey Decimal Classification System

000-099 GENERAL WORKS
010 Bibliographies and Catalogues
020 Library and Information Sciences
030 General Encyclopedic Works
050 General Serial Publications
060 General Organizations, Museums
070 Journalism, Publishing, Newspapers
080 General Collections
090 Manuscripts and Book Rarities

100-199 PHILOSOPHY AND RELATED DISCIPLINES
110 Metaphysics
120 Knowledge, Purpose, Man
130 Popular and Parapsychology, Occultism
140 Specific Philosophical Viewpoints
150 Psychology
160 Logic
170 Ethics
180 Ancient, Medieval, Oriental
190 Modern Western Philosophy

200-299 RELIGION
210 Natural Religion
220 Bible
230 Christian Doctrinal Theology
240 Christian Moral and Devotional
250 Local Church, Religious Orders
260 Social, Ecclesiastical Theology
270 History and Geography of Church
280 Christian Denominations, Sects
290 Other Religions and Comparative

300-399 THE SOCIAL SCIENCES
310 Statistics
320 Political Science
330 Economics
340 Law
350 Public Administration
360 Social Pathology and Services
370 Education
380 Commerce
390 Customs and Folklore

400-499 LANGUAGE
410 Linguistics
420 English, Anglo-Saxon
430 Germanic Languages, German
440 French, Provencal, Catalan
450 Italian, Romanian, Romanic
460 Spanish and Portuguese
470 Italic Languages, Latin
480 Hellenic, Classical Greek
490 Other Languages

500-599 PURE SCIENCES
510 Mathematics
520 Astronomy and Allied Sciences
530 Physics
540 Chemistry and Allied Sciences
550 Earth and Other Worlds
560 Paleontology
570 Life Sciences
580 Botanical (Plant Life)
590 Zoological (Animal Life)

600-699 TECHNOLOGY (APPLIED SCIENCES)
610 Medical Sciences
620 Engineering, Allied Operations
630 Agriculture and Related
640 Home Economics
650 Managerial Services
660 Chemical and Related
670 Manufactures
680 Misc. Manufactures
690 Buildings

700-799 THE ARTS
710 Civic and Landscape Art
720 Architecture
730 Plastic Arts, Sculpture
740 Drawing, Decorative and Minor
750 Painting and Paintings
760 Graphic Arts, Prints
770 Photography and Photographs
780 Music
790 Recreational and Performing Arts

800-899 LITERATURE
810 American Literature in English
820 English and Anglo-Saxon Literature
830 Literature of Germanic Languages
840 French, Provencal, Catalan
850 Italian, Romanian, Romanic
860 Spanish and Portuguese Literature
870 Italic Languages Literature, Latin
880 Hellenic Languages Literature
890 Literatures of Other Languages

900-999 GENERAL GEOGRAPHY AND HISTORY
910 General Geography, Travel
920 Biography, Genealogy, Insignia
930 Gen. History of Ancient World
940 Gen. History of Europe
950 Gen. History of Asia
960 Gen. History of Africa
970 Gen. History of N. America
980 Gen. History of S. America
990 General History of Other Areas

Dear Reader

*T*his book was developed as a result of the frequent questions I received concerning unit studies and teaching my children in general. If it were not for those determined mothers seeking better and more practical methods for teaching their children, I probably would not have written this book.

It is very frustrating for me to see parents struggle through a curriculum only to find the curriculum does not meet their needs. The parents are unhappy and the children are even more displeased.

Educating our children does not have to be a complicated process; it just needs to be a thoughtful process. Evaluate your priorities and let those priorities be your guide.

I encourage you to send me your comments and questions. This enables me to stay in contact with the needs and interests of home-educating families. I am always looking for good teaching tips myself. I appreciate your input.

Those mothers who were most persistent in their questions will find our conversations between the pages of this book. I offer my thanks to you as you continue to be an encouragement to me.

Please address any comments or questions to:

Valerie Bendt

333 W. Rio Vista Court

Tampa, FL 33604-6940

Thank you!

Valerie Bendt
1990

2004 update – You may now visit our website at www.ValerieBendt.com

1. *American Dictionary of the English Language*, Noah Webster 1828, republished in facsimile edition by the Foundation for American Christian Education, San Francisco, California.

2. *Ibid.*

3. *Webster's Encyclopedia of Dictionaries, New American Edition*, Ottenheimer Pub., Inc., 1978, p. 121.

4. *Webster's New World Dictionary of the American Language*, The World Publishing Co., 1988, p.444.

5. Susan Schaeffer Macaulay, *For the Children's Sake*, Crossway Books, 1984, p. 8.

6. *Ibid*, p. 82.

7. Philippians 4:8, *New American Standard Version*.

8. Charlotte Mason, *Home Education*, Tyndale House Pub., Inc., 1989. Originally published by Kegan Paul, Trench, Trubner and Co., Ltd., London, England, 1935. p. 153. Now published by The Charlotte Mason Research and Supply Company.

9. *For the Children's Sake*, Op. cit., p. 112.

10. *Home Education*, Op. cit., p. 98, 99.

11. Ruth Beechick, *You Can Teach Your Child Successfully*, Arrow Press, 1988, p. 297.

12. *Ibid*, p. vii.

13. Donald Graves and Virginia Stuart, *Write From the Start*, NAL PENGUIN, INC., 1985, p. 231.

14. *Home Education*, Op. cit., p. 80.

15. Franky Schaeffer, *Addicted to Mediocrity*, Crossway Books, 1981, p. 39, 40.

16. Recorded by Sandi Patti, words and music by Phil McHugh and Greg Nelson, *That's the Love of God*, River Oaks Music Co., 1989.

17. James 1:5, *New American Standard Version*.

What Others Have Said About *How to Create Your Own Unit Study*

"I congratulate you on a wonderful book. I enjoyed the warm feeling it gave me just to read it. What a help it will be to free parents from slavery to the school model!"
Dr. Ruth Beechick, Author of *You Can Teach Your Child Successfully*

"Valerie has done the best job I know to translate theory into practical strategy."
Cathy Duffy, Author of *Christian Home Educators' Curriculum Manuals*

"Your book was a breath of fresh air and really gave me renewed hope."
D. D., Alberta Canada

"Your book is very practical. It adds so much to our preparations of our unit studies."
A.B., Seabrook, South Carolina

"My husband and I have enjoyed your book. It is a wealth of knowledge, inspiration, and guidance to us."
L.K., Falkville, Alabama

*T*imelines offer us a means for placing people and events in their proper sequence. A timeline that traditionally hangs on a wall in a classroom is effective; however, it is cumbersome as it takes up a great deal of space and is not easily *handled* by young learners. Children like to see, as well as touch, in order to assimilate information. Therefore, a timeline that can be placed in book form affords us a much more user-friendly means for housing our historical data. On the following page you will find instructions and diagrams for organizing a timeline book. Feel free to alter this plan to fit your budget and needs.

We originally purchased an oversized binder from an art and drafting supply store. This binder was approximately 30" x 30". This was a bit difficult to work with so we purchased another oversized binder, approximately 13" x 15". This binder includes 3 rings as found in a regular notebook and are spaced the same as the rings found in a regular notebook. This makes it easy to find paper, plastic sleeves, and so forth to fit the binder.

If you cannot find a binder that is about this size, choose a large photo album or a large ring binder from an office supply store. Purchase plastic sleeves designed for photo albums containing pockets to hold photographs. I suggest that you use the plastic sleeves that have six pockets per page for holding photographs.

You will also need poster board or some other sturdy paper to make divider pages. If using a regular sized notebook, you may want to purchase divider pages with tabs. The divider pages are used to separate one century from the next. Sometimes these divider pages will be used to separate larger periods of time such as periods before Christ. Here you may use 500 year increments. It will be helpful to use a book such as the *Timetables of History*, by Bernard Grun to sort out these dates. We use the ring binder in a calendar fashion as shown on the following page to make our timeline book.

Note: The drawings presented in this section were done by my daughter Michelle. When she was in high school, she did a unit study on World History. As a way to document what she had learned, she drew hundreds of pictures depicting relevant events, objects, and people she encountered in her studies. These drawings represent some of her work.

Children like to see, as well as touch, in order to assimilate information. Therefore, a timeline that can be placed in book form affords us a much more user-friendly means for housing our historical data.

Time Line Book

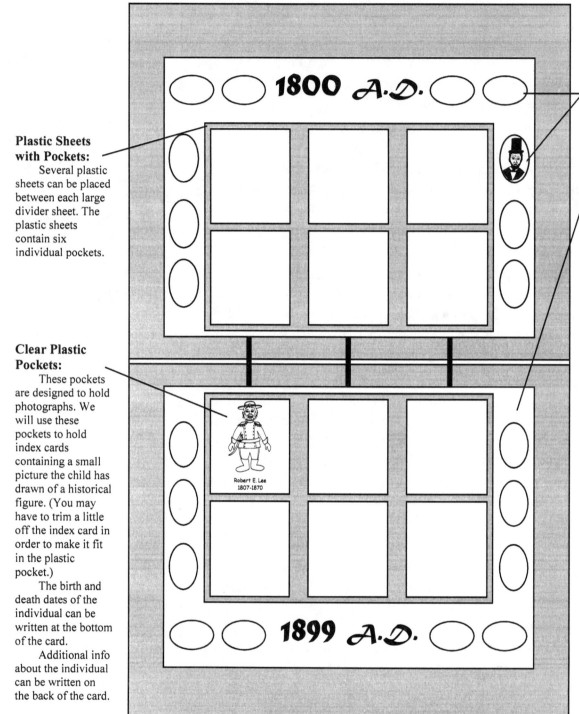

Plastic Sheets with Pockets:

Several plastic sheets can be placed between each large divider sheet. The plastic sheets contain six individual pockets.

Clear Plastic Pockets:

These pockets are designed to hold photographs. We will use these pockets to hold index cards containing a small picture the child has drawn of a historical figure. (You may have to trim a little off the index card in order to make it fit in the plastic pocket.)

The birth and death dates of the individual can be written at the bottom of the card.

Additional info about the individual can be written on the back of the card.

Small Pictures:

Small pictures representative of the time period can be drawn around the borders of the large divider sheets.

Large Divider Sheets:

The large divider sheets separate one century or time period from another. The large divider sheets can be cut from poster board for added strength.

Use the ring binder in a calendar fashion as shown. Write the beginning date for the time period on the top divider sheet and the ending date for the time period on the bottom divider sheet.

Directions for using a regular sized binder: If using divider sheets with tabs that you have purchased, they will be the same overall size as the plastic sheets with pockets. You can write the appropriate dates on the tabs.

Pictures representative of the time period can be drawn directly on the front and back of the divider pages, as there will not be any borders extending beyond the plastic sheets with pockets as shown in the diagram.

Photo Album or Large Ring Binder

Time Line Figures

Robert E. Lee	Mary Anne Randolph Custis Lee
1807-1870	1808-1873

Sample Historical Figures

Child can trace basic outline to
make any historical figure desired.

Sample Pictures for Divider Pages

Unit Studies Made Easy

The Unit Study Idea Book

Valerie Bendt

Dedication

This book is dedicated to my loving husband, Bruce, and my five wonderful children, who are also my friends, students, and often my instructors!

My children's names and ages at the time of publication (1992) are as follows: Michelle, 12 years old; Melissa, 10 years old; Robert, 8 years old; Raymond, 6 years old; and Mandy, 2 years old.

Table of Contents

Introduction

*T*his book is meant to be a book of ideas, not a curriculum guide. It is my hope that my ideas will serve as a catalyst to begin a chain reaction which will fuel your own ideas. Each one of us views things a little differently, and therefore we will be inspired to take a variety of avenues in our educational endeavors. This book is not meant to be exhaustive by any means, only inspiring and encouraging.

Many suggestions are given for each topic. Use only the suggestions that appeal to you. Your success will be greater if you enjoy what you are doing. Take one step at a time, not rushing through one project or task just to begin another. Realize that completing even *one* section or *one* project is a tremendous accomplishment. One single aspect of a unit is valuable and can stand on its own merits.

You will never be able to exhaust any given topic. Our Heavenly Father created such a vast and complex universe that even in a thousand lifetimes we could never learn all there is to know. Fortunately we are not limited by our lives here on earth, but have eternity to devote to our quest for knowledge of the Holy One and all that His works encompass.

It should be our desire to acquaint our children with a variety of ideas, people, and places. There is no set curriculum that should be imposed on all children. Children are individuals, and therefore their studies should be tailored to meet their particular needs and desires. Our Lord has given parents charge over their children, and therefore we are our children's best curriculum designers. Our studies should not focus on our interest areas alone. Rather, areas of interest are broadened as we dare to investigate unexplored topics. However, our emphasis in these new study areas can be centered on those disciplines we favor most.

I have chosen to compile this book in a very simple manner. As I plan units throughout the year, I try to choose topics from a variety of subject areas. Although a number of content areas are integrated into each unit, the main thrust of a particular unit lies in a specific area. For example, I choose units primarily based on history, geography, science, math, fine arts, or literature. Each unit is written in a manner to encompass one content area. I feel that selecting from a variety of key study areas enables us to achieve a well-rounded course of study.

It is my observation that many unit study curriculums overextend themselves as they try to integrate every discipline into each unit of study. This is often forced, and therefore the material integrated does not always make sense or truly benefit the study. It does not require the integration of all the content areas to be a valuable study. Some studies naturally lend themselves well to the integration of several content areas. I find that only a well-planned, uninspiring, no-room-for-creative-input, type of unit study can satisfactorily integrate every subject. So stop worrying about your children getting their daily shot in the arm of math, science, history, language, art, music, geography, and spelling. Let us get on with real learning and real life that is not compartmentalized into digestible doses of mediocrity. Still worried that your children will be lacking if they miss out on all these content areas? We must realize that the educational leaders in our society are trying to press our children into a mold to acquire the same (boring) skills. These skills have been allowed to overshadow true knowledge. Break the mold and allow a masterpiece to emerge!

Remember that this is only a book of ideas. Use your heart and mind to discern the path your family should take. Education does not need to be a complicated process, only a thoughtful one. May the Lord bless you in your desire to raise children for His glory.

Please use the margins in this book to make notes and to include a listing of additional books you discover as you compile materials for your unit study.

Suggestions for Making this Book Easier to Use

I encourage you to read my first book, ***How to Create Your Own Unit Study***, before attempting to use this book. It will provide you with pertinent information which will help you to receive the full benefit from this unit study idea book.

Although suggested library books are given for each unit, they are not meant to be a stumbling block in the event that you cannot locate some of them. In my book ***How to Create Your Own Unit Study***, a section is included on "Using the Library" along with a "Library Reference Guide." The information given will enable you to find books from your own library that pertain to each unit. Do not waste valuable time trying to locate books not owned by your library system. Use books available to you.

You may want to buy some books or materials to supplement your unit studies. Although it would be ideal to rely totally on your public library as a source for materials, this cannot always be done. However, if you are not buying textbooks and workbooks each year, it is easier to accommodate these occasional purchases.

I strongly urge you to buy ***Books Children Love***, by Elizabeth Wilson. This is a fabulous resource for locating interesting and morally sound books relating to your topic of study. I have had good success in finding the books in my public library that are suggested in ***Books Children Love***.

In this book of ideas, I list several activities and projects. This listing is meant to be a sampling from which you may choose. Do not try to undertake every suggestion. Too many activities and projects can be frustrating. Pace yourself, and most of all relax and enjoy your family!

LITERATURE

Library Unit

This is a good unit to help you and your children get acquainted with the library. You may also want to arrange a guided tour of your public library. Try to visit the largest branch in your area, as they will have the most services available.

Some churches maintain a library which is open to the general public for a small annual fee. Many homeschool support groups offer memberships for their lending libraries. As more people join, more materials can be purchased.

Library Books

I Took My Frog to the Library, by Eric A. Kimmel; *Book! Book! Book!*, by Deborah Bruss; *The Silver Balloon*, by Susan Bonners; and *Can You Guess Where We are Going?* by Elvira Woodruff are delightful picture books with a library theme. *Libraries and You*, by Pekay Shor. *Libraries and How to Use Them*, by Jeanne Hardendorff. *Check It Out! The Book about Libraries*, by Gail Gibbons. *Let's Visit the Library*, by Marianne Johnston. *The Way Things Work*, by David Macaulay, contains information about the printing press and book binding. *Learning about Books and Libraries: A Gold Mine of Games*, by Carol K. Lee and Janet Langford offers 47 games for K– 6th grade to acquaint children with books and the library. *The Inside-Outside Book of Libraries*, by Julie Cummins. *Library: From Ancient Scrolls to the World Wide Web*, by John Malam. *Most Beautiful Libraries in the World*, by Guillaume de Laubier offers lavish photos of libraries world wide as well as text tracing the history of libraries to the present day. *The Library in America: A Celebration in Words and Pictures*, by Paul Dickson presents the history of the public library in America. My favorite photo is the one of the first horse-drawn book wagon operated by a public library.

History

In 2700 B.C., the **Sumerians** established libraries to house tablets. One of the most famous of these libraries was built by the Babylonians in Nineveh. **Ptolemy I** established a library at Alexandria about 300 B.C. during the Greek rule in Egypt. **Eumenes II** (ruling from 197-159 B.C.) established a library at Pergamum, in northwest Asia Minor. By the 2nd century A.D., there were more than 25 public libraries in Rome. During invasions of the Roman Empire in the 3rd century, many libraries were burned.

Monasteries served as safeguards for culture and education. Read about **St. Benedict** during the Dark Ages. During the 11th, 12th, and 13th centuries, many universities were founded and libraries were needed. It was difficult to obtain books because hand-copying was slow. Many books were chained to the shelves as they were extremely valuable. Later, **Johann Gutenberg** (1398?-1468), a German inventor developed moveable type and later the printing press. This made it possible to print large quantities of books at affordable prices. He printed the Gutenberg

Bible in 1456. The Vatican Library was founded in the 15th century by **Pope Nicholas V. Reverend John Harvard** began the library at Harvard College. In 1731, Benjamin Franklin began a subscription library. **The Library of Congress** in Washington, D.C., was founded in 1800. The first free public libraries did not come about until the 19th century and were supported by taxes. As early as 1910, the first motorized book-mobiles were delivering reading material to people in rural communities.

Read about **Melvil Dewey**, a librarian who worked out a number system used in many libraries today. It is called the Dewey Decimal Classification System. There is another classification scheme used called the Library of Congress Classification. You may wish to zero in on a couple of individuals during this study, such as Gutenberg and Dewey by reading biographies about these individuals. The rest can be summarized by reading about the history of libraries in an encyclopedia.

Terminology

Use the glossary in a library book such as *Libraries and You*, by Shor, or use a dictionary to define the following terms before you advance in the unit study. Children may write the term on one side of an index card and the definition on the other side. These terms are: author card, bibliography, biography, call number, card catalog, Dewey Decimal number, fiction, index, Library of Congress, nonfiction, periodical, subject card, table of contents, and title card.

Activities

Visit your local library and have your children make a map of the interior. Have them include sections for fiction, nonfiction, easy readers, biographies, fine arts, fairy tales, records, audio cassettes, video cassettes, paintings, periodical indexes, computers, and so on. Also remind them to put in restrooms, tables, chairs, display cases, etc. If your children are young or your library is large, you may want to have your children only map out the youth department. This pictorial representation should help to familiarize them with the layout of the library.

Schedule an appointment with the librarian at your local branch to have him or her explain the library's computer system to you and your children. Your library's computer will contain information on the library's annual financial report; the members of the library board; branch locations and hours; services available — story times, book mobiles, and computer labs to name a few; the library catalog; and the history of the public library in your area.

Library Skills

Teach your children to read numbers containing several decimal places. Give them a list of such numbers to put in numerical order. Check out a number of books from each section of the youth department of your public library. (Older students may choose books from other areas in the library as well.) Assign books to each child and have them make catalog cards for their books using 3x5 index cards. Show your children examples of the catalog cards found in one of the suggested library books. (Although most public libraries use a computerized cataloging system nowadays, it is still fun and educational to complete this activity. It also helps the children understand how time consuming it was to locate library books only a few years ago!) Explain about author, title, and subject cards. Have them make an author, title, and subject card for each book. Some books may have more than one subject card. Help your children to determine the subject matter for each book. You will note that each type of card contains a brief description of the book. If your children have not read the books, they can read the inside front jacket flap for information about the book. A list of subject matter contained within each book is usually found on the copyright page as well.

Libraries vary in the arrangement of their card catalogs. Commonly they have a separate catalog for the subject cards, and the author and title cards are located in one catalog. Let each child take a turn at alphabetizing the cards they have made. You may want to combine all the cards, or separate them into groups by author, title, and subject before alphabetizing.

Once you have done this, your children may want to play "library." They can take turns "checking out" books. Place a slip of paper in the back of each book to be stamped when it is checked out. The children can also make their own library cards. All the activities mentioned above can be done with books you own as well as with library books. Use the Dewey Decimal Classification System (found in one of your library books on using the library) to determine call numbers. Remember, fiction as well as easy readers are classified by the author's last name.

Have each child make a book jacket to accompany his favorite book. These can be placed in your "library display case." The children can choose a book to read aloud and record on tape. A bell or musical instrument can be used to indicate that a page needs to be turned. This also provides hours of entertainment for toddlers who want to be read to frequently. They can listen to the tapes, and this will afford you extra time to help the older children with special schooling needs. A more complicated task would be to dramatize the story while making the tape. Children can be very creative when it comes to devising methods to simulate various sounds. Try it for fun sometime. You may find it helpful to check out a dramatized recording of a book from your library.

This is a good time to explain the parts of a book to your children. Begin with the cover or book jacket. Discuss the title, author, illustrator, and publisher. Point out that this information is on the spine of the book as well, and if it is a library book, point out the call number, too. Explain that the front inside jacket cover gives a brief description of the book. The back inside jacket cover tells about the author and illustrator. Often the back outside cover will contain brief reviews of the book.

Examine the title page. If there are two title pages, compare them. Point out the copyright, Library of Congress number, publisher, and other information listed. Many books indicate whether the book is fiction, nonfiction, or a biography on the same page as the copyright. Discuss the dedication, introduction, preface, acknowledgements, etc. Talk about the table of contents, and have the children locate a desired chapter or section of the book. Discuss other significant parts of a book such as the appendix, bibliography, index, and glossary. Locate books that contain these different sections.

Most books begin page one as a right-hand page. See if you can find any exceptions. Choose a book with an index. Explain that this is a listing of information that can be found in this particular book; it is in alphabetical order. Select several topics for your children to locate using the index. Find a book containing several different indexes. A poetry volume is a good choice. Choose one with a subject, author, and title index. Some poetry volumes have first line indexes, as well.

Have the children locate poems relating to specific topics such as cats, lightning, mountains, etc. Then have them use the other indexes in the volume. Read several of the books that you have chosen to conduct this unit with your children. These may be factual books about the library, or they may be books you have chosen to "catalog." Allow each child to select a book to be presented to the family as an oral narration. They can pretend they are the librarian giving a book talk.

You and your children can also make simple hand puppets and "act out" a book you have chosen. For simple-to-make, felt animal puppets see page 332 for information regarding my book *Successful Puppet Making*.

The children's reference section is an interesting place to explore in your public library. For information concerning this, read the "Guide to the Reference Section of the Children's Department of the Public Library" in my book *How to Create Your Own Unit Study*. This section will help you locate specific books pertaining to a particular unit study (see page 89).

Children's Authors Unit

*I*n my book, ***How to Create Your Own Unit Study***, I included a sample of a children's authors unit we did a few years ago. Since that time, we have done several children's authors units in conjunction with my children writing and illustrating their own books. Studying various authors, their writing styles, their works, and their lives has given my children a wealth of information to draw from in creating their own books. We also studied select illustrators, including some author-illustrators. I have seen vast improvement in my children's writing and drawing. Vocabulary is more vivid, storylines are more involved and interesting, and more attention is given to details. Their drawings show more skill, effort, and imagination.

The books developed by the children are carefully made, using art quality paper, markers, paints, cardboard for stiffening covers, fabric for decorative covers, and button thread for hand sewing the bindings. Six full weeks are taken to complete this project. The reward for this diligence is a collection of books that will be treasured for a lifetime. Yearbooks such as these provide a record of the children's progress and achievements. These books are something they can be proud of and will make a handsome addition to their portfolios.

I encourage you to assist your children in making professional quality, handmade books. Over the years we have made a variety of books using a number of book-making manuals. Since these manuals are written for the traditional classroom, I find that some of them are difficult to adapt to my homeschool classroom. Some of these books present a secular philosophy of education that is contrary to my biblical philosophy of education.

After gaining several years of experience in making books with my children, I decided to write my own book-making manual entitled, ***Creating Books with Children***. (See page 331 for more information.) This book is written as a six-week book-making unit study, and it includes reproductions from more than 50 books made by homeschooled children. The book chapters include:

Week One:	Pre-Writing Activities
Week Two:	Writing the Stories
Week Three:	Text Layout and Editing
Week Four:	Illustrating the Books
Week Five:	Developing the Beginning and Ending Pages and the Book Jackets
Week Six:	Assembling the Books

There are other books designed to help you make less complicated books. A book that we have used and enjoyed is ***How to Make Books*** *with Children*, published by the Evan-Moor Corporation. This book is to be used primarily with young children. *Creating Books with Children* can be adapted for use with all ages. For example, the younger children can dictate their stories to Mom or an older sibling. This is a helpful tip for any child who cannot write or who finds writing laborious.

Even young children can assist in putting the books together and learn much about the mechanics of book assembly. Additional information about book binding can be found in David Macaulay's book, *The Way Things Work*. It also includes an explanation of the printing press. In *Creating Books with Children*, I stress that the final stories should be typed, resulting in a more professional looking product. My capable children type their stories as well as assist me in typing the younger children's stories. This affords them extra typing practice, and it helps me out considerably. If you do not own a computer, word processor, or typewriter, then consider investing in one. Typing skills are important and can be learned on a typewriter (preferably electric). Later these skills can be transferred over to use on a computer. If necessary, you can hire someone, maybe a fellow homeschooler, to type your children's stories.

This past year we chose to study two European children's authors. We studied Robert Louis Stevenson and Hans Christian Andersen. Robert Louis Stevenson was born in Scotland in 1850. We read his famous novel, *Treasure Island*, in an unabridged form. Although the language was somewhat complicated, the children enjoyed the book, especially my two boys. I read this book aloud to the children, and my two older girls occasionally read aloud also. We watched the movie *Treasure Island* and compared it with the book. We also checked out some library books on boats, as we encountered many navigational terms during our readings. We briefly studied pirates, using the *Pirates and Buccaneers Coloring Book* by Dover Publications, Inc. This interesting book includes pictures and historical information on pirates, buccaneers, and privateers.

We produced a video of an excerpt from *Treasure Island* entitled, "What I Heard in the Apple Barrel." This selection was found in the book *Play a Part*, by Bernice Carlson. Each child helped cut out and sew the costumes. My oldest daughter Michelle filmed the production and my daughter Melissa was the narrator. My two boys along with two other homeschooled boys made up the cast. The boys copied some of their lines from the play as a writing activity.

While studying Robert Louis Stevenson, we also read his book, *A Child's Garden of Verses*. Each child chose a number of poems to read aloud. The children copied some of these poems from the book, and I verbally dictated several other poems to the children, which they wrote in their notebooks. I had the children make a list of words relating to childhood. Then they found rhyming words for each word in their list.

Following this activity, they wrote poems about childhood and illustrated their poems. My girls then typed the poems and we glued them onto their illustrations.

I could not find a suitable biography about Stevenson, so we read the biographical information found in our encyclopedia. It was interesting to find that he became a proficient writer in his youth because he practiced "day in and day out." Wherever he went he carried two books, one to read and another to write in.

We also studied Hans Christian Andersen. We read a biography of his life that was very interesting entitled, *The Story of Hans Christian Andersen, Swan of Denmark*, by Ruth Manning-Sanders. We read many of his works which are located with the fairy tales in the library. We noticed there were several versions of each book; some were translated and illustrated by different individuals.

Andersen was born in Denmark, and therefore his books were originally written in Danish. It is interesting to get two different translations and compare them. Sometimes the titles are slightly different also. For example, *The Steadfast Tin Soldier* and *The Brave Tin Soldier*. Some translators choose to simplify the tales for younger children. After studying a few different versions of Andersen's tales, I had the children retell the tales in their own words.

Some of the tales we read were: *The Nightingale, The Emperor's New Clothes, The Snow Queen, The Steadfast Tin Soldier, The Swineherd*, and *The Ugly Duckling*. I had the children read these aloud. Sometimes they made illustrations to accompany the tales. The children also enjoyed writing their own fairy tales.

Andersen's tales provide excellent material for discussion. As you read the biography of Andersen and some of his well-known tales, you will begin to see why he wrote the tales. *The Ugly Duckling* is said to be an autobiographical account of Andersen's life. As a child, Andersen was unattractive and strange. He lived in a dream world of his own. He was teased and tormented by other children. Through his determination though, he became a famous writer and in later life dined with kings and queens.

Andersen often told his tales in the palaces of kings and queens; therefore, he used them frequently as subjects for his stories. One good example of this is the tale, *The Emperor's New Clothes*. Perhaps Andersen was trying to convey to the people in the king's court that they should learn to think for themselves. As you read his other tales, you will find interesting ideas to discuss with your children.

After studying these two authors, my children began writing their stories for their book projects. Since we had studied quite a bit about

Stevenson, I thought they might like to write about pirates. My two older girls composed their stories on their own while my younger boys dictated their stories to me. This took about one week. My oldest daughter Michelle wrote a pirate story, but I could tell she was not really happy with it. I told her to write about anything she wanted. She chose to write a storybook for her baby sister, Mandy, entitled *Mandy's Day at the Zoo*. Michelle has a strong interest in art; therefore, she focused primarily on her illustrations. After she had written her story I read it and helped her edit it. I had her rewrite the story in present tense. She had written in past tense as if Mandy was telling the story. After she wrote it in present tense, with Mandy still telling the story, Michelle said she realized that it sounded much better this way. Then Michelle typed her story on our word processor.

Melissa wrote a story about a little boy who was searching for buried treasure in his backyard. She was very descriptive in her account of his expeditions. She typed her story on the word processor, and I helped her with the punctuation, which is her most difficult area. Melissa concentrated a lot on her illustrations, looking through some books to find pictures to aid her. She did not trace the pictures, but she used them as examples for some of her drawings. Since she types and spells better than I do, she helped me type my boys' stories.

I was very encouraged to see the progress that Robert and Raymond had made in the year's time since they wrote and illustrated their first books. Their choice of vocabulary and their story content showed great advancements. I was also amazed at how they were able to carry an underlying theme throughout their stories. This is something we had discussed briefly as we read other books. Each day I was more and more amazed as they dictated their stories to me. Even I was anxious to find out how their stories would end! It was also exciting to see the evidence of their personalities in their stories.

Raymond thought he was going to write a three hundred page novel! After writing eighteen pages on notebook paper that Raymond had dictated to me, I informed him that he had better wrap up the story. He said he would end it, but that he was going to write a sequel! Very quickly he came up with a terrific ending that surprised me.

Robert's story was almost as long. Since my hand was worn out, he dictated much of his story to his sister Melissa. I was amazed at how Robert managed to keep three different parts of the story going at once. He used phrases such as, "Meanwhile back at the palace..." and "Out in the middle of the ocean ..." He had so many ships and subplots that it was fascinating to see how he kept track of them all and managed to neatly wind up the entire story. Robert also took great care with his illustrations. He said that his story could have been real, so he wanted his pictures to look real. In his book the year before, he was not as concerned with his art work.

From these few examples, you can see numerous skills that each child has been able to develop. I did not specifically teach my children spelling, vocabulary, composition, how to develop a plot, and so on. But, through reading many, many well written books and discussing them, they were able to absorb much information and have a good time doing it. Each child is already talking about the books they will write next year. They have also informed me that they want to pick their own topics next time. You see, I am learning too! Writing books with my children is the most rewarding project we have done. It is also a project that can be shared with family and friends and treasured for a lifetime.

Often you can take a classic, such as *Heidi* or *The Swiss Family Robinson*, and make a complete unit study out of it. Literature-based units are fun and fairly easy to create. It is not necessary for you to completely read the book beforehand. Just glancing through it will give you some ideas of related topics to pursue in the course of your study.

When you begin to plan the unit, there are some pertinent questions you should ask yourself. Where does this story take place? Is this story a true account, based on a true account, or fictional? What character qualities do the individuals in the story possess? (Often you will discover the answer to this question as you read the book with your children.) Is there a biography about the author in print? If not, you can use a reference book at the library such as *Yesterday's Authors of Books for Children* or *The Junior Book of Authors* which will include a few pages about the author. You may photocopy these few pages since the reference books are not available for circulation. Usually an encyclopedia will offer some information about the author, too. Are there any key historical persons mentioned in the book? What about inventions and discoveries pertinent to the time and locale of the story? What other books did the author write? Do they in any way relate to the book you are studying? In what country and time period did the author live?

As you read along, many opportunities will arise which will stimulate areas of interest to investigate. Since you can not be dashing off to the library every other day, an encyclopedia will prove helpful in these instances. For example, if you are reading and you come across a person or place you had not noted earlier, you can look up brief information concerning these topics in the encyclopedia. Most of us do not have time to read the book in its entirety and make elaborate lesson plans ahead of time. It is often these unplanned, spur-of-the-moment interruptions that provide us with the best educational opportunities. I believe it is important to purchase reference materials as opposed to multitudes of textbooks and workbooks. You will get many miles out of reference materials. A new or even old set of encyclopedias may not be feasible for each family to acquire. An affordable handy reference book which we use frequently is entitled *A First Dictionary of Cultural Literacy: What Our Children Need to Know*, by B.D. Hirsch, Jr. Families with older students may prefer *The Dictionary of Cultural Literacy: What Every American Needs to Know*, also by Hirsch. The Internet has also opened up a quick and easy means for us to reference information quickly.

Getting back to our literature-based studies, you will sometimes come across something interesting as you read, such as an invention of the day, unusual animals, various land formations, plants, peoples, battles, bodies of water, political terms, geographical terms, and the list continues. The next time you are in the library you can select books describing some of the more appealing topics. You can keep a list of topics to explore further as you read along. This is also a beneficial activity for the children. As you are reading them a classic, have them compile a list of other topics to investigate. Then have the children research those particular topics at the library or in an encyclopedia or in another reference book you may own. In this way the children are learning to be observant, and they are participating in the research of the unit study.

Literature-based units are also beneficial in that they provide us with excellent writing models. Many textbooks and workbooks today are written in short, choppy, uninteresting sentences. Classics and other outstanding literary works offer us a feast of literary delicacies. Scenes are vividly described. Characters come alive as the author unveils their personalities. We are able to experience the political, geographical, and economical climate of the story. We can learn many things while being entertained by the author.

This exposure to good literature broadens our vocabulary and our understanding of the world in which we live. Many writing activities naturally flow from this encounter with inspiring literature. Dictate favorite passages to your children noting spelling, punctuation, grammar, vocabulary, and capitalization. Occasionally you might have them rewrite the passage, replacing adjectives with words they choose. Another time they could change the tense or voice of a passage you are studying. Younger children can copy the selections. They might circle words they do not know. They could circle the phonics patterns in the words they do know and tell you how the rules are applied. Other times they could circle all the words with capital letters and explain why these words are capitalized. For more ideas on copying and dictation, I urge you to read *You Can Teach Your Child Successfully* by Ruth Beechick. After reading this book you will be able to incorporate many of Ruth's ideas into your own unit studies. This has been one of the most beneficial books pertaining to homeschooling that I have read.

The next several pages contain sample literature-based units. Hopefully these will give you some ideas so that you can branch out and conduct a literature-based unit that appeals to your family. Generally, I read the classic aloud to my children. The older children also take turns reading aloud. This gives them good practice with their oral reading skills. If your library has several copies of the classic you have chosen, you may want each child to have his or her own copy. Often children like to follow along as they listen. This of course depends on their learning style. Other children, especially younger children do better if they draw while Mom is reading. They can illustrate something from the story.

For information about a literature-based unit study guide I created for my children based on Russell Hoban's "Frances" books, see page 330. This guide is chock full of cut-and-paste activities, puzzles and games.

*J*ohanna Spyri, the author of the well-loved classic *Heidi,* lived from 1827-1901. For information about the author use a reference book from the library like *Yesterday's Authors of Books for Children.* Often the volume of *Heidi* that you choose will have biographical information at the end of the book. This is the case in the volume that I have chosen of *Heidi* published by Grosset and Dunlap, Inc., the Illustrated Junior Library edition. Read the biographical information before you begin to read the story. As you read the story, see if your children can detect the similarities between Heidi's childhood and the author's childhood. Explain that the author chose to write about things with which she was acquainted. This is helpful to keep in mind as your children compose their own stories. Books originally written in other languages come to us by way of a translation. The volume of *Heidi* that I chose was translated by Helen B. Dole.

Check your library for other books written by Johanna Spyri. My library has a book entitled, *The Children's Christmas Carol,* adapted by Darlene Geis. The Swiss Alps are the setting for this enchanting tale as well. This book is a good choice for capable children to read to themselves or to read to their younger siblings. It helps to reinforce the visual image of the Swiss Alps portrayed in *Heidi*, as well as to further acquaint them with the character of Johanna Spyri.

Setting

The story takes place predominantly in the mountains of Switzerland. Parts of the story take place in Frankfurt, Germany. Obtain library books with information about Switzerland and Germany. Look for books with good pictures so the children can get a glimpse of the vast mountains and beautiful valleys described in *Heidi*. Use maps and a globe to locate Switzerland and Germany. Find out pertinent information about these two countries such as their major exports, religion, education, and government.

As you read with your children, stop at the end of each page or chapter and have them make a list of the words they recall from the story that describe the setting. Have them look for words that describe the scenery, topography, and geographical character of the passages read. What words are used to describe the living quarters? At first you might do this assignment at the end of each page to help your children develop their abilities for locating these descriptive attributes. Later, you can reserve this activity for the end of each chapter. This activity may be oral or written; done on an individual basis or as a group. Are there certain words the author uses frequently? Are her words colorful? As you progress with this word-finding assignment, your children can describe the feelings that are evoked by the author's choice of vocabulary.

Characters

Discuss the characters brought to life in each chapter. Have your children write a list of the phrases used to describe each character. From these descriptions have the children make an illustration of each character. It is not necessary to do this assignment for every chapter. Choose some interesting passages from each chapter to dictate to your children. Discuss punctuation, capitalization, grammar, spelling, and vocabulary. Have the children look up words they cannot define. I find it helpful to have the children look up the unfamiliar words in a simple thesaurus. Have them read the passages inserting their own words for various adjectives. Can they describe the person as accurately or as interestingly as the author can? Does the author use any words that have a different meaning today? If so what are those words?

Bible

Biblical themes are evident throughout the book. In chapter fourteen Heidi relates to the Grandfather the principles of Scripture she learned from the Grandmamma in Frankfurt. She then reads the story of the Prodigal Son to the Grandfather from her beautiful book given to her by the Grandmamma. Realizing that he has been a wayward son, the Grandfather repents and asks the Lord for forgiveness. Read the story of the Prodigal Son with your children and compare the story of the Grandfather's life with the Biblical story.

Heidi also learned that when we pray, we must pray for the Lord's will to be done in our lives. Often He does not answer our prayers immediately because the timing is not right. He frequently has lessons for us to learn beforehand, and often He has a plan different and better than ours. Heidi's faith is strengthened as these principles become evident in her own life. She learns to trust the Lord in all things and to share her faith with others.

Make a list of the character qualities of the main characters of the story. Using a topical Bible, such as *Nave's Topical Bible*, look up these attributes and read Bible verses pertaining to each character quality. Have your children try to identify which verses go with which individuals. The traits portrayed by the persons in the story may be positive as well as negative.

Narration

Whether oral or written, narration is a great memory building tool. It also enables us to determine if our children are not only understanding and retaining the story, but if they are improving their vocabulary. If done orally, we can evaluate their progress in verbal presentation. From time to time, we should tape our children giving an oral narration. This will allow them, as well as us, to hear the progress that has taken place. It is easier to compare written narrations, and this should also be done to see if their writing skills have improved.

I find that dinnertime provides an excellent opportunity for the children to give oral narrations. They have an audience, including Dad who often cannot be part of the regular studies. This oral narration helps keep Dad apprised of the children's studies.

General Information

As mentioned on the preceding pages, the children can make a list of topics that arise as you read. The classic *Heidi* offers many avenues for further research. Switzerland, Germany, mountains, goats, flowers, trees, hymns, physical handicaps, and cheese are just a few. As you read, you will encounter more topics than you could possibly study, so choose to investigate only those of real interest.

To add a little variety to your study of *Heidi* you can check out a book about the famous legendary Swiss hero, William Tell. Several storybook versions exist depicting this gallant individual. In 1829, Gioacchino Rossini's opera, *William Tell* was performed. Today the *William Tell Overture* is very well known and loved. You may also be able to check out an audio cassette tape or record containing this famous overture.

It is evident from the story that Heidi loved old people, others less fortunate than herself, animals, and nature. Search for evidences of these qualities as you read. These can also be noted in the life of the author as you read her biographical information.

The Swiss Family Robinson Unit

*T*his beloved classic was written by Johann Wyss. The version we own was published by Grosset and Dunlap Publishers, an Illustrated Junior Library edition. William H.G. Kingston edited this version. This edition was illustrated by Lynd Ward, who also wrote and illustrated the well known book, **The Biggest Bear**.

I found another edition of **The Swiss Family Robinson** at the library. It was complete and unabridged like the one we own, and was also translated by W.H.G. Kingston, but it was published by Children's Press, Chicago. The final section of this edition contains biographical information about the author. Originally the story was written by Pastor John David Wyss who was an expert in farming and nature. He was born in Bern, Switzerland, in 1743. He created this story for his four children and although he recorded it, he filed the papers away. Years after the pastor's death, his son Johann Rudolph Wyss, who was a professor of philosophy at Bern and chief librarian, discovered the manuscript among his father's papers. He made some changes, touched up the story here and there, and took it to a Zurich publisher. It was an immediate success.

The after word in this version goes on to explain about the translation of the book into French and English. This information is beneficial for understanding how books are translated from one language to another and how we end up with so many different versions of the same story.

Another pleasing feature about this version of **The Swiss Family Robinson** is the informative material located in the margins. Difficult words from the text are defined, often accompanied by diagrams, and many of the animals and vegetation mentioned are depicted.

As an interesting activity, you may read a portion from one version of **The Swiss Family Robinson**, and compare it with the same portion from another version. Which translator portrayed a more vivid picture? What other comparisons can you make? Find an abridged version and compare it with an unabridged version. Do they evoke the same feelings? Why or why not?

As in the classic **Heidi**, the predominant characters in **The Swiss Family Robinson** are from Switzerland. The authors of both classics are Swiss. Locate a few library books about Switzerland to enhance your study. Choose books with quality pictures enabling your children to get a glimpse of the incredible geography of Switzerland. You will want to compare the geographical characteristics of Switzerland with the island that the family comes to inhabit.

This book provides an excellent basis for studying character qualities, animals, plants, land formations, geography, and the list multiplies as you read the book. An in depth study of the character qualities of perseverance, determination, patience, ingenuity, faith in the Creator, strong love of family, and hope can be made. Even the first page of this classic gives us a glimpse of the faith of the father, who is also the narrator of the story. We find the family on board ship in the midst of a raging storm.

> *My heart sank as I looked round upon my family in the midst of these horrors. Our four young sons were overpowered by terror. "Dear children," said I, "if the Lord will, He can save us even from this fearful peril; if not, let us calmly yield our lives into His hand, and think of the joy and blessedness of finding ourselves forever and ever united in that happy home above."*

This strong faith in the supreme Creator is carried throughout the book. Chapter one, Shipwrecked and Alone, offers an opportunity to view similar situations documented in Scripture. We read in Acts chapter 27 of Paul sailing for Italy and being caught in a violent wind. A similar event is described in the first chapter of **The Swiss Family Robinson**. Even the wording is similar. After reading the entire first chapter of the book, read Acts chapter 27 and have your children compare the two accounts. Of course one is a true account and one is not. (One area of contrast is that in the classic, only the Robinson family is spared, and in the biblical passage, all those on board are spared.) Another biblical passage that comes to mind when I read this first chapter of the classic is Jonah chapter one. This can be compared with the account in **The Swiss Family Robinson**. There is also the biblical account of our Messiah in the storm tossed boats with His disciples in Mark 4:35-41.

As you read chapter one, many areas of interest will surface. For example they contrived swimming belts for the mother and the boys who could not swim. This provides a good opportunity for discussing the principle of buoyancy. You can experiment by putting various items in a pan of water and finding which ones float and which ones sink. Once again I recommend David Macaulay's, **The Way Things Work**. Many topics such as levers, pulleys, buoyancy, floatation, and friction arise in our story and are simply and concisely addressed in Macaulay's book.

> *We immediately searched about for what would answer the purpose, and fortunately got hold of a number of empty flasks and tin canisters, which we connected two and two together so as to form floats sufficiently buoyant to support a person in the water, and my wife and young sons each willingly put one on.*

In the second chapter, A Desolate Island, we begin to see the development of the character of the coast. The children may begin keeping a list of the descriptions of the land and water. You will encounter terms such as bay and inlet which may require defining. A great number of birds appear in this chapter along with animals on the wrecked ship. The children may make a separate list with the names of these creatures.

As the family was making their way toward the island in their homemade vessel, the dogs were swimming along beside them and growing extremely weary. They occasionally rested their forepaws on the outriggers of the little craft and Jack wished to prevent them from this. The father intervened quoting from the Scriptures, "Stop, that would be unkind as well as foolish; remember, the merciful man regardeth the life of his beast." I looked up merciful in my topical Bible to locate the text for this passage. In **Nave's Topical Bible** it reads as follows. "A righteous man regardeth the life of his beast: but the tender mercies of the wicked are cruel." Proverbs 12:10. (I chose to carry the passage a little further.) You may wish to look up this passage in different versions and compare them. It is interesting because later these dogs serve as not only companions for the family, but as protectors.

Another incident which can be compared with a similar occurrence in Scripture appears in chapter two of the classic.

As soon as we could gather our children around us on dry land, we knelt to offer thanks and praise for our merciful escape, and with full hearts we commended ourselves to God's good keeping for the time to come.

In Genesis 8:20 we find that as soon as Noah was on dry land, he built an altar to the Lord and offered a sacrifice. A comparison can be made also between the animals on Noah's ark and the animals on *The Swiss Family Robinson's* ship. Can your children find any other similarities in the two accounts?

The personalities of the characters in the book become more evident as the story unfolds. Have the children locate a few phrases in each chapter that give evidence of each person's character.

In chapter two we get our first clue as to the whereabouts of the stranded family. Your children may keep a list of clues describing the location of the island. What kind of information would be useful to collect to make this determination? The scientific explanation below provides a good opportunity to integrate some physical principles of light.

The children remarked the suddenness of nightfall, for indeed there had been little or no twilight. This convinced me that we must not be far from the equator, for twilight results from the refraction of the sun's rays. The more obliquely these rays fall, the farther does the partial light extend; while the more perpendicular they strike the earth, the longer do they continue their undiminished force, until, when the sun sinks, they totally disappear, thus producing sudden darkness.

Have the children copy this passage and make a list of the words they do not understand. Look these words up in a dictionary to help clarify the meaning of the passage. Try creating this phenomenon with a globe or ball and a light. Perhaps the children could then make a diagram to illustrate this experiment.

Chapter three, We Explore Our Island, offers a beautiful illustration made with words. After reading this chapter with your children, re-read some of the more descriptive parts and have them make illustrations to accompany them. They might then copy a few pertinent sentences at the bottom of their pictures. You will encounter some interesting plant life in this chapter. Keep a list of the plants the Robinson family comes across and the uses they find for them.

Chapter four enables us to study another scientific principle. Fritz watches as his father sucks juice from a sugar cane. He too tries this and finds he cannot extract any juice. A simple library book that leads you through an investigation of the power of air is called, **Simple Science Experiments with Straws**, by Eiji Orii and Masako Orii.

> *"How do you get the juice out, Father?"*
> *"Think a little," I replied. "You are quite as capable as I am of finding out the way, even if you do not know the real reason of your failure."*
> *"Oh, of course," said he, "it is like trying to suck marrow from a marrow bone, without making a hole at the other end."*
> *"Quite right," I said. "You form a vacuum in your mouth and the end of your tube, and expect the air to force down the liquid from the other end which it cannot possibly enter."*

As you read on, you will find that the coconut milk which Fritz had in his flask had fermented from the heat of the sun. He tugged the cork from his flask and there was a loud pop as the milk came foaming out like champagne. Fritz said it tasted like excellent wine. Read about fermentation from an encyclopedia or library book. Try putting some apple juice or other sweet juice in a jar and setting it in the sun for several hours. What happens? Why?

More animals appear in this chapter. Add them to your list. Have the children relate the account of how Fritz adopts a baby monkey. Have one of your children look up monkeys in an encyclopedia or library book, and share some interesting bit of information with the family. Each child can research an animal and relay the findings with the family. Your family may choose to investigate animal classifications and categorize the animals you meet as you read. You can use an encyclopedia or the **Usborne Book of Animal Facts**, by Anita Ganeri. Anita Ganeri and Judy

Tatchell wrote another book which you may find helpful called *How to Draw Animals*, published by Usborne. Most library books about animals contain a great deal of evolutionary material. Often the evolutionary content can be overlooked. *Mammals and How They Live*, by Robert M. McClung, is a library book that contains information regarding the way animals are classified.

The *Character Sketches* books, published by Institute in Basic Life Principles, contain interesting information about numerous animals. There are three volumes in the series. Using the indexes found in each volume, you will be able to locate pertinent information about the animals you encounter in your study. These beautifully illustrated books integrate Scripture with the study of nature. They are a delightful addition to any nature study.

In chapter five, We Revisit the Wreck, the children awake to find that Fritz has placed a dead, stiff jackal in a life-like stance before the tent. The other children are quick to try and guess what sort of animal this is. One guesses a yellow dog, another wolf, and still another striped fox. The father ends the quarrel by telling them that a jackal partakes of the nature of all three. Using a library book or encyclopedia look up each of these animals, and compare them.

The father and the older boys maneuvered their vessel made of large kegs back to the wrecked ship. Once they arrived they decided to accommodate their craft with equipment suitable for sailing. Here you will find several nautical terms. Look these up under boats or ships in an encyclopedia or book from the library. Some of the terms you will encounter are: mast, sail, spar, lug sail, masthead, rudder, oar, and ballast.

Discuss the plan the father contrived for using flags for signals. Although their system was a simple one, you might want to investigate the signal flags that have been used by ships.

Many domestic animals are mentioned in this chapter. They also have an encounter with a shark. Have one of the children read about sharks and share some interesting information with the family. What category would "sharks" be classified under?

Now that I have gone through five chapters and given you suggested activities and writing assignments for each, investigate some chapters on your own.

I would like to make a few suggestions for writing assignments that you can integrate as you choose. You may select a sentence or paragraph from each chapter that you feel emphasizes the most valuable character qualities. Have your children copy these selections or take them from dictation. Using a topical Bible you can investigate what the Bible has to say about the various character traits.

Choose a paragraph that is very descriptive. Have your children look up those descriptive words in a thesaurus, and re-write the paragraph substituting the new words. Discuss the feeling evoked by this change. Is the message as clear? (Often a thesaurus can be checked out of the library.)

Many difficult words appear in the text. Their meanings, however, can generally be discerned through context. Choose a couple of sentences with complicated words. Have the children verbally replace these words with words from their own vocabulary as they are able to discern the unfamiliar words from context. Later try this as a written exercise and have the children copy the sentences, omitting the unfamiliar words and leaving a blank in their place. Then have them fill in their own words.

Do not try to define every difficult word as you read to your children. This causes reading to be choppy and uninteresting. A few exercises involving unfamiliar words from time to time will be far more beneficial.

I am just going to touch on some of the remaining chapters of the book. Chapter seven, We Build a Bridge, exemplifies some engineering principles as they seek a way to complete their task. In chapter eight, The Journey to the Wonderful Trees, we find that these magnificent trees are fig-bearing mangroves of the Antilles. Locate a book on trees for an accurate description and illustration. What were some of the peculiarities of the trees mentioned in the chapter? What new animal appears and how does it prove useful to the family?

In the next chapter, The Tree-House, we find the father using geometry to aid in the task of constructing a ladder of proper height to reach a desired branch.

> *"Geometry will simplify the operation considerably; with its help the altitude of the highest mountains are ascertained. We may, therefore, easily find the height of the branch."*

The following passage offers an explanation for determining unknown heights by similar triangles. The triangle EBA is similar to the triangle EDC because angle E is the same in both triangles and the angle ABE and angle CDE, by construction are both right angles. Therefore this equality results:

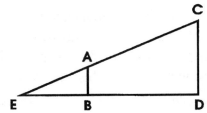

Thales, a mathematician of Ancient Greece, surprised the Egyptians when he was able to tell them the height of their Great Pyramid. By comparing the shadow of his staff to the height of the staff and the shadow of the pyramid to the height of the pyramid, he was able to find the height very quickly. He was using this same principle of similar triangles.

The father also constructs a bow and arrow. Most boys are interested in bows and arrows. You may wish to find a library book about archery. This is a sport that my boys really enjoy. Read Psalms 127:3-5.

A Visit to Tentholm, chapter 10, begins with the father quoting from Scripture:

"Six days shalt thou labor and do all that thou hast to do, but on the seventh, thou shalt do no manner of work. This is the seventh day, "I replied, "on it, therefore, let us rest." "The leafy shade of this great tree is far more beautiful than any church," I said; "there will we worship our Creator."

These passages and the dialogue that goes along with them offer good material for discussion. Read the Genesis account of creation noting what the Lord has said about the seventh day. It is interesting that the father realized that they did not need a church to worship the Creator. What is the church?

As you read, you will find that the family gave names to their various abodes and bodies of water on the island. Can the children recall all the names? Maybe your children will want to re-name some of the landmarks, bodies of water, buildings, and parks in your area. Perhaps they can think of names that would be significant to them. (If you have read the Anne of Green Gables series, you will find that Anne always made up names for various places in her town. She felt the original names lacked imagination.)

There are 44 chapters in all. Therefore, I could not possibly discuss them all in this book. You will encounter many forms of plant and animal life which you can investigate and classify. You will read about many ingenious devices which the family contrives to make their life more agreeable. You will experience their family unity and dependence on the Creator.

One last activity I would like to mention is to encourage your children to keep a simple log or journal. Buying or making a special book to record life's daily happenings will prove helpful. Chapter nineteen supplies us with an encouragement in this endeavor.

In the evening, when our room was illuminated with wax candles, I wrote a journal of all the events, which had occurred since our arrival in this foreign land. And, while the mother was busy with her needle and Ernest was making sketches of birds, beasts and flowers with which he had met during the past months, Fritz and Jack taught little Franz to read.

The Plant Sitter Unit

*T*his literature-based unit study for the early grades features Gene Zion's charming story *The Plant Sitter*, which was written in 1959. Margaret Bloy Graham's friendly illustrations make this book a delight for young children. The book centers on a young boy, Tommy, who begins a plant sitting business to occupy his summer days. His father says he is too busy to take a vacation this year, so Tommy makes valuable use of his free time by caring for his neighbors' plants while they are away for the summer. He earns two cents a day for each plant he tends. Tommy trots away with his wagon to gather the neighbors' plants, and soon his house is overflowing with greenery. The plants continue to flourish under Tommy's care and they seem to almost engulf the house. One night, Tommy has a dream that the plants destroy his house.

The next day he rushes to the library to do some research on plants. Following the advice he finds in the library books, Tommy increases his plant business. Soon the neighbors return and are very pleased with the condition of their plants. Then Tommy gets a real reward. His father, who constantly grumbled that the plants were a nuisance, now realizes he misses the plants. Therefore, he decides the family should take a trip to the country.

About the Author and Illustrator

Gene Zion has written a number of books for children including: *Harry the Dirty Dog*, *Dear Garbage Man*, *No Roses for Harry*, and several others. Margaret Bloy Graham illustrated these books as well as *The Plant Sitter*. Your children will probably enjoy these stories too.

Library Books

Drawing from Nature, by Jim Arnosky, contains a very informative section on drawing plants. The text, as well as the illustrations, gives insight into creating life-like images. *Linnea's Windowsill Garden*, by Christina Bjork and Lena Anderson, is a terrific little book filled with fascinating facts and fun projects for grades 3 and 4. It includes a section about making cuttings. You will find this handy information because Tommy makes cuttings from his neighbors' plants in *The Plant Sitter*. (He did this to prevent his house from being strangled by the plants!) *Linnea's Windowsill Garden* also gives a brief but interesting explanation for the Latin names for plants. Another project filled book is *Green Thumbs: A Kid's Activity Guide to Indoor and Outdoor Gardening*, by Laurie Carlson for ages 4-8.

A First Look at Leaves, by Millicent E. Selsam is a great book to help you and your children discover the many different characteristics of leaves. It also includes a section on making leaf prints. *Usborne First Nature Flowers*, by Rosamun K. Cox and Barbara Cork, includes a good explanation about pollination. (Keep this simple with young children.) *Plant Families*, by Carol Lerner, is an examination of twelve of the world's largest and most familiar plant families. *How a Seed Grows* by Helene J. Jordan offers a simple introduction to the basic understanding of how seeds work. *From Seed to Plant* by Gail Gibbons includes a simple introduction to how plants reproduce, discussing pollination, seed dispersal, and growth from seed to plant. We have always loved Gail Gibbons' books for their appealing illustrations and simple, straight forward text. *A Seed Grows: My First Look at a Plant's Life Cycle* by Pamela Hickman includes flaps for kids to lift and see what is going on under the soil and inside the plants. *The Young Scientist Investigates Seeds and Seedlings*, by Terry Jennings is a good choice to read aloud to your children. It offers an introduction to seeds and seedlings without using complicated terms. Several art projects and simple experiments are included. This book is out-of-print, but may be available in your public library.

Anna's Garden Songs, and *Anna's Summer Songs*, by Lena Anderson include poems about vegetables, trees, flowers, ferns, and fruits depicted in charming pictures. *Linnea in Monet's Garden*, also by Lena Anderson, (this is the same Linnea who has a windowsill garden listed previously) offers a look at fine art as it encompasses nature. In *The Random House Book of Poetry for Children*, selected by Jack Prelutsky, use the subject index to look up "flowers and plants," and you will find a listing of related poems. *Seeds and More Seeds*, by Millicent Selsam, is an I-Can-Read book. *Little Owl and the Weed*, by Constance Boyle, is a wonderful child's storybook. *The Tiny Seed*, by Eric Carle, tells the fascinating story of the life cycle of a flower using colorful collage illustrations.

Robert Quackenbush makes use of his unique storytelling abilities and child-appealing illustrations to bring to life Luther Burbank, the world famous plant breeder in *Here a Plant, There a Plant, Everywhere a Plant, Plant!: A Story of Luther Burbank. Cactus*, by Cynthia Overbeck, contains color photographs depicting the great variety of shapes and sizes in the cactus family. (If you cannot locate this book, find a colorful book about cactus plants.) *An Eyewitness Book: Plants*, like most of the books in the Eyewitness Series is well written and includes terrific photographs.

You will want to read *The Plant Sitter* with your children several times during the course of your unit study. If you have a child who is able, have him read aloud portions of the story after you have read them aloud at least once. If the child is just learning to read, it is best if he is familiar with the story before he attempts to read it himself. He will not be pre-occupied with trying to follow the storyline as well as trying to decipher each word. (This is why I advocate that a beginning reader dictate a story to his mom or dad and then read it, or a portion of it, out loud. His familiarity with the story will allow him to coast over the more difficult words. His self-confidence will be boosted and much real learning will take place.)

The Plant Sitter is especially appealing to young children. Tommy, the star of the show, is a young boy who uses his initiative to start a productive business.

Bible

There are a multitude of references to plants in the Bible, and because this unit is designed primarily for young children, we will only investigate a few. Remember, it is best to keep a unit simple. More in depth studies can be made at a future date. It is not important that your child learn everything there is to know about plants at this time. It is not even important that they learn the "typical" information about plants that is expected for their age level. Most of what is written in textbooks for young children on this topic consists of phrases like, "Plants are nice. Plants have leaves. Plants are green. Plants help us." Most preschoolers have figured this out for themselves. Let us put away the "twaddle" and let our children get on with real learning.

I used *Nave's Topical Bible* and *The Biblical Cyclopedia Index* found in *The Open Bible, New American Standard, Expanded Edition*. To begin our study, let us go back to the beginning. I suggest reading the first chapter of Genesis with your children, focusing on:

Genesis 1:11-13. (NASV)

Then God said, "Let the earth sprout vegetation, plants yielding seed, and fruit trees bearing fruit after their kind, with seed in them, on the earth;" and it was so. And the earth brought forth vegetation, plants yielding seed after their kind, and trees bearing fruit, with seed in them, after their kind; and God saw that it was good. And there was evening and morning a third day.

Genesis 1:29-30 (NASV)

Then God said, "Behold, I have given you every plant yielding seed that is on the surface of all the earth, and every tree which has fruit yielding seed; it shall be food for you; and to every beast of the earth, and to every bird of the sky and to every thing that moves on the earth which has life, I have given every green plant for food;" and it was so.

Discuss words with your children such as seed, fruit, kind, yielding, sprout, vegetation, and bearing. Note that the plants were created on the third day. Ask your children why they think that the Lord created plants on the third day. When were the animals created? When was man created?

Another interesting passage to study and perhaps even memorize is the first Psalm. A variety of plants are found in the Bible. Although it would be tedious to investigate them all, I have listed some that you may want to examine.

Aloe..........................Psalm 45: 8, Prov. 7:17

Bramble.........................Judges 9:14,15

Brier..............................Judges 8:7,16

Broom ("Juniper").............Psalm 120:4

Calamus........................Song of Solomon 4:14

Camphire ("Henna")...........Song of Solomon 1:14

Crocus..........................Isaiah 35:1

Cummin.......................Isaiah 28: 25, 27

Dill..............................Matthew 23:23

Garlic...........................Numbers 11:5

Gourd...........................2 Kings 4:39

Grass...........................Psalm 103:15

Hyssop.........................Exodus 12:22

Lily.............................Song of Solomon 5:13

Mallows.........................Job 30:4

Mandrakes......................Genesis 30:14-16

Mint............................Matthew 23:23

Mustard........................Matthew 13:31

Myrtle.........................Isaiah 55:13

Nard............................Song of Solomon 4:13,14

Rue.............................Luke 11:42

Saffron.........................Song of Solomon 4:13,14

Spelt............................Ezekiel 4:9

Thorn...........................Judges 8:7

Vine of Sodom.................Deuteronomy 32:37

Wormwood....................Deuteronomy 29:18

Wheat...........................Matthew 13:25, Luke 16:7

Using *Nave's Topical Bible*, look under botany to find a listing of many other plants found in the Bible. It is interesting to note the Lord's laws concerning hybridization. See Leviticus 19:19 and Deuteronomy 22:9-11. Hybrid plants and animals are sterile and frustrate the purpose of creation. Note that in Genesis the Lord created the plants yielding seed and the fruit trees bearing fruit after their kind. Through hybridization, man seeks to improve on the Divine Creator's work. Quoting from *Institutes of Biblical Law*, by Rousas John Rushdoony:

> *Knowledge and science require a basis of law, fixity, and*

pattern. Without this there can be neither science nor progress. Hybridization is an attempt to deny the validity of law. Its penalty is an enforced sterility. In every area, where man seeks potentiality by a denial of God's law, the penalty remains the same, limited gains and long-range sterility.

As you read the biography of Luther Burbank, you will see why many religious and civic groups were appalled when he published his catalog entitled, "New Creations in Fruits and Flowers." I suggest reading Luther Burbank's biography by Robert Quackenbush at this time. Another interesting avenue to explore is grafting. Grafting is different from hybridization. Look up both grafting and hybridization in your dictionary. A biblical analogy to grafting can be found in Matthew 11:17-24. It is interesting to note that an olive tree was grafted into another olive tree; it was not grafted into a peach tree or an almond tree.

Activities

Have your children make a list of all the different kinds of plants they can name. It may be helpful to write each letter of the alphabet down the side of your paper and have them think of a plant name for each letter. This is a good activity to do as a group. Older children may want to try this activity on their own. In conducting this study, I find that I know the names of a very limited number of plants. I feel ignorant when people, generally older people, can rattle off the names of hundreds of plants. Charlotte Mason in her book *Home Education* states that this familiarity with nature used to be common among people. Somehow we have lost this bond with our Heavenly Father's creation, but you and your children have the opportunity to recapture it. Take frequent nature hikes and invest in a good field guide for plant identification purposes.

Supply each child with a paper sack to begin your nature hike. We have an alley behind our house which abounds with interesting vines, weeds, acorns, pinecones, twigs, and blossoming beauties (dandelions, buttercups, and so forth). Allow each child to fill his sack, encouraging him to find leaves and stems that look interesting, not necessarily pretty. When you arrive home, spread a table with newspapers and empty the sacks on the papers. Ask the children to draw the specimens of their choice. They may want to draw any bugs that sneaked in too! Using a field guide, you may be able to identify most of the specimens that your children have collected.

A review of the book *Drawing from Nature* will give you and your children some hints about drawing plant life. Discuss the various leaf formations, stems, roots, and so on. *A First Look at Leaves* is a great book to read with your children at this time. Try classifying the specimens gathered according to their leaves. For example, group the plants together that have leaves with smooth edges, wavy edges, or saw-like edges. Discuss symmetry found in nature. A useful library book pertaining to this is *Symmetry*, by Ed Emberly. Leaf prints are fun to make. Follow the directions given in *A First Look at Leaves*. I have included brief instructions in case this library book is not available to you.

<u>How to Make Leaf Prints</u>

Materials: ink roller, printing ink, printing paper, magazine with a slick cover, tweezers, leaves, newspapers.

Spread the newspapers on a table. Lay the magazine on the newspapers and squeeze a generous amount of ink on the slick surface of the magazine. Spread the ink on the roller. Place a leaf on a clean piece of paper and spread the ink on the smooth side of the leaf. Carefully lift the leaf with the tweezers and lay it face down on the printing paper. Place a clean piece of paper over the leaf and rub it gently with your hand, being careful not to move the leaf. Remove the top paper and the leaf to expose your beautiful leaf print. You might like to try pressing leaves too. My son Raymond pressed a bug once, and he decided never to do that again!

Perhaps your children will want to compose a poem about some of the specimens they gathered. Read some of the poems from *The Random House Book of Poetry for Children*. (Use the subject index to locate poems about flowers and plants.) We particularly liked "Old Quin Queeribus," by Nancy Byrd Turner; and "Wild Flowers," by Peter Newel. *Anna's Garden Songs* and *Anna's Summer Songs* are both full of delightful poems about plants. Encourage your children to use the words they have chosen in describing their nature specimens to write a poem. It is often helpful to make a list of any words that relate to your topic; for instance the descriptive words about the specimens, and then find words to rhyme with them.

Now is a good time to read *The Plant Sitter* again with your children. Have your children list some of the ways that Tommy took care of his plants. Have the children copy the portions of the book that explain how Tommy cared for the plants. If your child needs help with proper letter formation, write out the selections for him neatly. I suggest you write one line and then skip a line. This enables your child to write directly under the words you have written. You might want to have capable children write the passages as you dictate them. You will find that two key elements are water and sunlight. Using a library book about plants read selections pertaining to these topics. *Linnea's Windowsill Garden* contains informative sections that will prove helpful such as "The Art of Watering," "The Water Cycle," "My Own Little Water Cycle," and "What do Plants Need to Survive?"

We noted that Tommy gave the cactus plants very little water. I chose a library book on cactus plants and read significant portions that explained why they need so little water. The pictures were interesting also. Tommy did some research at the library and found that he could make cuttings from the plants, and that these cuttings would grow into new plants. ***Linnea's Windowsill Garden*** contains a section entitled, "Here's How You Make a Cutting." This book is loaded with easy projects for your children to enjoy. Help your children keep a log of their plant experiments. List the materials needed, procedure followed, and a daily record of their observations. I suggest they make sketches to accompany their journals.

You may choose to expand your study to include flowers, pollination, fruit and seeds, germination, roots, shoots, and so on. I suggest reading ***The Young Scientist Investigates: Seeds and Seedlings***, by Terry Jennings. <u>Do not overextend yourself on this unit</u>, but make it fun and interesting. Use the additional library books recommended, or others you may find, to enhance your study, not to complicate it!

Read some of the storybooks about plants that I listed in the library section. Allow capable children to read aloud from these books. Perhaps your children will want to write a book of their own about plants. Shape books are an excellent choice for this unit.

If you care to take a closer look at fine art, read ***Linnea in Monet's Garden***. Claude Monet was an impressionistic artist. Much of his work focused on the elements of his garden at Giverny. Use the subject card catalog in the fine arts section to look up plants and flowers. This resource will direct you to a variety of artists' works pertaining to your unit. Select a few books with reproductions of art that include interesting plants and/or flowers. Allow your children to look at a picture for one minute and then tell you as many things as they can remember about the picture. Then have them look at the same picture again to make more observations. This activity helps to strengthen their observation skills. If your children like to draw or paint, they might like to copy a favorite botanical painting.

And lastly, you may want to visit a botanical garden in your area. Be sure to take along a camera and a pocket field guide. Show the children how to look up the plants they encounter in the field guide. They can make a scrapbook featuring photos of their favorite plants.

SCIENCE

Aviation Unit

*T*he study of aviation can be broken into several basic categories. I have chosen to focus on the history of aviation and the elements of flight, which include the workings of a plane and the effects of air and weather in aviation.

Library Books and other Materials Pertaining to the History of Aviation

The Wright Brothers for Kids: How They Invented the Airplane with 21 Activities Exploring the Science and History of Flight, by Mary Kay Carson. Woven throughout this heartwarming account are activities that highlight the brothers' ingenuity and problem-solving abilities. ***The Smithsonian Book of Flight for Young People***, by Walter J. Boyne, contains outstanding photographs. Choose sections from this book to read to your children, particularly Part 1, From Dream to Reality. This section gives a good overview of the history of aviation. An older child may wish to do further reading in the book, but the text is quite extensive.

Flying Machine: An Eyewitness Book, by Andrew Nahum is a photo essay outlining the history and development of aircraft from hot-air balloons to jetliners. It includes information on the principles of flight and the inner workings of a variety of flying machines. ***History of Flight Coloring Book***, by A.G. Smith, published by Dover. ***My Brothers' Flying Machine: Wilbur, Orville, And Me***, by Jane Yolen is told in free verse from the perspective of the Wright Brothers' little sister. ***First Flight: The Story of Tom Tate and the Wright Brothers***, by George Shea is an I-Can-Read chapter book.

Childhood of Famous American series: ***Wilbur and Orville Wright: Young Fliers***, by Augusta Stevenson. Childhood of Famous American series: ***Amelia Earhart: Young Aviator***, by Meryl Henderson. We love the Childhood of Famous America series books! ***Lost Star: The Story of Amelia Earhart***, by Patricia Lauber is a suspenseful and exciting account. ***Clear the Cow Pasture, I'm coming in For a Landing! A Story of Amelia Earhart***, by Robert Quackenbush. We love Robert Quackenbush's simple yet entertaining biographies.

The Glorious Flight: Across the Channel with Louis Bleriot, by Alice and Martin Provensen. ***The Glorious Flight*** won the Caldecott Medal for the most distinguished American picture book for children published in 1983. ***Charles A. Lindbergh: A Human Hero***, by James Cross Giblin is written for grades 4 and up. This biography presents Lindberg's controversial personality as well as his heroic side. A biography for the middle grades is ***Charles Lindbergh***, by Blythe Randolph which includes frequent quotes from Lindbergh's autobiography.

The Way Things Work, by David Macaulay. This book includes easy-to-understand explanations of flight, the airplane, flying machines, an airliner wing, the helicopter, the jump jet, the hydrofoil, the jet engine, the rocket engine, and more.

Library Books and Other Materials Pertaining to the Elements of Flight

The World's Greatest Paper Airplane and Toy Book, by Keith R. Laux offers 40 different aircraft designs. *Kids' Paper Airplane Book*, by Ken Blackburn includes all the materials and information kids need to make 16 paper airplanes. Also includes a field guide to real planes, a log to record flight distances, and ideas for activities. For example, one activity demonstrates the principles of aerodynamics. *Flying*, by Gail Gibbons offers an easy-reader-type book about aircraft. *Flight, Flying Start Science*, by wildlife photographer Kim Taylor offers an introduction to the science of flight in nature and in human technology. *Why Can't I Fly?*, by Ken Brown, is a picture book about an ostrich that wants to fly.

Experimenting with Air and Flight, by Ormiston H. Walker, uses examples found in nature and presents experiments you can perform. The author guides you through the basic principles of aerodynamics. You will investigate the properties of air and the four forces at work on an aircraft in motion: lift, thrust, drag, and gravity. *How Birds Fly*, by Russell Freedman. *How Birds Fly*, by Bobbie Kalman. *The Miracle of Flight*, by nature photographer Stephen Dalton, combines high-speed photography, line drawings, and text to explain the basic principles of winged flight, whether by insect, bird, or man.

Simple Weather Experiments with Everyday Materials, by Muriel Mandell. *Little Cloud,* by Eric Carle, will delight your preschooler. *The Book of Clouds*, by photographer and scientist John Day introduces us to earth's great skyscape. *Weather Words and What They Mean*, by Gail Gibbons is another easy-reader-type book. *Weather Forecasting*, by Gail Gibbons offers a simple look at predicting the weather. *The Kid's Book of Weather Forecasting: Build a Weather Station, 'Read the Sky' & Make Predictions!*, by Mark Breen and Kathleen Friestad is designed for grades 4-6. Readers are encouraged to use their powers of observation and some homemade equipment to become weather forecasters.

The History of Aviation

I suggest reading a couple of the biographies mentioned previously to help your children get a feel for the circumstances surrounding the early years of aviation. You may want to choose biographies of other pertinent individuals such as Eddie Rickenbacker, Richard Byrd, James "Jimmy" Doolittle, and Charles "Chuck" Yeager. Several of the books mentioned provide a brief overview of the history of aviation which will prove beneficial. Of course, it would be difficult to read biographies about everyone who played a part in aviation's past.

As you read, note the ideas of flying expressed by early man in mythology and legend. For example, research the Greek god Hermes. Read about Pegasus, Phaeton, Daedalus, and Icarus, Sinbad the sailor and his Roc, and Arabs and their flying carpets. Others to include are Simon, a Roman magician who tried to fly from a tower, and Wan-Hoo, the

Chinese ruler who attached 47 large rockets to his chair to fly to the moon. Compare ancient myths and legends about flight to modern tales about space creatures. What happens when people reject the knowledge of a Divine Creator? They are left to devise their own explanations of man and the universe. Observe early designs for flying machines such as those of Leonardo DaVinci, early gliders, balloons, and all types of powered aircraft from the Wright brothers to modern times.

Investigate the Japanese custom of flying kites to celebrate children's growth. Obtain a library book about kite making and create your own kite. Discuss the principles of aerodynamics that come into play. How does a tail help a kite? Does it correspond to any part of an airplane? A terrific library book about kites for young children is *Catch the Wind!: All about Kites*, by Gail Gibbons. *Easy-to-Make Decorative Kites : Step-by-Step Instructions for Nine Models from Around the World*, by Alan and Gill Bridgewater offers complete instructions for making kites as well as an introduction to the history of kite making.

Read the poem, "Darius Green and His Flying Machine" by John T. Trowbridge, from *Best Loved Poems*, by Garden City Publishers, NY. If you cannot locate that particular poetry volume, look for *The Oxford Book of American Light Verse*, chosen and edited by William Harmon. I found this in the reference section and photocopied the poem. (Be sure to have plenty of change for the copy machine as the poem is about five pages long!) Discuss the poem noting examples of cause and effect relationships, clues to time and location, and foreshadowing of later events.

Check out video tapes relative to your study. Compare the information given in these tapes with the information you have read. Read about and discuss the parts of an airplane and their functions: wing, fuselage, tail assembly, and landing gear. Construct a model airplane and identify the plane's basic parts. Use an atlas to locate the latitude and longitude of five cities. Read a library book about the magnetic compass with your children. Discuss and examine the pocket compass that hikers use. Learn about the differences between magnetic north and true north. Construct a simple, working compass. A simple book entitled, *What Makes a Magnet?*, by Franklyn M. Branley provides hands-on activities that include making a magnet and a compass.

Investigate aeronautical charts, the altimeter, the tachometer, time in aviation, and the airspeed indicator, using an encyclopedia or library book. Read about internal combustion engines and jet engines. You will find David Macaulay's *The Way Things Work* helpful for finding much of the information. The ages of your children and the amount of information you want to cover will dictate how in depth your study will be. Some of the more complicated topics can be further investigated at a later date.

Conduct several experiments that show the properties of air. *Experimenting with Air and Flight* is an excellent book. It includes experiments investigating such topics as: Is Air Real?, Air Pressure and the Power of Air, Wing Shapes, Drag and Streamlining, Finding the Best Shape, Thrust, Propellers and Helicopters, Auto Gyros, Jets and Jet Engines, How Birds Fly, Speed and Balance, Birds and Insects, Gliders, Parachutes, Detecting Air Currents, Measuring Airspeed, Wind Tunnels, Outdoor Observation with Plants, Balloons, Rocket Propulsion, Into Orbit, Weightlessness, and more. Have the children keep a notebook describing their experiments, noting procedures and observations.

Atmospheric conditions have a great influence on aviation. Weather and climate conditions must be carefully observed. Using books you have chosen from the library, investigate the basic causes of weather. Study about atmospheric pressure, wind, temperature, humidity, dew, frost, and clouds. The nature of clouds is determined by temperature, turbulence, foreign particles, and water vapor content. Have your children keep a weather calendar during the course of your study. Design symbols to represent sunny, cloudy, rainy, or snowy conditions.

Record variations in weather during the day, noting cloud formations as well. What types of clouds are visible? Note the degree of visibility: haze, fog, rain, etc. Note the forces of wind. High winds mean there will be a change in weather conditions. Using a weather experiment library book, make a chemical hygrometer to show the moisture content in the atmosphere. Measure precipitation and record temperature.

Additional Activities

Visit an airport. Make a timeline depicting aviation history. Have the children draw or trace pictures to go on this timeline. Investigate careers in aviation. Discuss the uses of the general aviation airplane: battling forest fires, reforesting clear cut areas, law enforcement, highway traffic control, planting crops, fertilizing crops, studying wildlife, feeding livestock, detecting plant disease by use of infrared photography, commuter airlines, mail operations, banking operations, business flying, sport flying, etc.

Have your children write to the addresses below or visit the websites for information.

Department of Transportation
Federal Aviation Administration
800 Independence Ave, SW
Washington, DC 20591
www.faa.gov

U.S. Centennial of Flight Commission
Washington, DC
www.centennialofflight.gov

Many writing activities can be integrated into this unit. Have the children copy or take from dictation significant information. Keep a list of aviation terms and their meanings as you encounter them in your reading. There is a lot of material available on this unit of study. Do not get bogged down trying to integrate too many subjects into this study. I specifically wrote a separate unit on birds because it is too tedious to study birds and aviation at the same time. The library books regarding aviation should offer enough material concerning birds for the present time. At a later date you may wish to study birds in more detail. At that time, you may briefly review some of the points of aviation.

Integrate music, poetry, and art as it suits your needs. Listen to a musical recording of "The Flight of the Bumble Bee." Your children can write a paragraph about how this music makes them feel. Can your children write a poem about the history of aviation? For a challenging activity, write a group of poems utilizing the aviation terms your children have compiled. Have each child draw pictures of his favorite aircraft. This can include some of the early forms of aircraft from hot air balloons to supersonic jets.

Bible

Since weather plays a vital role in aviation, we can investigate the properties of weather found in the Bible. Using a concordance, you can look up wind and find a number of passages. **Nave's Topical Bible** has a listing for weather. It suggests Matthew 16:2,3. I want to also include Matthew 16:1.

And the Pharisees and Sadducees came up, and testing Him asked Him to show them a sign from heaven. But He answered and said to them, "When it is evening, you say, 'It will be fair weather, for the sky is red.' And in the morning, 'There will be a storm today, for the sky is red and threatening.' So you know how to discern the appearance of the sky, but cannot discern the signs of the times?" (NASV)

You may also find Job chapter 37 and 38 to be interesting as well. These give reference to our Maker's mighty power over the elements of the world. Discuss the importance of the verses mentioned and how we should respond to man's forecasting.

The heavens are telling the glory of God; And their expanse is declaring the work of His hands. Psalm 19:1 NASV

Videos

Look for videos on space and space exploration in your public library and video rental stores.

Books and Activities

I highly recommend the following two books to be used as your basics "texts" for this study: *Astronomy and the Bible, Questions and Answers*, by Donald B. De Young, is a wonderful resource, as many library books present a humanistic view of the solar system. *The Astronomy Book*, by Jonathan Henry is also presented from a Christian perspective and is geared for older children and early teens. The pictures and layout of this book make it a pleasure to use. An additional valuable resource for this unit is *Great Science Adventures: The World of Space*, published by Common Sense Press, which contains a host of reproducible activities and graphic organizers to bring your astronomy study to life. *Creation Astronomy: A Study Guide to the Constellations!*, by Felice Gerwitz and Jill Whitlock presents astronomy from a Creation perspective. Contains over 250 activities. *Janice Vancleave's Constellations for Every Kid: Easy Activities That Make Learning Science Fun* teaches children how to locate the most prominent constellations in their own backyard.

Library Books

Find the Constellations, by H.A. Rey. My children really liked this book. It was always disappearing from the schoolroom! *Ancient Astronomy*, by Isaac Asimov. *Space Songs* and also *Sky Songs*, by Myra Cohn Livingston, poet; Leonard E. Fisher, painter. *Worlds Beyond: The Art of Chesley Bonestell*, by Frederick C. Durant, III and Ron Miller. Bonestell desired to accurately depict the planets of the solar system. He said he was disillusioned by artists' conceptions of the planets. Many of these incredible paintings date from the 1940s. (This book is located in the fine arts section of the library.) *There's No Place Like Space,* by Tish Rabe, is a fun space book to share with your preschoolers. The Cat in the Hat (along with beloved Thing One and Thing Two) straps on his space suit and rhymes his way among the nine planets, presenting important facts along the way. *Papa Please Get The Moon For Me*, by Eric Carle, offers the young child a splendid introduction to the monthly lunar cycle, ingeniously designed with fold-out pages. You may want to choose a simple book on telescopes. David Macaulay's book, *The Way Things Work*, is an excellent choice for brief information about telescopes. It also contains material on space telescopes, space probes, and satellites. You will find a multitude of books on astronomy in the youth section as well as the adult section of the library.

Bible

Use a concordance and look up words like star, constellation, heavens, moon, sun, and so on. If you have a topical Bible, like *Nave's Topical Bible*, you can look up astronomy, and it will lead you to many passages which you might not find using a concordance. These passages make great selections for the children to type or copy. The Genesis account of creation is very appropriate to study at this time. As your children copy or type these passages, have them make a list of the words that pertain to your study. This is a good time to teach them how to use a topical Bible and a concordance. You will also find the book previously mentioned, *Astronomy and the Bible*, to be a tremendous resource.

Projects

I do not like to get hung up on a lot of projects, but this unit begs for one. Use *Great Science Adventures: The World of Space* listed previously or a library book that has instructions for creating a mobile of the solar system. You can use Styrofoam balls, or balloons and papier-mâché. We chose the messier papier-mâché version. I read to the children about the different planets as they constructed their models.

This is also a good unit for conducting experiments pertaining to light. Purchase some solar paper from a school supply store for some interesting fun with sunlight.

Games

Good Heavens: Astronomy Game manufactured by Ampersand Press. (See Resource section for ordering information.)

Arts

Have your children paint or draw space pictures. Pastels done on rough paper give a nice effect. The books, *Space Songs* and *Sky Songs* have very interesting pictures, and Chesley Bonestell's paintings are extremely appealing. The library usually has a number of books with instructions on making a variety of spacecraft. My boys enjoy those craft books. *Crafts for Kids Who Are Wild About Outer Space*, by Kathy Ross, looks interesting.

History

I suggest you read two or three biographies of famous astronomers. It is helpful if you read them in chronological order, as most astronomers based their research on the findings of earlier astronomers. Isaac Asimov's *Ancient Astronomy* gives a brief account of the works and beliefs of many of these early astronomers. Their biographies can easily be located in the junior biography section of your public library. Choose simple or more complicated biographies as suits your needs. Two interesting biographies by Jeanne Bendick published by Beautiful Feet Books that focus on early scientist/astronomers are *Along Came Galileo* and *Archimedes and the Door to Science*.

You may also be interested in studying about space exploration. You could read a biography of Neil Armstrong such as *Neil Armstrong: Young Pilot.* This title is in The Childhood of Famous Americans series.

Language Arts

Read **Space Songs** or **Sky Songs**, or other books with poems about the sun, moon, planets, comets, etc. Have your children copy selected poems or take them from dictation. In the two books mentioned above, the poems are printed in various ways so as to create an appropriate design. If these books are not available to you, choose a large poetry volume with a subject index and look up words pertinent to your study. You should be able to find a number of poems relating to our solar system.

Read information about the planets, sun, moon, stars, asteroids, comets, etc. (For this use library books; **The Astronomy Book**, by Jonathan Henry; or **Astronomy and the Bible**, by Donald B. De Young.) Have your children make a list of significant words relating to each category. They can compile these lists as you proceed through the unit study. After their lists are finished, have your children use them to write space poems. They may choose to write about the planets, comets, the moon, or the solar system in general. It is helpful for them to make a list of words that rhyme with the words they have already listed. You may choose to introduce several forms of poetry, such as Haiku, a Japanese form of poetry usually dealing with nature. It contains seventeen syllables in lines of 5, 7, and 5 syllables. This type of poetry does not usually rhyme.

You can think of many language arts assignments for this unit. Sometimes you may have your children copy or take from dictation information about the planets or other relative topics. For younger children, dictate simple sentences from the books you read, and discuss the phonics rules in the words they have written. Have your children illustrate the passages they write. Your children may want to write a fictional story about space travel and utilize facts about our universe. You can explain that many authors write fictional stories that take place in real places and historical time periods. You might also discuss science fiction. Jules Verne used his knowledge of science to create believable science fiction. He wrote his famous book, **From the Earth to the Moon** in 1866. Your children may enjoy listening to this book while studying about space. Another fun activity is to make an A to Z listing of terms relating to astronomy and the solar system.

Ants Unit

Go to the ant, O sluggard, Observe her ways and be wise, Which having no chief, Officer or ruler, Prepares her food in summer, And gathers her provision in harvest. Proverbs 6:6-8 NASV

Books

If you own or have access to any of the **Character Sketches** books published by the Institute in Basic Life Principles, use the indexes found in these books to locate interesting information concerning ants. (Ordering information is included in the reference section.) **Great Science Adventures: The World of Insects and Arachnids** is available from Common Sense Press and offers reproducible activities and graphic organizers. (See resource section for ordering information.) **Go to the Ant Coloring Book: Learning from Proverbs**, by Judy Rogers, illustrated by Vic Lockman.

Library Books

An Ant Colony, by Fischer-Nagel. **Ladis and the Ant**, by Sanchez-Silva. **The Ants Go Marching**, by B. Freschet. **Ant Cities**, by Arthur Dorros. **Ants**, by Yazima. **The Visit**, by Diane Wolkstein. **The Random House Book of Poetry for Children. Hidden Messages**, by Van Woerkom. **It's an Ant's Life**, by Steve Parker. **The Little Red Ant and the Great Big Crumb**, by Shirley Climo. **Thinking About Ants**, by Barbara Brenner, **Two Bad Ants**, by Chris Van Allsburg. (This book was a favorite of mine. It is predominantly a picture book, but it is wonderful for any age. It also offers a good opportunity to discuss the consequences of disobedience.) You will probably find many books on ants, so pick a few that look interesting.

Terminology

Have your children keep a record of terms and their meanings as you encounter them in your reading. They should also make a diagram of an ant and list the body parts. **Great Science Adventures: The World of Insects and Arachnids** contains reproducibles for making a terrific ant model!

Activities

My mother bought the children an ant farm and we stocked it with ants from the park behind our house. You can get ants through the mail, but you cannot get queen ants because they are protected by law. We raided a large ant bed (red ants) and were able to get many queens. Some of the ants were in the larvae and pupae stage. They were fascinating to watch. (We did get bit trying to get them in the farm! Wear gloves. We also roasted our ants by placing them in a window with a sunny exposure. Try not to do that.) The children took turns feeding and watering the ants. It is a good idea to keep a record of the ants' activities. This can be done in a simple manner, and it teaches the children observation skills.

Games

My children each made an ant colony game. I gave them simple books about ants and had them make up 25 questions and answers pertaining to ants. This activity was very educational as they learned to read to locate specific information. They also had to put this information in the form of a question. They used index cards to write the questions, and the answers were included on the bottom of each card. My daughter Michelle typed all her question cards and used color coding dots (used for coding files) to indicate specific categories.

The children made "event cards" as well as factual cards. These cards helped to liven up the game. For example, one of my children's event cards read: "You forgot to pick up the Queen's gown at the Royal Ant Dry Cleaners. Go back 4 spaces." The children made game boards out of poster board. Underground ant tunnels and rooms served as excellent game routes. They made ant playing pieces out of Styrofoam pieces used for packaging material. The children also wrote their own game rules. The older girls typed their rules while the younger boys dictated theirs to me. It is a good idea to play several kinds of games before the children devise their own game. This game making was a lot of fun. We spent a week making the games.

Bible

Proverbs 6:6-8; 30:25. It is interesting that the Lord uses something as simple as ants to convey His principles. As you continue this study, you will find there are over 10,000 different kinds of ants! This is an excellent opportunity to discuss the complexity of creation. Each kind of ant was designed for a special purpose. We are much more precious to our Heavenly Father than the ants. He created each of us for a special purpose also.

Language Arts

I dictated passages about ants to the older children. The younger children copied sentences I chose pertaining to ants. These selections were taken from library books and *Character Sketches*. As the children did these writing exercises, we discussed punctuation, capitalization, vocabulary, spelling, nouns, verbs, and adjectives. We also read a number of poems about ants. *The Random House Book of Poetry for Children* has two funny poems: "Ants, Although Admirable, Are Awfully Aggravating" and "The Ant Olympics." The first poem offered a good opportunity to discuss alliteration (the repetition of the same sounds or of the same kinds of sounds at the beginning of words). After brainstorming words relating to ants, the children wrote their own ant poems and illustrated them. The older children typed their poems.

Birds Unit

Most people think of John James Audubon, the American woodsman, when they think of birds. He was probably the greatest American naturalist and obviously the greatest of all bird painters. He traveled the frontier country of America and painted birds in their natural habitats. He was born April 26, 1785.

As I began to look for books about birds in my public library, I found them in three basic areas. First, in the children's section I found factual books pertaining to birds. Then I located poetry books with various poems about birds. Next I looked for a biography of Audubon. You will find a number of biographies available at your public library. ***Into the Woods: John James Audubon Lives His Dream***, by Robert Burleigh, is a picture book biography including excerpts from Audubon's journal as well as beautiful illustrations. ***Audubon: Painter of Birds in the Wild Frontier***, by Jennifer Armstrong, is a stunning picture book presenting intriguing episodes from the life of the Audubon. Your children may enjoy ***Audubon's Birds of America Coloring Book*** published by Dover.

I found the fine arts section had beautiful books with paintings of birds. I also found an interesting book entitled, ***John James Audubon's Birds in Cross Stitch***, by Ginnie Thompson. This book includes color photographs of finished cross stitch birds as well as the patterns and directions. Each plate contains quotations taken from John James Audubon's five volume ***Ornithological Biography*** (1831-1839). It is interesting to compare the cross stitched color plates with the reproductions of Audubon's original paintings in the book listed above or in his great work, ***The Birds of America***. This is a good skills activity, as well as a good observation activity, because the children must use the index in Audubon's books to locate the desired reproductions. The third place I found books pertaining to birds in my library was in the Science and Technology Department. I could have literally come home with hundreds of books on birds! I realized that I had to put some boundaries on our study.

I want to encourage you to read the preface, introduction, or foreword to some of the books you choose. These sections supply informative details concerning Audubon's works and life. Years ago, I never read these parts of books because I felt it was a waste of time, but I now realize that valuable information can be gained from reading them. This is generally true for any book you read.

Library Books

The following books were located in the Fine Arts Department of my public library. ***Audubon, Homer, Whistler, and 19th Century America***, by John Wilmerding. (Although this only contains one color reproduction of Audubon's works, it contains biographical information about Audubon and beautiful color plates of other American artists who lived during the same time period.) *Painting Birds*, by Susan Rayfield. *Draw Birds*, by David Brown, a simple yet very informative paperback book that will enable your children to draw birds fairly easily. It even details the anatomy of various birds. *The Art of Robert Bateman,* by Ramsay Derry. Mr. Bateman is a modem naturalist. His book includes many paintings of birds. *John James Audubon's Birds in Cross Stitch*, by Ginnie Thompson (mentioned previously). *Bird*, an Eyewitness Book, published by Alfred A. Knopf. Contains great pictures. (Most of the books in the Eyewitness series are very well written. This series covers a vast range of titles from *Ancient Egypt* to *Tree*. Many libraries carry this series as well as many homeschool catalog companies.) *An Illustrated Guide to Attracting Birds,* Sunset Publishing Corporation. This focuses on bird identification, plant lists, feeders, houses, and baths. Use the subject card catalog in the Fine Arts Department to locate other books pertaining to birds.

The following books were located in the Science and Technology Department of my library. *The Miracle of Flight*, by nature photographer Stephen Dalton, combines high-speed photography, line drawings, and text to explain the basic principles of winged flight, whether by insect, bird, or man. *The Birds of America*, by John James Audubon (mentioned previously). *Tunnicliffe's Birds, Measured Drawings,* by C.F. Tunnicliffe.

The following books were located in the Children's Department of my library. *How Birds Fly*, by Russell Freedman. (This book gives a simpler explanation than *The Miracle of Flight*.) *How Birds Fly,* by David Goodnow is a beautifully illustrated book presenting a fascinating beginner-level study of birds in flight.

State Birds, by Arthur Singer and Alan Singer. Since there are so many kinds of birds that you can study, a simpler task would be to focus on our state birds. During this study the children can brush up on the location of each state. Arthur and Alan Singer worked together to paint the 1982 commemorative stamp block of birds and flowers for the fifty states for the U.S. Postal Service. If your children collect stamps, this may interest them. *Birds with Bracelets: The Story of Bird Banding*, by Susan F. Welty. In the junior biography section I found several biographies about Audubon. I chose, *Audubon, The Man Who Painted Birds*, by Norah Smaridge.

The last area where I found bird books was in the poetry section of the children's department. Browse through these books of poetry, using subject indexes to locate poems about birds. Some books I selected were: *Wings from the Wind: An Anthology of Poems Selected and Illustrated by Tasha Tudor. Sing a Song of Popcorn*, selected by Beatrice Shenk De Regniers. *Feather or Fur*, by Grete Manheim. Using a poetry index in the reference section will help you to locate more poems about birds. You will also find many easy readers containing stories about birds. The subject card catalog will direct you to some of these books.

A related topic of study is of course the study of flight, predominantly the achievements man has made in aerodynamics. This can become very involved, and I think it best to give only an introduction into this now, and focus on the history of flight at a later time. *The Miracle of Flight* or *How Birds Fly* should be sufficient at this time for introducing the children to aerodynamics.

The *Character Sketches* books, published by Institute in Basic Life Principles, contain fascinating information about various kinds of birds. These books are a superb reference for any nature study.

If you own a pet bird, that is great. Your children can observe the bird, making notes about behavior and making sketches. They can do this with birds in your neighborhood or a nearby park as well. A pair of binoculars would prove helpful for bird watching. Check out a simple library book on binoculars and find out how they work. Try to identify the birds in your neighborhood. How about buying or making a simple bird feeder to attract birds to your home? *Backyard Bird Watching for Kids: How to Attract, Feed, and Provide Homes for Birds*, by George H. Harrison and Kit Harrison, covers 20 favorite backyard birds, directions for designing gardens to attract them, plans for building feeders and birdhouses, tips for photographing birds, and a log to list birds observed. Is there a zoo with an aviary in your area? Take sketch pads to make drawings and record notes. Have the children compose a poem to go with their favorite sketch.

Your children can write to the following organizations for information or check out their websites:

National Audubon Society
700 Broadway
New York, NY 10003
Phone: (212) 979-3000
www.audubon.org

The National Wildlife Federation
National Wildlife Federation
310 Tyson Drive
Winchester, VA 22603
800- 822-9919
www.nwf.org

Bible

Investigate Bible verses that mention birds. A topical Bible would prove helpful. Some suggested verses are: Genesis 1:20-30, the creation of birds on the fifth day and man's dominion over them along with the other creatures. Leviticus 11:13-20 concerning species that are unclean. Job 38:41, Psalm 147:9 concerning ravens. Matthew 10:29 and Luke 12:6, 24 concerning sparrows and ravens. Psalm 84:3, 124:7. Matthew 6:26, 8:20. Revelation 19:17. You will find many more and you may also look up "snare" in your concordance or topical Bible.

As is evident in all our studies, we are made aware of the complexity and beauty which our Heavenly Father created. Man can only make an inferior duplicate of the complicated wing of a bird. You will find that you could never complete a study of every kind of bird. And what scientist can explain bird migration apart from the plan of a Divine Creator?

Happy bird watching!

Human Body Unit

I will give thanks to Thee, For I am fearfully and wonderfully made; Wonderful are Thy works, And my soul knows it very well.

Psalm 139:14 NASV

Books and Materials

Backyard Scientist, Series Three, by Jane Hoffman. This book of experiments allows you to explore the life sciences. Some of the experiments included are: The Blinking Experiment, The Digestion Experiment, The Vocal Cord Experiment, The Nerve Cell Experiment, The Lung Experiment, The Ear Experiment, and more. The experiments found in Jane's books use items found around the home or items that are easily accessible. Another pleasing feature about the ***Backyard Scientist*** books is that each experiment includes a solution at the end. You are not left to figure things out for yourself if you are having trouble!

The Gray's Anatomy Coloring Book, published by Running Press. This book includes over a hundred adaptations of the original illustrations from the classic reference book, ***Gray's Anatomy***. It includes descriptive captions, and the terminology has been limited to the basics in order not to be overwhelming. ***The Body Book: Easy-to-Make Hands-On Models That Teach***, by Donald M. Silver, offers reproducible patterns enabling you and your children to make bone and stomach "books," a "movie" that shows how a tooth grows and more! These manipulative models give students a clear understanding of how our bodies are put together and how they work.

Creation Anatomy: A Study Guide to the Miracles of the Body! by Felice Gerwitz. With this K-12 text your family will learn what a remarkable living machine the human body is! See how all the systems of the body are interrelated and cannot function without each other. God compares the human body to the Body of Christ as each needing the other, and we can understand how each function of our body is related to all the others.

Another fun resource is ***The Cat in the Hat's Learning Library: Inside Your Outside: All About the Human Body*** by Tish Rabe, where The Cat in the Hat takes Sally and Dick for a ride through the human body. ***My Five Senses***, by Aliki, will interest the youngest readers and listeners.

Somebody, the human anatomy game by Aristoplay, is a game/puzzle activity that helps teach the names, locations, and functions of the body parts.

Library Books

Your Body and How It Works, by Ovid K. Wong, Ph.D. I used this book for dictation exercises and for conducting interesting experiments. The chapters included are: The Covering System, The Supportive System, The Muscular System, the Circulatory System, the Breathing System, The Digestive System, The Waste-Disposal System, The Hormonal System, The Nervous System, and the Reproductive

System. The book also includes a glossary of terms. Each section contains pertinent experiments which also include conclusions. (The conclusions are to help us moms!) I really enjoy this book as it is clear, concise, and uncomplicated. It even provides older children with a good functional study of the body. (Ignore the introduction about the body being a complicated machine, or use it to discuss this humanistic falsehood.) *Your Body is Wonderfully Made*, by Fred B. Rogers, M.D. A simple yet refreshing little book that emphasizes the biblical reference in Psalms that man is "wonderfully made." It states that the body functions more smoothly and intricately than any engineering marvel ever envisioned. (A sharp contrast to the "we are machines" concept.) This book can be read in one sitting and is a good choice for your children to read aloud.

Play and Find out about the Human Body, by Janice Van Cleave offers 50 fun-filled experiments for children ages 4 to 7. This book addresses questions such as: Why doesn't my hair hurt when it gets cut? How does my back bend? Why don't my fingerprints match yours? *The Skeleton Inside You*, by Philip Balestrino is a simple book that young children can read aloud. *Leonardo DaVinci, Art for Children*, by Ernest Raboff. This is a simple book about Da Vinci; however, you can locate other books in the fine arts section of your library that contain quality reproductions of his work. Among other things, DaVinci was an artist who studied portraiture which involved the study of anatomy. It is interesting to observe the accuracy with which he painted the human form. *How the Body Works: 100 Ways Parents and Kids Can Share the Miracle of the Human Body*, by Steve Parker, contains hundreds of practical, safe experiments to help the whole family learn by doing.

The following books are about individuals who worked to improve the quality of life for man. These biographies offer a bit of historical emphasis to your study. *Dr. William Harvey and the Discovery of Circulation*, by William C. Harrison. The answers that Harvey found about the circulation of the blood did not agree with the beliefs and practices of his time. (He was born in 1578.) He knew it was dangerous to express ideas that opposed those then in acceptance. Even the brilliant Galileo had been persecuted for expressing new truths about the universe. *Dr. Beaumont and the Man with the Hole in His Stomach*, by Sam and Beryl Epstein. As a result of a shooting accident, a frontiersman was left with a hole in his stomach that would never close up. Doctor Beaumont performed experiments on digestion through this passageway.

The Mysterious Rays, Marie Curie's World, by Nancy Veglahn. Marie Curie discovered radium. During the First World War she equipped a mobile x-ray unit and accompanied it to hospitals on the battle field. The unit was used to locate broken bones and shell fragments. *Marie Curie's Search for Radium*, by Beverley Birch is geared for ages 9-12. *Famous Firsts in Medicine*, by Bette Crook and Charles L. Crook, M.D.

Patriot Doctor, the Story of Benjamin Rush, by Esther M. Douty. Benjamin Rush was a doctor, teacher, patriot, and humanitarian. As physician-general of Washington's armies, he fought death and disease through the desperate years of the Revolution. ***Gifted Hands: The Story of Ben Carson***. This amazing story details the life of a black surgeon who has successfully separated thirty Siamese twins who had little hope of survival. Ben Carson describes his own inspiring life story, recounting his rise from inner-city kid to renowned surgeon. Ben's mom decided when he was young that he and his brother would read good books and not watch TV.

Bible

This unit provides us with an opportunity to study the most magnificent handiwork of the Creator. Naturally the first place we turn to is the book of Genesis.

Genesis 1:26-27

And God said, 'Let us make man in our image, after our likeness; and let them have dominion over the fish of the sea, and over the fowl of the air, and over the cattle, and over all the earth, and over every creeping thing that creepeth upon the earth.' So God created man in his own image, in the image of God created he him; male and female created he them.

Genesis 2:7

And the Lord God formed man of the dust of the ground, and breathed into his nostrils the breath of life; and man became a living soul.

Some other verses are Job 10:8-12, Job 33:4, Job 43:19, Psalm 119:73, Psalm 138:8, Psalm 139:13-16, Isaiah 64:8, Job 32:8, Matthew 6:22-23.

Using a concordance, look up words relating to the body such as body, bone, blood, breath, circumcise, ears, face, feet, finger, flesh, forehead, hand, heal, heart, illness, infection, infirmities, knee, life, mouth, multiply, neck, physician, sick, skin, skull, soul, taste, tears, teeth, temple, thirst, throat, tongue, tooth, vessel, voice, weep, and womb.

My favorite passage for this human body unit is Psalm 139:13-16. My children and I memorized this passage. I prefer the New American Standard Version that reads:

For Thou didst form my inward parts;
Thou didst weave me in my mother's womb.
I will give thanks to Thee,
For I am fearfully and wonderfully made;
Wonderful are Thy works,
And my soul knows it very well.
My frame was not hidden from Thee,

When I was made in secret,
And skillfully wrought in the depths of the earth.
Thine eyes have seen my unformed substance;
And in Thy book they were all written,
The days that were ordained for me,
When as yet there was not one of them.

This passage and others make excellent typing exercises. We use a large print Bible for typing practice. Another interesting Biblical passage to study in the course of this unit is Ephesians 6:13-17.

Therefore, take up the full armor of God, that you may be able to resist the evil day, and having done everything, to stand firm. Stand firm therefore, having girded your loins with truth, and having put on the breastplate of righteousness, and having shod your feet with the preparation of the gospel of peace; in addition to all, take up the shield of faith with which you will be able to extinguish all the flaming missiles of the evil one. And take the helmet of salvation, and the sword of the Spirit, which is the word of God.

Have your children note the various body parts mentioned and what protects them.

Language Arts and Science

Using one or two of the books you have chosen for this unit, allow your children to either copy or write from your verbal dictation, pertinent passages relating to the systems of the body. As you explore each body system, have your children color corresponding illustrations from the ***Gray's Anatomy Coloring Book***.

Then choose several experiments to perform using either Jane Hoffman's ***Backyard Science, Series Three*** or ***How the Body Works: 100 Ways Parents and Kids Can Share the Miracle of the Human Body***. I encourage you to have your children copy the experimental procedures outlined in the books and then to record their findings. This provides them with a good model for posting experimental data. While undergoing the experiments, have your children make accompanying illustrations to help fix the new found information in their minds. This can be as simple as tracing a picture from the ***Gray's Anatomy Coloring Book*** that corresponds to the system you are investigating.

After studying each system, have your children make a list of all the words they can think of that relate to that particular system. Children who are more artistic can write the words in such a manner as to *form* a picture of something indicative of that body system.

Take some large butcher paper, bulletin board paper, or poster paper (available at Staples and Office Depot.). Have your child lie on it, while you trace his basic body shape. Then let him add hair, nails, skin color, eyes, nose, mouth, ears, teeth, heart, lungs, blood vessels, and all the other organs. He will probably need to use a book or the game *Somebody* to help him out. He can even tape overlays on his body that flip up to reveal other body parts underneath. These "bodies" can be rolled up for easy storage.

Poetry is always fun to explore. Psalm 139:13-16 is a beautiful poem about the marvelous formation of an infant in the womb. The children can take the word lists they compiled for each system and make a poem about one or all the systems combined. You may need to help them think of adjectives and verbs relating to each system as most of the words on their lists may be nouns. Remind them that poems do not have to rhyme. The feeling evoked by the poem is more important.

You will find many library books about the human body. Choose some books you like to read aloud with your children or have them read on their own. The book I chose to use as our basic text was rather simple. I wanted to give my children an overview of the workings of the body. Later we will study each individual system in greater depth. Focusing on two systems at a time, it will take five units to complete this more in depth study. Other units will be interspersed between them. Do not think you must cover everything in just one unit. Remember, learning lasts a lifetime. The body is our Maker's most magnificent creation, so it is fitting that we should come back to it time after time. It helps us to recall that we are fearfully and wonderfully made, and we are precious in His sight!

*T*his fascinating study lends itself to hands-on investigations. Feel free to take a break from the academic nature of the study and learn from doing!

<u>Library Books</u>

Giants of Electricity, by Percy Dunsheath. This book includes biographical information about numerous scientists who contributed to the harnessing of electricity: Ampre, Davy, Faraday, Franklin, Galvani, Gauss, Henry, Kelvin, Maxwell, Oersted, Olim, Volta, and Weber. *The Quest of Michael Faraday*, by Tad Harvey, offers an interesting biography of Faraday. Faraday discovered how to produce electricity from magnetism. *Michael Faraday: Physics and Faith*, by Colin Archibald Russell, is a more detailed biography for grades 8 and up. *Charles Proteus Steinmetz, Wizard of Electricity*, by Erick Berry. This is the story of a crippled mathematical genius with a humped back and large head.

How Did We Find Out About Electricity?, by Isaac Asimov. Asimov tells the history of electricity from the early Greek philosophers to Volta's battery and Faraday's electromagnetism. *Benjamin Franklin's Adventures With Electricity*, by Beverley Birch, is for ages 9-12. Childhood of Famous American series: *Thomas Edison: Young Inventor*, by Sue Guthridge for ages 9 –12.

The Thomas Edison Book of Easy and Incredible Experiments, by James G. Cook and the Thomas Alva Edison Foundation. Experiments in this book encompass magnetism, electricity, electrochemistry, chemistry, physics, energy, and environmental studies. We really enjoyed this book! *The Way Things Work*, by David Macaulay. Yes, I am recommending this book again. Macaulay is both entertaining and instructive in his comprehensive book that explains the mysteries behind the things we encounter everyday. Specifically pertaining to this unit are the sections on electricity in general, magnetism, electromagnetism, the electric bell, the electric horn, the electric motor, the electric generator, the two-way switch, batteries, circuits, current, and more. Macaulay's reference book should be included in the homeschooling family's home.

Electricity and Magnets, by Barbara Taylor. This is a nice simple book. The table of contents reads: Using Electricity, Sparks and Flashes, Batteries, Circuits, Magnetic Forces, and Electromagnetics. The book also includes step-by-step investigations.

Young children will enjoy, *Switch On, Switch Off*, by Melvin Berger, which explains how electricity is produced and transmitted, and how generators, light bulbs, and electrical plugs work. *The Magic School Bus and the Electric Field Trip*, by Joanna Cole takes us on a trip through the town's power lines to discover how electricity works. *Science Experiments With Magnets* and *Science Experiments With Electricity*, both by Sally Nankivell-Aston, are designed for ages 9 –12.

Bright Lights to See By, by Miriam Anne Bourne, is a delightful story about a period in history when electricity was still a wonder.

You will find several biographies of the famous scientists who contributed to the harnessing of electricity. If you have trouble locating some of the suggested books, look for biographies of the men mentioned. You will also find many books relating to electricity in the children's section of your library. Use your subject card catalog to locate them.

When undertaking scientific units, I am more successful if I stick with simple books that present basic facts. Later, these scientific topics can be studied in greater depth, but a good foundation must first be laid. Tedious facts are often difficult to memorize, but basic concepts that are presented in a simple and concise fashion enable us to progress to more difficult concepts. Therefore, we build upon previous knowledge rather than memorize nebulous facts.

An exciting aspect of science is that the so-called "laws of nature" are fixed and unchanging. This is because an omnipotent and immutable Creator designed our universe. If the universe just happened, how could we rely on these laws of nature to remain constant?

Quoting from **Scientific Creationism**, by Henry Morris:

It seems obvious that the evolution model would predict that matter, energy and the laws are still evolving since they must have evolved in the past and there is no external agent to bring such evolution to a halt.

Creationists obviously would predict that the basic laws, as well as the fundamental nature of matter and energy, would not now be changing at all. They were completely created - finished in the past, and are being conserved in the present.

Michael Faraday was an English scientist who we credit more than any other single man with giving us the Age of Electricity. He felt that all of nature was governed by a few fixed and unchanging laws. He was a great and thorough scientist. He set up experiments to test his theories, realizing that if an experiment failed to prove his theory, the flaw was with him, not with nature. Either his experiment or his theory was imperfect.

As you study electricity, or any science-based unit, it is fitting to also study the immutability of the Creator. Just as the laws of nature are unchanging, so are His ways, His thoughts, and His laws unchanging. He is the same yesterday, today, and tomorrow. Some verses (KJV) to reflect on are:

Ecclesiastes 3:14 *"Whatsoever God doeth, it shall be for ever; nothing can be put to it, nor anything taken from it."* Malachi 3:6 *"I am the LORD, I change not; therefore ye sons of Jacob are not consumed."* James 1:17 *"Every good gift and every perfect gift is from above, and cometh down from the Father of lights, with whom is no variableness, neither shadow of turning."*

Use a topical Bible and look up "GOD-Immutable" to find other pertinent verses. A very interesting and informative little book dealing with the attributes of the Almighty is entitled, ***The Knowledge of the Holy***, by A.W. Tozer.

As with most other science units, this unit on electricity lends itself well to projects or experiments. Using some simple library books you can conduct a few experiments with your children. I like the way the experiments are laid out in ***The Thomas Edison Book of Easy and Incredible Experiments***. (There are several library books available that offer simple experiments with electricity.) Part I of the Thomas Edison book is entitled, Simple Experiments in Electricity, Electrochemistry, and Basic Chemistry. Some of the experiments in this section are A Simple Electrical Circuit, How a Doorbell Circuit Works, How a Two-Way Switch Works, Conductors and Insulators, What is an Electrolyte?, Electricity from a Lemon, The First Electric Battery. Part II, Simple Experiments in Magnetism and Electricity, include some of the following experiments: The Variable Conductivity of Carbon, The Carbon Transmitter Principle, Making an Electromagnet, Magnetism and the Compass, the Fuse in Action, Faraday's "Ice-pail" Experiment, and Does Ice Conduct Electricity? This book offers many more experiments using inexpensive, easy-to-obtain materials. Another interesting feature of the book is that it contains photos of Thomas Alva Edison as well as a chronology of events in his life.

While conducting experiments with electricity, it is helpful for the children to keep a log of the materials used, procedures carried out, and the results noted. It is also beneficial to record the reasoning behind their findings. Making illustrations or taking photographs of the procedures will also aid your children's retention of their findings. The illustrations or photos can be labeled and placed in a notebook along with the data they gather.

The Power of Science Electricity Kit, by Learning Resources (see resource section for ordering information) offers everything you need to study about static and current electricity, circuits, switches, fuses, and electromagnetism through safe, hands-on activities for ages 9 -11.

A fun and inexpensive game you may want to purchase is ***AC/DC Electric Circuit Game***, manufactured by Ampersand Press. (See resource section for ordering information.) This game is played with a special deck of cards. The cards illustrate wires, switches, energy sources, energy users, and fuses. The object of the game is to build workable circuits. The players may get "shocked" or "shorted." This game offers an intriguing introduction to the study of electricity.

Use a simple library book about electricity and have your children write each word found in the glossary on one side of an index card. Then have them write the meaning of the word on the reverse side of the card. These cards can be used to quiz the children on their vocabulary. Another alternative is to write a word on one card and the meaning of that word on a separate card. Then the cards can be mixed and then matched.

Younger children can be sent on a hunt to find items in the house that operate on electricity. Older children can work some calculations using past electric bills. How much electricity do you use on the average per day in a given month? How much more or how much less electricity did you use this month than you used last month? How many kilowatt hours did you purchase this month? What is a kilowatt hour? How much do you pay per kilowatt hour? Discuss the other points of your electric bill. (Usually all the terminology and method of calculation are defined on the back of your bill.) Have your children make a list of things they can do to help conserve energy and thus lower your electric bill.

Remember, when you are conducting a unit requiring a lot of experiments or projects, lighten up on the more academic aspects of the unit. These projects "teach" so many principles and disciplines that you do not need to "pad" them with an abundance of written work. Keeping a record of the experiment should suffice in such units. Continue to read topic-related books with your children and have fun!

HISTORY AND GEOGRAPHY

Foreign Countries Unit

We open up new horizons for ourselves and our children as we examine the geography and culture of other lands. It can be difficult for our children to see beyond our neighborhood, let alone across the world. A useful book to read with younger children is, *Where in the World do You Live*, by Al Hine and John Alcorn. Another child-friendly book for young children is *Me on the Map*, by Joan Sweeney.

When we begin a study of another country, it is helpful to first examine the term "country." According to National Geographic Society's *Exploring Our World, The Adventure of Geography*:

> A country is a recognized territory whose government is the highest legal authority over the land and the people living within its boundaries. Each country has not only distinct boundaries, but also a unique name and flag. All but the smallest countries issue their own money.

Do you know how many countries there are in the world? Experts disagree on the number because they disagree about the status of some territories. An important measuring device is whether the governments of other countries recognize a region as independent and self-governing.

The term "state" is often used to mean "country," although it is a more formal term. "Nation" is also frequently used in place of "country." "Nation" denotes a group of people with a common culture who may be divided by political boundaries.

Spend some time with your children perusing a map of the world or a globe. Have the capable children read the names of a number of countries. Choose one continent and learn the names of all its countries. Aristoplay has a terrific game called *Where in The World?*, which offers an engaging way to learn the names and locations of countries. Many other pertinent facts can be learned as well. Select a country from the continent you have chosen and begin a study of it.

Learn the names of important bodies of water, mountains, and other geographical features located in and around the country you have chosen. *Exploring Your World, The Adventure of Geography* is an excellent resource that enables readers to explore the "how's" and "why's" of our planet as well as the "where's." Its concise text and vivid photographs acquaint us with terms such as canal, continent, desert, earthquake, grassland, island, mountain, plateau, and more. *National Geographic World Atlas for Young Explorers* can be used in place of this book. It may be easier to locate, and it is less expensive.

Two very simple books by Jack Knowlton that are useful for young children are *Geography from A to Z, A Picture Glossary*, and *Maps and Globes*. If your children like The Cat in the Hat they would enjoy *There's a Map on My Lap!: All about Maps*, by Tish Rabe.

Select library books pertaining to your country of interest, remembering to investigate clothing, art, sports, literature, music, cuisine, theatre, education, government, hobbies, economy, religion, language, alphabet, geography, and as many other areas as you can imagine. How does this country relate to the countries surrounding it, and what influences have these neighboring countries had on one another's pasts? Skim your local newspaper for information on political happenings today. *God's World Publications* offers interesting and well-written newspapers for children beginning at the kindergarten level and extending through high school and adult levels .

Video tapes offer us a bird's eye view of the country we are investigating. Public libraries or video rental stores are an excellent source for video cassette tapes pertaining to foreign countries. Your library will probably own audio cassette tapes featuring a study of the language(s) of your chosen country of study. Investigate the children's section for language tapes which present the language in a simple format. You and your children may want to learn a few phrases in the foreign tongue.

Audio Memory Publishing offers two audio cassette tapes that make learning the names of the countries a simple task. The states of the U.S., territories of Canada, and the planets of the Solar System are included as well. The tapes are simply titled, *Geography Songs* and *More Geography Songs*.

When conducting a historical unit, or most any other unit, it is advantageous to make a timeline and timeline figures to represent the historical figures of study.

For further information concerning timelines, see the section of *How to Create Your Own Unit Study* entitled **A Word about Timelines** on page 109.

Korea Unit

Korea lies in close proximity to both China and Japan, with only a short stretch of water separating the Korean and Japanese coasts. Both the Chinese and Japanese have exerted an influence over Korea in the course of history. At various times armies of both China and Japan have invaded Korea and imposed their social and political institutions on its people. Korea has therefore adopted some of the culture of these nations. However, the independent nature of Korea has enabled it to retain its own distinct civilization for thousands of years. In the 1800's Korea was known as the hermit kingdom.

Library Books

Korea: Land of the Morning Calm, by Carol Farley. A very informative book that offers a brief but well written account of modern Korea and its past. This book will direct you to many areas of interest. I suggest this as a basic text for your study. *Land of Morning Calm: Korean Culture Then and Now*, by John Stickler, also explores traditional and modern Korean culture. *Peacebound Trains*, by Haemi Balgassi, is a beautiful picture book that evokes the landscape and people of Korea and a special grandmother-granddaughter relationship during the Korean war. *My Freedom Trip*, by Frances Park and Ginger Park, offers another recounting of a family's struggle during the Korean war.

The Trip Back Home, by Janet S. Wong, offers a treatment of modern Korea for the youngest readers. *When You Were Born in Korea*, by Brian E. Boyd, focuses on an adopted Korean child's life prior to adoption. *We Don't Look Like Our Mom and Dad*, by Harriet Langsam Sobol, is a photo-essay on the life of an American family and their two Korean-born adopted sons. *My Best Friend, Mee-Yung Kim*, by Dianne MacMillan and Dorothy Freeman. *We Adopted You, Benjamin Koo*, by Linda Walvoord Girard.

Count Your Way Through Korea, by Jim Haskins. Korean life is explored as you learn to count from one through ten in Korean. Haskins describes such aspects as one ancient building and four parts of the traditional Korean costume for men. *Courage in Korea: Stories of the Korean War,* selected by Albert Tibbets. This volume contains ten stories of the U.N. resistance to the Red invasion of Korea. It is about men in foxholes, in rice paddies, in waist-deep mud, making a firm stand against the intruders. The courage and friendship of these men are evident as you are exposed to the hardships and suffering they endured as they said to the Communists, "No Farther." I stayed up late at night reading this book because it was so interesting. If you begin one story, you must finish it without delay. Most of the stories selected for publication in *Courage in Korea* were written in the early 1950's. This volume is out-of-print, but you may be able to locate a copy at your public library or through a used book source.

Bong Nam and the Pheasants, story retold by Edward Yushin Yoo. A delightful Korean tale. *Aekyung's Dream,* by Min Paek. A story of a young Korean girl who immigrated to America with her family; a contemporary tale from the North American Korean Community. The author has also translated the text into Korean. ***The Cat Who Went To Heaven***, by Elizabeth Coatsworth. This Newbery Award book relates the tale concerning a poor Japanese artist who was commissioned to paint the death of the lord Buddha. It is a fine literary work which will acquaint your children with the religious beliefs prevalent in much of the Far East, including Korea. Four newer books we have discovered that give a wonderful view into Korea's past are ***Seesaw Girl, The Kite Fighters, The Firekeeper's Son, When My Name Was Keoko***, and the 2001 Newbery Medal winner, ***A Single Shard***, all by Linda Sue Parks. We have really enjoyed Linda Sue Parks books. ***The Korean Cinderella*** by Shirley Climo. ***Cooking the Korean Way***, by Okwha Chung and Judy Monore. Besides offering simple Korean dishes you can make at home, the book gives a brief introduction to the land, history, food, and feasts of Korea.

Understanding Far Eastern Art, by Julia Hutt. A complete guide to the art of China, Japan, and Korea, detailing ceramics, sculpture, painting, prints, lacquer, textiles, and metalwork. ***The Oriental World***, by Jeannine Auboyer and Roger Goepper. Includes 228 illustrations of art from India, South-East Asia, China, Korea, and Japan. ***Chinese and Oriental Art***, by Michael Batterberry. Includes a very informative section on Korean art. Batterberry does an excellent job of weaving history and art into an interesting text.

Kiteworks: Explorations in Kite Building and Flying, by Maxwell Eden. ***Catch the Wind!: All About Kites***, by Gail Gibbons. A simple book telling about the basic materials for kites, how kites are made, who were the first kite flyers, and how kites take off and fly. Includes step-by-step instructions for building a kite. Bright and colorful; great for young children. ***Tae Kwon Do: The Korean Martial Art***, by Richard Chun. Tae Kwon Do literally means "The Art of Kicking and Punching." This book contains an interesting history of the Korean martial art. Another similar book is ***Tae Kwon Do: The Ultimate Reference Guide to the World's Most Popular Martial Art***, by Yeon Hee Park, Yeon Hwan Park, and Jon Gerrard.

Vocabulearn Korean, consists of two 90-minute audio cassettes and a 36 page Vocabulist. Another cassette tape program I found at my public library is entitled ***Language/30 - Korean***. This program consists of two audio cassettes and a phrase dictionary. Everyday words and phrases are emphasized. Your library may contain other instructional language cassettes. These are interesting to listen to, and they give you and your children an opportunity to experience the language. Your public library may also own videos on Korea. Video rental stores carry a variety of travel videos including presentations of Korea.

Other Books and Materials

Exploring Your World, the Adventure of Geography, and

National Geographic World Atlas for Young Explorers, both published by the National Geographic Society. These books are a valuable resource which will assist you as you encounter geographical terms. For example, when studying Korea you encounter inactive volcanoes, mountains, seas, rivers, peninsulas, islands, monsoons, the Pacific Ocean, and so on. These volumes offer superb pictures and text depicting geographical terms.

Operation World: When We Pray God Works, by Patrick Johnstone. A day-to-day guide to praying for the world. *Operation World* is a prayer calendar covering every country in the world. Background facts and figures include populations, peoples, economies, politics, religions and churches. Accompanying the book are prayer cards for spiritually needy nations. Each card represents one country and includes facts as well as a list of the basic prayer needs of that particular country. It is very exciting to read about the impact the Christian church has had in South Korea. Christianity, as well as other religions, has been harshly repressed in North Korea.

Korean Embassies and Consulates in the U.S.:

Embassy of Korea
2450 Massachusetts Avenue N.W
Washington, DC 20008
202-939-5600
www.koreaembassyusa.org

Korean Consulate General
3500 Clay Street
San Francisco, CA 94118
415-921-2251
www.koreanconsulatesf.org

There are many officials and their families living in the U.S. who are affiliated with the Korean Embassy. They would probably like to receive letters from children requesting information concerning their country. Your children may even find an intriguing pen pal amongst the children of the Korean Embassy officials.

Religion

The major religions of Korea are Buddhism, Confucianism, and Christianity. Koreans celebrate Buddha's birthday as the Feast of Lanterns. Lanterns are displayed in the temple courtyards as symbolic of the light Buddha brought to the world. Buddhism came to Korea as an influence of the people of India. Perhaps your children would like to construct a paper lantern fashioned after the Korean lanterns.

Confucianism was implemented in Korea through the influence of the Chinese. Confucius believed that a strict social order would benefit society. The Confucian teaching of social order still controls Korean life today. Confucius also sought to help people live a good life in the present, rather than planning for a future in heaven.

Christianity reached South Korea in the nineteenth century. The Christian church with the largest membership in the world today is located in Yoido. It has a membership of over 629,000. North Korea is said to have 10,000 Christians in Pyongyang.

Other Areas of Interest

Koreans are noted for their magnificent pottery called celadon, a pottery with a greenish blue glaze. Using books from the library such as *Chinese and Oriental Art* by Michael Batterberry, investigate this art form and read about its history. In the index of these library books, you can look up Korea, and find many interesting pictures and descriptions of beautiful Korean art. The Koreans have a fondness for dragons, as is evident from their ancient architecture. Kites offer another avenue to explore, as the Koreans enjoy kite flying contests. A library book about kites will enable you to make kites and have a contest of your own. (See page 152 for a listing of kite books.)

Investigate the Korean alphabet, Hangeul. Hangeul is a writing system that consists of 28 symbols based on sounds, rather than thousands of Chinese characters based on meanings. This system was developed during the reign of King Sejong, ruler of Korea from 1418 to 1450. He decided that a simpler writing system should be devised so that all people could learn to read and write. *The King's Secret: the Legend of King Sejong*, by Carol J. Farley, recounts the legend of how Korea's Hangeul alphabet was invented.

At certain times during Korea's history, Hangeul was forbidden. Today it is very highly regarded and the Korean people celebrate National Hangeul Day. The people of South Korea enjoy a very high literacy rate as a result of the implementation of this writing system. *The King's Secret: the Legend of King Sejong*, contains information in the back of the book about Hangeul writing system. *Aekyung's Dream* is written in English as well as Hangeul.

Note the formation of the symbols used in Hangul. Locate some examples of Chinese and Japanese writing and compare them with the symbols of Hangeul. Discuss how the use of a writing system based on sounds is more efficient than one based on characters representing separate ideas. During the same century Hangeul was developed, the Koreans were printing with movable type. This remarkable feat began in 1403, some 50 years before Johann Gutenberg invented his printing press!

Prepare a Korean meal or dish, decorating the table in Korean fashion for an added touch. *Cooking the Korean Way* offers a variety of recipes, including the Korean national dish, Kimch'i. It is made of pickled cabbage and ranges from mild to very spicy. *Korean Home Cooking*, by Soon Yung Chung, looks very tasty! The book claims to offer quick, easy, delicious recipes to make at home.

Traditional Korean dress is another area of interest. ***Understanding Far Eastern Art*** includes some information on the textiles of the Far East and concentrates on the design of the kimono. Costume books offer additional material concerning the traditional dress. The Amazon Dry Goods Company has authentic patterns for various far eastern dress for more industrious families. (See resource section for ordering information.)

Perhaps your family would like to learn the Korean national anthem, "Aegukga." As you study the history of Korea, you can discuss the differences between North and South Korea with your children. For example, in North Korea, state education is implemented at three months of age when babies must attend state-owned nurseries. Contrast this with South Korea where family life plays a vital role. A study of Tae Kwon Do, an ancient art of self defense will undoubtedly prove inviting to many children. Investigate other traditional and popular Korean sports.

Geography

Explore the vast mountain ranges of Korea. Investigate its extinct volcanoes, its fierce monsoons, its seas and rivers, its three thousand islands, and its green rice fields. Define these terms with your children. Also define the term peninsula which describes Korea as a whole. Video cassettes will probably offer the best views of Korea's geography. Unfortunately, I have not found many library books with numerous quality photographs of Korea. If you have an opportunity you might peruse some of the National Geographic Magazines. Investigate magazines and newspapers which will shed light on the political activity in Korea today. This can be done by skimming your local newspaper, or using the facilities provided at your public library. The internet has opened up a whole new area of research in recent years. Through searches you will be able to "tour" Korea as never before!

Activity

As your children study various countries of the world, have them compile an atlas. This can include copy or dictation work about the areas of interest pertaining to each country; maps the children have collected, traced, or drawn; facts about the people, land, government, and so on; pictures depicting the dress of the country; poems they have written or copied about the country; photographs of any projects they have made relative to their study; and other useful materials. These atlases can be kept for future reference and serve as a tool for review.

Now a new king arose over Egypt, who did not know Joseph.
Exodus 1:8 NASV.

Library Books

The Art of Egypt under the Pharaohs, by Shirley Glubok. This
text examines artistic Egyptian achievements through a discussion of the
history, mythology, daily life, customs, and religious beliefs of the ancient
Egyptians. ***The Art of Ancient Egypt***, by Shirley Glubok. An excellent
introduction to the art of ancient Egypt related in an uncomplicated style.
Looking at Architecture, by Roberta M. Paine. A book spanning the
centuries from ancient Egypt to the present day that describes the intellect
and human effort involved in the design and erection of many famous
buildings. ***The Buildings of Ancient Egypt***, written and illustrated by
Helen and Richard Leacroft. Archaeologists have been able to re-create an
image of life in Ancient Egypt more than three thousand years ago as a
result of exploring tombs and their contents.

Ancient Egypt, An Eyewitness Book, by George Hart. Real-life
photographs and an informative text present us with a mini-museum
through which we can view early Egyptian life. ***Science in Ancient
Egypt***, by Geraldine Woods. Chapter contents include: Geography and
Ancient Egyptian Science, The Pyramids, Mathematics, Astronomy and
Timekeeping, Medicine, Writing and Agriculture, Crafts and Technology,
and Our Debt to Egypt. ***Pyramid***, by David Macaulay. Pyramids stand
today as massive remnants of ancient Egyptian culture. Macaulay takes us
through the step-by-step construction of an imaginary pyramid.

Ancient Egypt, by Daniel Cohen. Each page is almost filled with
beautiful color drawings depicting life in early Egypt. ***The Way Things
Work***, by David Macaulay contains simple yet sufficient information
about levers, pulleys, inclined planes, and related topics. This works well
in conjunction with Macaulay's book, ***Pyramid***, which incorporates a
discussion of such mechanical devices. (Although this book is available in
most public libraries, it is a valuable reference tool to own.) ***Exodus:
Adapted From the Bible***, by Miriam Chaikin, illustrated by Charles
Mikolaycak. The beautiful illustrations are a result of careful research into
the ancient Egyptian world. ***The Egyptian Cinderella***, by Shirley Climo.

Other Books and Materials

***Great Science Adventures: The World of Tools
and Technology***, published by Common Sense Press, contains
reproducible activities and graphic organizers to teach grades K through 8
about gears, pulleys, wedges, inclined planes, and more. While learning
about simple tools you are building a foundation for understanding more
complex devices. A great hands on accompaniment for Macaulay's
Pyramid and ***The Way Things Work***. ***The Riddle of the Rosetta Stone:
Key to Ancient Egypt***, by James Cross Giblin, chronicles the lives of
several scholars who struggled to decipher Egyptian hieroglyphs and

break the code of the Rosetta Stone. For ages 8-12. *The Shipwrecked Sailor: An Egyptian Tale with Hieroglyphs*, by Tamara Bower, for grades 1-5.

I am delighted to have found an excellent resource for obtaining materials for historically based units. Rob and Cyndy Shearer of Greenleaf Press have written study guides for various time periods including *The Greenleaf Guide to Ancient Egypt, The Greenleaf Guide to Famous Men of Greece, The Greenleaf Guide to Famous Men of Rome*, and *The Greenleaf Guide to Famous Men of the Middle Ages*. They have written these guides to accompany *Pharaohs of Ancient Egypt* (Landmark Books), *Famous Men of Greece, Famous Men of Rome*, and *Famous Men of the Middle Ages*. (The latter three were originally written by Haaren and have been edited and updated by Rob and Cyndy.)

The Greenleaf Catalog includes additional materials for a study of these areas mentioned as well as materials for a study of Vikings, Renaissance and Reformation, Explorers, and U.S. History. Their catalog is a terrific resource for historically based units as some books included are available from the public library. Greenleaf offers very good prices on their study packages which include the *Famous Men of...* books, additional high quality publications relative to the study, and the *Greenleaf Guides*. The guides include suggestions for how to set your study of ancient civilizations in a biblical context. They also offer suggestions for utilizing the additional books included in the package. All the books may be bought separately.

Greenleaf's Ancient Egypt Study Package includes: *Greenleaf Guide to Ancient Egypt*, by Cyndy Shearer; *The Pharaohs of Ancient Egypt*, by Elizabeth Payne; *Usborne Time Traveller Book of Pharaohs and Pyramids*, by Tony Allan; *Usborne First Travellers: Deserts*, by Angela Wilkes; *Pyramid*, by David Macaulay; *Tut's Mummy Lost...and Found*, by Judy Donnelly; and *Mummies Made in Egypt*, by Aliki. Greenleaf also offers other pertinent books for a study of Ancient Egypt including: *Cultural Atlas of Ancient Egypt; Young Scientist Book of Archaeology*, by Usborne; *Mara, Daughter of the Nile*, by Eloise Jarvis McGraw; *The Golden Goblet*, by Eloise Jarvis McGraw; *Pyramid -The Video*, based on David Macaulay's book, *Pyramid*.

You may be able to locate a good number of these books in your public library as well as some I listed at the beginning of this unit. The Greenleaf guides are so well written that I strongly urge you to purchase them. I would like to give you a glimpse into these guides.

The Greenleaf Guides are primarily written for the elementary grades, but the information covered is so well laid out and interesting older students will definitely benefit from their use. When I was in high school, history was a blur of dates and wars. Because I had an ability to memorize material fairly quickly, I managed to make good grades. The understanding behind all those facts was missing. Had I first been introduced to stories about the people of various times and cultures, I would have had some background knowledge upon which to hang the new information presented to me. Knowledge builds upon knowledge.

Greenleaf holds to this same philosophy. Quoting from their guides:

> *Textbooks, by themselves, teach you facts. They do not introduce you to real people. Teaching history to elementary school students should be like calling a child to story time. You find a snug comfortable place, you curl up together, and you start with "Once upon a time."*

Before beginning a study of Ancient Egypt, Greenleaf suggests that you put the study in biblical context by reviewing the first few chapters of Genesis and noting the descriptions of those who followed Adam and his sons. They also suggest reading and discussing the story of the Tower of Babel. After this material is covered they urge you to move on to the first chapter of Romans to investigate what happens when man turns away from the truth and exchanges it for a lie. Next a review of Exodus is recommended. *The Greenleaf Guide to Ancient Egypt* gives suggestions for covering this material; however, Greenleaf now offers *The Greenleaf Guide to Old Testament History*. (This guide was not available when I first wrote *The Unit Study Idea Book* in 1991.) We have also more recently discovered *Old Testament Days: An Activity Guide* by Nancy I. Sanders, which contains more than eighty activities and projects to provide insight into life in the Middle East during the period covered by the Old Testament. This activity book is geared for grades 2 – 5.

The Greenleaf Guide gently takes you through the study of Ancient Egypt; making recommendations along the way, but taking into account that each individual family will tackle the unit in a different manner. Suggested vocabulary lists from the recommended books are given, and various projects are listed such as making a salt map of Egypt. Other interesting pertinent tidbits are included such as a cryptogram, directions for the Egyptian game Senet, and more. Other interest areas covered include a study of pyramids, levers, wheels, pulleys, inclined planes, basket weaving, the history of paper, deserts, irrigation, Egyptian boats, Pharaohs, the Nile River, archaeology, hieroglyphics, and more.

Ancient Greece Unit

As we studied about Ancient Greece, I was intrigued by the influence of this aged culture on today's society — from movies to literature to architecture to art to athletic shoes to automobile tires!

Library Books

Eyewitness: Ancient Greece, by Anne Pearson, traces ancient Greek achievements from the Bronze Age through the Hellenistic period using evidence found by archaeologists. The photographs and spectacular visuals make this book seem like a visit to a world-class museum. *Usborne Book of the Ancient World: Combined Volume: Early Civilization/the Greeks/the Romans* details Ancient Egyptian, Greek, and Roman civilizations. Includes colorful maps, pictures, and diagrams. *Art Tells a Story: Greek and Roman Myths*, by Penelope Proddow. The author tells the story of the myth behind each selected work of art after which she describes the work from the artistic point of view. *The Odyssey*, retold by Robin Lister and illustrated by Alan Baker. A colorful rendition of the ancient tale of Odysseus's journey from Troy. *The Children's Homer: The Adventures of Odysseus and the Tale of Troy*, by Padraic Colum. Mr. Colum proves himself a master storyteller in his retelling of these epic adventures. (See further discussion of this book later.)

Books and Other Materials

D'Aulaires Book of Greek Myths by Edgar and Ingri Parin D'Aulaire, includes all the great gods and goddesses of ancient Greece depicted in a big, beautiful classic, lovingly illustrated and skillfully told volume. The D'Aulaires' illustrations have a memorable quality. *Spend the Day in Ancient Greece: Projects and Activities that Bring the Past to Life*, by Linda Honan. This book is a more recent publication which offers more than a dozen activities to help bring ancient Greece to life such as: write a letter using the Greek alphabet, make a snake bracelet, create masks, and build a chariot. This book is designed for ages 8-12, but as with most materials can be adapted for both younger and older children. Another favorite of ours is *Classical Kids: An Activity Guide to Life in Ancient Greece and Rome*, by Laurie Carlson, which contains hands-on activities such as making a star gazer, chiseling a clay tablet, and making a Greek mosaic. Designed for grades 4-6.

Much of the culture of many ancient civilizations is still intact today. If you were to visit Egypt, Greece, or Rome, you would find that monuments and ruins exist as reminders of the past. Most of us have not been able to travel to these foreign lands, but we can learn from those who have. This can be accomplished by means of published materials such as books, maps, and videos, or on a more personal level by inquiring of friends or relatives who have traveled extensively. They may have returned from their excursions with articles, photographs, slides, or movies. Ask family members, friends, or church members if they have traveled to other countries. You may be pleasantly surprised to find someone who is more than willing to share their acquired knowledge with you. Investigate sources such as your public library or video rental store for movies of Ancient Greece.

Once again Greenleaf Press gets my vote for publishing excellent materials for historically based unit studies. (For further information about Greenleaf Press, refer to the *Ancient Egypt Unit Study.*) Rob and Cyndy Shearer, who founded Greenleaf Press, have revised, edited, and updated *Famous Men of Greece*. This work was originally written by John H. Haaren, LL.D. and A.B. Poland, Ph.D. in 1904. Quoting from Greenleaf's preface to *Famous Men of Greece*:

> *When we read about Moses leading a rebellious and grumbling people across a desert, we identify with Moses -- until it is not only Moses that we see, but ourselves, acting under seemingly impossible circumstances. The study of history becomes not merely the study of nations, but a moral training ground where the wise and the unwise are observed, and the consequences of wisdom and folly may be dissected under a teacher who charges less than Experience.*

> *Just as the child identifies with Moses, he can also identify with other historical figures and analyze the wisdom and folly of their actions. When at the center of all this is the question, "What does God think about this action, person, behavior?", then the study of history (even the study of very pagan nations) takes place in a way in which the God of History is ever present.*

> *We are firmly convinced that biography should be an integral part of a child's study of history.*

Greenleaf Press offers an Ancient Greece study package which includes: *Famous Men of Greece* (mentioned above), *The Greenleaf Guide to Famous Men of Greece*, *The Greeks* (by Usborne), and *The Children's Homer*. Greenleaf also offers several other titles which can be purchased separately. (For those pinching their pennies, I have found many of the titles they recommend at my public library. After reviewing some of these books at your library, you may decide to purchase them.) I recommend at least buying *The Famous Men of Greece* and *The Greenleaf Guide to the Famous Men of Greece*, which may be purchased separately. *The Greenleaf Guide to Famous Men of Greece* walks you through your study while integrating vocabulary, discussion questions, projects, and suggestions for supplementary reading assignments. This guide is well written and I find it satisfies at least two purposes. First, it acquaints us with an important and interesting part of history. Secondly, it offers an excellent example for preparing future historically based unit studies. After familiarizing ourselves with Greenleaf's plan of action, we can follow their model and create units of our own. This idea of copying can enable us to excel in a variety of areas. (As mentioned previously, Greenleaf's catalog is an excellent resource in itself!)

The third book included in the Ancient Greece Study package is **The Greeks**, from the Usborne illustrated World History Series. (I recommended the combined version at the beginning of this unit: *Early Civilization/the Greeks/the Romans*.) This book offers a glimpse of many aspects of early Greece. It will supply you with a variety of additional topical studies to include in your lessons. Areas of interest include: A Greek House, Clothes and Jewelry, Pottery, Architecture, Sculpture, Music and Poetry, The Theatre, Medicine, Greek Myths, and many more. Like all Usborne books, this book is loaded with child-appeal.

The fourth and final book included in the Ancient Greece study package is **The Children's Homer: The Adventures of Odysseus and the Tale of Troy**, by Padraic Colum. Padraic Colum combines the age old stories from Homer's **Iliad** and **Odyssey** into one enthralling adventure. Published in 1918, Padraic Colum's vivid re-telling of the Greek epics is an excellent introduction to the classic myths for young people.

Greenleaf offers a variety of other interesting books to enliven your study of Ancient Greece. Some titles are available at your public library. Ancient Greece book list: **Cultural Atlas of Ancient Greece**. Includes maps and other useful information pertaining to daily life in Ancient Greece. Recommended for use with junior high student. **Journey Through History: Greek and Roman Times**, by Verges. 2nd-3rd grade reading level with a higher interest level. **D'Aulaire's Book of Greek Mythology**. Appealing watercolor drawings depicting the Greek myths. The D'Aulaire's are Caldecott Medal winners. **Bulfinch's Mythology Coloring Book**, available from Greenleaf. **Tales of the Greek Heroes**, by Low. This book is beautifully illustrated and a delight to read. (I found this book in the reference section of my public library. Some libraries may own a circulating copy.)

More offers from the Ancient Greece book list: **Mythology**, by Edith Hamilton. A good text for junior and senior high school students. **The Golden Fleece**, by Padraic Colum. The author of **The Children's Homer**, reviewed earlier, retells the story of Jason's quest for the Golden Fleece. **The Golden Fleece** was awarded the Newbery Honor in 1922. **The Trojan War**, by Coolidge. **The Trojan Horse ... or How the Greeks Won the War**, a Random House "Step-up-to-Reading" book. **Adventures of Ulysses**, by Evslin. **The Iliad**, by Homer. (Penguin edition.) **The Odyssey**, by Homer. (Translated by Richmond Lattimore.) **The Last Days** *of Socrates,* by Plato. ***Ancient Astronomy,*** by Asimov. Great for use with young children.

You do not need to utilize a multitude of books to complete your study. Some books may be used only for their illustrations, others as read-aloud books with your children, some for children to read independently, and some for children to read aloud. Choose one or two books to act as your basic texts, such as ***Famous Men of Greece*** and ***The Children's Homer***. Conduct a few activities to liven up your study from a book such as ***Classical Kids: An Activity Guide to Life in Ancient Greece and Rome,*** by Laurie Carlson. The Greenleaf Guide will provide a sufficient number of suggestions to enhance your study. Use other books as they suit your needs, realizing that this study of Ancient Greece can be either a brief introduction or an all absorbing quest.

Greenleaf Press also offers the ***Famous Men of Greece Pronunciation Tape***. The names of the people and places found in ***Famous Men of Greece*** will not become a mess of jumbled syllables with the aid of this tape!

FINE ARTS

Most children enjoy drawing, and cartoon characters are often the first objects they attempt to re-create. This unit is an entertaining unit and a good one to interject between units more academic in nature.

Library Books

Walt Disney, Master of Make-believe, by Elizabeth Montgomery. *Walt Disney*, by Greta Walker. Childhood of Famous American series: *Walt Disney: Young Movie Maker*, by Marie Hammontree. *Bill Peet, An Autobiography*, by Bill Peet. *Draw 50 Famous Cartoons*, by Lee J. Ames. *Ed Emberley Drawing Books*, some titles are: *Ed Emberley's Great Thumbprint Drawing Book*; *Ed Emberley's Big Orange Drawing Book*; *Ed Emberley's Picture Pie, a Circle Drawing Book*. You will find many how-to-draw cartoon books at the library. Investigate the children's section as well as the fine arts section of your public library. Since animation involves the use of a movie camera, you may want to investigate this device. David Macaulay's *The Way Things Work*, includes a brief but concise explanation with terrific child-pleasing drawings of the movie camera.

Other Books and Resources

The Big Book of Cartooning in Christian Perspective, by Vic Lockman. Go to www.Disney.com and visit the Disney Family Museum.

In this unit I have chosen to focus on Walt Disney and Bill Peet. Walt Disney loved to draw cartoon characters and was fascinated with animation, which made characters look as if they were moving. He was making animated cartoon commercials for movie theaters as a young man, but was frustrated because he felt the figures moved too stiffly. He read all the books he could find on animation and developed a technique which made the characters move naturally. This required making a series of drawings and photographing them. It took much longer, but the animated characters were more lifelike.

As you read biographies of Disney, you will learn of the advancements being made while he was perfecting his films. First, sound appeared in movies, and then color was introduced. These two topics provide spring boards for further study for those who want to pursue them. You will be amazed at the number of academy awards Disney won for his animated films, true life adventures, and full length motion pictures.

Reading the autobiography of Bill Peet will be fascinating for both you and your children. I stayed up past midnight reading it myself. The book is filled with interesting tidbits. Mr. Peet casually takes us on a stroll through American life during the First World War. He acquaints us with his newspaper selling days as he shouts exciting headlines such as: "Lindberg Flies the Atlantic! Extra! Extra! Read all about it!" He gives us a glimpse of the desperate days of the Great Depression, he relates his memories of the great flood of the Ohio River, he recounts Amelia

Earhart's disappearance over the Pacific, he reminds us of the Hindenburg disaster, and he tells us of the continuing national problem of unemployment. Later he joins the artists at the Disney studios. He recounts his struggle to rise in the company.

Peet gives us a glimpse of what it takes to put together animated films. We learn about drawing in-betweens, composing story boards, developing screenplays, recording characters' voices, and more. In a brief, entertaining way, we experience the animation industry. In the midst of his work at the Disney studios, World War II breaks out and Disney begins producing animated training films, films to sell war bonds, and films to ridicule and vilify the enemy. After the war, work resumed as usual. Peet goes on to write and illustrate children's books. He has written more than thirty picture books.

In his autobiography, Peet explains that he drew pictures in a writing tablet during school. Often he was caught doing this so he began to draw directly in his school books on the margins of the pages, which was graphic evidence that he spent little time reading the text. At used book sales, Peet's illustrated books were best sellers. He said he supposed those books were the very first books he ever illustrated for children!

Bill Peet was amazed when Walt Disney asked him to write a feature length screenplay. He said it was a wonder that he could write much more than his own name after daydreaming and drawing his way through classes in school. Peet attributed his ability in language to his love for books and the hours he spent reading many of the best authors at the neighborhood library.

You will find this a delightfully fun unit to explore with your children. The children can have fun drawing still cartoons and inserting captions with dialogue. Look up animation in an encyclopedia or library book and investigate the techniques of animation. Make an animation booklet, having the children draw a character on each page of a booklet with the binding at the top. Use the same character on each page, changing the body position very slightly from one page to the next. Then flip very quickly through the book, and the figure will look as if it is moving. Compare this with the information you find on animation in the encyclopedia or library book.

The computer industry has changed the way cartoon films are animated today. This presents yet another avenue for you and your children to study. *Careers in Computer Animation*, by Jeremy Shiresor and *Getting Ready: A Career As a Computer Animator*, by Bill Lund are books you may want to borrow from your public library.

Music is a delightful avenue to explore with our children. It stimulates creativity and an appreciation for quality entertainment. Often this seems a difficult area to study because as parents we sometimes lack a musical background. This is all the more reason to investigate music with our children. The age of audio electronics has made it possible for us to obtain quality recordings of the great composers at affordable prices.

I suggest making the study two-fold: A brief study of the orchestra along with a study of two famous composers' lives. If you try to study several composers at once, the study can become confusing. Later in the year, or in years to follow, other composers' lives can be studied. At this time you may want to review the instruments of the orchestra or study a particular section of the orchestra in greater depth. I have listed five biographies of famous composers. Select two and enjoy.

<u>Library Books</u>

The Boy Who Loved Music, by David Lasker. Based on an actual incident from the life of Joseph Haydn. This book contains charming illustrations by the author's father, Joe Lasker. *The Twenty Children of Johann Sebastian Bach*, by David Arkin. Contains beautiful illustrations and provides a good introduction to the life and times of Bach. *Ludwig Beethoven and the Chiming Tower Bells*, by Opal Wheeler. Opal Wheeler has written many music biographies and is an interpreter of music to children. Her warm literary style and delicate skill make for pleasurable reading for all ages. This biography was first published in 1942. It certainly surpasses the short, choppy, slick-looking biographies often written for children today.

Handel at the Court of Kings, by Opal Wheeler. Handel was known as the Father of the Oratorio and was the composer of the magnificent *Messiah*. *Mozart, the Wonder Boy*, by Opal Wheeler. Mozart was a child prodigy. Opal Wheeler has caught Mozart's life-long fascination with children. Thirty-five full pages of Mozart's music are included. Many of the biographies written by Opal Wheeler may no longer be available, but if you can locate them through interlibrary loans at your public library, it will be well worth the effort.

The Pantheon Story of Music for Young People, by Joseph Wechsberg. Contains an historical overview of western music. Every major composer has been emphasized with a special treatment of the classical and romantic periods. The text is filled with interesting illustrations offering a glimpse of music history. Although this book is now out-of-print, you may be able to locate it at your public library. *Great Composers*, by Piero Ventura, is similar in content to the book listed above, but is a much more recent publication. This is evident in the illustrations which have a modern look rather than one which captures the feeling of the age as reflected in *The Pantheon Story of Music*.

The Magic Flute, based on the opera by W.A. Mozart, retold by Stephen Spender. Brief biographical information about Mozart is included at the end of the book. *The Magic Flute* was Mozart's last opera. This book is currently out-of-print, but may be available at your public library. There are several newer versions available in book form if you cannot find the one retold by Spender. *Meet the Orchestra*, by Ann Hayes. Each instrument of the orchestra — from oboes and violas to tubas, trumpets, and timpani is explained, with clear definitions as well as more information as to how each one sounds. Karmen Thompson's illustrations are silly — but musically correct — featuring an array of formally dressed animal musicians. *The Story of the Incredible Orchestra: An Introduction to Musical Instruments and the Symphony Orchestra*, by Bruce Koscielniak gives us a lively look at the history of the orchestra and the instruments that comprise it. *The Farewell Symphony*, by Anna Harwell Celenza is a delightful introduction to Joseph Haydn, his "Farewell Symphony," and 18th-century court life.

Books and Other Materials

Based in 19th century Vienna, *Beethoven Lives Upstairs* is a story of the idiosyncratic but creatively brilliant Beethoven who is struggling with his deafness as he composes his Ninth Symphony. This story is available in book form as well as audio cassette or CD. You may be able to find the video version of this story at your library; however, it is currently out-of-print in this format. *George Fredrick Handel: Composer of Messiah*, by Charles Ludwig, published by Mott Media. *Peter Ustinov Reads the Orchestra*, by Peter Ustinov with the Toronto Philharmonic Orchestra is a full-length cassette providing a demonstration of the wide variety of instruments in the orchestra.

Over the years we have thoroughly enjoyed the *Music Masters Series*. Each 60-minute CD highlights significant events from each composer's life through biographical narrative and selections from works he composed at the time. Much more stimulating than just reading a biography. The following composers are featured in this audio series: Vivaldi and Corelli, Bach, Handel, Haydn, Mozart, Beethoven, Schubert, Berlioz, Mendelssohn, Schuman and Grieg, Chopin, Verdi, Wagner, Strauss, Foster and Sousa, Brahms, Tchaikovsky, and Dvorak.

The Cornerstone Curriculum Project offers a full, four year music curriculum consisting of biographical narrative and representative music of the great composers entitled *Music and Moments with the Masters.* (See resource section.) This curriculum utilizes the CDs mentioned above as well as offers a study guide to enhance the program.

The *Famous Children Series*, by Ann Rachlin and illustrated by Susan Hellard, focuses on the childhood and early musical training of famous composers including: Bach, Beethoven, Brahms, Chopin, Handel,

Haydn, Mozart, Schubert, Schumann, and Tchaikovsky. My daughter, Mandy, read these biographies again and again. You can locate these biographies by looking up the author's name in the library catalogue.

The Way Things Work, by David Macaulay, offers several sections beneficial to this musical study: Sound and Music, Sound Waves, Amplifier, Electric Guitar, and Musical Instruments. He uses clever drawings and simple text to familiarize us with woodwind, brass, string and percussion instruments. (Watch out. If Dad gets a hold of this book the kids may never see it again!)

Another well written book is *The Gift of Music - Great Composers and Their Influence*, by Jane Stuart Smith and Betty Carlson. This book is written from a Christian perspective and contains an enlightening preface by Francis Schaeffer.

I do not suggest purchasing every, or even most, of the items listed. If your budget allows I think some of these will add an exciting dimension to your study. The library is a valuable source for recordings of selections by various composers. The value of purchasing your own cassettes or CDs is their availability. The narratives of the composers' lives are also helpful.

This study has far more educational benefits than first meets the eye. Geography and history take on a new perspective when viewed through the eyes of the great composers. It is evident that many publishers are turning once again to the study of music and composers, as many products are now available for educational use.

If you or your children play a musical instrument, this unit is a natural. Use these talents to enrich your unit. Several of the biographies by Opal Wheeler contain music by the representative composer. Perhaps your family can attend a classical concert in your area. Video tapes and television broadcasts offer another avenue for viewing and listening to concerts.

Writing assignments naturally flow from this study as the children are inspired to write while listening to the works of the great artists. Interesting passages from the composers' biographies can be copied or taken from dictation. Selections by favorite composers set the mood for children to create visual works of art. Use your imagination and make this unit enjoyable. Remember, it is best to keep things simple and concentrate on one or two composers at a time. You may also choose to study only one section of the orchestra for each unit. Later, when you choose to study one or two more composers, you can investigate another section of the orchestra. The key to a successful unit is simplicity. Simplicity affords the children better retention, less adult stress, and therefore greater enjoyment for all!

The Impressionists Unit

*T*he impressionists were different from the painters before them. They often left their studios and painted out of doors. They were concerned with capturing the passing moment to create an "impression" of what they saw. The impressionists put the colors on in little dashes and dots. They concentrated a great deal on light and how it made objects look different at different times of the day. They simply tried to spontaneously depict the world around them.

Several years ago I was taking an art class at a nearby college. Our assignment had been to do a detailed charcoal pencil drawing of a landscape. I drew a picture of a park with lots of trees. After looking at my picture, the teacher gave me a fat piece of wet charcoal and a cup of water for dipping. He asked me to use the wet charcoal to recreate in ten minutes what it had taken me four hours to accomplish. Upon completion of my picture he was very pleased and said I had captured the feeling of the landscape much better the second time. He put that picture in the school art show. It was a type of impressionistic expression. Impressionism conveys feelings. Impressionism may not be your favorite style of art, but it is certainly interesting and worth looking at. The paintings reproduced on the front and back covers of *Unit Studies Made Easy* are impressionistic paintings by Liz Ann Alvarez.

Library Books

Pierre-Auguste Renoir, by Ernest Raboff. Raboff, an artist himself, is well known for guiding children through the world of art and artists. *Young People's Story of Fine Arts: The Last Two Hundred Years*, by V.M. Hillyer. This is now out-of-print, but many libraries still own copies. There are a number of other titles in the "Young People's Story" series. If you come across any at a used book sale be sure to buy them. *Famous Painting: An Introduction to Art*, by Alice Elizabeth Chase, is an excellent choice for a beginning student for art appreciation. *Great Painters*, by Piero Ventura, is a very thorough yet uncomplicated treatment of fine art. Ventura uses his own artistic talents, particularly cartoon-like pictures to tell the story of the great masters. He includes narrative about the masters and their masterpieces. These books can be used for other fine arts studies as well.

The Impressionist Revolution, by Howard Greenfeld, focuses on Monet, Sisley, and Pissarro. This is a text for the more serious art appreciation student. *Mary Cassatt*, by Nancy Mowll Mathews, contains beautiful photographs of the works of Cassatt. *Renoir*, by Bruno F. Schneider. This book contains beautiful color photographs of Renoir's works. *Degas*, by Edward Huttinger. The works of Degas are depicted in appealing color photographs. *Monet at Giverny*, published by Mathews Miller Dunbar. Includes photographs of Monet's paintings as well as photographs of his family, home, and elaborate garden. *The*

Impressionists, by Michael Wilson. Contains reproductions of the works of many of the impressionists. The text is lengthy, however. ***Children in the World's Art***, by Marion Downer. Written in a clear simple style, this book focuses on the works of Degas, Cassatt, Renoir, and other artists who used children as their subjects.

Books and Other Materials

Cornerstone Curriculum Project offers a fine art curriculum entitled, *Adventures in Art*. There are several titles in the Ernest Raboff series of artist biographies. Most of these are out-of-print but are available through used book sources. Fine art prints can be ordered directly from the Washington, National Gallery of Art. (See address in resource section.)

The following books are story books relating to one of the great impressionistic masters. ***Linnea in Monet's Garden***, by Cristina Bjork is told from the view point of a young girl, Linnea. Her story is like a scrapbook, reliving a trip she took to Paris and Giverny to learn about Monet's water-lily paintings. ***Degas and the Little Dancer: A Story about Edgar Degas***; ***The Magical Garden of Claude Monet***; and ***Camille and the Sunflowers: A Story About Vincent Van Gogh***, all by Laurence Anholt. ***Katie Meets the Impressionists***, by James Mayhew. ***Once upon a Lily Pad: Froggy Love in Monet's Garden***, by Joan Sweeney. ***Suzette and the Puppy: A Story About Mary Cassatt***, by Joan Sweeney.

Discovering Great Artists: Hands-On Art for Children in the Styles of the Great Masters, published by Bright Ideas for Learning, by MaryAnn F. Kohl, offers 110 art activities for children to experience the styles and techniques of the great masters from Renaissance to the present.

For this unit I have chosen to focus on four of the impressionists. Units become complicated if we try to concentrate on too much at once. Even though we are concentrating on Renoir, Degas, Monet, and Cassatt, we come in contact with many others as we study these people's lives and view the works of many of the impressionists in the library books.

The French Impressionists formed a fellowship and jointly exhibited their works. After some time, they recruited an American woman to exhibit with them. Her name was Mary Cassatt, a great admirer of Degas. Later she was instrumental in gaining American support for Impressionist painting. Mary excelled at painting domestic subjects, mothers with their children, and young girls. This is why I find her work fascinating and an excellent choice for study.

It is often interesting to select a reproduction of a painting by Cassatt from a library book and create a story to accompany it. I find her paintings of mothers and their children particularly well suited for this purpose.

Edgar Degas, unlike his Impressionist contemporaries, showed a partiality to unnatural colors. He used gray and brown to convey dingy urban life and pinks and purples created by theater lighting. Other Impressionists used only colors that appear in nature. Degas painting centered on all aspects of Parisian life: circuses, racetracks, dance halls, the theater, and of course the ballet. His paintings of the ballet are most appealing. Boys would probably be more interested in his horse race paintings and drawings.

Pierre-Auguste Renoir predominately painted human subjects. He incorporated children, beautiful women, and festive groups into his paintings. He is well remembered for his lovely painting of a "Child with Watering Can." Another favorite of mine is "Girl with a Hoop." As you view the works of the various artists, allow your children to select a favorite painting and share with the family why he or she likes it. Have the child read the history of the chosen work, and present this information to the family as if he were a guide at an art gallery. Look for as many details as possible when observing the paintings. What can you conclude about the people in the picture? Are they happy, sad, confused, angry, or exuberant? Using a thesaurus, try to find a variety of words that describe the painting, focusing on the people, objects, background, and overall tone of the painting.

Every time we mention Monet, my children make some comment about his lily pond. He frequently used his garden at Giverny for his paintings. Monet is noted for having painted haystacks as well. This may seem an odd subject for painting, but Monet was seeking to capture the effects of light at different times of the day. He painted fifteen pictures of the same haystack. He painted twenty pictures of the front of a French cathedral at various times of day and each picture was different. Monet was not necessarily interested in the shape or form of an object, but in the light and color that could transform an object. Compare Monet's paintings with the other Impressionists. Did they all paint like Monet? Have your children make a list of some of the similarities and differences they note in paintings by each artist. Encourage them to note variations and likenesses in subject matter, mood, color, light, seasons, time of day, location, and so forth. You do not have to be an art expert to be observant and have an opinion.

In any art study you pursue, you will encounter the human form. The human figure has been a subject of continuous study throughout time. Many of the great masters have tried to capture the grace and perfection of the human body, and often of the nude form. For this reason please use discretion when allowing your children to freely look through books with art reproductions.

Additional Activities

Using library books such as *Young People's Story of Fine Art*; *Famous Paintings: An Introduction to Art for Young Readers*; *Great Painters*; or books in the *Ernest Raboff Series*, read information about the artists and works being studied. Have your children copy or take from dictation pertinent information about each artist.

Incorporate writing skills into your unit as your children record observations of selected works of the artists they are investigating. Locate the artist's native country on a map. As you read, you should discover some general information about the political climate in which they lived. How did this affect their work? Use some of the more technical library books offering high quality reproductions of the various artists' works. The books located in the fine arts section of the public library often have a better and larger selection of artists' works than those in the children's section. Occasionally read brief passages from these texts, but do not allow yourself to get bogged down with too much technical information.

Remember to keep the unit simple, stress free, interesting, and therefore truly educational. Buy some water-based paints — preferably acrylics — and allow your children to experiment, seeing if they can capture the impressionistic style on canvas. The children may choose to paint from real life, preferably outdoors or in a bright, naturally-lighted room. They may want to copy one of their favorite paintings. The great masters have been copied time and time again by many an aspiring art student. It is this same concept of copying well-written literature that provides us with an excellent model for our composition exercises. Mom and Dad must also try the paint and brush. You are never too old to learn and have fun!

I suggest buying paints in tubes, whether acrylics, oils, or water colors. Jars and bottles of paint have a short shelf life, and they are very messy. Boxed sets of watercolors quickly turn to "mud." I prefer to use water-based acrylic paints. Acrylics are thick enough to add texture to the children's paintings, but they clean up easily with water. Acrylics can also be thinned with water to produce a water-color effect. A nickel-sized dab of each color on a piece of aluminum foil or on a Styrofoam plate will suffice for each child. Purchase a variety of brushes. It pays to invest in middle-of-the-line brushes.

Canvases are not cheap, so canvas paper in a pad will do nicely at first; however, any art quality paper may be used with acrylics. Acrylics done on canvas have the "look" of an oil painting. Water color paints do better with water color paper. Oil paint works best with canvas paper, canvas board, or stretch canvas.

Make fine art a regular part of your yearly studies. Like music, art serves to stimulate our creativity and helps us appreciate the creative beings that we are, fashioned in the image of the Supreme Creator.

The Painters of the American Revolution Unit

*T*his unit focuses on four great painters who lived during the Revolutionary Era. These individuals made artistic contributions which aided in the historic documentation of this era. The four painters are: Benjamin West, John Singleton Copley, Charles Wilson Peale, and Gilbert Stuart. Many other artists' works and lives are reviewed as well, but on a lesser scale.

Library Books

Benjamin West and His Cat Grimalkin, by Marguerite Henry is an excellent book. We all enjoyed it so much! *The Boy Who Loved to Draw: Benjamin West*, by Barbara Brenner, illustrated by Olivier Dunrea is a pleasing picture book. *Copley*, by Elizabeth Ripley. *The Pantheon Story of American Art for Young People*, by Ariane Ruskin Batterberry and Michael Batterberry. *American Adventures*, by Elizabeth Coatsworth. In particular, we read the section entitled, *Boston Bells*, a story about Copley. *Painter of Patriots, Charles Wilson Peale*, by Catherine Owens Peare. *The Art of Colonial America*, by Shirley Glubok. *The Art of the New American Nation*, by Shirley Glubok. Look in the fine arts section of your library for books with reproductions of paintings by the four artists mentioned above. Several of the books I have suggested include works by these artists.

To help fill in background material for this unit, we also read a number of other books about individuals who lived in America during the Revolutionary Era. Most of these books were read at bedtime or breakfast. *Carry on, Mr. Bowditch*, by Jean Lee Latham. *Boat Builder*, by Clara Judson is the story of Robert Fulton. *Patrick Henry, Firebrand of the Revolution*, by Nardi Reeder Campion.

Language Arts

This unit requires a lot of reading aloud with your children, and the biographies are entertaining. Since these biographies are filled with dialogue, they are very good for dictation or copying exercises. This gives your children practice with using quotation marks and beginning a new line when a new character speaks. Use this opportunity to allow capable children to read aloud from the biographies. Younger children may narrate a portion of what has been read. This is a great activity for them as it builds vocabulary, expression, and retention of the material being read.

Once you have finished reading a biography, the front inside jacket flap makes an excellent selection for your children to copy or take from dictation as it encapsulates the book. Ask your children to write a summary that they would include in the front of the book if they were publishing it. Maybe they feel that some other information should have been added or that some information should have been deleted.

Allow your children to look at the reproductions of the artwork in the library books. Read about the history surrounding the individual paintings. Ask your children to examine a painting done by one of the artists you are studying. Give them two minutes to examine the painting. Then have them make a list of all the things they remember from the painting. This list may include, people, things, places, colors, feelings expressed, and so on. After doing this activity a few times, you can have your children make columns on their papers with headings for nouns, adjectives, and adverbs. Then they can write words describing the painting in the proper columns. Encourage your children to be more descriptive with each assignment. Later, see if your children can relate the story behind the paintings.

Art

Read an account of an historic event from the Revolutionary time period. Have your children illustrate this event with colored pencils, crayons, acrylic paints, watercolors, markers, or pastels. Then have them give their paintings a title.

GENERAL KNOWLEDGE

Our lives were touched in a significant way through this study. Prepare to be blessed!

Videos

Sign Language for Everyone, by Cathy Rice, includes a 170 page hard back book. This is the video series we used several years ago. Timberdoodle and Lifetime Books and Gifts offer a sign language curriculum entitled, *Signs for His Glory*, in which each lesson centers on a character quality. In this program Jennifer Lamp teaches over 500 signs through the use of two videos and workbooks designed for three age levels.

Public libraries often have sign language videos available. Check with a deaf service center in your area. They usually offer basic signing courses to the public for a nominal fee.

Books

The Joy of Signing, by Lottie Riekehof. Available at Christian book stores. *Sign Language for Everyone*, by Cathy Rice. (The book may be purchased separately from the video tape.) *Hue and Cry*, by Elizabeth Yates, is a fictional story that takes place in New Hampshire in the 1830's. Jared Austin, a faithful member of the mutual protection society that defends his community against thieves, struggles to temper justice with mercy when his deaf daughter, Melody, befriends an Irish immigrant youth who has stolen a horse. *Amelia Lends a Hand*, by Marissa Moss. When she learns her new neighbor is deaf, Amelia sets to learning sign language.

Library Books

I Have a Sister — My Sister is Deaf, by Jeanne W. Peterson. This book is illustrated with soft charcoal drawings and provides information on how the deaf compensate. Truly a heart warming text offering a perceptive portrait of a young deaf child. *Anna's Silent World,* by Bernard Wolf. Six-year-old Anna was born deaf. She receives special training in lip-reading and the use of hearing aids. Also available in Spanish, *Ana Y Su Mondo de Silencio. American Sign Language Dictionary*, by Martin Sternberg, contains over 7000 signs and 12,000 illustrations.

A Story of Nim: The Chimp Who Learned Language, by Anna Michel. This book has large print, easy text, and photographs. *Exploring Mime*, by Mark Stolzenberg. *Mandy*, by Barbara D. Booth. A sensitive story about a young deaf girl who does not like to go out at night because she can not read lips or signs in the dark. *The Way Things Work,* by David Macaulay. Among many other topics, this book contains interesting and informative material about sound and the ear. *Presenting Reader's Theater: Plays and Poems to Read Aloud*, by Caroline Feller Bauer. A collection of over 50 read-aloud scripts. A short but informative section is included on mime on pages 14 and 15. Select a few plays and have the children mime appropriate parts. Another book of interest is entitled *Mime Ministry*, by Susan K. Toomey.

Introduction

Quoting from the 1991 Timberdoodle catalog:

Just between us...Did you know that the population of the hearing impaired in the United States alone, is nearly equal to the entire population of Canada? If you find that fact as staggering as we did, then you'll readily see that there may be no more practical second language for your family to master. Plus, American Sign Language fulfills a foreign language requirement in many states!

Terminology

American Sign Language, Manually Coded English, Finger spelling, Manual Alphabet, Pidgin Sign English, Sign Language, Deaf Persons, Hard of Hearing Persons, Gestuno, etc.

Bible

Use a concordance and/or a topical Bible to locate passages dealing with hearing versus understanding. Example:

"You will keep on hearing, but will not understand; And you will keep on seeing, but will not perceive; For the heart of this people has become dull, and with their ears they scarcely hear, and they have closed their eyes lest they should see with their eyes, and hear with their ears, and understand with their heart, and turn again, and I should heal them." Matthew 13:14, 15 (NASV)

Look up other terms in your concordance or topical Bible such as ear, sound, hearers, deafness, etc. Parables are excellent selections for you and your children to pantomime. Remember, no talking allowed. The children have fun guessing which parable is being acted out. Look up pantomime in the dictionary before you begin. You may need to read and review a number of parables before undertaking this endeavor.

Vocabulary

You will begin to build a signing vocabulary, and you can continue to increase your signing vocabulary in units to follow. This will give added dimension to all your units and will build and maintain skills in signing. It is easiest to stick with signs for simple words at first like the names of animals.

Storytelling

Relate short stories using sign language. This is different from pantomime because the story is told using actions and sign language, not actions alone. Signed storytelling videos are often available at colleges, video rental stores, and public libraries. Watch one and see if you can interpret the story.

<u>Arts</u>
Mimes, Clowns
Costumes
History of mime
Slow motion and robot movements
Skit writing

<u>Science</u>
Ear
Larynx
Sound

Hands (Hands play an important role for the deaf person. Signing is also very good for increasing hand coordination and mobility.)

Choose some simple library books that explain about the ear and how it works. David Macaulay's book, *The Way Things Work*, is an excellent choice. Your library probably owns a copy, but it may be located in the adult section. This is a book well worth purchasing as it can be used with almost any unit that relates to science. The pictures are great for those of us who need to see something to understand it. The text is brief yet thorough.

<u>History</u>

The history of signing can be learned by reading biographies.

Gallaudet, Friend of the Deaf, by Etta DeGering and *A Deaf Child Listened*, by Anne E. Neimark, are both excellent biographies of Thomas Hopkins Gallaudet. *Cobblestone: Helen Keller/America's Disabled May 1983* offers interesting details about Helen Keller. *A Picture Book of Helen Keller*, by David A. Adler, is a wonderful introduction to Helen Keller for young children. *The Story of My Life*, by Helen Keller, is incredibly inspiring. (See the section of *Unit Studies Made Easy* entitled *For the Love of Reading*, for suggestions for using Helen's autobiography.) Childhood of Famous American series: *Helen Keller: From Tragedy to Triumph* is a favorite at our house.

Middle Ages: Monks during this era used signing when they took a vow of silence. Early Bibles have been found with signs drawn in them.

<u>Music</u>

Today we find more interest in signed interpretation of music. This portrays lyrics, rhythm, and emotions of songs. This form of expression helps deaf people and hearing people to enjoy and experience music together.

<u>Language Arts</u>

Give your children a spelling test and have them fingerspell the words. Fingerspell words for your children and have them write these words as you spell them. Write skits to be performed by pantomime. Dictate or copy selections from the books you have chosen. Write a letter using pictures of signs to convey your message. Write a description of a fair, carnival, or some other usually noisy affair from the perspective of a deaf child. Write a letter to the organizations listed below for information about deafness.

Activities

Visit a nursing home and communicate with the deaf patients. They are happy even if you only fingerspell with them. Have your children sign a song or a Bible verse for them. Choose their best pantomime of a parable and have the children act it out.

Let signing be the only communication between you and your children for a specified length of time. Try 30 minutes. It is interesting to see how they try to get your attention and how frustrated they become when they can not easily do it. Discuss how discouraging it might be at times for deaf children to live in a world of silence.

Have children draw the hand positions to spell their names. A good reference book for this activity is *The Handmade Alphabet*, by Laura Rankin.

Sources for Information

Gallaudet University
800 Florida Avenue, N.E.
Washington, DC 20002
www.gallaudet.edu

Registry of Interpreters for the Deaf, Inc.
333 Commerce Street
Alexandria, VA 22314
www.rid.org

I decided it was time for each of my children to plan a unit that appealed to their individual tastes. We spent a week discussing choices while finishing up another unit. They changed their minds several times during the week of discussion. I explained why some units would be more difficult than others, and that some topics needed to be narrowed down as they were too general. Once they made up their minds, we visited the public library. I helped each child search for appropriate books. Yes, this did take time. We spent over three hours. You must realize, however, that I was helping four children hunt for books, and our busy two-year-old was also "helping." This was before our library catalog was available on computer. Now it is much easier to research a topic. The internet has also opened up new avenues for research.

Kids Create a Unit

Civil War Unit

Michelle, my oldest daughter, chose to study the Civil War time period. Her fascination with the clothing of that time enticed her to make that era her topic of study. One of the books relating to clothing that she chose was *Corsets and Crinolines*, by Norah Waugh. Another was *Uniforms of the Civil War*, by Francis A. Lord and Arthur Wise. For her project, she made a dress from that era. (Eventually she made costumes from this era for all her siblings!)

Other selected books: *The Art of America from Jackson to Lincoln*, by Shirley Glubok. *I Varina, A Biography of the Girl Who Married Jefferson Davis and Became the First Lady of the South*, by Ruth Painter Randall. *Abraham Lincoln*, by Ingri and Edgar Parin D' Aulaire. *Ulysses S. Grant, Encyclopedia of Presidents*, by Zachary Kent. *America's Robert E. Lee*, by Henry Steele Commager, illustrated by Lynd Ward.

I read *Invincible Louisa*, by Cornelia Meigs to my older girls. This is the Newbery Award Winning biography of Louisa May Alcott, the author of *Little Women, Little Men*, and many other titles. Louisa lived during the Civil War era and served as a nurse in a Union hospital for a short time. Her relationships with wounded soldiers spurred her to write articles for a newspaper concerning their lives, which were later published under the title *Hospital Sketches*. Miss Alcott was acquainted with Ralph Waldo Emerson, Henry Thoreau, and Henry Wadsworth Longfellow. Reading the writings of some of these men added a literary flair to the study.

My daughter selected several fictional books based on true accounts from the Civil War. *Phantom of the Blockade*, by Stephen Meader. *Across Five Aprils*, by Irene Hunt. *North by Night*, by Peter Burchard. *Uncle Tom's Cabin*, by Harriet Beecher Stowe. *Rifles for Watie*, by Harold Keith. (Newbery Award Book.) *Freedom Crossing*, by Margaret Goff Clark. Two fictional books relative to this time period were purchased from a Christian book distributor. They were *The Dixie Widow* and *The Last Confederate*, both by Gilbert Morris. (These are books eight and nine in the Winslow series.)

As we began to investigate this era, we realized we could study for several months, even years! The main emphasis was to become acquainted with this time period, and in the future more in depth studies would prevail.

One important thing to realize when undertaking a study like this is that when you read the biography of one individual, many individuals are brought to light as they interact with the biographee. It is not necessary to read dozens of biographies for each unit you pursue.

My daughter also checked out a video on the Civil War. Each day

Michelle read from a selected book and wrote a paper concerning her findings. Some days this was a summary of what had been read, and other days this was a selection she chose to copy from one of the books. Each evening she would share some interesting bit of information with the family.

For her project, she chose to make a dress from the time period. Initially she wrote to a historical pattern company seeking information. After receiving the pattern, she selected fabric and began to make the dress. She even made wire hoops! (The historical pattern was ordered from Amazon Dry Goods. See resource section.)

For another project Michelle wrote a simple, fictional play situated in the South during the Civil War. This play was based on the book, **Freedom Crossing**, by Margaret Goff Clark. She made full color plates depicting the costumes of each character. She designed the clothes using costume books from the library and an Amazon Dry Goods catalog.

I feel that this study is a good example of how a specific unit can be tailored to fit a student's interests. Most of the library books were located by using the subject card catalog. Others were found by using a reference book entitled **American Historical Fiction and Biographies for Children and Young People**, by Jeanette Hotchkiss.

Dolls and Stuffed Toys Unit

My next daughter, Melissa, chose to undertake a unit on dolls and stuffed toys. She selected some books on making dolls, doll houses, and stuffed toys. She also chose some storybooks relating to those topics. She decided to study A.A. Milne's *Winnie-the-Pooh* books in particular. The following are titles of the books Melissa chose: *William's Doll*, by Charlotte Zolotow. *Dollhouse Mouse*, by Natalie Standiford. *Bear and Mrs. Duck*, by Elizabeth Winthrop. *Katherine's Doll*, by Elizabeth Winthrop. *The Best-Loved Doll*, by Rebecca Caudill. *Satchelmouse and the Doll's House*, by Antonia Barber. *Winnie-the-Pooh, The House at Pooh Comer, The World of Pooh*, and *The Pooh Storybook*, by A.A. Milne. She also read a biography of A.A. Milne.

Edith and the Bears, *A Gift From the Lonely Doll*, and *The Lonely Doll*, all by Dare Wright. *Making Your Own Toys*, by Pamela Peake. *Dolls and Toys from A to Z*, by McCall's Needleworks and Crafts. *Creative Soft Toy Making*, by Pamela Peake. *Dollhouse Magic*, by P.K. Roche. *Dollhouse People*, by Tracy Pearson. *The Pooh Craft Book*, by Carol Friedrichsen. *Hittie, Her First Hundred Years*, by Rachel Fields. She also located a number of story books about dolls by Rumer Godden including: *The Story of Holly and Ivy*, *Four Dolls*, *The Doll's House*, and *Impunity Jane: The Story of a Pocket Doll*. She enjoyed these books the most.

Melissa chose to make a stuffed doll. She selected a pattern from a library book and used graphing techniques to enlarge the pattern. She calculated the amount of material needed and purchased it. After she made the doll, she wrote and illustrated a book featuring the doll as the main character. She also wrote each day from the books she read and shared information from her studies with the family. Melissa typed the front jacket flap information from each library book. She maintained a folder with the information from each book she read.

I was amazed at how many research skills Melissa gained as she searched for materials for this unit. She learned to read the front and back book flaps, bibliographies, and summaries of each book as she found these often contained information that lead her to other materials. Often these materials were not in our library, so she requested interlibrary loans to obtain the books from other libraries within our state library system. Later, she was able to transfer the research skills she learned to other areas of study.

My younger boys, Robert and Raymond, decided to conduct a unit together. They chose construction. Since my boys are only 8 and 6 years old, we did not study this topic in great detail. We selected some simple books for Robert to read to Raymond and me. Other books were chosen primarily for their illustrations.

Library Books

Round Buildings, Square Buildings, & Buildings That Wiggle Like a Fish, by Philip M. Isaacson. *Stone and Steel*, by Guy Billout. *Tunnels*, *Up Goes the Skyscraper!*, and *Tool Book*, all by Gail Gibbons. *Towers and Bridges* including simple experiments, by Julie Fitzpatrick. *Pyramid*, *Castle*, *Cathedral*, and *City*, all by David Macaulay. Our library has the video *Castle*, based on Macaulay's book. *The Ultimate Wood Block Book*, by Sam Bingham. *What It Feels Like to Be a Building*, by Forest Wilson.

We purchased an impressive book called *The Art of Construction, Projects and Principles for Beginning Engineers and Architects*, by Mario Savadori. Even I was able to understand the principles described in this book. It includes projects that use ice cream sticks, paper, string, and paper clips to demonstrate construction principles. My husband and I read selections from this book to the boys.

Robert read the simpler books, like those by Gail Gibbons, to Raymond and me. Then I asked the boys questions concerning these books. I chose sentences for them to copy. They circled the phonics rules in each word and we discussed these rules along with pertinent punctuation and capitalization rules.

The boys looked for examples of the construction principles we studied in things around us. For example, they looked for triangles in objects. Triangular formations give a structure support. They found some of these formations under the seats of chairs, on the bottom of stools, in bicycle frames, in the swing set, and in roof trusses.

My boys really enjoy playing with Lego blocks, which fit right in with their studies! Robert and Raymond each dictated a story to me that was in some way related to building. Robert's story was entitled, *The Tiny Builders*, and Raymond's story was called, *How to Build a Castle*. Each day I would neatly write out several sentences from their stories and the boys would copy them, read those portions aloud to me, and circle the phonics rules in each word. It was through this process that my younger son, Raymond, began to show a great improvement in his reading ability. He was certainly pleased with himself.

Take some time out to allow your children to create their own units. The experience will be both educational and rewarding.

Acknowledgements

Portions taken from the preface to **Famous Men of Greece** and **The Greenleaf Guide to Ancient Egypt**, page 4, are used with permission by Greenleaf Press, Lebanon, Tennessee.

Portions taken from **The Institutes for Biblical Law**, page 262, are used with permission by Ross House Books, P.O. Box 67, Vallecito, California, 95251.

Portions taken from **Scientific Creationism**, page 18 are used with permission by the Institute for Creation Research.

Portions taken from **Exploring Your World: The Adventures of Geography**, page 148 are used with permission by the National Geographic Society.

Portions in the Introduction of the Sign Language Unit are taken from the **1991 Timberdoodle Catalog**. For current Sign Language Materials visit their website at: www.timberdoodle.com.

For the Love of Reading

Valerie Bendt

Dedication

I dedicate this book to my daughter, Melissa, and my mother, Hope Connelly, who both graciously worked on typing the manuscript of this book from my handwritten copy. I know that deciphering my scrawl was not an easy task. Thanks! — V.B. 1994

My children's names and ages at the time of publication (1994) are as follows: Michelle, 14 years old; Melissa, 12 years old; Robert, 10 years old; Raymond, 8 years old; and Mandy, 4 years old.

Table of Contents

Introduction

There are numerous reading programs available to enable you to teach your children to read. These programs vary in content. Some have: workbooks, games, activities, phonetic readers, spoken audio tapes, sing-a-long audio tapes, and teacher's manuals. There are programs to suit most every type of learner. There are programs to suit most every type of instructor. Many of these programs are geared to teach writing, composition, and spelling, too.

In a society where we are inundated with so many reading programs, why am I writing still another book about reading? My desire is to share my experiences in teaching my children to read. I want to show you how you can personalize your reading program so your children not only learn the mechanics of reading, but they develop a love for reading; a love that will cause them to be life-long readers and, therefore, life-long learners.

First, it is my hope that children learn to be expressive and creative at an early age, or rather I should say, that their creativity and expressiveness that are so ripe at an early age be encouraged to blossom rather than be discouraged by too formal and stilted a program. Reading is an important part of our entire lives. Let it be an enjoyable, integral part right from the start.

Reading is an important part of our entire lives. Let it be an enjoyable, integral part right from the start.

Secondly, for those with older children who need to be motivated to read, it is my hope that some of the ideas set forth in this book will provide an avenue by which to nurture the desire to make reading an important part of their lives as well.

Thirdly, it is my hope that the ideas presented in this book will enable you to draw your language arts lessons from the books you share as a family.

2004 note: Since the publication of the first edition of *For the Love of Reading* in 1994, I have written a phonics program entitled *Reading Made Easy: A Guide to Teach Your Child to Read*. Please see pages 333 and 334 for an explanation of this program.

*U*nfortunately, the first child in a family is often taught by the trial and error method. This has been the case with my oldest daughter, Michelle. My husband and I knew we would homeschool our children even before they were born. We did not exactly know how, but we knew in our hearts that it was the best practice for our family. Back in the early days of homeschooling there were few voices offering instruction to parents desiring to homeschool, so we were terribly excited by any materials we could locate on the subject. Through a friend we found out about a Christian correspondence school that would accept homeschooled children. We enrolled Michelle immediately when she reached the acceptable age of four years. I was so excited that she was finally old enough to homeschool. (Years later I realized that I had been successfully homeschooling her before her official enrollment. After the enrollment, our methods began to digress.)

I very promptly induced this independent, creative, intelligent child to sit quietly and complete X number of worksheets, in a given period of time, for five days each week. She rebelled almost instantly. "Mommy this is boring. Mommy I know this stuff already." But like the thorough mother that I am, I insisted that she complete *every* page. After all, she might miss a concept or a rule that might tarnish her academically for life!

Now during this time period, I was doing my homework, being careful to learn every phonetic rule. I did not concern myself with math too much because it was a favorite subject of mine, and I had already had several years experience in tutoring children in math. Phonics presented somewhat of a problem, not because I was not a good reader, but because I was not familiar with the rules of the game.

After applying myself diligently to the mastery of the rules, I needed a subject on which to try out this newly acquired knowledge. Naturally, Michelle was my target, but the problem was that by the age of four and a half she was burned out on schoolwork. I can not fully describe what happened as Michelle progressed from age four to four and a half, but the following incident may give you some idea.

As I explained earlier, Michelle is a very creative child. She loves to draw and make things out of paper. One day during her fourth year, she was supposed to be completing her worksheets, and I was rather upset with her because she could not read. After all she was four and a half, and according to the teacher's manual she should have been reading by now! I could see her academic future being washed down the drain. Ready to give up, I left her in the dining room with her pencils, scissors, and paper and decided to read to her little sister, Melissa, who was two and a half years old at the time. Melissa wanted to be read to all of her waking hours, and I decided that this was a comfortable idea since I was pregnant

Unfortunately, the first child in a family is often taught by the trial and error method.

Phonics presented somewhat of a problem, not because I was not a good reader, but because I was not familiar with the rules of the game.

with our third child.

Melissa and I sat in the rocking chair reading in the living room, while Michelle busied herself in the adjacent dining room. Michelle had given up the phonics workbooks in favor of creating dollhouse furnishings from paper. Let me further describe what she was doing. Michelle would draw a figure on her paper, cut it out, fold it, tape the ends, and produce a china hutch, television, chairs, washer and dryer, and so forth.

Meanwhile, Melissa and I were reading. By this time Melissa had learned the alphabet, and now she was working on learning the sounds those letters generally make when used at the beginning of a word (initial consonant sounds). She then progressed to detecting the letter sounds at the end of a word (final consonant sounds). As I read to Melissa, I casually pointed out the letters in some of the words and emphasized their sounds. Next, we worked on short vowel sounds in words like *cat, dog, cup, pig,* and *bed.* Melissa loved this attention and progressed rapidly. (After all, this was really just a game to her.) Michelle was taking all this in from the other room, more extensively than I realized.

I began pointing out more difficult phonetic combinations to Melissa like *bl, cl, fr, tr,* and other blends. Later she was ready for the more complex phonetic sounds like *oo, ow, au,* and *or* that appear in the middle of words. I would say to Melissa, for example, "See this word *f-o-o-d,* well, *oo* says *oo* in this word. The word is *food.*" Then I would point out other *oo* words, still rather casually, as we read along. Days, and probably weeks, passed and each day I would sit and read with Melissa, and Michelle would draw or create something out of paper.

It was not long before Michelle was interrupting as I read with Melissa in the next room; she was shouting out the sounds for the letter combinations that we were reviewing. Melissa was learning to read in a pleasurable relaxed way on Mother's lap, and Michelle was learning to read by eavesdropping! (I am convinced that if your child is having difficulty with a concept, go in the next room, whisper the information, and he will get it!)

This teaching strategy benefited Melissa, Michelle, and me. Melissa wanted to be coddled and read to, Michelle wanted to be free to work with her hands, and I needed to be able to share this new phonetic knowledge that I had acquired with someone!

Things have not changed much through the years in our household. While I am reading aloud to my children, Melissa still wants to look over my shoulder and read along, and Michelle listens better if her hands are busy either drawing or sewing, and I still have a need to share new thoughts and ideas with them. I learned an important lesson 10 years ago from our first schooling experiences; I learned that children are

Melissa was learning to read in a pleasurable relaxed way on Mother's lap, and Michelle was learning to read by eavesdropping!

individuals. They have varying needs, desires, strengths, and weaknesses. I learned to be flexible while still remaining goal oriented. My goals have not varied too much over the years; however, my teaching strategies have varied to fit the needs of my children and our family's situation.

I learned that I could not recreate school in the home effectively and more importantly that I should not! If anything, the schools should be trying to emulate the atmosphere prevalent in the home. I used to look back on the early years of homeschooling and feel a sense of failure. But I have come to look on those years as a growing period — a period of growth and learning for me, my husband, and my children. What is important is that we grow as a family and learn from our experiences.

I would like to relate another situation that occurred while teaching my son Robert to read. When Robert was five years old, I began teaching him to combine letter sounds to form short words like *cat, dog, bit, rug,* and *bell.* After he had fairly mastered some simple words like these, I handed him a small, very easy, phonetically controlled reader. One of the pages in the book read something like, "Hop Fred, hop, hop, hop." He dutifully proceeded to read the book when suddenly he looked at me quite frustrated and said, "Mom, don't you know that people don't really talk like that!"

I was astounded at this five-year-old's perceptiveness, and I decided that I would not offend his intelligence by having him plod through such monotonous books any longer. I said, "Robert, would you like to write your own readers?" He quickly agreed to this, and I immediately asked him to dictate a story to me. Still not sure what was to be the outcome of this, but delighted that he was not going to have to read anymore little readers, Robert began enthusiastically telling me a story.

I carefully wrote each word, inserting proper capitalization and punctuation as I went along, meticulously forming each letter. I had large kindergarten-lined paper on hand, so this is what I used to transcribe his story. After he dictated about 6 or 8 pages to me, I read his story to him, and he drew a picture to accompany his story. Then I handed the papers to him and said, "Now, here is your reader. Read it to me."

Robert exclaimed, "Why, I can't read that! It's too hard!" I reminded him that he wrote the story, so how could it be too hard for him to read? (Presented in that manner, it did sound logical to him.) He skeptically took the pages from me and slowly began to read the words. Suddenly, the story began to flow more naturally, and a bright smile came over his face. When he reached a difficult word, he managed to decipher it. After all, it was *his* story, so he was familiar with the storyline and the vocabulary. Occasionally, I would help him with a word or two. Robert and I were both so excited that we could hardly contain ourselves. He had progressed in one sitting from reading sentences like, "Hop Fred, hop,

I learned to be flexible while still remaining goal oriented.

I learned that I could not recreate school in the home effectively and more importantly that I should not!

hop, hop," to reading sentences like, "The knight lived in the dazzling castle on the hill."

Our excitement was contagious, and Raymond, who was only three years old at the time, was anxious to "tell Mommy a story, too." I carefully wrote out Raymond's story, and then I read it to him. Afterward, he illustrated his story. I began to see how successful this teaching method could be. In only six months, Robert progressed from reading on a Kindergarten level to reading on a third-grade level. (I confess, I succumbed to temptation and pulled out a third-grade reader which Robert read flawlessly. He also noted that these stories were much more interesting than those in the beginning readers.)

Not only did this simple method of reading instruction produce a terrific reader, it produced two terrific storytellers.

Not only did this simple method of reading instruction produce a terrific reader, it produced two terrific storytellers. Yes, every time Robert dictated a story, little Raymond had to dictate a *longer* story. And out of this love for storytelling arose a desire to make books, real books.

I want to explain that I did continue giving Robert phonics instruction using a manual that supplied me with appropriate exercises. We would spend a short time each week mastering the rules, and the remainder of the time Robert would spend dictating stories and reading them to me.

We also played games to help with difficult sounds. Most of these were card games that I made up, but more recently I have found a book called **Games for Reading**, by Peggy Kaye. This book includes over 75 easy-to-make games that are not only fun to play, but that are beneficial for building the child's vocabulary, for helping him to hear letter sounds more accurately, and for training his eye to see patterns of letters. I find that I am more consistent in using games that I make rather than using purchased games, because I already have time invested in the game. My children seem to appreciate that I have taken the time to make something for them, and many times they are also able to help make the games, which makes them even more valuable!

Games put children in exactly the right frame of mind for learning difficult things. Children throw themselves into playing games the way they never throw themselves into filling out workbook pages. [1]

As Peggy Kaye states:

Games put children in exactly the right frame of mind for learning difficult things. Children throw themselves into playing games the way they never throw themselves into filling out workbook pages. [1]

Combine your favorite reading program with **Games for Reading**, have your child write (dictate) his own readers, and you will have a winning phonics program — a program that encourages creativity and a love for reading!

Robert and Raymond's ability to create stories did not just happen in a day or two. For a number of years my husband, my two older daughters, and I had been reading to them daily. They also listened to stories on audio cassette tapes. Story time was part of our daily routine (and it continues to be). This story time included selections from picture books, novels, biographies, poetry books, Bible stories, the Bible, and numerous other kinds of books. They had assimilated many stories, and when asked to compose stories of their own, they had little trouble. Occasionally, they would be stumped when they could not evoke the right name for a character or place. However, after a little contemplation, they would devise a satisfactory title.

Recently my son Robert, who is now ten years old, was dictating a poem to me for inclusion in one of his most recent books entitled *Fine Art Pictures and Poems*. First, I allowed him to brainstorm, thinking of many words that related to his poem's topic. After compiling a list which he dictated to me, I encouraged him to think of words that rhyme with the words in his list, and I wrote these down also. It was then time for him to compose the poem. We sat for what seemed a very long time with no utterance from Robert. I guess I displayed a sense of annoyance as I told him I would be back after I did some laundry. When I came back, he dictated a simple but excellent poem to accompany his re-creation of Monet's painting entitled, *Houses of Parliament*. Robert's poem reads as follows:

The River Thames

On the quiet River Thames,

The House of Parliament sits,

The fog and bog surrounding it,

Enclosed in gloom and mist.

I was obviously impressed with his poem, and Robert smiled and said, "Now Mom, some things are worth waiting for!" So now when I try to hurry my children or press them too hard, I remember, "There are some things that are worth waiting for!"

A mother who attended one of my seminars related an interesting story to me. She said her family was studying the fruits of the Spirit and her little daughter said, "Mommy, I can tell you all the fruits of the Spirit." She began, "Love, joy, peace, patience, kindness, goodness, hope, gentleness, self-control, and *hurrying*." Her mother was rather astounded and said, "Hurrying?" Her daughter explained, "Oh, yes, I figure that's the most important one because you're always telling us to hurry, hurry!" That mother said that now when she catches herself hurrying her children, she stops and remembers her time with them is really very short, and she must take the time to enjoy them.

They had assimilated many stories, and when asked to compose stories of their own, they had little trouble.

So now when I try to hurry my children or press them too hard, I remember, "There are some things that are worth waiting for!"

We should not be speeding our children on to adulthood, but rather nurturing, loving, and simply enjoying them.

It is important for us to consider these thoughts when teaching our children, whether it is teaching them how to read or how to tie their shoes. We should not be speeding our children on to adulthood, but rather nurturing, loving, and simply enjoying them.

"Children are a gift from the Lord, the fruit of the womb is His reward."

Naturally, very young children seldom have the necessary attention span to sit through an entire book. Even a simple board book may be overwhelming for an adventuresome youngster. Some (like my daughter Melissa) will show an interest in books at an early age, but many are too busy with important matters like building block towers, or more often, un-building (otherwise known as knocking down) block towers built by someone else.

I learned through the years of homeschooling my children how stimulating it is for young children to be present when their older siblings are having their lessons. Often the very young are busy at play while I am reading aloud to the older children. It is amazing to me how much they absorb while I am reading, even though they are not planted next to me on the sofa. We often think that the children must be sitting close by with eyes fastened to us or the book. (Remember the incident I related earlier about Michelle learning to read by overhearing?)

Last spring I was preparing for a workshop detailing a sign language unit study we had done the year before. My daughter, Mandy, who was three and a half years old at the time, accompanied me to the library to select books to use during my presentation. As I pulled a copy of **The Story of My Life**, by Helen Keller, from the shelf, Mandy looked at the photograph on the cover and exclaimed, "That's Helen Keller. You read that book to us." I was astonished at this remark, for Mandy was only two and a half years old when I read the book to my children!

Mandy has absorbed much information by being in the room during schooling hours. Her experiences are not confined to traditional preschool lessons, but to real literature, history, science, math, and so on. Preschool subjects are taught naturally through daily life experiences. Mandy did not complete a series of worksheets on squares to learn about squares. Squares and other preschool topics were a part of her real world.

People sometimes ask, "What type of kindergarten program do you have planned for Mandy?" Well, she already enjoys sign language, spouting off definitions for Greek and Latin roots, learning about electricity and magnetism, dictating and illustrating stories (her art work is somewhat non-descript as she spent too much time studying Picasso), "typing" on the computer, learning about Ancient Egypt, and more. I guess she will keep on learning right along with the rest of the family!

Mandy did not have much of an interest in the alphabet in printed form before age four, but she was very intrigued by the manual sign alphabet. Now as I sign the alphabet, she can say the names for each letter that I sign, regardless of the order in which I sign them. I initially taught her the *ABC* song, signing each letter as I sang the names for the letters. Recently she has begun making the signs for the letters with her own chubby hands. It may seem unusual, but she has learned the manual sign

I learned through the years of homeschooling my children how stimulating it is for young children to be present when their older siblings are having their lessons.

Mandy has absorbed much information by being in the room during schooling hours. Her experiences are not confined to traditional preschool lessons, but to real literature, history, science, math, and so on.

alphabet before learning the printed form. The printed form will be mastered later. Incidentally, I am using her knowledge of the manual sign alphabet to teach her the printed letters and their sounds. (I do not recommend this procedure for all children, but I mention it to emphasize that it is beneficial to use a child's interests to teach him basic skills.)

All my children have learned their alphabet with help from **Dr. Seuss's ABC** book. (We are presently on our second copy.) Now as I read this book with Mandy, I make the letter sign with my right hand and point with my left hand to the corresponding letter on the page. Then Mandy proudly tells me the letter's name printed on the page. One evening I told Mandy that we need to read **Dr. Seuss's ABC** book everyday and practice her letters and that soon she will be able to read. She said, "You mean I will be able to read all by myself?" I told her that she would if we really worked at it. Well, early the next morning while I was still asleep, Mandy brought me her *ABC* book and wanted to read it! This was a good sign that Mandy was ready to begin some simple phonics instruction in a fun, non-stressful manner. (I've found many of the suggestions in **Games for Reading**, by Peggy Kaye, are appropriate for Mandy at this stage.)

Mandy has recently reached the point where she loves to sit while I read to her. She does not have to busy herself "undoing" what someone else has just finished "doing." She also enjoys "reading" to me. She will take a favorite book that is partially or completely memorized and "read" it to me. It is special when Mandy invents her own story to accompany the illustrations in a book. On a recent visit to the library, we saw three little girls about Mandy's age sitting at a small table. Mandy pulled up a chair and began "reading" them a story from a book she had not seen before. The little girls sat mesmerized as she wove her tale. Mandy had a captive audience and she loved it. When the children's father asked if he could read them a book, they all responded with, "No, no! We want Mandy to read us another story!"

All of the processes I have mentioned are paving the way for Mandy to learn to really read. Let us review these pre-reading processes. First when she was very young, Mandy played nearby while I read to the other children. Then as her attention span increased, she sat, looked, and listened (and commented) while I read to her. (Even when Mandy was an infant we read baby board books.) Then Mandy "read" to me and created her own stories. We have always made books available for her to freely look through, and we have also always insisted that she have a respect for books and not destroy them. Now she is learning the names for the letters of the alphabet and the sounds they generally make.

Earlier this year, Mandy dictated and illustrated her first book entitled **Brown Bear Gets Lost**. My four older children also made books during the same time period. Mandy was thrilled that she was actually making a real book, too. She had often looked at the books her siblings had previously made. (For information on *Creating Books with Children* see page 331.)

Mandy dictated her story to me over the course of three days. Initially I wrote the story in longhand and then my daughter, Melissa, typed it into the computer. Each day Mandy made an illustration to be included in her book. I taught her to draw a bear by making a series of circles with her pencil. Then she colored her pictures. Once the illustrations were complete and the text was printed on the pages, Mandy helped me glue the pages and sew the book binding.

Afterward we made a book jacket which Mandy illustrated. This book jacket contains a front flap with information about the book and a back flap with information about the author/illustrator. My boys dictated the information for their book jacket flaps to me as I sat at the computer, and Mandy "typed" on another computer, listening to every word they uttered. (She was probably "typing" what they were saying.)

Then it was Mandy's turn to dictate her passages to be used for her book jacket flaps. She was excited to tell about herself as her brothers had done. She even understood, without my explanation, that the back jacket flap was to read as if someone other than the author had written it. She was copying or mimicking what she had heard her brothers say, and she was applying it to herself. (Children often do this while engaged in a pretend conversation on the telephone.) This is the passage she dictated to me concerning herself, the author/illustrator.

> *Mandy is three years old, and she likes to ride her bike, read books, and "type" on the computer. She loves hamsters and birds. Mandy likes bears and dolls too. This is Mandy's first book and she wants to write some more books soon.*

I then added:

Mandy is the youngest of five children.

Well, I had typed what Mandy dictated, printed it, pasted it on the back inside flap of her book jacket, and she was *still* telling me all about herself! She then asked, "Mommy, did you get all that?" I explained that she would have to write an autobiography next!

Raymond, who turned eight years old this summer, made great progress in his reading abilities as we were making books. The children spent a week getting their basic stories written or dictated. As Raymond dictated his story for his book, I typed it into the computer. Then each day we began with Raymond reading aloud the portion of his story that he had dictated to me the day before. The benefits of this were twofold as it served as a review of what Raymond had previously dictated, which

The benefits of this were twofold as it served as a review of what Raymond had previously dictated, which enabled him to logically begin the next episode of his story, and it served as an enticing reader which kept his interest, challenged him sufficiently, but did not overwhelm him.

enabled him to logically begin the next episode of his story, and it served as an enticing reader which kept his interest, challenged him sufficiently, but did not overwhelm him. Once again, as I mentioned earlier when relaying a similar experience with my oldest son Robert, the student was not overburdened with deciphering and following a storyline. Decoding was less difficult due to familiarity with the vocabulary, the child's own spoken vocabulary, and the storyline was naturally interpreted as it was created by the child.

Some children, like my son Raymond, have a natural ability to tell stories. Raymond's difficulty usually lies in his inability to *end* a story. His imagination seems to run away with him. But, there are children who find it troublesome to develop a story of their own. This is where the narration method for mastering composition is extremely useful. Read a story to your child, have him orally narrate the story while you write it down, and then allow him to use his own version of the story as a reader. (You might find that you will be more successful if you tape the narration, and then transcribe it.)

As I explained in the previous chapter, the story flow and vocabulary are familiar, thus there is less difficulty with decoding than with an unfamiliar story. This method also gives the child practice with developing a story without the burden of creating characters and plot. By this simple narration process, he makes the story his own.

I received a letter from a mother who used my book, **Creating Books with Children**, to lead her children in making books. Her older child had no difficulty in developing a story, but her younger child was stumped as to what to write. I had mentioned that in devising a story, a child might retell a favorite Bible story. So this mother asked her son, "What's your favorite story?" He chose the story about David and Goliath. She proceeded to read him the story a few times, reading several different versions, and then she asked him to retell the well-loved Bible story. As he dictated, the mother wrote her son's own words. This transcription became his story, and he made illustrations to accompany it.

This simple process will probably contribute more toward building that child's future ability to read and write on his own than any number of teacher contrived worksheets. Often a child can decode words far above his typical grade level, but cannot put a simple story in his own words or compose a few sentences representing his own thoughts.

Young children can successfully be encouraged to narrate storybooks containing lots of illustrations. After the story has been read, once or twice, the children can narrate the story by following the pictures. This helps them to keep events in their proper sequence. Older children will also find this beneficial if they are having difficulty with narration.

Initially, if the older children's narration is based on a long book, have them narrate each chapter as it is read aloud. (The difficulty of the book to be narrated can be determined by the ability of the children to comprehend the story as it is read aloud.)

Later, written narration should be encouraged as well as oral narration of material that is read aloud. Sufficient practice with oral narration at a young age will greatly facilitate the ability of a child to give a written narration when he is older. It is important that oral narration be

Narration: The Simple Yet Effective Method for Mastering Composition

Read a story to your child, have him orally narrate the story while you write it down, and then allow him to use his own version of the story as a reader.

By this simple narration process, he makes the story his own.

This simple process will probably contribute more toward building that child's future ability to read and write on his own than any number of teacher contrived worksheets.

Because a child can read on his own, does not mean he no longer needs to have stories read aloud to him.

Oral narration is also important in that it opens up the gate to discussion.

Dinnertime can serve as an appropriate time for narration exercises, as a captive audience is already established.

continued with older children, just as it is important that older children continue to participate in the family read-aloud time.

Because a child can read on his own, does not mean he no longer needs to have stories read aloud to him. And following this same manner of thought, it does not mean that because he can write he should no longer participate in oral narration. Oral narration is also important in that it opens up the gate to discussion. And it is as we discuss our readings with our children, that thinking skills are developed. I will elaborate further on the aspects of discussion in the next chapter.

Dinnertime can serve as an appropriate time for narration exercises, as a captive audience is already established. Children, and people in general, tend to perform at a more proficient level if they have an audience. Sometimes our children need to perform for someone other than Mom.

I would like to give you an example of a successful dinnertime narration given by my daughter, Michelle, awhile ago. This narration came about in a rather spontaneous manner as she had recently finished reading an exciting book, and she just had to tell someone about it. The book she had just completed was Gary Paulsen's suspenseful novel **Hatchet.** In this drama a young teenage boy is flying in a small plane to visit his father in Canada. The plane crashes after the pilot dies of a heart attack. The young boy manages to escape from the plane with only his hatchet secured to his belt. This hatchet was a going away gift from his mother. He manages to survive nearly two months alone in the wilderness with the aid of his hatchet.

Michelle did a wonderful job of slowly unfolding the tale, enunciating each suspenseful episode as her siblings sat perched on the edges of their chairs. In turn, each would quickly ask her an important question hoping to resolve the current dilemma facing the main character. Michelle would very slowly answer this question with a "Well …" and then she would draw out her sentences, carefully choosing each word to keep her listeners enticed.

Michelle had an eager audience and took full advantage of this situation. I too was listening with strained ears and wide eyes as I cleaned up the after-dinner dishes in the kitchen. Michelle was surprised at the end of her performance when I announced that she had spent 55 minutes narrating the story. I was careful to log this as part of Michelle's schoolwork for the day under **Narration.** I also logged it as part of the other children's schoolwork under **Listening Comprehension.** They were listening and comprehending as was evidenced by their questions and their attentiveness.

Let me warn you that this practice of narration can be dangerous too. One day this past summer, my son, Robert, was absorbed in a historical book about Egypt, which specifically describes the processes of mummification. He was so interested in what he learned that he was eager to share this new found information. He wanted to *narrate* what he had read.

The problem was that his brother and two older sisters *did not* want to learn about mummification, and Robert was banished from the family room. I was in the shower and my youngest child, Mandy, was sitting on my bed reading books to herself. Robert came in and found a willing subject.

Mandy was listening intently as Robert elaborated on the finer points of mummification. I walked into the room as Mandy was saying, "Yeah, then what did they do?" I knew that Robert had been reading about the mummies of Ancient Egypt when I left the room to take a shower, so I quickly asked him what he was telling Mandy. He confessed saying, "Well, she's the only one that would listen to me!" I nicely explained that you do not tell a four-year-old child about mummies. And I was right because every night thereafter for about two weeks, Mandy took refuge in our bed in the middle of the night. Remember, narration is a powerful tool, so use it wisely!

We have numerous Bible storybooks, Bible story audio cassettes, and even a few Bible story video cassettes. My youngest daughter, Mandy, now four years old, has fallen in love with one particular Bible storybook. Each day we read many stories from her book, and although we read a variety of stories, we must read several favorites over and over again.

Her three favorite stories are currently, "The Prodigal Son," "A Wise King" (about Solomon when he ordered that the dispute between the two women over the baby be settled by cutting the baby in half), and "David Fights a Giant."

One day I was conducting a **Creating Books with Children Workshop**, and upon entering the church where the workshop was held, Mandy immediately noticed a rather large painting of David slaying Goliath. She looked puzzled as she stared at the picture. Then she asked, "Why is David so small? He doesn't look like the David in my book." Now I could see the wheels turning inside her head. I tried to explain that each artist draws David and Goliath differently because we do not really know what they looked like. Then she wanted to know, "Is this a real story?"

I could guess that she was wondering that if this was a real story, then why the pictures were not real. We talked about it some more, and for days she kept asking about the painting in the church. I got out several of our Bible storybooks and read her the story of David and Goliath from each book. She studied the various likenesses of the characters and

He was so interested in what he learned that he was eager to share this new found information. He wanted to narrate what he had read.

criticized them as if she knew fact from fiction.

Through this sequence of events, Mandy's world was broadened. She was really thinking about what she heard and what she saw. One of the Bible storybooks contains a very useful follow-up to each story. It includes individual pictures from the story, such as a picture of David, another of his sling, another of the brook, another of the stones, another of Goliath, another of Goliath's sword, and so forth.

Then the book asks the child to name each person or article. Following this game, they ask the child to retell the story in her own words. This is a terrific device for encouraging a child to narrate. The picture of each person and article helps to place those people and objects in the child's mind, so she is able to snatch them up while recalling the story.

This is a good narration technique that can be used with any picture book. Pictures are useful when a child retells a story, as they help her to keep the sequence of events in proper order. Naming each character and article depicted <u>before</u> the narration is given helps the child to look for details as well. It makes the process of narration seem more like a game.

Mandy loves to offer her biblical knowledge at family Bible study time. One day my husband was discussing Galatians with the children, and he mentioned Paul. Immediately Mandy latched onto that name. She knew Paul; she met him in her Bible storybook. She then proceeded to tell her father, "Paul was blinded by a bright light!" He asked her a few questions, which helped her to recount the entire story.

There have been several occasions when the mention of a person from the pages of Scripture has caused a light to turn on in Mandy's head, and she excitedly relates the story that she has learned about this person. She is pleased that she knows about the Bible too, and that she can participate in the discussion.

Familiarity with a well-loved story can also offer an opportunity to extend a young child's attention span. The Bible storybook that Mandy has grown to love so well is very simple. Each story only spans two or three pages with large illustrations and large type. Mandy has memorized a number of stories and portions of several others. Her interest in the painting of David and Goliath in the church spurred questions causing us to read the account of David's triumph in several other Bible storybooks, which offered longer narratives. Because she was acquainted with the story and took a special interest in it, she was ready to listen to a longer, more detailed version of that story.

Now she is anxious for me to read from these longer Bible storybooks, which did not interest her earlier. Mandy searches through the

Pictures are useful when a child retells a story as they help her to keep the sequence of events in proper order.

Familiarity with a well-loved story can also offer an opportunity to extend a young child's attention span.

more lengthy stories, studying illustrations, which are of course depicted differently from the pictures in her simple book. Once she locates a familiar picture she asks, "Is this Jonah and the Big Fish?" and is this "The Prodigal Son?" Then I proceed to read those stories to her. It has now become a game for her to cart in a number of Bible storybooks and find "Daniel in the Lion's Den," or "David and Goliath" in each book.

Older children may enjoy drawing pictures to accompany a story you are reading aloud. Then they can use their pictures to help them narrate the story to you. This is especially helpful for stories that have few or no illustrations accompanying them.

Children do not have to physically draw to paint pictures in their minds. You might read aloud a passage or two from a story you are sharing and ask what images come to mind as you speak. You can assist them with this activity by asking questions such as: "What do you think the man looked like?", "Can you describe the kitchen in the old farm house?", "What color do you think the big cat was?", and so forth.

As we read we form images in our minds, images that are very real to us. Besides describing a visual image with words, your children can describe the personalities and character traits of the individuals in the story. This is less difficult if they describe how a person behaved in a particular segment of the story.

Another suggestion is to read a passage that is spoken by one of the characters from a book you have been reading aloud, without disclosing the character's identity. See if the children can guess which character is speaking. What makes them think that this particular character made that statement? We found this to be a fun game to play while reading *Little Women,* as each of the four March sisters have very distinctive personalities. We noticed that it is easy to detect a passage spoken by Jo, as she has bold mannerisms. And conversely, Beth's patient, kind disposition is clearly evident in her dialogue.

For more ideas on teaching narration and composition while integrating grammar studies, see Karen Andreola's text, *Simply Grammar* for grades 4 - 8 and Cyndy Shearer's book, *English for the Thoughtful Child* geared for the primary grades.

Older children may enjoy drawing pictures to accompany a story you are reading aloud. Then they can use their pictures to help them narrate the story to you.

Reading Broadens Our World

It is exciting to be able to take what has been read and relate it to our own lives.

Love and enthusiasm for reading is nurtured as the children begin to see parallels between the different books we share as a family.

*T*he parameters of our world and those of our children are broadened as we read aloud with them and as they advance in their own readings. It is exciting to be able to take what has been read and relate it to our own lives. The children take an active part in reading as they listen, discuss, narrate, read aloud, or write about a book or a segment of a book that has been shared by the family. They are encouraged to be a part of several aspects relating to reading.

Love and enthusiasm for reading is nurtured as the children begin to see parallels between the different books we share as a family. For example, I have read **Dangerous Journey**, a retelling of Paul Bunyan's **Pilgrim's Progress** with my boys several times. My husband has also read it aloud to all the children. My daughter, Melissa, read it aloud to the boys, and Robert read it to himself. This all occurred over the course of perhaps two years. It is a well-loved book, and even my younger son, Raymond, has read parts of it to himself, primarily enjoying the incredible illustrations. This particular version of **Pilgrim's Progress** uses portions of the original text, carefully chosen by Oliver Hunkin and wonderfully illustrated by Alan Parry.

Recently at a home school curriculum fair, we bought another adaptation of Bunyan's **Pilgrim's Progress** for young children entitled **The Progress of Pilgrim Mouse,** which is written by Linda Parry and illustrated by her husband, Alan Parry. (Mr. Parry also illustrated **Dangerous Journey**.) This is a somewhat simpler version than **Dangerous Journey**, but it is also expertly written and illustrated.

I read this rendering of **Pilgrim's Progress** aloud to my boys over the course of two or three days. I was thoroughly pleased with their enthusiasm over the story. Without any prompting from me, they were continuously comparing the two adaptations of Bunyan's classic story. **Dangerous Journey** more closely depicts the original work, while **The Progress of Pilgrim Mouse** is based on the pilgrimage of Christopher Mouse. Therefore, the characters in the latter version are depicted as animals: mice, rats, a cat, an owl, a fox, a badger, a frog, a lamb, and so forth.

Robert and Raymond loved to tell me which of the creatures in **The Progress of Pilgrim Mouse** paralleled the characters in **Dangerous Journey.** One of the boys would say, for example, "Oh, Mom, you know who the two tethered owls in **The Progress of Pilgrim Mouse** represent don't you?" And as I tried desperately to remember, he would excitedly tell me, "You remember, they're like the two chained lions at the lodge in **Dangerous Journey.** "Oh yes, of course I remember – now that you've refreshed my memory," I replied.

They could not wait for me to read further from **The Progress of Pilgrim Mouse** so that they could discover which creatures, places, and events represented or paralleled the characters, places, and events in **Dangerous Journey.** Now, as if this was not enough excitement to see parallels in two books we had read aloud together, we unexpectedly stumbled upon still another story whose underlying theme was based on Bunyan's classic.

The next book we selected to read after **The Progress of Pilgrim Mouse** was Louisa May Alcott's, **Little Women.** (I had previously read **Little Men** to the boys, and we decided we should back up and read **Little Women.** Oops!) My girls had read these books independently, so I did not get the benefit of reading them aloud beforehand. Since the girls had read an abridged version of **Little Women**, I am now reading the original with them, too.

As we embarked on our reading of **Little Women**, we were greeted with the preface which was adapted from John Bunyan's, **Pilgrim's Progress**. The significance of this entry was not apparent to me until we read the first chapter, "Playing Pilgrims." This first scene opens with the girls lamenting over the dismal reality that their Christmas was going to be a poor one.

> *You know the reason mother proposed not having any presents this Christmas was because it is going to be a hard winter for everyone; and she thinks we ought not to spend money for pleasure, when our men are suffering so in the army.* [2]

The four March girls continued to grumble over their circumstances, each showing a very self-centered side of her character. The dialogue proceeds in this manner for awhile when the girls are suddenly brought back to their senses by the striking of the clock. Soon their mother would be home. They decided then to spend the small amount of money they each possessed on their beloved mother. After supper Mother read the letter she received from Father, who had entered into the military as a chaplain during the strife-torn Civil War years.

> *Give them all my dear love and a kiss. Tell them I think of them by day, pray for them by night, and find my best comfort in their affection at all times. A year seems very long to wait before I see them, but remind them that while we wait we may all work, so that these hard days need not be wasted. I know they will remember all I said to them, that they will be loving children to you, will do their duty faithfully, fight their bosom enemies bravely, and conquer themselves so beautifully, that when I come back to them I may be fonder and prouder than ever of my little women.* [3]

Following this touching letter, the girls each expressed shame for their selfish attitudes and resolved to be better so as not to disappoint their

Now, as if this was not enough excitement to see parallels in two books we had read aloud together, we unexpectedly stumbled upon still another story whose underlying theme was based on Bunyan's classic.

father.

Mrs. March broke the silence that followed Jo's words, by saying in her cheery voice, "Do you remember how you used to play Pilgrim's Progress when you were little things? Nothing delighted you more than to have me tie my piece-bags on your backs for burdens, give you hats and sticks and rolls of paper, and let you travel through the house from the cellar, which was the City of Destruction, up, up, to the house-top, where you had all the lovely things you could collect to make a Celestial City." [4]

Each girl related her favorite part of the game. Then the girls' mother remarked:

We never are too old for this, my dear, because it is a play we are playing all the time in one way or another. Our burdens are here, our road is before us, and the longing for goodness and happiness is the guide that leads us through many troubles and mistakes to the peace which is a true Celestial City. Now, my little pilgrims, suppose you begin again, not in play, but in earnest, and see how far on you can get before Father comes home. [5]

The mother went on to explain that the girls' bundles were the burdens that each was carrying now.

"We were in the slough of despond tonight, and Mother came and pulled us out as Help did in the book. We ought to have our roll of directions, like Christian. What shall we do about that?" asked Jo, delighted with the fancy which lent a little romance to the very dull task of doing her duty."

"Look under your pillows Christmas morning, and you will find your guidebook," replied Mrs. March. [6]

Chapter two begins with Jo waking in the gray dawn of Christmas morning feeling a sense of disappointment.

Then she remembered her mother's promise, and slipping her hand under her pillow, drew out a little crimson-covered book. She knew it very well, for it was that beautiful old story of the best life ever lived, and Jo felt that it was a true guidebook for any pilgrim going the long journey. [7]

The four girls each received their guidebooks and decided to read a little each morning as soon as they awakened.

After reading these chapters, Robert and Raymond decided it would be fun to play Pilgrim's Progress at our house.

After reading these chapters, Robert and Raymond decided it would be fun to play Pilgrim's Progress at our house. They announce that the garage would make a suitable City of Destruction as its present condition lends itself well to that descriptive title, and their loft bedroom would be a satisfactory Celestial City as it is the loftiest (excuse the pun) point within the house. The boys remarked that they would let their bundles or burdens drop from their backs as they ascended the ladder to the Celestial City as the March girls had let their bundles totter down the stairs in *Little Women*. They went on enthusiastically describing how they would play Pilgrim's Progress in our home.

Let us review the significance of the knowledge my boys and I gained through reading three books with an overlapping theme. First, we read *Dangerous Journey* and my children expressed their understanding of this classic tale by paralleling it to Scripture. As Oliver Hunkin states in the introduction to *Dangerous Journey*:

> *But rapidly the fame of Bunyan grew, and his work has become recognized by millions of readers not as an idle tale at all but as a story with a hidden meaning – an "allegory" of that Dangerous Journey which is, in fact the journey of Everyman from this world to the next.* [8]

After several readings of this version of Bunyan's classic tale, we later read a younger child's rendering of this story called, *The Progress of Pilgrim Mouse*. The boys paralleled the details of this version with those of *Dangerous Journey*. And thirdly we read *Little Women* in which we were given a more realistic glimpse of the journey of the pilgrim as played out by the March sisters. This journey was revealed to us through their present trials and in a more humorous tone as we learned how the March sisters had played Pilgrim's Progress as young children. (Additional references are made to the Pilgrim's journey throughout *Little Women*.) It is interesting to note that the author of *Little Women*, Louisa May Alcott, assumed that her readers were familiar with Bunyan's, *Pilgrim's Progress*.

My girls also joined in our Pilgrim's Progress unit study. As literary and handwriting exercises, they copied, or took dictation on alternate days, from the text of *Dangerous Journey*. Difficult words were researched, and we discussed their meanings. The girls also read *The Progress of Pilgrim Mouse* and made a list of the creatures in this narrative and the characters they parallel in *Dangerous Journey*.

The boys copied the text from *The Progress of Pilgrim Mouse*. I would write out the selection for them to copy the night before. Sometimes I would write the passage, skipping lines which enabled them to write directly below my writing. On other days, they would copy directly from a separate sheet of paper on which I had neatly copied the passage. And every few days I would personally dictate the day's passage to them. After they copied their selection for the day, they read it aloud to me individually, and then we discussed it. I also drew spelling words from these passages, and the boys typed the chosen words three times each on the computer. I gave assistance if they needed it, explaining various rules as we proceeded, such as changing the *y* to *i* before adding a suffix as in the word *tried.* I also explained phonetic combinations such as *aw* as in *hawk.* (**The Natural Speller,** by Kathryn Stout, will prove beneficial for brushing up on all those spelling rules!)

Typing the spelling words gave the boys' hands a break from writing and allowed them to practice their keyboard skills.

Typing the spelling words gave the boys' hands a break from writing and allowed them to practice their keyboard skills. It also enabled me to evaluate their typing abilities during this activity, making certain they were using the correct key strokes. (We have a computer typing program that the children use frequently.) Each day we printed their spelling lists to keep in their folders with their copying exercises.

As we read through **Little Women,** we discussed the allusions made to the **Pilgrim's Progress** story, which were even more evident as all the children had been copying from an adaptation of Bunyan's timeless classic. We found it interesting to note that more copies of Bunyan's original, **Pilgrim's Progress** have been printed in history than any other book except the Bible.

The children each decided to make a **Pilgrim's Progress** game. In the front of both **Dangerous Journey** and **The Progress of Pilgrim Mouse,** appears a map of the country through which Christian, or Christopher Mouse, must travel. These maps reminded my son, Raymond, of a game board, and so the idea of making a game came to life.

When using textbooks, children are often required to answer questions at the end of each chapter. When designing a game, children are required to not only answer questions, but they must also formulate questions.

Making games to accompany a unit study is an extremely valuable project. When using textbooks, children are often required to answer questions at the end of each chapter. When designing a game, children are required to not only answer questions, but they must also formulate questions. This requires much effort as they must search for facts and accurately compose a question.

Index cards, poster board, and dice are often all that is necessary to make fun and interesting games. The game cards can feature questions pertaining directly to the study, as well as include material to liven up the game. This may include cards indicating, for example, that the player must go back a designated number of spaces, or that the player may roll again. So, some cards are included just for fun to add adventure to the game, while others ask factual information pertaining to the study.

It is obvious to see that there is a great deal that can be learned during the game-making process, and the unit study material is easily reviewed through playing the games.

I generally suggest that my children make up twenty-five question cards and ten additional fun cards. Then they write the rules for their games. It is obvious to see that there is a great deal that can be learned during the game-making process, and the unit study material is easily reviewed through playing the games.

After spending several weeks copying from **Dangerous Journey** and **The Progress of Pilgrim Mouse**, we began reading from the original version of Bunyan's **Pilgrim's Progress**, which contains unusual grammatical structure and difficult vocabulary. Because we had first read the two adaptations of this wonderful story, we were better able to follow the original version. It is full of treasures and offers much material for meaningful discussion. Many allusions are made to biblical characters, and even little Mandy picked up on this as she listened while playing at my feet.

In more recent years I have discovered **A Little Pilgrim's Progress,** by Helen Taylor, in which the main character, Christian, is a child. This is a beautifully recounted, simplified version of Bunyan's classic tale. My children enjoyed this book as well as the other adaptations of **Pilgrim's Progress**.

It was obvious that my children took pleasure in being able to participate in a discussion of **Pilgrim's Progress**, because they had some previous knowledge of the subject from which to draw. *Reading broadens our world.* This holds true whether we are reading the newspaper, a magazine, a novel, a picture book, a poetry book, a history book, a science book, or any number of different kinds of worthy books. Breadth in our reading helps us to see relationships, develop concepts, and apply knowledge.

Breadth in our reading helps us to see relationships, develop concepts, and apply knowledge.

Where to Find Good, Worthy Books

A book that is read, re-read, highlighted, filled with notes, and referred to often is far more beneficial than ten wonderful books that sit on your shelf gathering dust.

Limit your purchases and increase the use of those few purchases.

It is also beneficial for our children to see that we read, study, and grow in wisdom and knowledge.

Many parents realize the need to provide their children with good books. Even more importantly, good books should be read aloud to the children. But finding these worthy books may present a problem, especially since there is such an overabundance of unworthy books. These unworthy books range from time wasters to those harmful in content.

I am going to gladly recommend a number of excellent guides to excellent books. I am not suggesting you buy and read all of these books initially, but that you choose one or two, read them, use them, and six months or so later, choose another book or two to read and use. Continue this process until you have read all or most all of these books. I often meet with zealous homeschooling parents who buy numerous books at a curriculum fair only to find that when the next year's fair comes around, they have still not read the previously purchased books.

A better method is to limit your book purchasing and to increase your reading and utilizing of those books. A book that is read, re-read, highlighted, filled with notes, and referred to often is far more beneficial than ten wonderful books that sit on your shelf gathering dust. This holds true for all curriculum materials whether they are geared for the parents or the children.

Owning a plethora of quality educational materials will not benefit our children unless they use them, and you can only use so many items effectively at one time. So do not fret if your budget does not allow you to purchase all those wonderful materials you want for your children. Limit your purchases and increase the use of those few purchases. Let the children saturate themselves in a given area for a given time.

I make it a point to only buy enough materials for one or two unit studies at a time. Once these studies have been completed, I plan for only one or two more. In this manner I do not overwhelm myself, and I am free to be sensitive to the Lord's leading in another direction if necessary. I am not locked into a schedule for the year that can't flex to meet the needs of my family and to follow the direction of the Lord.

I do not mean to sound as if I am giving orders or a class assignment, but each of these books I am going to recommend has been a blessing to me and my family. It is also beneficial for our children to see that we read, study, and grow in wisdom and knowledge.

The first book I would like to suggest is ***Honey for a Child's Heart***. This book is first in line as it is full of encouragement and ideas for developing a read-aloud-habit in the home. It also contains references to specific books for children categorized by age group. As the author of ***Honey for a Child's Heart***, Gladys Hunt, states:

That is what a book does. If introduces us to people and places we wouldn't ordinarily know. A good book is a magic gateway into a wider world of wonder, beauty, delight, and adventure. Books are experiences that make us grow, that add something to our inner stature. [9]

As I stated in the last chapter, reading broadens our world. Secondly, I am pleased to suggest **Books Children Love: A Guide to the Best Children's Literature**, by Elizabeth Wilson.

Mrs. Wilson has carefully arranged books listed into categories such as Art and Architecture, Bible/Spiritual Teaching, Biography, Crafts, Dance/Drama, Geography and History, Language, Literature, Mathematics, Music, Physical Education, Reference and Research, Science, and more! Each book listing includes the complete title, author, publisher, year published, number of pages, and approximate grade level.

Each book also receives a one paragraph description of its contents. Many books fall into more than one category, and therefore they are cross-referenced to those additional listings. **Books Children Love** is a terrific resource and a valuable timesaving reference book. Books for pleasurable reading or reading pertaining to a topic of study are easily found.

My daughter, Melissa, now 12 years old, has been using this guide for several years to locate enjoyable books for herself and her siblings. We call her our family librarian, as she reads numerous commentaries on books in her search for appealing books for the other children. She makes a list containing book titles and authors and takes it when we visit the library. She has been fairly successful in locating the desired books, and her brothers and sisters are usually excited over the selections she makes for them.

Melissa is a doll collector and loves to read all kinds of books about dolls. By using various book guides and making inquiries into the library's computer, she has located many and varied books on dolls. Through her diligence, she has also been able to locate unreferenced books about dolls by thoroughly reading the books she has been able to obtain. She has found that information about additional books on her topic of interest is located in the front and back jacket flaps, prefaces, introductions, forewords, and bibliographies.

Failing to completely read a book may mean leaving a treasure buried for a more inquisitive explorer. Melissa has cultivated her love for reading into a love for researching. Although her research seems to be in a pleasure-related area, the skills she has acquired can be transferred to any field of study.

Thirdly, I would like to recommend that parents read *A Family Program for Reading Aloud*, developed by Rosalie June Slater. The information contained in this guide includes: The Purpose and Importance

Books are experiences that make us grow, that add something to our inner stature. [9]

Although her research seems to be in a pleasure-related area, the skills she has acquired can be transferred to any field of study.

of a Family Program, Skills Needed in Reading Aloud, Books to Read to Younger Children, Introducing America in Your Reading Aloud, Evaluating Your Family Interests Through Reading in Depth, and Restoring Heroes and Heroines to our Reading Aloud.

Excellent material is included for the study of a select group of authors such as: Charles Dickens, Sir Walter Scott, Washington Irving, Nathaniel Hawthorne, Anne Bradstreet, Marguerite Henry, and others. A significant portion of the book is also donated to the study of America through the reading of biographies of great men and women. This guide is published by the Foundation for American Christian Education, and it contains rich information useful for conducting meaningful unit studies.

Fourthly, I would like to suggest a wonderful book that I recently read entitled, *Let the Authors Speak*, by Carolyn Hatcher. This book is subtitled: *A Guide to Worthy Books Based on Historical Setting*. Mrs. Hatcher also includes pertinent information on the importance and process of narration. She emphasizes that parents do not need to be educational experts, only guides. Mrs. Hatcher states:

> *I'm not sure how anyone else will react to this idea, but it certainly removed a burden from my shoulders knowing that to give my children the best I only needed to be a guide to the best.* [10]

And lastly I would like to encourage you to read, *Honey for a Teen's Heart.* This book was written by the author of *Honey for a Child's Heart*, Gladys Hunt, along with Barbara Hampton. Not only does this guide contain more than 300 books reviewed by Barbara Hampton, but it includes inspirations from Gladys Hunt on how to read a book; what makes a good book; and how to distinguish between good, better, and best. This book offers a truly delightful literature course for teens and parents. If you thought literature was boring in high school, you are in for a surprise!

You may be saying to yourself, "This woman is crazy to suggest I read five books — all guides to the best in literature!" Remember, I did not say to read them all at once. Read one of the books, familiarize yourself with it, and really use it! This will be far more beneficial than trying to scan each book briefly and never getting thoroughly acquainted with any of them. Later, as time and finances permit, choose another of these excellent guides and immerse yourself in it.

Each author is an expert in conveying her thoughts from her viewpoint. Each author brings to light different ideas, suitable for certain people, at certain times, under certain circumstances. We are truly blessed to have at our disposal the insights of these gifted women. Each of these guides contributes to "Honey for a Mother's Heart."

She emphasizes that parents do not need to be educational experts, only guides.

Read one of the books, familiarize yourself with it, and really use it!

When you continue to study and learn, you offer your children a special example — an example that says, as Charlotte Mason put it, "Education is a Life."

When you continue to study and learn, you offer your children a special example — an example that says, as Charlotte Mason put it, "Education is a Life."

Taking What We Read to Heart

As we conduct our unit studies or spend time reading enjoyable books together, there inevitably springs up a gem, a delightful morsel, that is worthy of our contemplation. My desire is to memorize some of these gems, but too often this is a difficult task as we tend to devour many excellent books in a condensed period of time.

While studying poetry and poets, we decided to investigate Robert Louis Stevenson. Not only were we enchanted by his poems, but we stumbled over a gem as I previously described. Mr. Stevenson said that wherever he went, he took two books with him, "one to read and one to write in."

I figured he must use that writing book for putting down thoughts that came to him so they did not slip away. But after thinking about it for awhile, I deduced that perhaps he also used that writing book to record passages, gems, from the books he was currently reading. This gave me an idea. We should keep a *Reader's Journal*. Often in book stores you will see beautifully decorated blank journals of all types, some with no titles, and others that say *Mother's Journal*, *Author's Journal*, and so on.

Often times I am stumped when I try to recall a particular book. Reading so widely makes it difficult to remember where we read *what* and exactly *how* the author constructed the thought. A *Reader's Journal* solves this dilemma and provides a good literary exercise.

As we copy pertinent passages from works we read, we become intimately acquainted with the authors and receive the benefit of their ideas and literary expertise. This is why copying good writing is a fine tool for learning to write well. It is a simple practice, yet effective. Because it is so uncomplicated a task, its effectiveness is multiplied as it enables us to perform it on a regular basis. If we are able to follow through with something consistently, it becomes habit; if it becomes habit, it becomes a part of who we are.

It is important to implement this habit of copying worthy excerpts, or gems, from the books we read. These literary passages to be copied, whether from history, science, novels, classics, or poetry, become the focus of our studies. This eliminates the need for dry workbook exercises and offers a richer, more meaningful dimension to our studies. While copying a passage, or taking that passage from dictation, many elements come into play. We must focus on spelling, punctuation, and grammatical structure.

Another benefit of this process of copying significant excerpts from books we read is that it stimulates discussion. It enables us to take a closer look at what the author is saying. It also allows us a means to compare one book or idea to another book or idea. It strengthens our observation skills as we search for gems to add to our personal *Reader's*

As we copy pertinent passages from works we read, we become intimately acquainted with the authors and receive the benefit of their ideas and literary expertise.

Journals.

Hopefully, the incorporation of a ***Reader's Journal*** in our academic pursuits with our children will encourage them to keep a journal for excerpts taken from books they read on their own. Of course, some books do not lend themselves to this sort of activity, especially humorous books or books for young children. But as the reader matures, he should be reading more and more books with gems worthy of notation. Even humorous books may fall into this category as everyone needs a good laugh from time to time.

*It strengthens our observation skills as we search for gems to add to our personal **Reader's Journals**.*

As I read the chapter, I searched for a valuable passage, a gem, to include in our Reader's Journals.

As I mentioned in the last chapter, if we instill the habit of developing **Reader's Journals** based on books we read together as a family, our children may be motivated to keep **Reader's Journals** based on books they read for personal enjoyment.

I would like to offer a sampling of excerpts I chose to include in our **Reader's Journals** when we studied sign language. We read numerous books during the course of this study, and one of our favorites was **The Story of My Life**, by Helen Keller.

Each night I pre-read the chapter I planned to read aloud to my children the next day. (No, I did not spend days and weeks preparing ahead of time!) As I read the chapter, I searched for a valuable passage, a gem, to include in our **Reader's Journals**. Usually, this passage jumped out at me as it contained valuable information or insights I deemed worthy of notation. Often this passage exemplified a specific character trait that I wanted to impress upon my children.

I would like to relate some background information drawing from Helen Keller's autobiography. Before Anne Sullivan came to teach Helen, her life was marred by darkness: darkness brought on by deafness and blindness. After her teacher came, she felt as if a veil of oppression had been lifted from her life. As Helen explains in her autobiography:

> *Thus I came up out of Egypt and stood before Sinai, and a power divine touched my spirit and gave it sight so that I beheld many wonders. And from the sacred mountain I heard a voice which said, "Knowledge is love and light and vision."* [11]

As we read through Helen's autobiography, we noted the numerous references to biblical passages or events. These made excellent excerpts for inclusion in our **Reader's Journals** and offered research exercises as we sought to locate these references in the Bible.

One of my favorite passages from **The Story of My Life** recounts how the mystery of language was first conveyed to Helen. Until this time, finger spelling was only a game to Helen; she did not realize everything had a name.

> *We walked down the path to the well-house, attracted by the fragrance of the honeysuckle with which it was covered. Someone was drawing water and my teacher placed my hand under the spout. As the cool stream gushed over one hand she spelled into the other the word "water," first slowly, then rapidly. I stood still, my whole attention fixed upon the motions of her fingers. Suddenly I felt a misty consciousness as of something forgotten — a thrill of returning thought; and somehow the mystery of language*

was revealed to me. I knew then that "w-a-t-e-r" meant the wonderful cool something that was flowing over my hand. That living word awakened my soul, gave it light, hope, joy, set it free! There were barriers still, it is true, but barriers that could in time be swept away. [12]

Following this passage was another entry offering biblical inference.

I learned a great many new words that day. I do not remember what they all were; but I do know that "mother," "father," "sister," "teacher" were among them – words that were to make the world blossom for me, "like Aaron's rod, with flowers." [13]

If we do not know the story of the departure of the children of Israel from Egypt and the miracle of Aaron's rod, these words of Helen's will have no meaning for us. The following selections are remarks Helen made about the Bible.

I began to read the Bible long before I could understand it. Now it seems strange to me that there should have been a time when my spirit was deaf to its wondrous harmonies...

But how shall I speak of the glories I have since discovered in the Bible? For years I have read it with an ever-broadening sense of joy and inspiration; and I love it as I love no other book.

The Bible gives me a deep, comforting sense that "things seen are temporal and things unseen are eternal" [14]

Helen's account of her experience at the well-house offers several avenues for discussion. What words does Helen use to describe the bower enveloping the well-house? What sensations did she feel as the water flowed over her hand? How did she feel after the "mystery of language had been revealed" to her? Realizing that Helen was both deaf and blind will help us to understand her perception of the incident.

Before reading the **Story of My Life**, by Helen Keller, we read a biography about Thomas Hopkins Gallaudet who pioneered education for the deaf in America. This wonderful biography, which is now out of print but still available in many public libraries, is entitled **Gallaudet, Friend of the Deaf**, by Etta DeGering. (Another excellent, biography about Gallaudet that is currently in print is titled, **A Deaf Child Listened**, by Anne Neimark.) Using either of these biographies, it is interesting to note comparisons between the teaching methods employed by Gallaudet and those used by Anne Sullivan to teach Helen Keller.

Gallaudet's first experience with teaching the deaf was when he taught his neighbor, little Alice Cogswell, that "h-a-t" written in the sand

Helen's account of her experience at the well-house offers several avenues for discussion.

represented the hat he held in his hand. A beneficial exercise is to compare this incident with Helen's revelation of language at the well-house.

The following excerpt is from **Gallaudet, Friend of the Deaf**, by Etta DeGering. First, I will fill in a little background information. Thomas Gallaudet is home for a visit from Andover Theological Seminary and is sitting on his front porch watching his brothers and sisters playing with the neighborhood children.

He called Theodore, his nine-year-old brother, from the circle. "Who is the little girl sitting over there by herself?"

Teddy looked in the direction he indicated "Her? Why don't you know? She's Alice Cogswell. Doc Cogswell's girl – lives next door."

"Why doesn't she play with the group?"

Teddy shrugged "She can't. She's deaf and dumb."

Deaf and dumb. So that was it. "Bring her to me. Maybe I can think of a game she can play. She looks lonesome."

Teddy ran over to Alice, made a sweeping motion "to come," left her with Thomas, and hurried back to the circle.

Thomas smiled and patted the step beside him. Alice sat on the very edge like a pink butterfly — if there are pink butterflies — ready to take flight.

Now what? His granny story was of no use here. College B.A. and M.A. degrees offered no solution. He thought fast. With all his soul Thomas longed to open this child's "silent prison," find a way for her to be one with the other children. Her need was some way of conversing. Could she be taught to write, he wondered.

Picking up his hat, the only thing he had at hand, he gave it to her, and stooping, wrote "hat" in the sand of the path.

Alice looked at him blankly. The marks in the sand meant nothing to her. Again and again, Thomas handed her the hat and wrote "hat" in the sand. He pointed to the writing and then to other things and shook his head. He pointed to the hat and nodded vigorously.

Her forehead puckered. She was trying to understand. She looked from the hat to the writing. What did those marks in the sand have to do with the thing she held in her hand?

Thomas breathed a prayer.

It may take the children several days to transcribe such a lengthy passage as the one I excerpted from Gallaudet, Friend of the Deaf, *into their* Reader's Journals.

Finally a glimmer of light shone in the hazel eyes. Her forehead smoothed. She smiled and nodded. For the first time in her life, Alice understood that things had names, names that could be written in the sand. [15]

We can also note other similarities between these two life stories, such as the circumstances surrounding Alice Cogswell's deafness and the deafness of Helen Keller.

It may take the children several days to transcribe such a lengthy passage as the one I excerpted from **Gallaudet, Friend of the Deaf**, into their **Reader's Journals**. Younger children may write from dictation or copy only one or two key sentences from the passage, although the entire passage is re-read to them. (Passages are copied or taken from dictation after the selection has been read aloud.)

For instance, they may copy, "Again and again, Thomas handed her the hat and wrote 'hat' in the sand."

Phonetic rules that appear in the words in the copied sentence can be circled and discussed. For example, the *ed* ending such as in *handed* can be explained. The children can write additional words that rhyme with *hat*. They may even wish to draw a hat to accompany their sentence. Even young children can learn to capitalize the first word of a sentence and the names of people. Explain that most sentences end in a period. The commas and quotation marks may prove to be too difficult for young children at this point, but they can be made aware of them and their purposes without expecting mastery at this level.

We can learn much about effective writing by reading Helen's own words, as she causes us to see the world in a new light. Helen beckons us to use all of our senses to express our thoughts, just as she employed all of her functioning senses to produce descriptive narratives. As you read various selections from her writings, try to note which senses evoked the choice of words she used to convey her message.

The following passage offers a superb exercise in observation and description techniques. Helen has been recently left high in a tree by her teacher who thought her quite safe for a few moments while she went to prepare a picnic for them to enjoy from this lofty position.

Suddenly a change passed over the tree. All the sun's warmth left the air. I knew the sky was black because all the heat, which meant light to me, had died out of the atmosphere. A strange odor came up from the earth. I knew it, it was the odor that always precedes a thunderstorm, and a nameless fear clutched at my heart. I felt absolutely alone, cut off from my friends and the firm earth. The immense, the unknown, enfolded me. I remained

Younger children may write from dictation or copy only one or two key sentences from the passage, although the entire passage is re-read to them.

The commas and quotation marks may prove to be too difficult for young children at this point, but they can be made aware of them and their purposes without expecting mastery at this level.

still and expectant; a chilling terror crept over me. I longed for my teacher's return; but above all things I wanted to get down from that tree.

There was a moment of sinister silence, then a multitudinous stirring of the leaves. A shiver ran through the tree, and the wind sent forth a blast that would have knocked me off had I not clung to the branch with might and main. The tree swayed and strained. The small twigs snapped and fell about me in showers. A wild impulse to jump seized me, but terror held me fast. I crouched down in the fork of the tree.

The branches lashed about me. I felt the intermittent jarring that came now and then, as if something heavy had fallen and the shock had traveled up till it reached the limb I sat on. It worked my suspense up to the highest point and just as I was thinking the tree and I should fall together, my teacher seized my hand and helped me down. I clung to her, trembling with joy to feel the earth under my feet once more. [16]

What a gripping account this blind and deaf woman has related through the use of well chosen words! She causes us to feel her desperation, tremble along with her, and then almost collapse with relief once security has been attained. Much oral discussion can ensue from this suspenseful account. How did Helen know a storm was approaching? Describe each warning of the upcoming storm as Helen perceived it. Describe Helen's terror, what sensations did she feel during the storm? Relate the security she felt as she was rescued by her teacher.

Older children can copy the passage or write it as it is dictated to them. Longer passages, such as this account of Helen's trial in the storm-tossed tree, may require more than one day to copy or write from dictation. Naturally, copying is a less difficult activity than writing a passage from verbal dictation. This technique can be used by children who find dictation laborious. Often, if the passage to be studied is above my girls' dictation level, containing difficult vocabulary and/or punctuation, I allow them to copy the selection directly from the book.

I like to tape record passages beforehand for my older girls to take from dictation to include in their **Reader's Journals**. As I slowly read the passage onto the tape, I add in uncertain punctuation. Long sentences may contain numerous commas and semicolons which the ear is not always able to discern. If I feel there is a word that might be difficult to spell, I read the entire sentence containing the word, and then I pause and spell the word. This gives them an opportunity to spell it themselves first and correct the spelling if they have made an error. I feel it is more important that the children write the correct spelling with my assistance than make a futile guess and reinforce a negative spelling. This also holds true for punctuation. As the children become more proficient in their writing, I omit some of these helps.

Numerous writing activities can center on the pertinent passages taken from the books we read in the course of our studies. For example, on one day the children may copy or take the selection from dictation. On the next day, they may rewrite the passage in their own words or with the help of a thesaurus. They may write the definitions for specific words from the selection, being sure to choose the definitions that best fit the context of the passage. They can rewrite the passage in another tense or as if related from another individual's perspective. For example, the incident with Helen in the storm-tossed tree could be rewritten from her teacher's point of view, or with a good dose of imagination, from the tree's perspective!

Younger children may copy a portion of the passage you have neatly written out for them. I write a selection to be copied on lined paper, skipping every other line as I proceed, so the children can write directly under my writing. I pay close attention to letter formation, size, and spacing. Although the younger children may only copy a sentence or two from the passage of study, they can listen carefully to the re-reading of the entire passage and participate in oral discussion pertaining to the selection. Many excerpts, such as this particular one relating Helen's frightful episode in the tree, also make excellent sketches for the children to pantomime or act out. Younger children especially enjoy this activity.

We also find it advantageous to select a simple biography about the individual we are studying. This shorter, less detailed biography offers an overview as the capable children read it aloud to the younger children. It also provides them practice with their oral presentation skills. Sometimes these less difficult biographical sketches offer suitable material for the younger children to copy. I try to locate a passage from the simple biography that parallels the passage from the more detailed biography we are implementing in our literary exercises. While conducting our sign language unit study, we chose a simple biography of Helen Keller entitled, *A Picture Book of Helen Keller*, by David A. Adler, to use along with her autobiography.

It is easy to see the benefits of a **Reader's Journal** are far reaching. The passages copied or taken from dictation offer a variety of literary exercises relating directly to the children's topic of study. (I know I have personally benefited from them as well!) Time is not usurped by tedious, irrelevant, fill-in-the-blank workbook assignments. These exercises based on excerpts from our reading encourage the children to become more observant and more critical of what they read. Furthermore,

Numerous writing activities can center on the pertinent passages taken from the books we read in the course of our studies.

We also find it advantageous to select a simple biography about the individual that we are studying.

These exercises based on excerpts from our reading encourage the children to become more observant and more critical of what they read.

capitalization, spelling, punctuation, sentence structure, and grammar can effectively be taught through copying and dictation exercises. This concept is succinctly expressed in **The Elements of Grammar**, by Margaret Shertzer.

> *In order to use English correctly and gracefully, it is necessary to recognize and practice using good grammar. Listening to speakers who are accustomed to speaking grammatically helps to train the ear to recognize correct usage.*
>
> *Good habits of speech will improve one's writing, but the best training may be to read examples of effective writing.*
> 17

I believe that reading effective writing is essential to improving one's own writing, as Margaret Shertzer affirms, but I believe that copying and taking from dictation samples of effective writing will further enhance writing abilities.

If you are questioning this teaching method of copying and dictation, you will find useful suggestions in Ruth Beechick's information packed book, **You Can Teach Your Child Successfully**.

For those desiring further assistance, I recommend using the **Learning Language Arts through Literature** series to help acquaint you with this teaching method. Excellent exercises and activities are developed based on passages taken from fine literature. After utilizing this material for a while, you will be able to integrate the teaching strategies incorporated in the **Learning Language Arts through Literature** series with selections you have chosen relating to your unit of study.

A plan such as the following may work for you. Have your children spend five weeks, or so, conducting a Basic Skills Unit, utilizing their math textbooks and/or math manipulatives, using the **Learning Language Arts through Literature** series, completing typing exercises, practicing handwriting skills, brushing up on *spelling dragons*, studying Greek and Latin Roots (perhaps using Joel Lundquist's, **English from the Roots Up)**, playing educational games, reading classics, and so forth.

Then undertake a planned unit study spanning the next five-week period in which you integrate the skills you practiced into your own unit of study. Conducting these Basic Skills Units throughout the year will help to give you a base from which to formulate lessons to accompany your unit studies.

A good composition/grammar handbook will be a treasured resource for conducting your literary exercises. I recommend **Write Source 2000** and other titles in the Write Source series of handbooks. These manuals cover nearly every aspect of writing including writing

Conducting these Basic Skills Units throughout the year will help to give you a base from which to formulate lessons to accompany your unit studies.

plays, poetry, journals, paragraphs, essays, biographies, autobiographies, news stories, stories, classroom reports, business letters, friendly letters, and more. They also contain significant information about the use of punctuation, spelling, capitalization, grammar, Greek and Latin roots, using the library, and so on. You will find other interesting data such as the manual sign alphabet, cuneiform, Morse code, semaphore, the periodic chart of elements, a chart of the solar system, maps, calendars, etc.! (After I gave a similar description of *Write Source 2000* at a unit study seminar, one mother stood up in the back of the room and shouted, "Sold!")

The Write Source Company publishes handbooks for each grade level. However, I find that I can use *Writer's Express* (designed for grades 4 and 5) with all my elementary students, *Write Source 2000* (designed for grades 6-8) with my middle school students, and *Writer's Inc.* (designed for grades 9-12) with my high school students. Another helpful resource for writing effectively is *The Clear and Simple Thesaurus Dictionary*, published by Grosset and Dunlap.

As I mentioned in a previous chapter, I like to acquaint myself with one or two books on a given topic and make good use of them. If I buy a composition/grammar handbook designed for each age/grade level I am teaching, I will never become sufficiently familiar with any of them to use them effectively. This goes for the children as well. If they become acquainted with a reference book they can refer to year after year, they will reap a harvest of benefits. A familiar friend is one that is turned to again and again.

If they become acquainted with a reference book they can refer to year after year, they will reap a harvest of benefits.

There is More to Language than Meets the Ear

*L*et us saunter back to the last chapter where I discussed excerpts taken from **The Story of My Life**, by Helen Keller. Helen's limitations can also be used to help us realize there is more to language than meets the ear. This concept is illustrated by Helen in the following passages :

> *The deaf and the blind find it very difficult to acquire the amenities of conversation. How much more this difficulty must be augmented in the case of those who are both deaf and blind! They cannot distinguish the tone of the voice or, without assistance, go up and down the gamut of tones that give significance to words; nor can they watch the expression of the speaker's face, and a look is often the very soul of what one says.* [18]

Following the inclusion of this passage in our **Reader's Journals**, we can perform a simple exercise to help us visualize Helen's words. Read an excerpt from a well known children's story, such as **Goldilocks and the Three Bears**, and employ no expression in either facial features or tone of voice. Make your voice very bland, almost robotic, and your face dull and placid. Then read the selection again, adding expression in both voice and countenance. Have the children compare the two readings.

As we are concentrating on the tone of voice and expression, I would like to share a thought provoking passage from **A Family Program for Reading Aloud**, published by Foundation for American Christian Education.

> *Noah Webster, in his Introduction to the Origin of Language in the 1828 **American Dictionary of the English Language** states: "It is therefore probable that 'language' as well as the faculty of speech, was the 'immediate gift of God.'"*
>
> *This gift includes the "Voice," source of sound, "Tone," or accent and inflection of the voice, and "Expression," that which identifies the ideas, convictions, and feelings of the speaker. These three elements are both internal and external. They make the difference between reading aloud that is monotonous and difficult to listen to, and that which is modulated. Modulation refers to "the act of inflecting the voice in reading or speaking; a rising or falling of the voice." This becomes the instrument of the Reader. If you love what you are reading; if you are interested in arousing the feelings of your listeners; if you know the message of the author and you wish to help convey it; all of these aspects will help you to use your voice effectively.* [19]

"It is therefore probable that 'language' as well as the faculty of speech, was the 'immediate gift of God.'" [19]

One of my favorite teachers is Charlotte Mason, who taught in England and lived from 1842 to 1923. She authored a number of books which have been reprinted in recent years including, *Home Education*. Her ageless methods offer us a vast wealth of knowledge bearing careful meditation. Among her many suggestions are the implementation and development of a special awareness and relationship with nature.

Through this relationship, we are directed to the One who orchestrates the wonders and complexities of nature. It is interesting to me that Helen Keller's teacher, Anne Sullivan, also realized the importance of this special relationship to be cultivated. The following excerpt from *The Story of My Life* illustrates this point:

> *We read and studied out of doors, preferring the sunlit woods to the house. All my early lessons have in them the breath of the woods – the fine, resinous odor of pine needles, blended with the perfume of wild grapes. Seated in the gracious shade of a wild tulip tree, I learned to think that everything has a lesson and a suggestion. "The loveliness of things taught me all their use." Indeed everything that could hum, or buzz, or sing, or bloom, had a part in my education – noisy-throated frogs, katydids and crickets held in my hand until, forgetting their embarrassment, they trilled their reedy note, little downy chickens and wildflowers, the dogwood blossoms, meadow-violets and budding fruit trees. I felt the bursting cotton-balls and fingered their soft fiber and fuzzy seeds; I felt the low soughing of the wind through the cornstalks, the silky rustling of the long leaves, and the indignant snort of my pony, as we caught him in the pasture and put the bit in his mouth – ah me! how well I remember the spicy, clovery smell of his breath!* [20]

Jessica Hulcey, co-author of the popular KONOS Character Curriculum, encourages the implementation of "discovery learning" techniques with children. It is exciting for me to see that Anne Sullivan was a proponent of the "discovery learning" method as well.

> *Our favorite walk was to Keller's landing, an old tumble-down lumber-wharf on the Tennessee River, used during the Civil War to land soldiers. There we spent many happy hours and played at learning geography. I built dams of pebbles, I made islands and lakes, and dug river-beds, all for fun, and never dreamed that I was learning a lesson. I listened with increasing wonder to Miss Sullivan's descriptions of the great round world with its burning mountains, buried cities, moving rivers of ice, and many*

Authors that Encourage Us to Cultivate a Special Relationship with Nature

All my early lessons have in them the breath of the woods – the fine, resinous odor of pine needles, blended with the perfume of wild grapes. [20]

other things as strange. She made raised maps in clay, so that I could feel the mountain ridges and valleys, and follow with my fingers the devious course of rivers. [21]

Those using the **Greenleaf Guides to History** will find that they offer instruction in creating salt maps of Egypt, Greece, Rome, and so forth. This helps to "fix" the geographical features of each place in the children's minds.

There are a number of fine authors who have helped us to cultivate a relationship with nature. As we read the tales of Beatrix Potter and investigate her life through biographies, we find that she was an avid nature student. This special bond she possessed with nature aided her in making effective, true-to-life drawings of wood and creatures. Although her creatures took on human characteristics, it is obvious she studied real specimens to create her illustrations. Her stories began as illustrated letters to her dear friend's children when they were ill. Friends and family encouraged her to publish these in book form. (Keep this in mind when reading the next chapter.)

Jim Arnosky, a modern day naturalist, offers us inspiring glimpses into the natural world. Effective drawing instruction will assist even young artists. Arnosky's easy readers focusing on raccoons, foxes, and other wildlife, encourage young readers to take a closer look at the wonders of creation while offering them simple, yet interesting beginning reading material. You should be able to find these books in your public library. (For a listing of books by Jim Arnosky, see the Other Recommended Books on page 327.)

It is fascinating to me how authors and illustrators use their gifts to introduce little-known or unexplored areas of life and present to us in-depth knowledge to further pursue those areas of interest.

Quoting once again from *A Family Program for Reading Aloud*, published by the Foundation for American Christian Education:

But there are other purposes in the teaching and learning of literature. One of these purposes is to minister to the individual student. Through skillful teachers who are able to inspire and delight the mind and heart, new horizons are opened up, and new fields envisioned which provide challenge.

The wider the range of reading, and the more focused, the greater are the opportunities for self-discovery.

The purpose of reading in a specific field is to extend the horizons of our mind to contemplate the implications of a particular subject. [22]

Learning from Letters

I find it intriguing to read the letters included at the end of Helen Keller's autobiography. Some of these letters were written by Helen at different stages in her childhood, and others were written to Helen by various individuals. As we are on the subject of letters, I would like to share a little of the importance of letters. In our day of mass communication, letter writing is becoming a dying art. It seems to me that in general, people write less as they are more occupied with mechanical distractions.

If we observe biographies we read in the course of our studies, we find that letters, diaries, journals, and other writings provide the foundation of much of the person's life story. (Read the bibliography located at the end of each biography for a listing of the supportive materials.) It is important to point out to our children the significance of the written word. The Bible is our Heavenly Father's letter of love to us. "Thy word is a lamp unto my feet and a light unto my path."

Returning our thoughts to the letters following Helen's autobiography, let us look at what we can learn from them. As illustrated in this next quote from *The Story of My Life*, we understand how difficult it is for a deaf child to acquire language.

> *This process was continued for several years; for the deaf child does not learn in a month or even in two or three years, the numberless idioms and expressions used in the simplest daily intercourse. The little hearing child learns these from constant repetition and imitation. The conversation he hears in his home stimulates his mind and suggests topics and calls forth the spontaneous expression of his own thoughts. This natural exchange of ideas is denied to the deaf child.* [23]

It is amazing to me that at the writing of her autobiography at age 22, Helen possessed the ability to skillfully express her thoughts and ideas, although encumbered by almost overwhelming physical hindrances. It is helpful to look at her earlier years, when the mystery of language was newly disclosed to her.

> *Miss Sullivan began to teach Helen Keller on March 3rd, 1887. Three months and a half after her first word was spelled into her hand, she wrote in pencil this letter.*
>
> *TO HER COUSIN ANNA (MRS. GEORGE T. TURNER)*
>
> *(Tuscumbia, Alabama, June 17, 1887.)*
>
> *helen write anna george will give helen apple simpson will shoot bird jack will give helen stick of candy doctor will give mildred medicine mother will make mildred new dress*

If we observe biographies that we read in the course of our studies, we find that letters, diaries, journals, and other writings provide the foundation of much of the person's life story.

It is important to point out to our children the significance of the written word.

(No signature) [24]

It is remarkable to see the progression from one letter to the next.

By the following September Helen shows improvement in fullness of construction and more extended relations of thought. [25]

The following is a short excerpt from a letter Helen wrote to her teacher while Miss Sullivan was away. This letter was written only two years after her first. Note the improvement in all areas of style, vocabulary, composition, and sentence structure.

TO MISS ANNE MANSFIElD SULLIVAN

Tuscumbia, Alabama, August 7, 1889.

Dearest Teacher – I am very glad to write to you this evening, for I have been thinking much about you all day. I am sitting on the piazza, and my little white pigeon is perched on the back of my chair, watching me write. Her little brown mate has flown away with the other birds; but Annie is not sad, for she likes to stay with me. [26]

As we read these letters with our children, we can make comparisons between them. It is this type of comparing and contrasting of writings that develops and nurtures our thinking skills. Children are beckoned to offer their thoughts and inspirations about a matter, rather than to read a paragraph and then select the best answer from a multiple choice listing. Much of this discussion can take place orally and can gradually develop into written essays.

Turning our discussion back to Helen's letters:

Helen Keller's letters are important not only as a supplementary story of her life, but as a demonstration of her growth in thought and expression — the growth which in itself has made her distinguished.

One cause for the excellence of her letters is the great number of them. They are the exercises which have trained her to write. [27]

Another excerpt taken from the collection of Helen's letters reads:

Like a good many of Helen Keller's early letters, this to her French teacher is her re-phrasing of a story. It shows how much the gift of writing is in the early stages of its development the gift of mimicry. [28]

And so these two quotes emphasize two important methods utilized in good writing instruction. It is evident that exercises comprised of copying, dictation, and narration (a retelling or rephrasing of what has been read), offer excellent training in writing. It is also important to spend

It is this type of comparing and contrasting of writings that develops and nurtures our thinking skills. Children are beckoned to offer their thoughts and inspirations about a matter, rather than to read a paragraph and then select the best answer from a multiple choice listing.

sufficient time writing, as Helen did. Writing letters were the exercises that trained her to write.

We can glean a bit of history as we read Helen's autobiography and the letters she both wrote and received. She was intimately acquainted with Dr. Alexander Graham Bell at an early age. Dr. Bell was greatly responsible for encouraging Helen's education. She recollects her first encounter with this great man.

> *Child as I was, I at once felt the tenderness and sympathy which endeared Dr. Bell to so many hearts, as his wonderful achievements enlist their admiration. He held me on his knee while I examined his watch, and he made it strike for me. He understood my signs and I knew it and loved him at once. But I did not dream that that interview would be the door through which I should pass from darkness into light, from isolation to friendship, companionship, knowledge, love.*

> *Dr. Bell advised my father to write to Mr. Anagnos, director of the Perkins Institution in Boston, the scene of Dr. Howe's great labors for the blind, and ask him if he had a teacher competent to begin my education.* [29]

We chose a short biography of Dr. Alexander Graham Bell to read after we encountered him in Helen's life story. We selected a newer biography filled with excellent photographs, including a photograph of Helen and Anne Sullivan with Dr. Bell. The children and I were excited to see them pictured together. We did not launch an in-depth study of Dr. Bell and his accomplishments at this time, as I wanted our focus to remain on our initial study of sign language; however, investigating Dr. Bell briefly at this point added a significant dimension to our study.

Later, when we conduct a unit study more intensely focused on Dr. Bell, his accomplishments, and his inventions, we will be able to say, "Oh yes, we remember that Alexander Graham Bell and Helen Keller were friends. Dr. Bell played an important part in Helen's education."

Several letters between Dr. Bell and Helen are included in the afterword of Helen's life story. Helen even dedicated her autobiography to Dr. Bell:

TO ALEXANDER GRAHAM BELL

Who has taught the deaf to speak and enabled the listening ear to hear speech from the Atlantic to the Rockies,

I DEDICATE

This Story of My Life. [30]

There were several other famous individuals that we encountered

It is also important to spend sufficient time writing, as Helen did. Writing letters were the exercises that trained her to write.

along with Helen. She wrote and received letters from prominent persons such as John Greenleaf Whittier, Dr. Oliver Wendell Holmes, Rev. Phillip Brooks, Mrs. Grover Cleveland, and Dr. Edward Everette Hale.

It is this personal encounter of individual with individual that helps us to see history as it truly is — not a series of dates and wars to be memorized, but a series of relationships between people, places, ideas, and events. History comes alive as we feel the sufferings, joys, defeats, and accomplishments of people throughout time.

Although not every autobiography or biography we read will offer as much food for thought as ***The Story of My Life***, it is easy to see that unit studies, based on the lives, triumphs, and sorrows of real people, in real space and time, gives us a more enthralling picture than dry textbooks. We should provide a vast supply of good books for our children to read and listen to. For as Gladys Hunt states in the book she co-authored, ***Honey for a Teen's Heart***:

Good stories put flesh on abstract ideas. It's difficult to fathom what it means to be noble, valiant, courageous, or even unselfish, unless we meet people in stories whose actions show us what these things mean.

We learn how to use the English language when we read good writing. It's a by-product. We come to admire the right word in the right place – and we are amazed at what it can convey. [31]

A good writer has something worth saying and says it in the best possible way and respects the reader's ability to understand. Language is used well. The word choices make us see, feel, hear, taste, smell, decide. The action of the story and the descriptions have a crisp leanness because strong verbs and simple descriptions are used. The Bible is a model for this kind of writing. With an economy of words, lasting pictures are painted. [32]

There is much more that we learned while reading the autobiography of Miss Keller that I would like to share, but space does not allow it; and it is better that you and your children have the opportunity to newly discover these gems for yourselves. (For more information about our sign language unit study see page 201.)

I hope these excerpts will help you to see how we conduct our studies and how our ***Reader's Journals*** contribute to our love for reading and our life-long habit of reading. For it is not profitable to bury our noses in books, but we must be able to learn from these books and act upon the knowledge gained. Furthermore, reading leads to writing, which enables us to enjoy communication and self-expression in a vital way.

History comes alive as we feel the sufferings, joys, defeats, and accomplishments of people throughout time.

It's difficult to fathom what it means to be noble, valiant, courageous, or even unselfish, unless we meet people in stories whose actions show us what these things mean. [31]

Acknowledgements

Portions taken from *The Story of My Life*, by Helen Keller, are taken from the Bantam 1990 edition. Bantam Doubleday Dell Publishing Group, Inc., 666 Fifth Avenue, New York, NY 10103.

Portions taken from *Honey for a Child's Heart*, by Gladys Hunt, are used with permission by Zondervan Publishing House, Grand Rapids, MI 49530.

Portions taken from *Honey for a Teen's Heart*, by Gladys Hunt and Barbara Hampton, are used with permission by Zondervan Publishing House, Grand Rapids, MI 49530.

Portions taken from *The Elements of Grammar*, by Margaret Shertzer, are used with permission by Macmillan Publishing Company, 886 Third Avenue, New York, NY 10022.

Portions taken from *A Family Program for Reading Aloud*, by Rosalie June Slater, 2nd Edition, are used with permission by Foundation for American Christian Education, P.O. Box 9588, Chesapeake, VA 23321-9588.

Portions taken from *Let the Authors Speak*, by Carolyn Hatcher, are used with permission by Old Pinnacle Publishing, P. O. Box 698, Joelton, TN 37080.

Portions taken from *Gallaudet, Friend of the Deaf*, by Etta DeGering, are taken from the edition published by David McKay Company, Inc., New York, NY.

Portions from *Little Women*, by Louisa May Alcott, are taken from the edition published by Outlet Books, a division of Random House Publishers, Avenel, NJ.

References

1 *Games for Math*, Peggy Kaye, author of *Games for Reading*, introduction.

2 *Little Women*, by Louisa May Alcott, 1987 edition, distributed by Outlet Book Company, Inc., a Random House Company, p. 3.

3 *Little Women*, by Louisa May Alcott, 1987 edition, distributed by Outlet Books Company, Inc., a Random House Company, p. 9.

4 *Little Women*, by Louisa May Alcott, 1987 edition, distributed by Outlet Book Company, Inc., a Random House Company, p. 9.

5 *Little Women*, by Louisa May Alcott, 1987 edition, distributed by Outlet Book Company, Inc., a Random House Company, p. 10.

6 *Little Women*, by Louisa May Alcott, 1987 edition, distributed by Outlet Book Company, Inc., a Random House Company, p. 10.

7 *Little Women*, by Louisa May Alcott, 1987 edition, distributed by Outlet Book Company, Inc., a Random House Company, p. 12.

8 *Dangerous Journey,* by John Bunyan, edited by Oliver Hunkin, Published by Wm. B. Eerdmans Publishing Company, Grand Rapids, MI., Introduction.

9 *Honey For a Child's Heart*, by Gladys Hunt, p. 13-14.

10 *Let the Authors Speak*, by Carolyn Hatcher, p. 23.

11 *The Story of My Life*, by Helen Keller, Bantam 1990 edition, p. 14.

12 *The Story of My Life*, by Helen Keller, Bantam 1990 edition, p. 16.

13 *The Story of My Life*, by Helen Keller, Bantam 1990 edition, p. 17.

14 *The Story of My Life*, by Helen Keller, Bantam 1990 edition, p. 84-85.

15 *Gallaudet, Friend of the Deaf,* by Etta DeGering, p. 40-43.

16 *The Story of My Life*, by Helen Keller, Bantam 1990 edition, p. 18.

17 *The Elements of Grammar*, by Margaret Shertzer, p. 2.

18 *The Story of My Life*, by Helen Keller, Bantam 1990 edition, p. 23.

19 *A Family Program for Reading Aloud*, by Rosalie J. Slater, p. 5.

20 *The Story of My Life*, by Helen Keller, Bantam 1990 edition, p. 24-25.

21 *The Story of My Life*, by Helen Keller, Bantam 1990 edition, p. 25.

22 *A Family Program for Reading Aloud*, by Rosalie J. Slater, p. 61-62.

23 *The Story of My Life*, by Helen Keller, Bantam 1990 edition, p. 22.

24 *The Story of My Life*, by Helen Keller, Bantam 1990 edition, p. 115.

25 *The Story of My Life*, by Helen Keller, Bantam 1990 edition, p. 116.

26 *The Story of My Life*, by Helen Keller, Bantam 1990 edition, p. 137.

27 *The Story of My Life*, by Helen Keller, Bantam 1990 edition, p. 109.

28 *The Story of My Life*, by Helen Keller, Bantam 1990 edition, p.135.

29 *The Story of My Life*, by Helen Keller, Bantam 1990 edition, p. 13.

30 *The Story of My Life*, by Helen Keller, Bantam 1990 edition, dedication page.

31 *Honey For a Teen's Heart*, by Gladys Hunt and Barbara Hampton.

32 *Honey For a Teen's Heart*, by Gladys Hunt and Barbara Hampton.

Notes

Success with Unit Studies

Valerie Bendt

Table of Contents

I dedicate this book to my loving husband, Bruce, who is always eager to listen as I share the little everyday affairs of our household. He is my head cheerleader.

My children's names and ages at the time of publication (1996) are as follows: Michelle, 16 years old; Melissa, 14 years old; Robert, 12 years old; Raymond, 10 years old; Mandy, 6 years old; and Randall 1 year old.

Dedication

What are Unit Studies Anyway?

Is it not far better to be able to relate one subject to another and see how they work together?

When conducting a unit study, I generally try to find at least one biography to read aloud about a person that relates to our topic of study.

Biographies allow us to become intimately acquainted with an individual and walk in his path.

I think it might be best to start by explaining what unit studies are <u>not</u>. Unit studies are not textbook studies. Textbook studies entail the study of as many as eight separate subjects, having little or no correlation to each other. For example, you may study **Literature**, focusing on British poets, while your **Geography Studies** center on the Middle East. At the same time your **History Studies** may be concentrated on the Civil War era. You may be studying biology in **Science** and geometry in **Mathematics**, while learning about the accomplishments of the Greek mathematicians. Your **Music Studies** may take you to the baroque period, while your **Art Studies** are focused on the paintings of American Indians, and last but not least, your **Bible Studies** are centered on Noah and the Flood. You can put all of this into a pot and serve a very unappetizing helping of mush. Each of these studies has merit, but is it best to study them all at the same time? Is this the best way to learn? Is it not far better to be able to relate one subject to another and see how they work together?

For example, a few years ago, our family studied sign language. This was a topic that I was very interested in, so I decided that the best way to learn about it was to study it with my children. When conducting a unit study, I generally try to find at least one biography to read aloud about a person that relates to our topic of study. It is as we study real people in real space and time that history comes alive for us. History is not a series of dates and wars to be memorized, but rather the interacting of individual with individual.

Biographies allow us to become intimately acquainted with an individual and walk in his path. While studying sign language, I chose a biography of Thomas Hopkins Gallaudet entitled, ***Gallaudet, Friend of the Deaf***, to read aloud to my children. Gallaudet was the founder of deaf education in America. History came into play as the Gallaudet College in Washington, D.C. was used as an army hospital during the strife-torn Civil War years. Next we read ***The Story of My Life***, by Helen Keller. Helen's father was a captain during the Civil War, so we were able to draw a parallel to Gallaudet's biography.

Both biographies gave us an **Historical Perspective** of sign language. We used a sign language instruction video and book and learned hundreds of signs, thus developing **Communication Skills** and **Manual Dexterity**. As we read the autobiography of Helen Keller, we were introduced to Alexander Graham Bell. Helen Keller and Dr. Bell were intimately acquainted, and Dr. Bell was responsible for Helen beginning her education. We did not dive into an in-depth study of Dr. Bell and his accomplishments at this time, such as the invention of the telephone, but rather we focused on his work with sound, hearing, and the ear. This added a **Scientific Dimension** to our study.

We also studied the **Anatomy** of the hand, the instrument of communication of the deaf. The children drew their hands as they formed the letters of their names as designated in the manual sign alphabet, thus stimulating **Artistic Abilities** and appreciation for the complexities of the anatomy of the human hand.

The children copied and took from dictation select passages from the biographies we read. Our spelling, vocabulary, punctuation, grammar lessons, and reading comprehension exercises centered on these passages, thus enhancing our **Language Arts Studies**. We wrote and talked about what it would be like to be a deaf person in a noisy world, therefore adding **Social Studies** to our curriculum. My older girls made books with a sign language theme, thereby encouraging **Creative Writing and Art**.

We researched Bible verses pertaining to hearing and the ear. We noted the importance of each part of the human body and how it parallels the relationship of the members of the body of Christ. Bible stories were read and then pantomimed. These activities enhanced our **Bible Studies**.

We went to the park and I pretended to be a deaf person. My children had to communicate with me without speaking for an hour. This was very frustrating for them as I sat in the swing, not paying them any attention. Soon they forgot the rules of our game and called to me from the top of the slide. After getting no response from me, the children learned that they had to come and tap me on the shoulder or stand in front of me in order to be noticed. We discussed this afterward, thus strengthening **Observation Skills** and **Thinking Skills**.

We visited Helen Keller's home in Tuscumbia, Alabama and saw the out-door play about her life entitled, *The Miracle Worker*, therefore adding a **Dramatic Element** to our study. **Geography Studies** were strengthened as the children followed the road map from state to state as we journeyed to her home.

As you can see, we touched on many subject areas during this unit study on sign language. Our attention was geared to our primary study of sign language; however, skills in other subject areas were strengthened along the way. Basic skills can be taught and enhanced in a meaningful way through unit studies. Children see the necessity for learning skills as they need them to study a topic.

It is obvious that this is a natural way to learn — focusing on one topic at a time. Our energies are not consumed by dividing our efforts in five or six subject areas that have no correlation. Multiply this confusion times two, three, four, or more children working at different levels on different subjects, in different textbooks, and calamity results! With unit studies, the entire family can study a topic together. Naturally, the older children will pick up more than the younger children, and their studies will be more in depth.

The children copied and took from dictation select passages from the biographies we read.

Basic skills can be taught and enhanced in a meaningful way through unit studies.

A unit study is what each person makes it. It can be a brief topical study or a life-long quest. It can be tailored to meet the needs of individual families.

However, areas of interest are opened as we explore new topics.

My sons' zeal for knowledge in a specific area caused them to study on their own.

Hopefully this illustration will explain what a unit study encompasses. <u>It is simply a study that focuses on one topic at a time</u>. As this topic is explored, a variety of subject areas are explored. A unit study is what each person makes it. It can be a brief topical study or a life-long quest. It can be tailored to meet the needs of individual families.

As I plan unit studies throughout the year, I try to choose topics from a variety of <u>key subject areas</u>. A number of other subjects are integrated into each study; however, the main thrust of a particular unit study lies in a specific area. For example, during the year I select unit studies primarily based on **History**, **Geography**, **Science**, **Fine Arts**, **Literature**, and so forth. Each unit study is conducted in a manner to encompass one main content area.

I feel that selecting from a variety of key subject areas enables us to achieve a well-rounded course of study. The children and I may wish to conduct a unit study that corresponds to an interest we may have. This is fine from time to time, especially for children who are difficult to motivate or who are burned out on traditional textbook and workbook studies. However, areas of interest are opened as we explore new topics. I would like to relate a story that illustrates these two points. That is, how an interest can act as a catalyst to launch us into a study, and how an area of interest can be discovered as we investigate a new topic.

About a year ago, I purchased materials to conduct a unit study on flight. My boys, Robert and Raymond, had been begging me to do this study with them, but my disinterest in the topic caused me to be lax about pursuing it. I finally gave into their desires, and we began our formal unit study on flight. The books I had previously purchased had been patiently waiting for us on the shelf, or so I thought. As we began our study and I assigned chapters for the boys to read, I learned that they had already devoured all of the books! I said to them, "You've been begging me and begging me to do this study, and I find out that you've already done the study on your own." They explained they were not going to wait around for me!

Now this is a perfect example of what Gregg Harris describes as a delight-directed study. I would like to offer a brief quote from Gregg's new edition of ***The Christian Home School***, page 123:

... Remember that delight-directed study is the goal for your students. As adults, this approach is the only way they will be able to be the life-long learners God wants them to be. Delight-directed study will teach them how to learn and how to keep up with all the changes in their field of interest. Textbooks must one day make way for reading "real books." Required classes must yield to voluntary study groups.

My sons' zeal for knowledge in a specific area caused them to study on their own. They were so enthusiastic that they decided to continue their study of flight with me joining them this time! We went to the library and selected some additional books on the topic of flight. Several of these library books were biographies. Reading about the lives of real people brings a unit study or topical study to life. Biographies and autobiographies allow us to experience the triumphs, defeats, excitement, and perils of the individual. Our studies take on a new dimension through this encounter with real people and real events.

While studying flight, we read a brief biographical sketch of Eddie Rickenbacker from *A Family Program for Reading Aloud*, which caused us to seek out his autobiography from the library. Eddie Rickenbacker designed numerous airplanes, as well as the Rickenbacker automobile. His autobiography is quite long, perhaps 600 pages, so we chose to read certain chapters that pertained to our study. One of these chapters was entitled, *Lost at Sea*.

Eddie's gift for expressing himself was evident as I read aloud this incredible account of how his plane crashed in the middle of the Pacific Ocean. Mr. Rickenbacker was on his way to give General MacArthur a top secret message that had been entrusted to him by the Secretary of War. Eddie and his crew languished through 24 days in life boats. He kept his crew alive through prayer and the singing of hymns. He said that there were three agnostics out of the eight men when they began their journey; however, there was not an unbeliever among them after the 8th day. Now, I will not tell you what happened on the 8th day, because you need to read the account with your children!

My children sat nearly motionless for two full hours while I read this excerpt to them, and I often had to choke back the tears. Even my six-year-old daughter, Mandy, was spellbound. This story has left an impression on me and my children that will be with us for a lifetime. The children still come to me, months later, and initiate a discussion about Eddie Rickenbacker's perilous account on the sea.

His autobiography offers us excellent material for a character study, as well as a glimpse of history and further insights into our key study of flight. I do not know of any textbook that would have entranced my children the way this autobiography did. My own interest in our study of flight was ignited in a way I would never have realized except through this incredible drama. Reading broadens our world. It is amazing what we can learn while absorbed in good literature. Basic skills and thinking skills can be taught and enhanced in a meaningful way through this intimacy with books. (For more ideas on how to effectively utilize good literature, please see my book, *For the Love of Reading*.)

Often parents come to me and say, "My child just doesn't like to read." My response is that he must like *something*, and that interest can be used to encourage him to read — to learn to love to read. If a child has a

Reading about the lives of real people brings a unit study or topical study to life.

My children sat nearly motionless for two full hours while I read this excerpt to them, and I often had to choke back the tears.

I do not know of any textbook that would have entranced my children the way this autobiography did.

delight or interest, he will immerse himself in studying about that delight or interest in a way in which he would never immerse himself in textbook studies.

But what about textbook studies? Let us look at what Charlotte Mason says about textbooks in her book, **School Education,** which she wrote in the early 1900s. On page 171. Miss Mason states:

> *We give him miserable little textbooks, mere compendiums of facts, which he is to learn off and say and produce at an examination; or we give him various knowledge in the form of warm diluents, prepared by his teacher with perhaps some grains of living thought to the gallon. And all the time we have books, books teeming with ideas fresh from the minds of thinkers upon every subject to which we can wish to introduce children.*

She also relates the idea that textbooks are an abridgement of an abridgement, and all that is left for the student is the dry bones of his subject, devoid of the stir of life.

I do not mean to disregard the use of textbooks in our educational endeavors; however, I want to emphasize that there is more education than is contained between their pages. Do not allow textbook studies to swallow up all your time so there is no time left for real books — books that will get your child excited about learning.

For those who feel rather insecure utilizing the unit study approach, textbooks can supply you with the framework around which to base your unit studies. Peruse your child's textbooks, searching for an interesting chapter or section. Utilize the information located within this chapter or section to develop a unit study. Select library books and other books you may wish to purchase that relate to the topic. You will be amazed at how easily many subjects can be integrated into this unit study.

Allow the child's other textbooks to rest on the shelf while conducting this unit study. Perhaps you will want to limit your unit study to two weeks, after which you can continue with your regular textbook studies. Then at a later date, select a chapter or section from another of your child's textbooks and conduct a unit study based on that. You will find that unit studies can easily be developed from literature textbooks, science textbooks, and history and geography textbooks. If you are working with a number of children of different ages, I suggest you use the older child's textbooks as a spring board for unit studies. The younger children can join in as they use materials geared for their reading and comprehension levels.

My daughter, Melissa, will be fifteen years old this summer. She has chosen to conduct textbook-based unit studies for the next school

Do not allow textbook studies to swallow up all your time so there is no time left for real books — books that will get your child excited about learning.

year. She utilized textbooks to a certain degree this school year and found she enjoyed the framework they gave her. (We school year round; however, we still talk in terms of beginning at the start of the typical school year.) Melissa is a good candidate for this type of study because she wants to work on her own, and the textbooks offer her a system by which to organize her lessons. She is also an avid reader, and therefore will read ample material to supplement this textbook method of learning.

It is important you use a system that works for both you and your children. Do not try to model your schooling efforts after a person or methodology that is not in keeping with your educational philosophy. (For additional information on developing your philosophy of education, please see the chapter in my book, *How to Create Your Own Unit Study*, entitled, *Defining Our Goal*.)

People often ask me, "Are unit studies appropriate for the high school student?" I feel that the answer to this is, "Absolutely!" In the example above I explained how one of my teenage daughters is utilizing a textbook-based unit study approach. She has also participated in a number of real life experiences that have strengthened skills in many areas. For example, at age thirteen, Melissa typed nearly the entire manuscript of my book, *For the Love of Reading*. She did this from my handwritten scrawl, which was not an easy task! As she was typing, she was constantly calling me to the computer and offering comments such as, "Mom, don't you need an apostrophe here?" And, "Your spelling is terrible, but I expected that," and so on.

I was amazed that this child who has difficulty editing her own work had no trouble in editing mine! I then realized that this is generally true of most people. It is difficult to edit your own work. (I know this from personal experience with my own books!) I told Melissa to change anything she felt needed changing, and that I would go over it later. I cannot think of any language arts exercises that would have been more beneficial. This real-life experience tuned her editing skills, and she was paid real money to do it!

Melissa has conducted a number of self-directed unit studies. She is a serious ballet student. This love has caused her to study various related topics. First she conducted a study of ballet, including the historical aspects as well as the technical aspects. This led her to a study of France, and now she is studying the French language. Melissa's enthusiasm for dance, singing, and drama has encouraged us to find alternate means for nurturing these desires. She has been taking ballet since she was three years old, and this coming school year she will be taking chorus at a local private Christian school. She is currently undertaking a unit study on Shakespeare. The highlight of this study will be a family outing to see a *Shakespeare in the Park Production*. This is an

It is important you use a system that works for both you and your children.

She has also participated in a number of real life experiences that have strengthened skills in many areas.

This real-life experience tuned her editing skills, and she was paid real money to do it!

outdoor event, and this year's drama is entitled, *All's Well That Ends Well.* This annual occasion has been a family tradition for several years.

My oldest daughter, Michelle, has just recently graduated from her home education program. She was registered with a private school, which maintained her transcripts and provided annual testing. Fortunately, the administrator of this school is an avid proponent of unit studies. She does an excellent job of translating unit studies into course credits. During her high school years, Michelle conducted several self-directed unit studies.

Nearly two years ago we were blessed with the birth of our sixth child, Randall. In preparation for this special event, Michelle read a 600 page midwifery manual, along with several books related to the human body and nutrition. She also did most of the cooking while I was pregnant and during Randall's first year, thus integrating her findings in her nutrition studies in a very real way. (Fortunately, she is an excellent cook. This she did not inherit from me!) She received hands-on practice as she learned to detect the position of the baby within the womb, take blood pressure, and listen for the baby's heart beat. She assisted in the actual delivery as well.

How is that for biology lab! And to think if she was in a traditional high school, she could have been dissecting frogs! (She did dissect the placenta, but I will not go into that!) This summer Michelle is going to a midwifery school for three months. She will live at the clinic-school which accommodates four students per session. Michelle will assist with between 50 to 100 births while at the school. She took a class this spring at a local community college, studied numerous midwifery textbooks, assisted in deliveries at a local birthing center, and participated in childbirth classes, all in preparation for attending the school this summer.

Some of Michelle's other endeavors included organizing our catalogue business. In 1995 she did the entire layout for our 48 page catalogue. This also involved reviewing materials to be included in the catalogue. This provided an excellent outlet for her to practice her computer, layout, writing, and editing skills. She has illustrated several books that I have written including **The Francis Study Guide**. (2004 note: A few years after **Success with Unit Studies** was first published, Michelle designed the puppets for my book **Successful Puppet Making**, described on page 332. We are currently working together on a Bible story puppet making book to be released in 2005.)

Michelle has designed logos and fliers for sporting events too. She is an accomplished martial arts student as well as a student teacher. She is currently working at a health food store where she is learning about herbs and nutrition. This herbal knowledge will prove useful in her midwifery studies.

By engaging in these various activities, her writing skills have

During her high school years, Michelle conducted several self-directed unit studies.

improved through note taking, her spelling abilities have been strengthened, her computer skills have vastly improved, her ability to read technical information and assimilate it has soared, and her organizational skills have been well developed. Through collaborating on the catalogue, our mother-daughter relationship has been nurtured.

Often the teenage years are difficult years for our children. As parents we tend to shy away from them because they are so moody. I realize, however, this is the time to cultivate a new relationship with our teens. Teens need to be able to express themselves and use their talents at this time more than ever. I have found through the years of conducting unit studies this method of instruction has allowed my children to develop the talents and abilities the Lord has given them. They have not been forced into a mold that stifles creativity and does little to prepare them for real life.

If Michelle attended high school or even college, what classes would offer her practice with the skills outlined? Perhaps a biology or physiology class, a journalism or publishing class, a graphic arts course, Business 101, and home economics. In order for students to participate in hands-on activities such as Michelle has done, often contrived or artificial means are employed. For example, students may be given an assignment whereby they pretend they are designing logos for a sporting event or creating a catalogue for a book store. At the end of the course, the instructor reviews the projects and then what? The student receives a grade and the project is often laid aside. It is exciting that homeschooled children can participate in real-life events, not just teacher-contrived situations.

I mentioned earlier that my boys, ages 10 and 12 were intrigued by their study of flight this year. They are also involved in martial arts. They have a keen interest in computers, which continues to be a source of study. Because I have teenage daughters who conduct their own studies now, the three younger children generally study the same topic. My daughter Mandy is nearly seven years old, and although she participates in the studies I conduct with the boys to some degree, I carry on special studies with her. Often we are able to include her little brother, Randall, who is nearly two years old, in these studies. He definitely wants to be one of the gang!

This year I have been reading the Little House on the Prairie series, by Laura Ingalls Wilder, with Mandy. (I am on my third time reading this series aloud. I read it to my other children when they were younger.) These excellent books generate activities and academic exercises. Each day I read one or two chapters from one of the books to Mandy. Then we discuss the chapter, and I devise simple sentences relating to the chapter for Mandy to read. Mandy enjoys composing

I have found through the years of conducting unit studies this method of instruction has allowed my children to develop the talents and abilities the Lord has given them. They have not been forced into a mold that stifles creativity and does little to prepare them for real life.

sentences about what we read too. This helps to strengthen her observation skills as she must recall the story. I write the sentences we make on index cards, one or two words per card. I lay the cards out on the table in the proper sequence, and then Mandy reads the sentences aloud.

Separating the words onto cards enables her to focus on one word at a time. The large print is also effective. I try to use words that Mandy is capable of reading. When Mandy is introduced to an unfamiliar word, I teach her the sound for the phonetic combination used at that time. For example, the sentence may read: **Pa fed the cow some hay.** If Mandy has not yet learned the rule that *ay* says **a** as found in the word *hay*, then I will teach her that rule at this time. We will write numerous other words on index cards utilizing this same rule such as: *bay, day, ray, may,* and *clay*. Then Mandy will copy the sentence on large lined paper.

This Little House unit study has allowed us to incorporate many educational and fun activities. Although there are several excellent Little House study guides, we have not used them, but rather we have let the study take its own course as we read the books aloud. Mandy's personality and academic skill level dictate the course this study takes. We have found many related materials such as ***My Book of Little House Paper Dolls, My Little House Cookbook, The Little House Calendar, My Little House Sticker Book, Laura Ingalls Wilder: A Biography, Dear Laura: Letters from Children to Laura Ingalls Wilder***, and the picture book series entitled, ***My First Little House Books***. The books in this series are beautiful full-color books with simple text based on the book, ***Little House in the Big Woods***. There are currently eight books in this series. See page 323 in the Resources section for listing of all the books. We have gone Little House crazy, but we are enjoying ourselves! Mandy helps make goodies from ***My Little House Cookbook***, and Randall helps eat them. (I told you he likes to participate in our studies too!)

I even made prairie dolls for Mandy and Randall. In ***The Little House in the Big Woods***, we read that Laura had a rag doll named Charlotte. Mandy decided it would be nice to have a rag doll too. She named her doll Laura Elizabeth Rose. Elizabeth is Laura's middle name, and Rose is Laura's daughter's name. Randall decided that he needed a doll also. So we have named his doll Almanzo after Laura's husband. I found a pattern for a rag doll complete with a cloth carrying case and wardrobe. With a little improvising, the clothes were transformed into prairie clothing complete with calico dresses and bonnets for Mandy's doll, and plaid shirts and overalls for Randall's doll. Mandy selected the fabrics for the clothes; after all, she is certain she knows what Laura and her family wore! Reading the stories has created a visual image in her mind.

When we selected the fabric for Randall's doll, he insisted on

Although there are several excellent Little House study guides, we have not used any of them, but rather we have let the study take its own course as we read the books aloud. Mandy's personality and academic skill level dictate the course this study takes.

carrying the large bolts of cloth to the cutting counter. He is not about to be left out! I am sure that many of you will be anxious to know what pattern I used, so I have included that information in the Resources section on page 328.

My daughter, Michelle, made some additional clothing patterns for me to complete the prairie doll wardrobe. These include two different bonnet patterns and an apron pattern. I have included these special patterns for you to copy in the Appendix on pages 296-299. The children were so enthralled with their prairie dolls that they wanted me to make prairie costumes for them too!

I succumbed to their desires and Mandy and Randall were transformed into "Laura" and "Almanzo." It is rewarding to see them playing "Little House" together rather than being held hostage to the imaginary play produced by television and animated movies. (See page 328 in the Resources section for information about the clothing patterns I used for the children.)

Mandy has several authors that are her favorites. Besides her admiration for Laura Ingalls Wilder and The Little House on the Prairie series, Mandy enjoys Beatrix Potter's works such as **The Tale of Peter Rabbit** and **The Tale of Mrs. Tittlemouse.** Her love for these two authors has inspired her to start her own special book series entitled, The Little Mouse on the Prairie series. Her first book in this series was "published" recently. It is titled, **The Little Mouse Family on the Prairie.** Mandy spent two weeks dictating the story to me, which I wrote on notebook paper. Her big sister, Melissa, typed it on the computer.

Mandy's creativity flourished while composing this manuscript. It is evident to see that she is modeling her writing after these two favorite authors. Mandy's story was about 33 pages handwritten in length! Mandy helped to make this book into a beautiful hard-bound, hand-sewn edition, which she illustrated herself. This book will be treasured for a lifetime! (Please see page 331 for details about my book, **Creating Books with Children,** which will lead you and your children through a six-week, book-making unit study.)

I could go on telling you more about my children's studies and activities, but I do not want to bore you! In the next chapter, I will explain how we integrate the **Five R's of Unit Studies** in our homeschooling. This includes: **Research**, **Reading**, **Writing**, **Recording**, and **Reporting**. Read ahead to discover how the incorporation of these disciplines gives the children the foundation they need to be self learners.

It is rewarding to see them playing "Little House" together rather than being held hostage to the imaginary play produced by television and animated movies.

Research

If we can cultivate research skills throughout our children's educational endeavors, then we will have life-long learners.

I then realized the research skills she was developing could be transferred to any field of study.

Literature can also be an effective vehicle for transporting us to another place and time.

*I*f we want our children to be life-long learners, we must teach them how to learn on their own. Most published curriculum materials foster a multiple choice or fill-in-the-blank mentality. They also employ the popular, "read the chapter and answer the questions at the end" method of instruction. Children learn only to do what they are told; they do not learn to be independent information seekers. Research is often treated as a separate skill to be covered once a year at the junior and senior high levels. If we can cultivate research skills throughout our children's educational endeavors, then we will have life-long learners.

The importance of research became evident to me years ago when my children were first creating their own unit studies. My daughter, Melissa, chose to study dolls and stuffed animals. I admit that I was a little apprehensive as I wondered how much educational value this type of study might hold. I was pleased to see how Melissa threw herself into her research to find all the information she could that related to her topic. I then realized the research skills she was developing could be transferred to any field of study.

Research is an integral part of learning. We should not lay all the material out for our children in nice neat packages, for in doing so we neglect a very crucial part of their education. After all, we want our children to develop the proper techniques to be able to teach and lead their own children one day. What is research? Research as defined in the **American Dictionary of the English Language, Noah Webster, 1828**:

> *To search or examine with continued care; to seek diligently for the truth.*

When conducting research about a unit study topic, it is helpful to gather information from a number of resources. I mentioned previously how effective biographies are in strengthening a unit study. They add a personal element to our studies that can not be found in most non-fiction materials. I usually try to find at least one biography about an individual that relates to our topic of study. Literature can also be an effective vehicle for transporting us to another place and time. Stories, both fictional and true, offer vital information about our topic of study. For example, a historical novel can convey us to another time and location as real events and places are portrayed in vivid detail.

The Bible is of course the one source we should always include in our research. A concordance or topical Bible will lead us to many verses pertaining to our topic of interest. (See the chapter entitled, *Using the Bible*, in my book **How to Create Your Own Unit Study**.)

Magazines, especially those such as *National Geographic*, contain useful material for a number of studies. These can be accessed through your public library's periodical catalog. Often a reference book such as a dictionary, encyclopedia, atlas, or almanac enables your children to glean useful information about their topic. This information will often direct them to other areas for additional materials. For example, an encyclopedia may list key people, places, inventions, discoveries, or related topics which can be explored. *The World Book Encyclopedia* contains excellent outlines about key topics of interest. My children enjoy using the Encarta Encyclopedia on CD ROM with our computer. I have noticed that they enjoy researching topics using this high-tech approach.

You will find a host of non-fiction books about a myriad of topics in the public library. Use both the adult and children's sections of the library. (More about this later.) Often a good library book will contain valuable information about your study which will enable you to find related materials. This book may mention pertinent people, inventions, and so forth that your children may want to investigate. For example, while studying about oceans, my boys decided they wanted to learn about the *Titanic*. After selecting a book about the *Titanic*, my sons sat at the library's computer and skimmed the book looking for key people and other interesting data. They used the subject key word function to locate books about various individuals, exploration devices, and historical material pertaining to their topic.

If you have access to a public library where the books are computer catalogued, your children will find many ways to investigate their topics. This is what a typical screen looks like. (See diagram on page 280.) Each menu has additional menus which can help narrow your topic of interest. My children are much faster at locating books pertaining to their topic than I am. We are able to access the library's catalog via the internet using our home computer. This is a great time saver as books can be located and pulled for us before we leave the house.

If you feel intimidated by the computers at your library, just let your children loose and they will figure them out! If you are still having difficulty, find an intelligent looking child in your library and ask him to show you and your children the ropes. My children love helping adults at the library who are floundering at the computer keyboard! (Of course, you could always ask a librarian for help.)

2004 note: Many online bookstores such as Amazon.com, Barnes and Noble, and various homeschool educational suppliers have search engines that allow you to search for books relating to most any topic of study. I have found this is a convenient way to search for books pertaining to our units, as most of these online stores display the front and back book covers and often sample pages from the books. Detailed reviews are usually included as well. This allows me to shop from home. If a book seems interesting, I check to see if my public library has a copy. If one is available, I place a hold for the book over the internet and pick it up at my

Often a good library book will contain valuable information about your study which will enable you to find related materials. This book may mention pertinent people, inventions, and so forth that your children may want to investigate.

We are able to access the library's catalog via the internet using our home computer. This is a great time saver as books can be located and pulled for us before we even leave the house.

convenience. Sometimes we will purchase a copy of a book we have borrowed from the public library. When conducting a unit study, I like to use the library as much as possible, but I also like to build our home library with quality books my children will turn to again and again.

Look for maps, sound recordings, videos, art work, poetry, newspapers, and additional materials to enhance your study. Ask yourself, "Are there organizations that we can write to for free or inexpensive materials? Are there people in my church or community that can offer their expertise in our area of study? Are there any museums or other areas of interest we can visit? What about plays and orchestral performances? What are some additional field trips that we might like to incorporate? What job opportunities can we explore that relate to our topic?

Do not feel you need to use every book or resource you find. That would make for a very stressful study; however, be aware there are *many* avenues to explore. Select those materials that will work best for your family situation. For more related information, see the chapter entitled, *Using the Library* in my book, **How to Create Your Own Unit Study.**

I would like to relate a story that Pat Wesolowski tells in her workshop entitled, *Information Please!* Pat says:

> *I heard a true story told by a lady that had visited Israel. While on her trip, she saw some sheep in a barren pasture digging in the ground. She asked the shepherd, "What in the world are these sheep doing?" He told her that when there is a drought, and there is nothing green on which to graze, the sheep have to dig in the dirt until they find the seed. It only takes 1 ½ tablespoons to give them a day's nourishment. He said it broke his heart to watch them have to work so hard for their food, but if he were to hand feed them now, when the grass grew again they would no longer graze. They would continue to expect to be hand fed and would starve to death.*

In response to this, Pat adds:

> *Isn't this what the school system has done with our children? They have hand fed them for so long that they no longer know how to feed themselves. Why would we want to emulate such a failed system? Why do we feel so compelled to meet the requirements set by an educational system that is secular and whose goals are, for the most part, in direct opposition to our goals and values?*
>
> *Our current educational goals are three-fold:*
>
> *1) To encourage our children to be inquisitive and have a desire to learn.*

2) To avail our children with the tools and ability to access information needed in order to learn.

3) To teach our children how to use the information they access and to verify whether it is accurate or not.

Pat has authored several books pertaining to research. These books are part of the *Information Please!* series written on three different levels. These levels are Beginning (K-5), Intermediate (6-8), and Advanced (9-12). Perhaps the best book to begin with is ***Information Please!: Getting Started***. This volume gives parents specific guidelines to follow when introducing children to reference materials. The various chapters are dedicated to using a number of resources including: libraries, thesauruses, dictionaries, encyclopedias, concordances, telephone books, newspapers, almanacs, atlases, maps, timetables, computers, grammar books, and other reference materials. Many chapters include questions, games, puzzles, and additional activities to familiarize your children with using each reference source. Sample pages from each level of ***Information Please!*** are included at the end of the book to allow the children to utilize the research skills they have learned. As Pat states:

Oftentimes the only barrier to knowledge is the lack of knowing how to find the information one needs. Education should not be equated with how many facts one can recite, but rather with one's ability to retrieve information and use it.

2004 note: The Internet has opened up new doors in the area of research for us and our children. It is important that we verify the information we find. One general method for verifying information is to be able to acquire the same information from at least two sources. Primary documents, diaries, letters, and newspaper articles are a good choice. I have asked Pat Wesolowski to offer some advice on using the Internet. Here is what she has to say:

*When I first wrote **Information, Please!** the Internet was new and not readily available to everyone. Now that the Internet is commonplace to every library and most homes, research has taken on a whole new dimension. Although it is true that one can find obscure information more quickly on the Internet, dependence on gaining information this way should not replace the ability to find information without using the Internet. Another caution to dependence on the Internet as an exclusive source for information is the possibility of receiving erroneous information. Almost anyone can set themselves up as an expert (whether they are or not) by creating websites filled with incorrect information. When doing research always ask these two questions: 1. Where did the information come from? 2. Is*

Oftentimes the only barrier to knowledge is the lack of knowing how to find the information one needs. Education should not be equated with how many facts one can recite, but rather with one's ability to retrieve information and use it.

—*Pat Wesolowski*

Although it is true that one can find obscure information more quickly on the Internet, dependence on gaining information this way should not replace the ability to find information without using the Internet.

—*Pat Wesolowski*

the source reliable?

*It would be ideal if the information you are seeking can be traced back to its original source, but that is not always simple or possible. When I assign a page of ten research questions to my children out of **Information, Please!** I tell them that they cannot use any one source more than twice. By doing this they are forced to choose which two questions they will save for the Internet (usually they choose the most difficult questions).*

Personally, I love how quickly I can find the information I need on the Internet when I am doing research. My favorite search engine is Google. A tip I learned last year (many of you may be aware of this, but I was not) has greatly reduced the amount of time it takes to find the information I need. When you put the words in the search box, if you enclose a phrase within quotation marks then the search engine will only look for those words as they appear in the quotation marks. For instance, if you type "George Washington" then the search engine will only come up with sites that include those two words together. If you exclude the quotation marks then the search engine will come up with every site that contains the word "George" as well as every site that contains the word "Washington" (without discernment to whether Washington is a place or a person).

*Another tip I learned this year with Google, which has made my life as a newsletter publisher much easier, is the fact that you can search for images on Google. When publishing an article on biscotti I thought it would be nice to include a picture. Although I had my doubts that a search would produce any pictures I was surprised and happy to have Google image search come up with pages of biscotti pictures from which to choose. To access these pictures I typed **biscotti** in the Google search box and clicked on the button labeled **Images** above the box.*

Has the Internet made research quicker and easier? Absolutely. Should it ever replace encyclopedias, almanacs, atlases, and other reference books? Not in a million years. How many times have you found a child reading page after page in a reference book when they were only looking up one item of information? This is a common occurrence in our household, but this won't happen very often with Internet research because once you

---

It would be ideal if the information you are seeking can be traced back to its original source, but that is not always simple or possible.

—Pat Wesolowski

Has the Internet made research quicker and easier? Absolutely. Should it every replace encyclopedias, almanacs, atlases, and other reference books? Not in a million years.

—Pat Wesolowski

find the information for which you are looking, there is usually little more to read.

Even though the Internet is a tool that can be used for good, it is also very dangerous. I would not allow any children to conduct unsupervised research on the Internet without a filter that prohibits access to objectionable sites. These filters can be purchased through Internet Service Providers, downloaded from websites, or added on to your Internet service from independent sources. One would be amazed at the sites that appear even when innocent searches are conducted.

This is what the main menu looks like on the computer at my public library. If I select item 1 then I can access the Library Catalog.

13 Aug 96   **North Tampa Branch**   06:53pm
Public Access Catalog

You can search any of the resources listed below. Enter the number of the database you want to use.

1. Library Catalog
2. American Heritage Dictionary
3. Bestsellers & Other Reading Lists
4. Clubs and Organizations
5. Frequently Asked Questions
6. Library Bulletin Board
7. Library Events Calendar
8. Your Library Record
9. Online Indexes or Articles {VISTA}
10. Print Saved List
11. TRAILS- Tampa History Index
12. Quit Searching

Enter your selection {s} and press {return} : PRT

This is what the Library Catalog menu looks like. I can easily locate desired materials by selecting from this menu.

13 Aug 96   **North Tampa Branch**   06:53pm
Public Access Catalog

Welcome to the Library Catalog
Please select one of the following search methods.

1. QUICK SEARCH-Look for any Keyword
2. Look for Exact TITLE
3. Look for Keyword {s} in TITLE
4. Look for AUTHOR by Keyword {s}
5. Look for Alphabetical AUTHOR List
6. Look for Keyword {s} in SUBJECT
7. Look for SERIES
8. Look for CALL NUMBER
9. Look for ISBN
10. Return to Main Menu
11. Quit Searching

Reading

Very young children utilize all of their senses to learn and gather information about the world around them. They taste, touch, smell, look, and listen. As they mature, they develop the ability to glean information through more structured means, such as direct instruction and reading.

While conducting unit studies, most of the knowledge about a topic will come through the medium of the written word. Books can be used in a variety of ways. Some books will be read aloud by the parent, some will be read aloud by the capable children, some will be read silently by the capable children, some will be used for their illustrations, and some will be used for reference purposes.

While conducting unit studies, most of the knowledge about a topic will come through the medium of the written word.

I want to mention again when conducting our unit studies, I try to select at least one biography about an individual relating to our topic that will enhance our study. I use this book, and generally one or two other books, as our basic "texts" which I read aloud to the children as a group. These are the books that provide us with discussion material and exercises for copying and dictation.

I select at least one relatively short book about our topic corresponding to each of the younger children's reading levels. We use these books to help build the beginning readers' skills. These skills include decoding abilities, sight word recognition, recognizing and understanding word meanings from context, and oral narration. I tailor these skills to accommodate each child. For example, I may read the words of each sentence aloud, pausing at a word the child can read. I encourage him to read that specific word. This progresses to allowing him to read an entire sentence from each page and then an entire sentence from each paragraph. Later, he will read an entire paragraph from each page. Eventually, he can read the whole page by himself. Then we use a system by which he reads one page, and I read the next. After a time, he may read two pages to my one, and so on, until he is able to read a whole book aloud to me. All of this happens so gradually the child feels no pressure.

I select at least one relatively short book about our topic corresponding to each of the younger children's reading levels.

All of this happens so gradually the child feels no pressure.

A child who is just learning his alphabet can be motivated to search for specific letters on the page or from chapter titles, which tend to have large print. Perhaps he will search for all of the *m*'s on the page. This is a good exercise in visual discrimination. I have found that the little ones do not like to be left out! They want to do schoolwork too.

Older children are also asked to read aloud. Often they will read aloud to a younger sibling from a relatively simple book relating to our topic. This helps to occupy a younger child who requires supervision, thus enabling me to work with one of my other children. This aids in developing the sibling relationship and the older child's teaching capabilities. The younger child feels he is part of the learning experience as well.

The younger child feels he is part of the learning experience as well.

Every child needs some individual attention. Every child needs to be able to learn some material on his own, and every child needs to be able to teach someone else.

I find it effective to select one book pertaining to our topic for my husband to read aloud to the children in the evening.

An interesting picture, chart, or graph may lure him into reading text that is a bit of a challenge for him.

Often times my older children will assist me by reading aloud portions from the main "text" that we read as a group. This enables me to review their oral reading skills.

While I am working with a child who is a beginning reader, and an older child is reading aloud to a younger child, my other children are reading silently from books geared to their reading levels and pertaining to our topic. A system of this type allows those of us with large families to effectively conduct unit studies. Not only does this system work well for organizational purposes, but it fosters the development of numerous skills.

Every child needs some individual attention. Every child needs to be able to learn some material on his own, and every child needs to be able to teach someone else. (And every mother needs to be able to maintain her sanity while homeschooling!)

I find it interesting to read newspaper articles about the new and innovative teaching methods that various schools are employing; that is using the older children to teach the younger children. We homeschoolers have been innovative for years!

I find it effective to select one book pertaining to our topic for my husband to read aloud to the children in the evening. This draws him into our study in a special way. As he reads, certain events or subjects related to our study emerge. This stimulates discussion and enables the children to narrate or retell the day's findings. It was very distressing when my husband would come home from work and ask the children, "What did you learn today?" and the only answer he received was, "I don't know!" His reading aloud helps them to recall the day's lessons.

I mentioned that some books may only be used for their illustrations. This can include diagrams, charts, graphs, drawings, and photographs. Often the books with the most appealing illustrations are found in the adult section of the library. The accompanying text may be too difficult for your study, but do not let that dissuade you from the benefit of a pictorial perspective. Sometimes these intriguing illustrations will cause a child to read the surrounding text, and before you know it, he is drawn further and further into a book, which would not usually interest him. This same principle may hold true for various books in the children's section of the library which are above your child's reading level. An interesting picture, chart, or graph may lure him into reading text that is a bit of a challenge for him.

And lastly, some books will be used as reference materials. Although not all of the information contained in these books may be pertinent to your study, certain key facts can be gleaned. For more ideas on effectually utilizing books, see *For the Love of Reading*.

A simple yet effective way to integrate language arts into a unit study is through the use of copying and dictation methods of instruction. As we emulate gifted authors, we learn the art of writing. Writing should not only be destined to the realm of creative writing, but should permeate all areas of study. We should strive to effectively write non-fiction as well as fiction.

Ruth Beechick does a wonderful job of expounding on the process and effectiveness of implementing copying and dictation methods in her book, ***You Can Teach Your Child Successfully***. I will briefly explain how we use this system in our studies. I generally review the material we read as a group the evening before. This usually means only scanning one section or chapter of a book. As I read, I search for a passage that clarifies or defines key elements pertaining to our study. Depending on the study, this may be relevant, factual information, or it may be a passage exemplifying a character trait I deem worthy of notation.

Initially, a paragraph provides us with ample material for copying or dictation. For certain children, I will copy the material onto lined paper, skipping every other line as I proceed. The child will then write directly under my writing. This enables the child to focus on letter construction and spacing.

I select an appropriate portion for each child to copy. For example, one child may copy the entire paragraph, while another copies one sentence from that paragraph. For a more advanced child, I may copy the selected passage at the top of his paper without skipping lines, and he will write at the bottom of the page. Afterwards, we will discuss various elements in the passage such as spelling, punctuation, grammar, phonics, and comprehension. Often, I will discuss elements from a passage collectively with the children, such as the use of quotation marks, without expecting mastery for every child. Many skills are only *introduced* to children in the early grades. These skills are reviewed year after year in order to develop proficiency.

An older child may take the passage directly from my verbal dictation, which entails the incorporation of more difficult skills as he must recall various rules. If the child has trouble with spelling, punctuation, capitalization, or some other element, a lesson can be devised to strengthen this weakness.

Gayle Graham has created a program which enables the child to use the words he misspells in his writing to create his own spelling notebook. The spelling notebook that Gayle has developed is called ***Tricks of the Trade***. It allows the child to categorize misspelled words according to spelling rules. He is not forced to learn tedious rules that he does not need; however, he is able to focus on the rules he does need in order to spell troublesome words. Gayle has written a companion book for

As we emulate gifted authors we learn the art of writing. Writing should not only be destined to the realm of creative writing, but should permeate all areas of study.

Often I will discuss elements from a passage collectively with the children, such as the use of quotation marks, without expecting mastery for every child. Many skills are only introduced to children in the early grades. These skills are reviewed year after year in order to develop proficiency.

parents called, *How to Teach Any Child to Spell*.

A good composition/grammar handbook is a valuable resource, which will allow your children to effectually tone their writing. I recommend the *Write Source* series. First I recommend **Writer's Express**, which is geared for the elementary grades. Next I suggest **Write Source 2000** for the middle grades, and finally **Writer's Inc** for the high school grades. These student-friendly books are packed with information.

Some of the topics covered in these manuals include: The Writing Process, Developing Essays, Building Paragraphs, Improving Your Writing, Journal Writing, Writing Biographies and Autobiographies, Writing the News Story, Writing Letters, The Business Letter, The Friendly Letter, Writing Poetry, Story Writing, Writing Plays, Using the Library, and Improving Vocabulary. Many other helpful elements are included as well as a list of prefixes, suffixes, and word roots and their meanings. You will find a glossary of literary terms such as allegory, melodrama, and tragedy. Other features are special punctuation and grammar sections. Full color maps, various charts, and historical documents are a few of the other components that make these guides so handy. You may own several books which contain some of the information found in one of these manuals, but having all this information packed into one easy-to-read book makes it an indispensable guide.

Let us return to the discussion of incorporating writing into our unit studies. When a child is first learning to talk, we use words and phrases we know he does not comprehend. Interaction with unknown words is the key to developing vocabulary. Although my children may be at different levels of the copying and dictation process, we are all concentrating on the same basic passage. This allows us to discuss the passage as a group. This discussion is not only centered on the technical elements such as grammar and punctuation, but also entails the essence of what the author is trying to convey.

A host of exercises can be implemented to help us benefit fully from the passage copied or taken from dictation. Key words may be selected as spelling and vocabulary words. A dictionary or thesaurus can be used to help clarify the meanings of these words. Passages may be rewritten in another tense, or rewritten so that a younger child might better understand the material presented.

I find my beginning readers to do well to read aloud the passage they have copied, and oral discussion can follow. Do not overwork these passages. You will be amazed at the progress your children will make as they continue to copy or take passages from dictation. It is not necessary to make a long drawn out assignment based on each passage.

For certain scientific unit studies, the children can copy or take from dictation an experiment that is planned for the following day. As you

---

A good composition/grammar handbook is a valuable resource, which will allow your children to effectually tone their writing.

When a child is first learning to talk, we use words and phrases we know he does not comprehend. Interaction with unknown words is the key to developing vocabulary.

Do not overwork these passages. You will be amazed at the progress your children will make as they continue to copy or take passages from dictation.

proceed with your studies, you will find more creative ways to incorporate copying and dictation exercises into your lessons. ***The Learning Language Arts through Literature*** curriculum makes effective use of the copying and dictation method of instruction. Utilizing these books will provide you with pertinent exercises and ample ideas, which can be transferred to any unit study topic.

Recording

It is useful for the children to record important facts or information about their topic of study. Generally, this will be material gleaned through reading or observation. Let's examine the recording of information derived from the books the children read.

There are several ways the children can record important facts they encounter. These facts can be recorded as notes on index cards, which can easily be categorized at a later time in order to construct a report. This report may be oral or written. For example, you may give a child one or two books geared to his reading and comprehension level, which he can use for compiling notes. You may tell him you want him to find a specific number of interesting facts, perhaps ten, and record these facts on index cards, one fact per card. Initially he may copy the passage, a brief passage, directly from the book. (Remember we discussed the effectiveness of copying previously.) Then he can turn the card over and rewrite the passage in his own words.

Each child can be responsible for gathering information that he will later share with the family.

Each child may search for different types of information. For instance, if you are studying about the human body, one child may be researching the circulatory system, while another is searching for facts pertaining to the to respiratory system. Each child can be responsible for gathering information he will later share with the family. (We will discuss more about sharing information in the next chapter *Reporting*.)

By taking notes specifically geared to a defined portion of the study, the children's abilities to scan for desired information are strengthened.

By taking notes specifically geared to a defined portion of the study, the children's abilities to scan for desired information are strengthened. The children can first read the book or chapter to be used for note taking and then scan for specifics.

We have found it fun to turn this note taking around a little and formulate questions from our reading, rather than only record facts as statements. We use this system to allow the children to create games. For example, give each child 25 index cards and a book or two about your topic of study suited to each child's reading level. Have the children write both the question and the answer on each card. Some cards will be what we call Event Cards. These tell the players to move ahead or backward, select another card, lose a turn, and so forth. With a bit of creativity on the part of the children, these cards can be interesting and add a fun dimension to the game. The next section of my book is entitled, Reporting. In this section I detail how to create a report or project to encapsulate material gleaned during a unit study. At this time each child can design a game board to accompany his game cards. These game boards can be constructed from poster board or foam board. Following this each child can write the instructions for his game. Games can be made individually, or their construction may be a family effort.

Games can be made individually, or their construction may be a family effort.

Recently my boys, Robert and Raymond, were engaged in a unit study about oceans. I told them they could write a report about anything they found interesting in their study. They both decided to write about shipwrecks. They further narrowed this down to a report about the *Titanic*, including information concerning the wreck itself and the discovery of the wreck some 70 years later. As they gathered information for their report, they realized their findings would make an excellent board game. Diligently, they worked to devise pertinent questions and create a suspenseful game. While most of the questions were about details surrounding the *Titanic*, some questions focused oceans in general. They developed Event Cards to make the game more interesting. Here are several examples of their Event Cards: "Iceberg Warning. Go back three spaces." "Man overboard. Lose one turn." "Bonus Card: Iceberg Repair Kit." "Find some stowaways and make them shovel coal. Progress quickens. Go ahead five spaces." Using our computer, they created and printed the game cards, and they even printed a clip art picture of a ship on the back of the game cards. They made the game board out of foam board, which included three-dimensional icebergs in the middle of the Atlantic Ocean. It was obvious that many skills came into play as the boys created their game. Not only did they learn a lot, but they had fun in the process!

This system encourages note taking, creativity, and offers a way to review material in a fun and interesting manner. This procedure will encourage learning far better than any workbook. After all, would your children rather complete worksheets or play a game? Obviously a number of skills are developed as the children devise their own games. Be careful not to overuse this learning method, but to use it sparingly so as to keep it a special and exciting activity.

You may want to purchase games for certain topics that you study. This would be a good idea when you are not making games of your own. Playing these commercially produced games will give your children ideas to incorporate when making their own games. Playing a variety of games will encourage them to implement numerous strategies and layouts for the games they construct to accompany future unit study topics. Aristoplay produces a number of excellent, educational games. (See Resources for ordering information.)

There are many other methods for recording information about a topic of study. Perhaps the children will make a list of key words pertaining to the study. These can be used as vocabulary and spelling lists. Allowing the children to select the words may foster a desire for them to learn their meanings and spellings. (We discussed earlier that we can draw vocabulary and spelling words from our copying and dictation passages as well.) The chosen key words can be written on index cards, one word per card, with the definition on the back. Often it may be more suitable for the child to use the key word in a sentence rather than write the word's definition. We like using a thesaurus to find an alternate, more familiar

Diligently, they worked to devise pertinent questions and create a suspenseful game.

It was obvious that many skills came into play as the boys created their game. Not only did they learn a lot, but they had fun in the process!

This system encourages note taking, creativity, and offers a way to review material in a fun and interesting manner.

word to represent the key word. I suggest using **The Clear and Simple Thesaurus Dictionary**, published by Putnam.

Another way to use key words from the topic is to write the letters from A to Z down the left side of a sheet of paper. As the children read, they can select a key word for each letter of the alphabet. For example, when studying the human body, the children may select A for artery, B for blood, C for circulation, and so on. The children can devise their own crossword or search-and-find word puzzles using the key words they select from their readings. There are several computer programs available that will allow you to make various word puzzles.

An alternate idea is to have the children make a list of key words, followed by two or three words that rhyme with each word. Then they can use their lists to compose a poem about their topic of study.

Diagrams offer another avenue for recording our findings. This is similar to composing an outline; however, the structure is less rigid.

Diagrams offer another avenue for recording our findings. This is similar to composing an outline; however, the structure is less rigid. I will use the study of the human body as an example. Let us suppose that each child is researching a different body system. Even if you have one or two children, it is natural to study one body system at a time. Breaking the study into smaller doses helps to eliminate confusion when gathering and recording information.

This type of recording process helps us to visualize our study in a way that is not grasped through note taking in general.

I have chosen to illustrate the circulatory system using a web diagram. (See diagram on page 289.) First the main heading is listed. Each main division will include smaller divisions. This type of recording process helps us to visualize our study in a way that is not grasped through note taking in general. It offers a systematic view of our study. (Please see page 310 in the Appendix for another example of a web diagram in which I have outlined the contents of this book.)

After sufficient practice with implementing this diagramming method, more formal outlining can be incorporated. Outlining not only gives us a diagramed approach to viewing the contents of our study, but it allows for more detailed observations to be included. Once again a good composition/grammar handbook, such as **Write Source 2000**, will be beneficial for formulating effective outlines. Several outline styles are reviewed.

There are many other kinds of diagrams that can be used to help our children organize data. One useful diagram is a compare and contrast diagram.

There are many other kinds of diagrams that can be used to help our children organize data. One useful diagram is a compare and contrast diagram. This type of diagram helps children to see how things are alike and how they are different. For example during a study of oceans, my boys compared and contrasted octopuses and squids. *(See diagram on page 291.)*

Human Body Unit Study

Circulatory System

Blood Vessels
- Arteries
- Veins
- Capillaries

Heart
- Atrium
- Ventricle
- Pump

Blood
- Red & White Blood Cells
- Platelets
- Liquid Plasma

Transportation System
- Carries Food
- Carries Oxygen
- Takes Away Wastes

Filtration System
- Kidneys
- 500 Gallons Of Blood A Day
- Urine

Heating System
- Blood Spreads Heat Thru Body
- Vessels Contract
- Vessels Dilate

Success with Unit Studies

You can also compare and contrast books. We did this when conducting a unit study based on the classic, *Pilgrim's Progress*. We compared and contrasted a child's version of the Pilgrim's Progress story called, *The Progress of Pilgrim Mouse*, with a more mature version entitled, *Dangerous Journey*. The Pilgrim's Progress story was also compared and contrasted with the well-loved story, *Little Women*. (For more information on this unit study see my book, *For the Love of Reading*.)

For more ideas on using a variety of diagrams, I suggest the book published by Critical Thinking Press entitled, *Organizing Thinking Skills: Graphic Organizers*. In the Appendix I have included some basic organizing diagrams you can copy and use with your children. I have included examples of how we have used them in our studies as well. (See pages 300-318.)

General note taking, in a more free form style using notebook paper, can be done as well. Often this is a more difficult way to record information as there are no boundaries or guidelines to help us organize our thoughts. This method entails recording interesting or important facts as the child reads along. This offers a summary of the material covered, and is more appropriate for certain studies. Some of your studies will center on experiments or other activities that require recording of observations. Many experiment books include lab sheets for recording data. These can be copied and used to post findings from additional experiments you conduct as well.

And let us not exclude illustrations as a means of recording pertinent information. This is particularly useful to employ when working with young children who cannot read and research on their own. They can listen to a reading, by you or a sibling, and draw an appropriate picture. This helps them to feel included in the study. However, illustrations as a means of recording are not only for young children. Older children will enjoy this approach for a change of pace. Photography offers still another avenue to document your findings. Children can photograph activities, experiments, and projects relating to your study.

Illustrations, charts, graphs, diagrams, and photographs enhance factual information that has been recorded and make a superb beginning for a book. We will discuss this more in the last chapter on Reporting. It is beneficial to incorporate each of these recording techniques during the course of your studies. Because there are a variety of recording techniques to employ, it is best not to overuse any one technique. Surely as you progress, you will devise recording methods of your own that we have not discussed.

Some of your studies will center on experiments or other activities that require the recordings of observations.

And let us not exclude illustrations as a means of recording pertinent information. This is particularly useful to employ when working with young children who cannot read and research on their own.

Octopuses/Squid

Similarities

They both have ink sacs, chromatophores, two eyes, beaks, tentacles, and suckers. Both are considered delicacies and are eaten by humans. They both live in the ocean. They are both cold blooded. They both can move by jet propulsion.

Differences

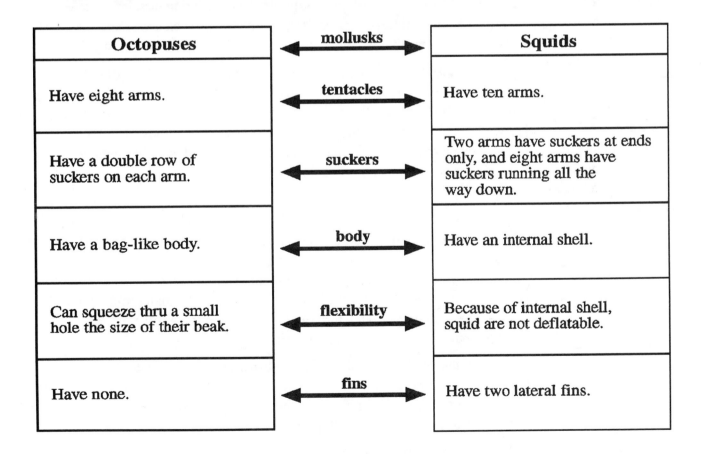

Octopuses		Squids
	mollusks	
Have eight arms.	tentacles	Have ten arms.
Have a double row of suckers on each arm.	suckers	Two arms have suckers at ends only, and eight arms have suckers running all the way down.
Have a bag-like body.	body	Have an internal shell.
Can squeeze thru a small hole the size of their beak.	flexibility	Because of internal shell, squid are not deflatable.
Have none.	fins	Have two lateral fins.

Reporting

I feel that keeping a study confined to five or six weeks is best.

It is best to keep the interest level high and return to the study at a later date, focusing more intently on one or two specific aspects of the study.

Note cards that may have been written during the recording stage can now be organized to compose a report.

I have included a section on reporting as I feel it is important to take the material that has been gathered and present it in an organized manner. This provides us with a finished product and helps bring closure to the study. As you will find when conducting a unit study, you could continue for many months depending on how much digging you want to do.

I feel that keeping a study confined to five or six weeks is best. This gives you ample time to do some research, read several pertinent books, conduct a few experiments or make some interesting projects, and present information in a formal or semiformal manner without dragging out the study. (When working with very young children, the study can span an even shorter period of time.)

It is best to keep the interest level high and return to the study at a later date, focusing more intently on one or two specific aspects of the study. For example when studying the human body, at first you may do an overview of all the systems. Then at a later date, you may focus on one or two single systems, researching them in further depth. If you are doing a basic study of oceans, you can return to the study in the future and concentrate on one element that you touched on in the initial study, such as whales. As you can see, the possibility for developing new unit studies out of previous studies is endless. Our Lord created such a vast and complex universe that we will never run short of material to investigate.

Returning our thoughts to reporting, let us take a look at several ways to utilize the information we have gathered and put it into a more finished form. Note cards that may have been written during the recording stage can now be organized to compose a report. The process of categorizing the note cards enables the children to put their findings in proper order. This encourages them to put like thoughts together in a paragraph.

For instance, if the note card material centered on the study of the human body, then those cards focusing on the circulatory system would be grouped together. Within this grouping, the cards relating to the heart would be placed in another group. Cards referring to the blood and its components would then be put in another group. Each small group would constitute a paragraph. This formula does not need to be followed too rigidly, but it should aid the children in composing a report.

It may be helpful for you to label small paper bags with the category divisions such as discussed above. The children can then easily sort their note cards. Even if you do not choose to make a formal report, this categorizing technique will prove a valuable and fun exercise.

An oral report can be presented utilizing the note cards as cue cards. Oral presentations should be encouraged for children of all ages.

An oral report or narration of material covered allows the child to make the material gleaned his own. If he can recount the events or facts presented, you know he is retaining the information. For additional tips regarding oral narration, see my book, *For the Love of Reading.*

Remember the key word lists we discussed earlier? Some words were used for spelling and vocabulary lists, devising poems, and making crossword or search-and-find puzzles. Now these elements can be combined to make a booklet. The booklet could be titled something like, *Key Words Relating to the Study of Space.* Dinah Zike's **Big Book of Books and Activities** offers many suggestions for making creative books to house data gathered during a unit study. The books and activities presented in Dinah's guide range from flap books to layered books, and from mobiles to pyramid dioramas. You will find Dinah's book a valuable tool as the necessary materials are easy to obtain, the directions are simple to follow, the projects can be made in a short period of time, and the children enjoy making the projects. Most importantly these books and activities offer the children a means by which to organize their findings.

A formal report is not always necessary or desirable. Mobiles, posters, dioramas, and other displays enable the children to organize and present the data they have recorded. Other suggestions for reporting include sewing costumes (perhaps historical costumes), putting on plays, creating puppets and performing puppet shows, making videos, and composing newsletters. We have done all of these at one time or another as the unit study allowed. In the last chapter, I mentioned that note cards can be transformed into game cards. Game boards and game instructions can now be developed. The games produced provide a creative avenue for reporting about a topic.

Our favorite means of reporting has been to make formal books. After several years of book making and experimenting with the book-making procedure, I wrote **Creating Books with Children**. (See page 331.) This book guides you through the process of making quality handmade books. The books are 8 ½" x 11", typed, illustrated in full-color, hand-sewn, cloth-covered, and hardbound. **Creating Books with Children** is designed as a six-week, book-making unit study that takes you through all the stages of writing, illustrating, text layout, editing, and other disciplines of book making. These books can be made to house stories the children have written or factual information they have gleaned from a unit study.

When studying sign language, my two oldest daughters made books with a sign language theme. I mentioned previously that my daughter, Melissa, conducted a self-directed unit study on dolls. She made two books about dolls during this time. My children have also made books to accompany a fine arts unit study we conducted where they tried

Oral presentation should be encouraged by children of all ages. An oral report or narration of material covered allows the child to make the material gleaned his own.

A formal report is not always necessary or desirable. Mobiles, posters, dioramas, and other displays enable the children to organize and present the data they have recorded.

Our favorite means of reporting has been to make formal books.

their hand at recreating famous works of art. They composed poems to accompany each picture.

A nature unit study inspired us to make books filled with drawings and factual information about unusual wonders from the natural world. This year my son, Robert, wrote a historical novel that took place in Ancient Rome. We studied Ancient Rome earlier this year and he was truly fascinated with it. He spent numerous hours ensuring his historical data was accurate, even though his main characters were fictional. My son, Raymond, wrote a fictional novel that took place during his favorite time period, the Middle Ages.

It is not important to make a formal book for every unit, and it would be tedious to do so. However, it is significant to develop some type of report, whether oral, written, or presented in some other form to help our children see the fruit of their efforts and be able to share this information with others. Allow your children to use their imaginations to present the material they have learned from your topic of study. You will be pleasantly surprised at how creative they can be when they move away from workbook and textbook oriented studies.

If we want our children to blossom, we must put away our preconceived ideas about education. Authorities are trying to force our children into a mold to acquire the same "knowledge." Break the mold and allow a masterpiece to emerge! I urge you to pray that the Lord will place people and events in your children's lives to help them become the individuals He wants them to be. May the Lord bless you as you seek His best for your family.

Allow your children to use their imaginations to present the material they have learned from your topic of study. You will be pleasantly surprised at how creative they can be when they move away from workbook and textbook oriented studies.

Break the mold and allow a masterpiece to emerge!

Acknowledgements

Portions taken from *The Christian Home School,* by Gregg Harris, 1988, revised 1995, are used with permission from Noble Publishing Associates.

Portions taken from *Information Please! Workshop,* by Pat Wesolowski, 1995, are used with permission by D.P. and K. Productions.

Portions detailing Internet research, by Pat Wesolowski, 2004, are used with permission by D.P. and K. Productions.

Portions taken from *School Education: Developing a Curriculum*, by Charlotte Mason, are taken from the 1989 reprint by Tyndale House Publishers Inc., Wheaton Illinois. Originally published in 1907 in England. Charlotte Mason's books are now published by The Charlotte Mason Research and Supply Co. (See Resources section for contact information.)

Prairie Doll Apron with Heart Pocket

Cut two apron pieces on fold (see pattern on page 297). With right sides together, sew the two pieces together. Leave an opening at the bottom about two inches long to turn the apron. Turn apron and stitch opening closed.

Cut two apron pockets. With right sides together, sew the two pocket pieces together, leaving an opening to turn the pocket. Turn pocket and stitch opening.

Sew pocket to apron where indicated on pattern. Leave top of pocket open as shown. Use snaps or Velcro closure to secure straps. Straps cross in back.

Prairie Doll Bonnet

Cut two bonnet brim pieces on fold (see pattern on page 298). With right sides together, sew pieces together. Leave side indicated open. Turn brim and baste opening closed.

Cut one bonnet back piece on fold. Hem bottom of bonnet back as shown. Sew a 1 ½ inch piece of elastic where indicated. Pull elastic taut as you sew with a zigzag stitch. Using a long machine stitch, gather bonnet back as shown on pattern.

Pin bonnet brim to bonnet back over gathered edge, matching right sides together. (You may choose either side of the brim to be the right side.) Adjust gathers to fit the bonnet brim. Sew brim to bonnet back. Add ribbons at sides for ties.

Prairie Doll Nighttime Bonnet

Cut one 10 inch circle of fabric (see pattern on page 299). Hem the edge with ¼ inch hem. Then sew a 6 inch piece of elastic around the circle ½ inch from the edge using a zigzag stitch. Pull elastic taut as you sew. Sew ribbons at sides for ties.

Prairie Doll Apron with Heart Pocket

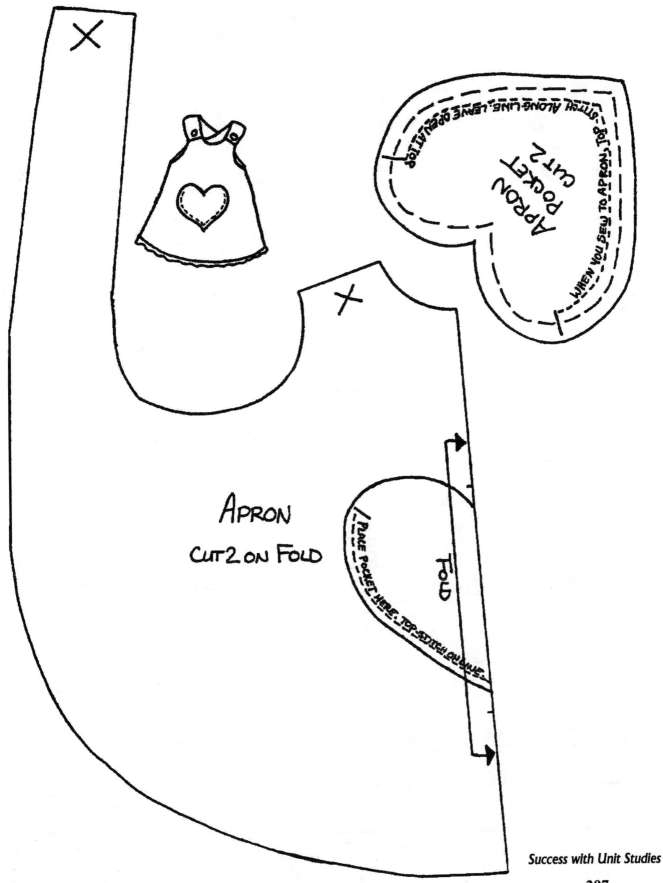

APRON

CUT 2 ON FOLD

FOLD

PLACE POCKET HERE. TOP-STITCH ON LINE.

APRON POCKET CUT 2

WHEN YOU SEW TO APRON, TOP-STITCH ALONG LINE. LEAVE OPEN AT TOP.

Prairie Doll Bonnet

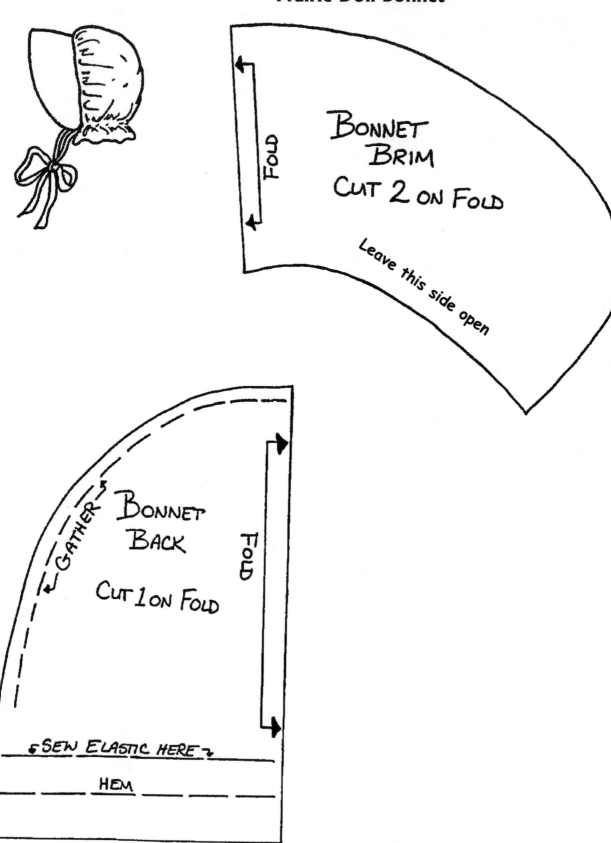

BONNET BRIM
CUT 2 ON FOLD

Fold

Leave this side open

GATHER

BONNET BACK

CUT 1 ON FOLD

Fold

SEW ELASTIC HERE

HEM

Prairie Doll Nighttime Bonnet

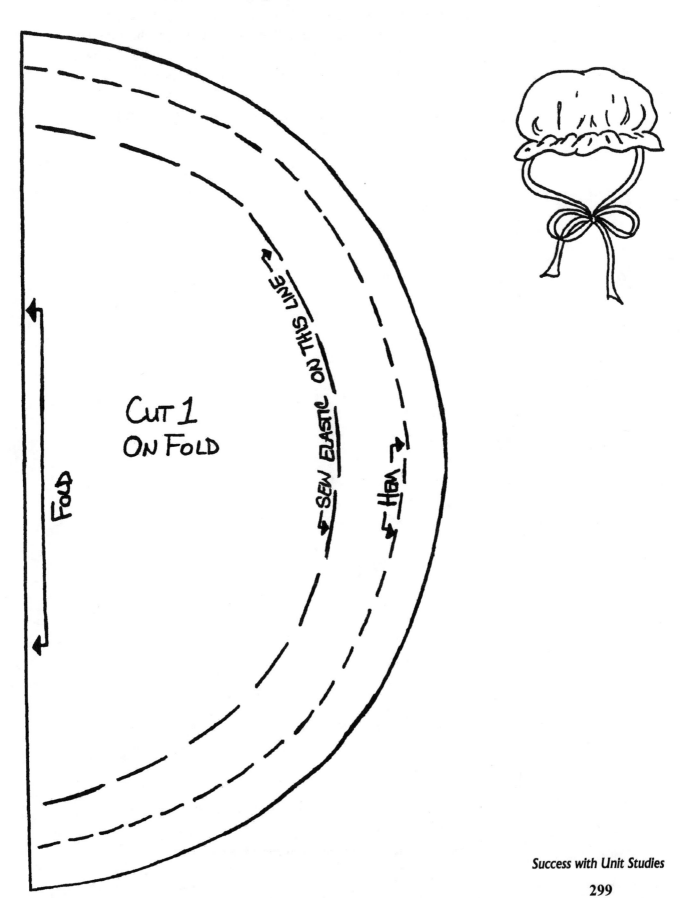

Cut 1
On Fold

Fold

SEW ELASTIC ON THIS LINE

HEM

Diagrams for Organizing Unit Study Material

I have included several blank diagrams on pages 301-309 that you may reproduce for use with your family or classroom. I have also provided examples on pages 310-318 that show how my children have used the diagrams to outline details from various unit studies we have completed. You will find the diagrams are versatile and can be used in many different ways. Hopefully the examples I have included will give you some ideas as to how to use the diagrams with your family.

The following charts and diagrams may be reproduced.

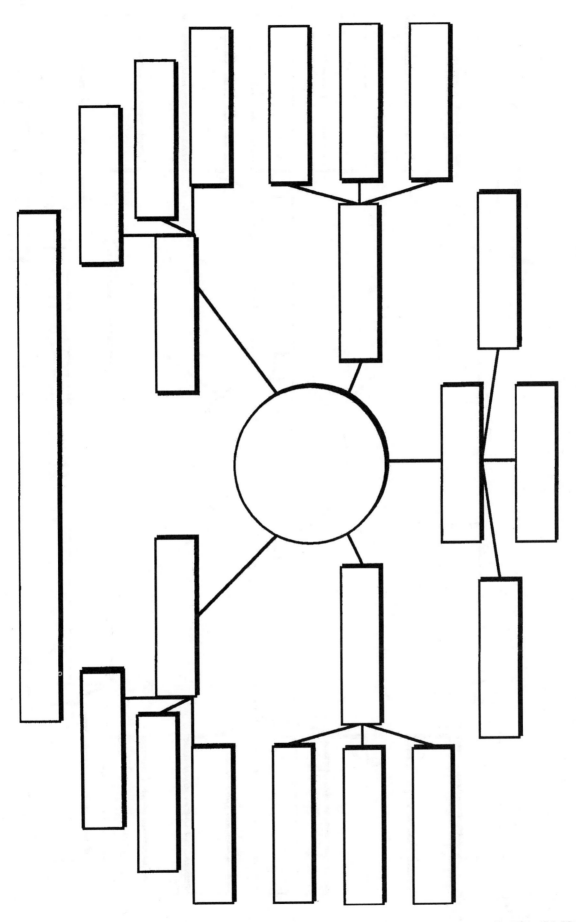

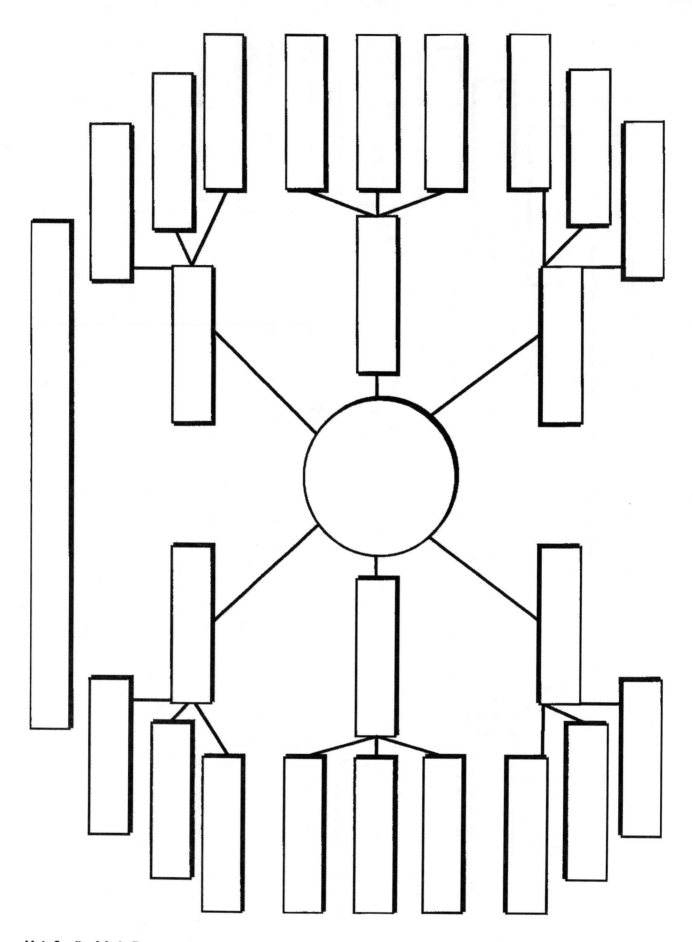

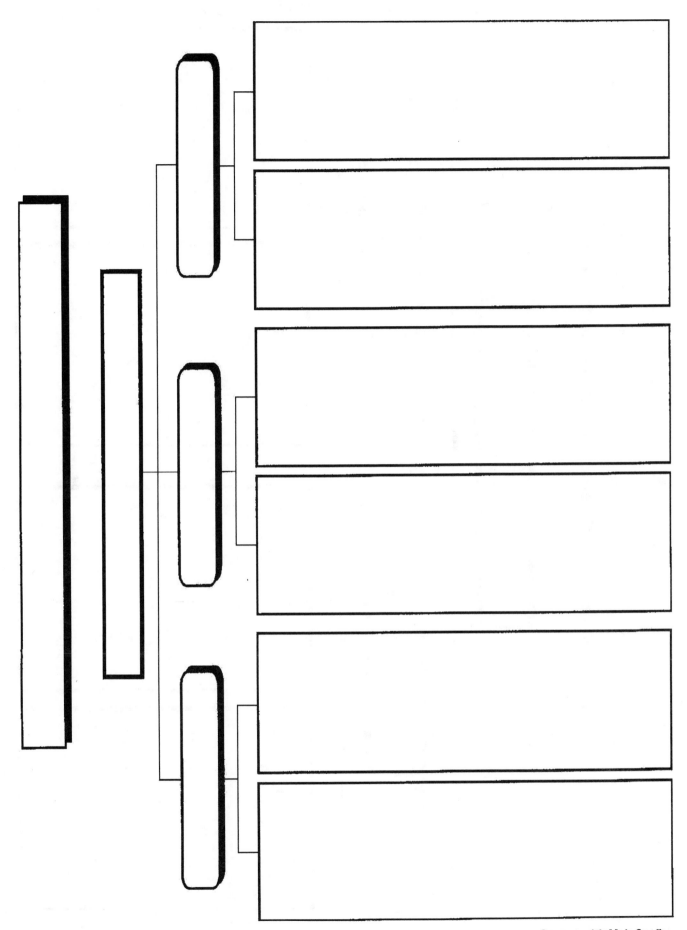

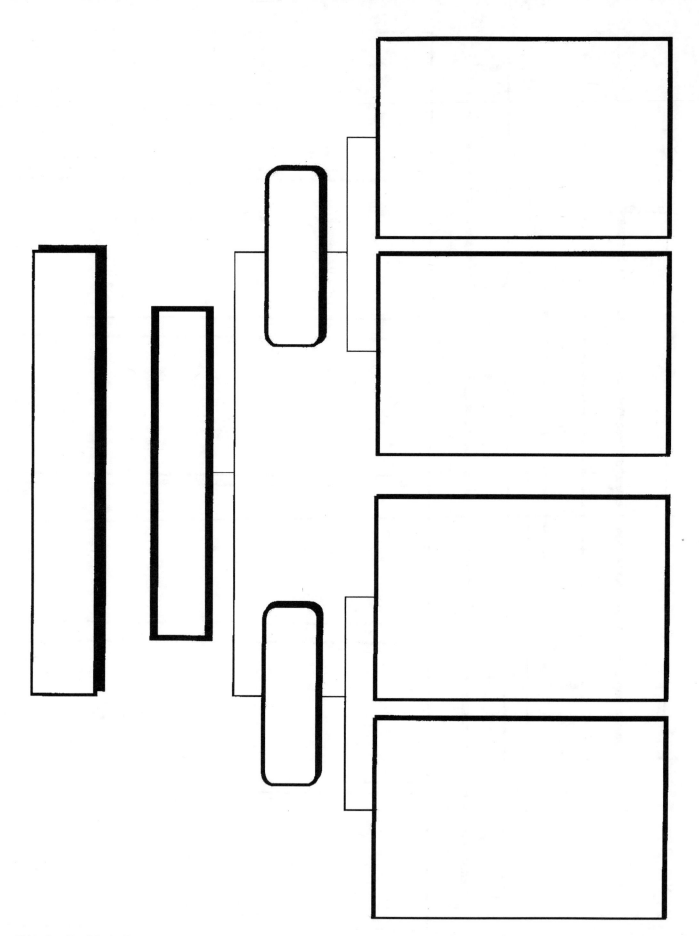

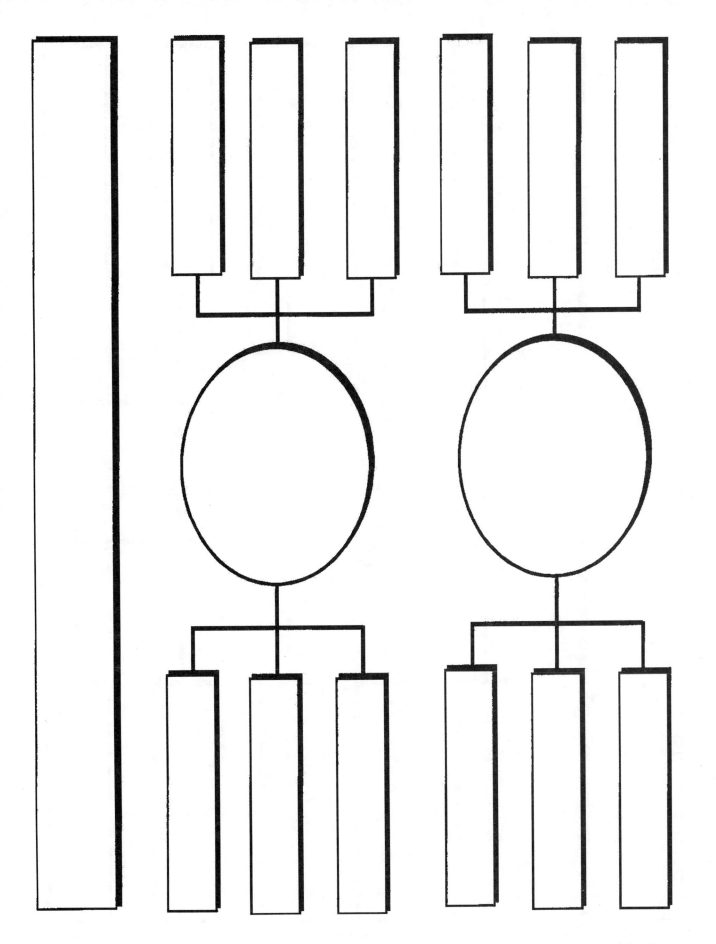

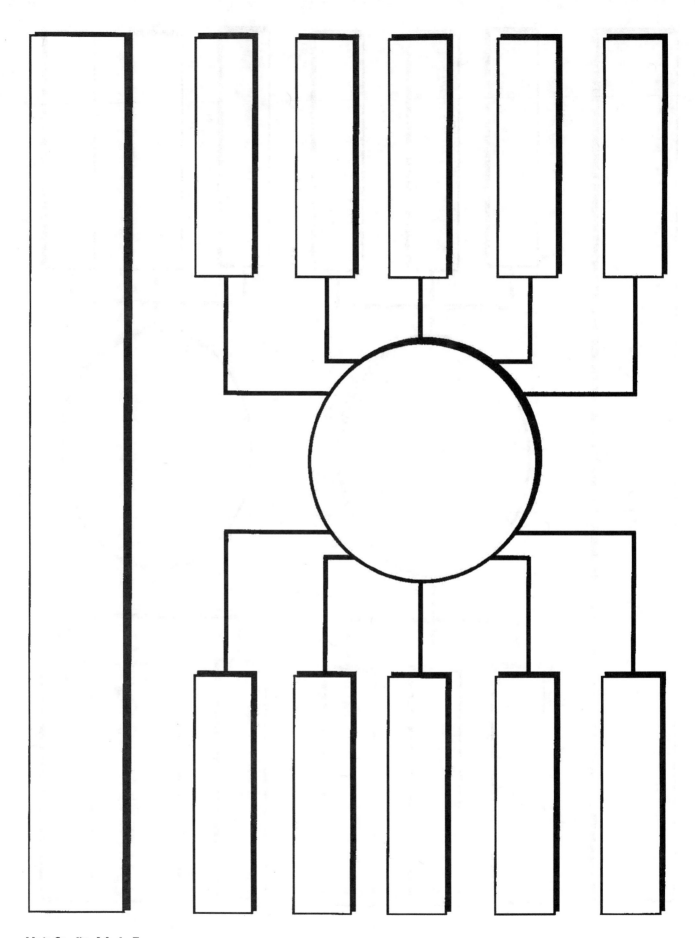

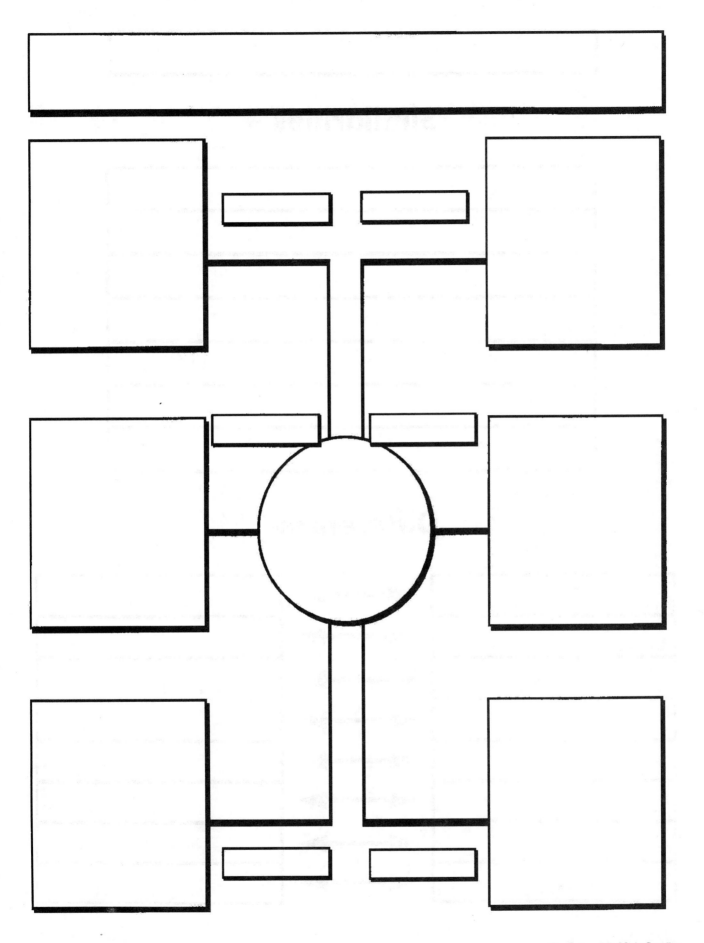

Similarities

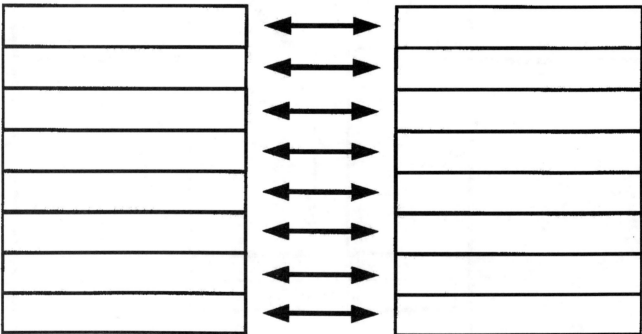

Differences

Similarities

Differences

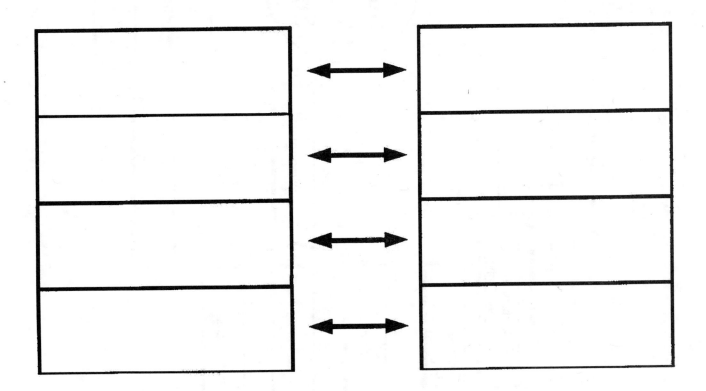

Success With Unit Studies

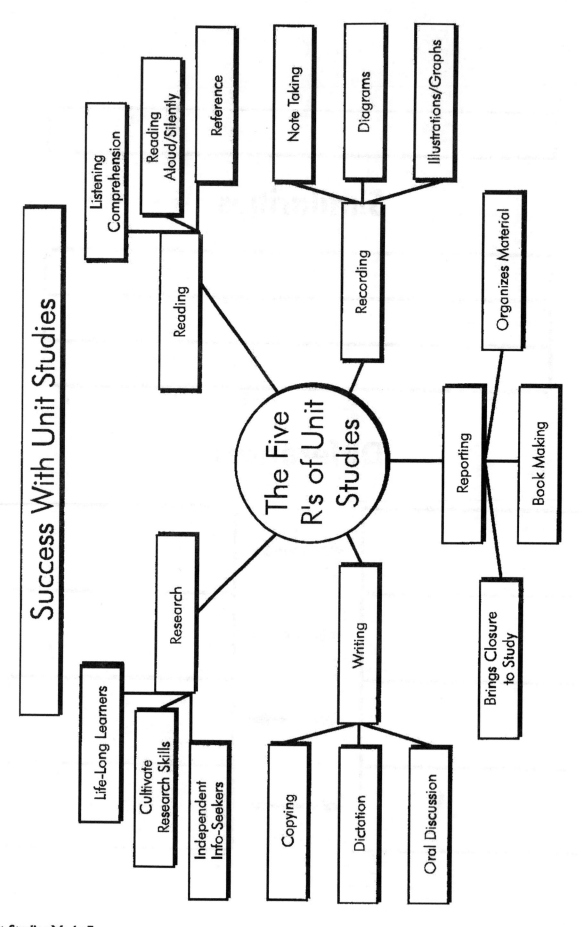

The Five R's of Unit Studies

Reading
- Listening Comprehension
- Reading Aloud/Silently
- Reference

Recording
- Note Taking
- Diagrams
- Illustrations/Graphs

Reporting
- Organizes Material
- Book Making
- Brings Closure to Study

Writing
- Copying
- Dictation
- Oral Discussion

Research
- Life-Long Learners
- Cultivate Research Skills
- Independent Info-Seekers

How the Bible Came to us Unit Study

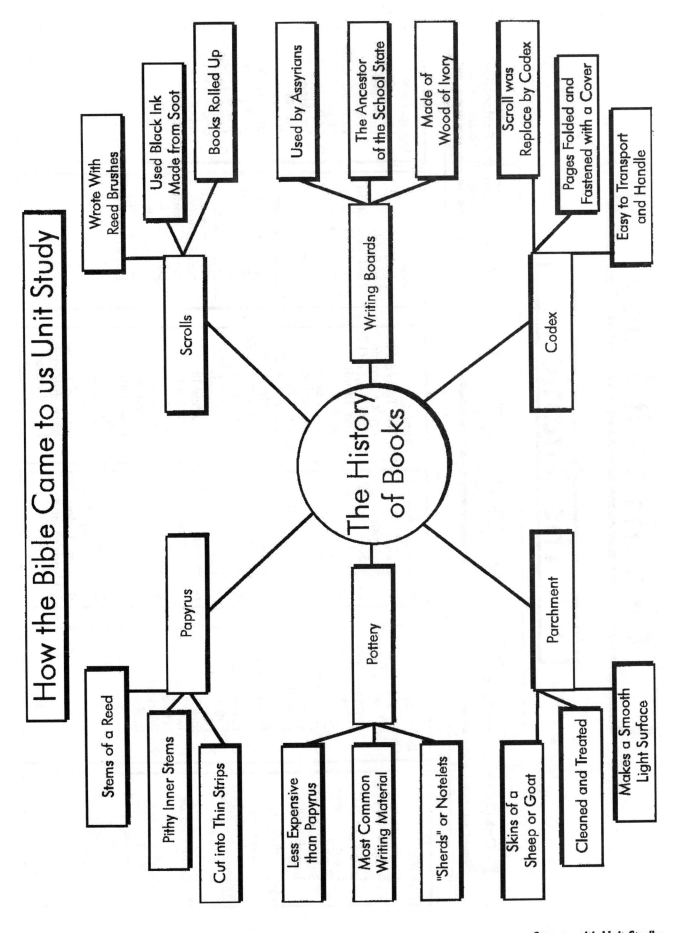

The History of Books

Scrolls
- Wrote With Reed Brushes
- Used Black Ink Made from Soot
- Books Rolled Up

Writing Boards
- Used by Assyrians
- The Ancestor of the School State
- Made of Wood of Ivory

Codex
- Scroll was Replace by Codex
- Pages Folded and Fastened with a Cover
- Easy to Transport and Handle

Papyrus
- Stems of a Reed
- Pithy Inner Stems
- Cut into Thin Strips

Pottery
- Less Expensive than Papyrus
- Most Common Writing Material
- "Sherds" or Notelets

Parchment
- Skins of a Sheep or Goat
- Cleaned and Treated
- Makes a Smooth Light Surface

Oceans Unit Study

The Titanic

Details about the Ship

Luxuries:
1. Gymnasium
2. Swimming Pool
3. Luxuriant 1st Class Quarters
4. Grand Staircase
5. Turkish Bath

Other Details:
1. Thought to be unsinkable
2. Most luxurious ship in the world
3. Sister ship of the Olympic
4. Built at the Harland and Wolf Shipyard
5. Owned by White Star Lines

Technical Details:
1. 16 Water-tight compartments
2. Three Million Rivets
3. Three Anchors
4. Three Propellers
5. Three Football Fields Long - 882 Feet
6. Eleven Stories High
7. Four Smoke Stacks
8. Two Ships Wheels
9. Wireless Radio

Details about the Catastrophe

People on Board:
1. 2,227 Passengers
2. 1,500 People Died
3. Captain- Edward J. Smith
4. President of White Star Lines- Bruce Ismay
5. Wireless Operator- Jack Philips
6. Philips' Assistant- Harold Bride
7. Ship's Designer- Thomas Andrews
8. Lookout- Frederick Fleet
9. Ruth Becker
10. Isadora and Ida Strass

Titanic:
1. The Titanic hit an iceberg on April 14, 1912
2. The Titanic sank to 2 1/2 miles below the surface
3. The Titanic broke in half
4. The stern and bow settle 650 miles apart
5. Life boats held 65 people- too few life boats on board
6. Enough life jackets for each person on board
7. 3rd- class passengers trapped below deck due to locked gates

Details about the Exploration of the Ship 73 Years Later

People:
1. Robert Ballard- led expedition in 1991
2. Ballard's partner- Jean Louis

Ship Condition:
1. Rusticles- Rust formations on ship
2. Ship found 400 miles off Newfound-land, Canada
3. Debris field- littered with artifacts from shipwreck

Equipment:
1. Manned submersible- Alvin
2. Camera sled- Argo
3. SAR- Sonar Tracking Device
4. Angus- camera sled - "Dope on a Rope"
5. Jason Junior- underwater robot

Shakespearean Unit Study

Details about Characters from two Shakespearean Plays

Much ado about Nothing

Beatrice and Benedict were always yelling at each other.
Hero, the prince, set them up so they each thought that the other liked them.
They eventually fell in love and got married.

Hero and Claudio were engaged to be married.
Hero was falsely accused of adultery.
In the end, her innocence was proved and the two were married.

Romeo and Juliet

Juliet was a Capulet.
She loved Romeo.
Her cousin, Tybalt, was killed by Romeo and he killed Mercutio.
Juliet killed herself after she found Romeo dead beside her.

Romeo was a Montague.
He loved Juliet.
His best friend, Mercutio, was killed by Juliet's cousin, Tybalt.
Romeo killed Tybalt.
Romeo killed himself after seeing Juliet in a death-like sleep.

Little House on the Prairie Unit Study

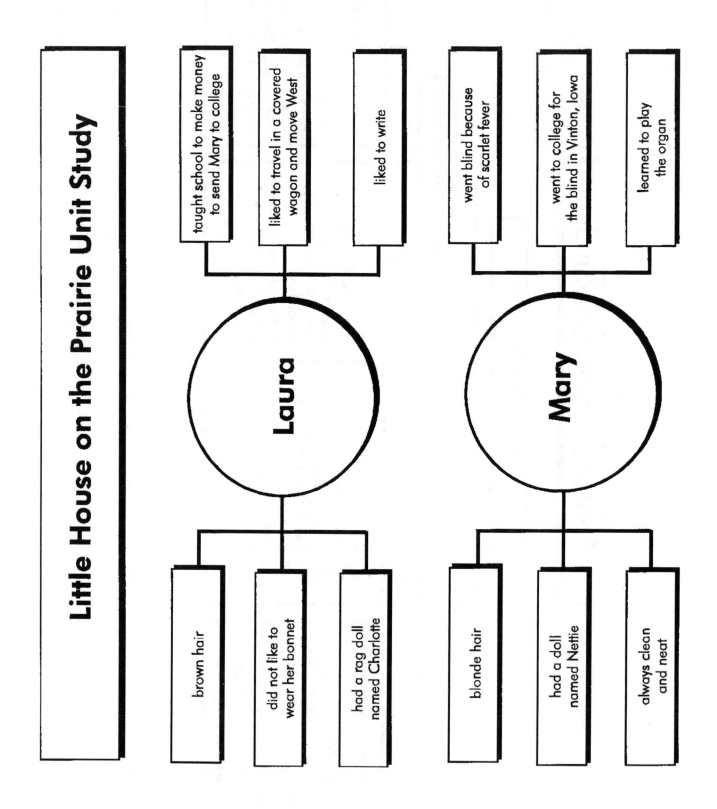

Laura

- taught school to make money to send Mary to college
- liked to travel in a covered wagon and move West
- liked to write
- brown hair
- did not like to wear her bonnet
- had a rag doll named Charlotte

Mary

- went blind because of scarlet fever
- went to college for the blind in Vinton, Iowa
- learned to play the organ
- blonde hair
- had a doll named Nettie
- always clean and neat

Little House on the Prairie Unit Study

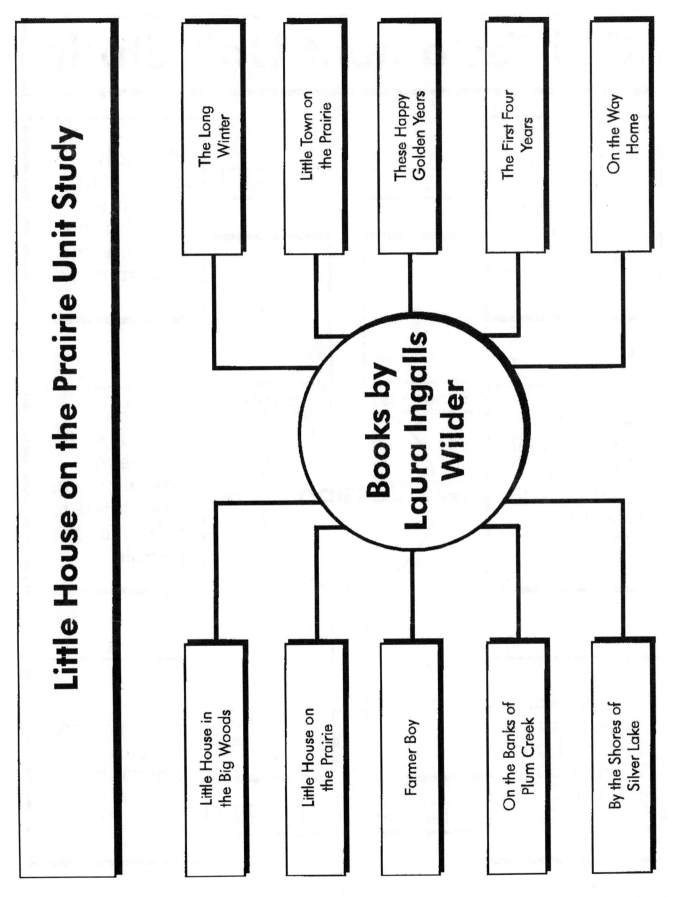

Books by Laura Ingalls Wilder

The Long Winter

Little Town on the Prairie

These Happy Golden Years

The First Four Years

On the Way Home

Little House in the Big Woods

Little House on the Prairie

Farmer Boy

On the Banks of Plum Creek

By the Shores of Silver Lake

Old Testament Unit Study

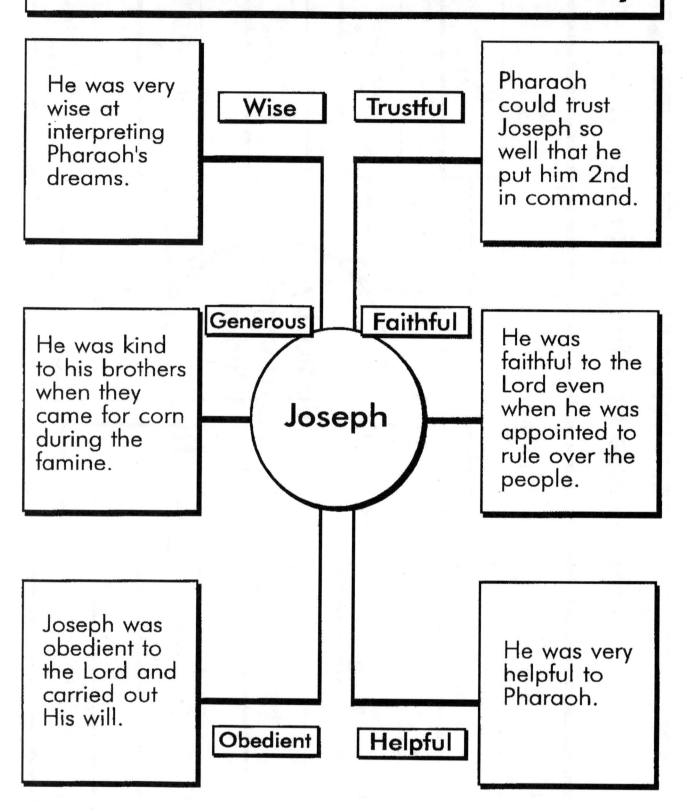

He was very wise at interpreting Pharaoh's dreams.

Wise

Trustful

Pharaoh could trust Joseph so well that he put him 2nd in command.

Generous

He was kind to his brothers when they came for corn during the famine.

Joseph

Faithful

He was faithful to the Lord even when he was appointed to rule over the people.

Joseph was obedient to the Lord and carried out His will.

Obedient

Helpful

He was very helpful to Pharaoh.

Hawaii and California

Similarities

They both have large cities, off islands, big beaches, and hot temperatures.
Both Hawaii and California are part of the United States of America.
Surfing is a popular sport in both states.
Both states have a large tourist industry.

Differences

Hawaii		California
Hawaii has volcanoes.	Natural Catastrophe	California has earthquakes.
Hawaii is an island.	Geography	California is on the mainland.
Hawaii has stone mines.	Mining	Gold discovered in CA.
Hawaii - 47th largest state.	Rank	California - 3rd largest state.
In Hawaii the temperature doesn't vary much.	Weather	Some areas have snow in California.
Hawaii is in the middle of the Pacific Ocean.	Regarding the Pacific	California borders the Pacific Ocean.

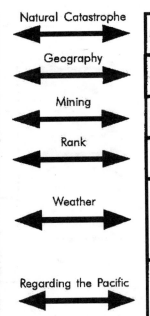

Jacob and Esau

Similarities

They were fraternal twins.
They were both Isaac's sons.
They both wanted the birthright.

Differences

Jacob		Esau
Jacob's skin was smooth.	Appearance	Esau was very hairy.
Jacob was Rebekah's favorite	Parents	Esau was Isaac's favorite.
Jacob preferred to stay at home.	Personality	Esau was a hunter
Jacob won the birthright.	Birthright	Esau swore he would kill Jacob.

AMAZON DRY GOODS

411 Brady Street

Davenport, IA 52801-1518

800-798-7979

Over 1,000 historic, ethnic, and hard-to-find clothing patterns.

AMPERSAND PRESS

750 Lake St.

Port Townsend, WA 98368

800-624-4263

www.ampersandpress.com

Games: *AC-DC: Electric Circuits Game*, *Good Heavens: Astronomy Game*, *Krill: Ocean Food Chain Game*, *The Garden Game*, and more.

ARISTOPLAY

Aristoplay, Ltd

8122 Main Street

Dexter, Michigan 48130

800-634-7738

www.aristoplay.com

Games: *Where in the World?*, *Somebody*, *Hail to the Chief*, *Made for Trade*, and other titles.

AUDIO MEMORY PUBLISHING

501 Cliff Drive

Newport Beach, CA 92663

800-365-SING

www.audiomemory.com

Audio cassettes: *Geography Songs*, *More Geography Songs*, and many others.

BACKYARD SCIENTIST

Jane Hoffman

P.O. Box 16966

Irvine, CA 92623

www.backyardscientist.com

Backyard Science Series I, II, and III.

BENDT FAMILY MINISTRIES

333 Rio Vista Court

Tampa, FL 33604

www.ValerieBendt.com

Reading Made Easy: A Guide to Teach Your Child to Read, The Frances Study Guide, Creating Books with Children, Successful Puppet Making, Making the Most of the Preschool Years, Unit Studies Made Easy.

CHARLOTTE MASON RESEARCH & SUPPLY COMPANY

P.O. Box 758

Union, Maine 04862

www.charlottemason.com

Home Education: Training and Educating Children Under Nine, by Charlotte Mason Vol.1 of the Original Home Schooling Series (6 vols.), *Simply Grammar*, and other titles by Karen Andreola.

COMMON SENSE PRESS

P.O. Box 1365

8786 Highway 21

Melrose, FL 32666

www.cspress.com

Learning Language Arts through Literature series.

Great Science Adventure series: *The World of Insects and Arachnids, The World of Plants, The World of Tools and Technology, The World of Space.*

How to Teach Any Child to Spell, Tricks of the Trade: A Student's Individualized Spelling Notebook.

CORNERSTONE CURRICULUM PROJECT

2006 Flat Creek

Richardson, TX 75080

972-235-5149

www.cornerstonecurriculum.com

Music and Moments with the Masters, Adventures in Art, Making Math Meaningful, Science the Search, and more.

CRITICAL THINKING COMPANY

P.O. Box 448

Pacific Grove, CA 93950-0448

www.CriticalThinking.com

Organizing Thinking Skills: Graphic Organizers.

CROSSWAY BOOKS

Good News Publishers

1300 Crescent Street

Wheaton, IL 60187

630-682-4300

www.gnpcb.org

Books Children Love: A Guide to the Best Children's Literature, by Elizabeth Wilson. *Teaching Children: A Curriculum Guide to What Children Need to Know at Each Level through Sixth Grade*, by Diane Lopez. *For the Children's Sake*, by Susan Schaeffer Macaulay. *The Gift of Music*, by Jane Smith and Betty Carlson.

DESIGN-A-STUDY

408 Victoria Avenue

Wilmington, Delaware, 19804-2124

www.designastudy.com

The Natural Speller and other titles, by Kathryn Stout.

DINAH-MIGHT ACTIVITIES

P.O. Box 690328

San Antonio, TX 78269.

210-698-0123

www.dinah.com

Big Book of Books and Activities and other titles, by Dinah Zike.

DP&K PRODUCTIONS

Pat Wesolowski

1285 Morgan Springs Road

Dayton, TN 37321

423-570-7172

850-385-1958

Email: bisb@juno.com

Information, Please! (5 levels); *The Civil War Unit Study*; *Inventions, Inventors & Entrepreneurs* (unit study); *Co-oping for Cowards -- Guide to Getting Started; Co-oping for Cowards: Volume 1*

"Cross Cultural Cruise with the books of Patricia Polacco"; *BIG Ideas/ Small Budget* (bi-monthly newsletter).

EVAN-MOOR CORPORATION

18 Lower Ragsdale Drive

Monterey, CA 93940-5746

800-777-4362

www.edumart.com

How to Make Books with Children, Grades 1-6 and other titles.

FOUNDATION FOR AMERICAN CHRISTIAN EDUCATION

P.O. Box 9588

Chesapeake, VA 23321-9588

www.face.net

A Family Program for Reading Aloud, by Rosalie June Slater; *American Dictionary of the English Language, Noah Webster 1828*; and other titles.

GOD'S WORLD PUBLICATIONS

P.O. Box 20001
Asheville, NC 28802-8201

800-951-KIDS

www.gwnews.com

God's World Newspapers, kindergarten through adult levels.

GREENLEAF PRESS

3761 Hwy 109 North
Lebanon, TN 37087

615-449-1617

www.greenleafpress.com

Great resources for historically based units: *The Greenleaf Guide to Ancient Egypt, Famous Men of Greece, The Greenleaf Guide to Famous Men of Rome, Famous Men of the Middle Ages, The Greenleaf Guide to Famous Men of the Middle Ages*, and lots more!

GROVE PUBLISHING

16172 Huxley Circle
Westminster, CA 92683

714-841-1220

www.grovepublishing.com

Christian Home Educator's Curriculum Manuals: Elementary and Junior/Senior High School.

HARPERCOLLINS CHILDREN'S BOOKS

10 East 53rd Street

NY, NY 10022

www.harperchildrens.com

My First Little House Books: *Going to Town, Winter Days in the Big Woods, Dance at Grandpa's, Christmas in the Big Woods, The Deer in the Wood, My Little House Songbook, Summertime in the Big Woods, My Little House Cookbook*. Adapted from the Little House books by Laura Ingalls Wilder, pictures in full color by Renee Graef. Several other titles have since been added in this series. A new series entitled Little House Chapter Books has also been published in recent years, as well as board books based on the Little House books.

My Book of Little House Paper Dolls: The Big Woods Collection; Dear Laura: Letters from Children to Laura Ingalls Wilder; Laura Ingalls Wilder: A Biography, by William Anderson; *Pioneer Girl: The Story of Laura Ingalls Wilder*, by William Anderson.

HISTORY ALIVE!

Diana Waring

P.O. Box 378

Spearfish, SD 57783-2331

605-642-7583

www.dianawaring.com

History Alive Through Music – America, and History Alive Through Music – Westward Ho! Also lots of other interesting history stuff.

HOMESCHOOLING TODAY MAGAZINE

PO Box 436

Barker, TX 77413

281-492-6050

www.homeschooltoday.com

A bi-monthly magazine designed specifically for Christian homeschooling families and those who take an active role in their children's education. Practical, easy-to-understand, and ready-to-use ideas are presented for every age group.

INSTITUTE IN BASIC LIFE PRINCIPLES

Box One

Oak Brook, IL 60522-3001

800-398-1290

www.iblp.org

Character Sketches: Volume I, II, and III.

"From the pages of Scripture, illustrated in the world of nature."

INSTITUTE FOR CREATION RESEARCH

10946 Woodside Ave. North

Santee, CA 92071

619-448-0900

www.icr.org

Scientific Creationism, by Henry Morris. ICR publishes many fine texts pertaining to the wonders of creation.

LEARNING RESOURCES

380 N. Fairway Drive

Vernon Hills, IL 60061

847-573-8400

www.learningresources.com

Cuisenaire Rods, *Hundreds Pocket Chart*, *1-100 Combination Kit*, and many other products.

LIFETIME BOOKS AND GIFTS

3900 Chalet Suzanne Drive

Lake Wales, FL 33859-6881

863-676-6311

www.lifetimebooksandgifts.com

Lifetime Books & Gifts is a home-based, family-run business supporting the homeschooler. Their resource guide contains thousands of books, music, games, and toys for all ages. *You Can Teach Your Child Successfully*, *A Strong Start In Language*, *An Easy Start in Arithmetic*, and *A Home Start in Reading*, all by Ruth Beechick, *Saxon Math*, *Honey for a Child's Heart*, *Honey for a Teen's Heart*, and many other wonderful titles!

MEDIA ANGELS

15720 S. Pebble Lane

Fort Myers, FL 33912-2341

www.mediaangels.com

Science study guides from a Creation viewpoint including: *Creation Science*, *Astronomy*, *Anatomy*, and *Geology*.

THE MOORE FOUNDATION

Box 1

Camas, WA 98607

360-835-5500

www.moorefoundation.com

Winston Grammar Kit, *Math-It*, *Home Style Teaching*, *Home Spun Schools*, *Home Grown Kids*, and *The Moore Report*.

MOTT MEDIA

112 East Ellen Street

Fenton, MI 48430

800-421-6645 (orders only)

810-714-4280 (other inquiries)

www.mottmedia.com

The Sower Series consist of biographies of historical figures written from a Christian perspective. Some titles include: *Abraham Lincoln*, *Robert E. Lee*, *George Fredrick Handel*, *Samuel F.B. Morse*, *Isaac Newton*, *The Wright Brothers*, and *Noah Webster*.

NATIONAL GALLERY OF ART

Washington, D.C. 20565

www.nga.gov

NOBLE PUBLISHING ASSOCIATES

1311 NE 134th St. Suite 2A

Vancouver, WA 98685

www.NoblePublishing.com

The Christian Home School, by Gregg Harris, and other titles.

SAXON PUBLISHERS

2600 John Saxon Blvd.

Norman, OK 73071

800-284-7019

www.saxonpublishers.com

Saxon math texts, and other curriculum materials.

TEACHING HOME MAGAZINE

P.O. Box 20219

Portland, OR 97294

503-253-9633

www.teachinghome.com

A Christian magazine for home educators.

THE WRITE SOURCE PUBLISHING HOUSE

P.O. Box 460

Burlington, WI 53105

www.TheWriteSource.com

Writers Express: A Handbook for Young Writers, Thinkers, and Learners; *Write Source 2000: A Guide to Writing, Thinking, and Learning*; *Writers Inc: A Guide to Writing, Thinking, and Learning*.

(I personally like the handbooks published by this company. I do not like the student workbooks or teacher's manuals.)

Games for Reading: Playful Ways to Help Your Child Read, by Peggy Kaye, Published by Pantheon Books (1984), a division of Random House Publishers, New York, NY.

Honey for a Teen's Heart, by Gladys Hunt and Barbara Hampton, Published by Zondervan (1992), Grand Rapids, MI.

Honey for a Child's Heart: The Imaginative Use of Books in Family Life, by Gladys Hunt, Published by Zondervan (1989), Grand Rapids, MI.

Let the Authors Speak: A Guide to Worthy Books Based on Historical Setting, by Carolyn Hatcher, Published by Old Pinnacle Publishing (1992), Joelton, TN.

The Story of My Life, by Helen Keller, Published by Bantam Books (1990), New York, NY.

A Picture Book of Helen Keller, by David A. Adler, Published by Holiday House (1991), New York, NY.

A Deaf Child Listened, by Anne E. Neimark, Published by William Morrow and Company (1983), New York, NY.

Little Women, by Louisa May Alcott, Distributed by Outlet Books, a division of Random House Publishers (1987), Westminster, MD.

Dangerous Journey, by John Bunyan, edited by Oliver Hunkin, Published by Wm. B. Eerdmans Publishing Company (1985), Grand Rapids, MI.

Secrets of a Wildlife Watcher, Drawing from Nature, Crinkleroot's Guide to Knowing the Trees, Crinkleroot's Guide to Walking in Wild Places, Crinkleroot's Book of Animal Tracking, Crinkleroot's Guide to Knowing the Birds, Raccoons and Ripe Corn (Early Reader), *Deer at the Brook* (Early Reader), *Come Out Muskrats* (Early Reader), *Watching Foxes* (Early Reader), all by Jim Arnosky, published by Beech Tree Books, a division of William Morrow & Company, New York, NY.

The Progress of Pilgrim Mouse, by Alan and Linda Parry, Published by Moody Press (2000). Originally Published by Thomas Nelson Publishers under the title of *The Evergreen Wood* (1992).

Knowledge of the Holy, by A.W. Tozer, Published by Harper San Francisco (1978). "A classic Christian testimony and devotion."

The Clear and Simple Thesaurus Dictionary, by Harriet Wittels and Joan

Greisman, Published by Grosset & Dunlap; Revised edition (August 1996), NY, NY. Available at most book stores.

Butterick 3668: 11 ½" Doll and Clothes with Carrying Case, Copyright 1994, Butterick Company, Inc., Butterick Pattern Service, 161 Avenue of the Americas, NY, NY 10013

Simplicity Costumes 9708 Child's and Girl's Puritan, Centennial and 18th and 19th Century Costumes, Copyright 1995, Simplicity Pattern Company, Inc., 2 Park Avenue, NY, NY 10016. This is the pattern I used for *Laura* costume.

McCall's 7843 Children's, Boy's, and Girl's Overalls in Three Lengths, Copyright 1995, The McCall Pattern Company 11 Penn Plaza, NY, NY 10001. This is the pattern I used for the *Almonzo* overalls. Any simple button-down shirt pattern can be used for the plaid shirt.

New by Valerie Bendt

Making the Most of the Preschool Years

Educational psychologists claim that more than half of a child's learning occurs in his first few years. Valerie discusses how you can make the most of these important years. She also offers tips on multi-level teaching, including teaching school-aged children with a toddler in the house, as she draws from her own experience in teaching her six children.

Valerie offers 100 activities for preschoolers to encourage independent play. Complete with illustrations, patterns, and diagrams! $20.00

Visit us on the web at www.ValerieBendt.com

329

The Frances Study Guide

by Valerie Bendt

This unit study guide offers lessons, reproducible activities, and puzzles based on the six Frances books by Russell Hoban. The Frances books are about a young badger and her family. They contain an old-fashioned charm missing in many of today's books for children.

Ages 3-7   **$16.00**

Storybooks sold separately.

Visit us at

www.ValerieBendt.com

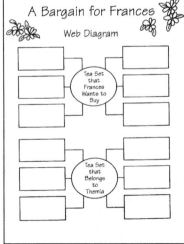

330

Creating Books with Children

In this six week, book-making unit study your children will study authors and illustrators while creating their own books. These books will become lifetime treasures! You will use this book again and again. Many subject areas are covered.

Week 1: Prewriting activities
Week 2: Writing the stories
Week 3: Text layout and editing
Week 4: Illustrating the books
Week 5: Developing the beginning and ending pages and the book jackets.
Week 6: Assembling the books $18.00

Visit us at www.ValerieBendt.com

ILLUSTRATING THE BOOKS

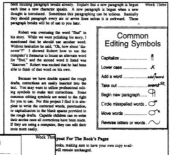

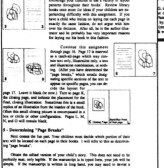

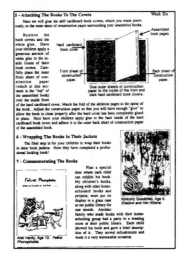

Successful Puppet Making

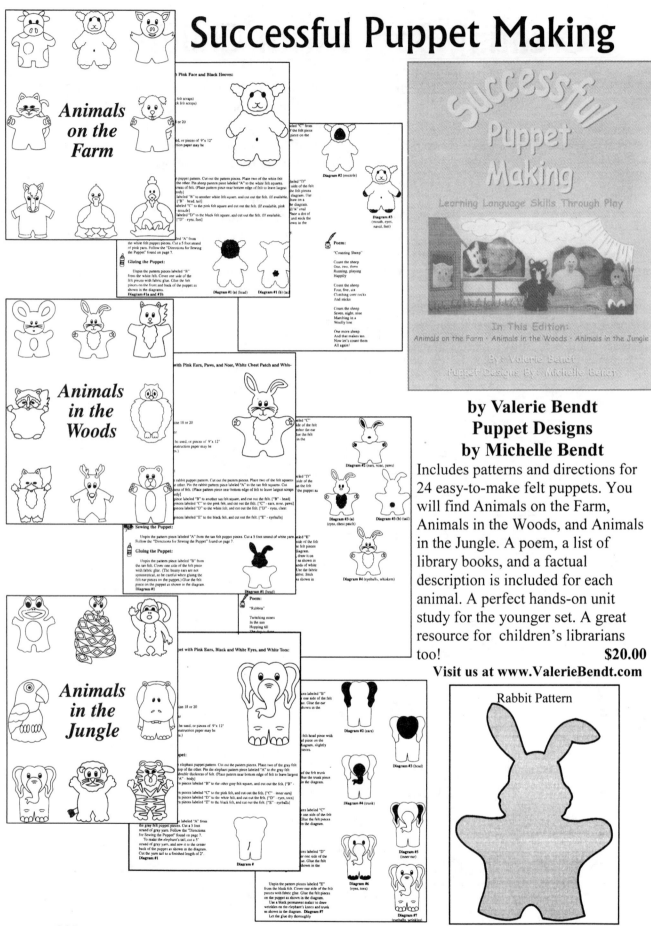

Reading Made Easy
A Guide to Teach Your Child to Read
by Valerie Bendt, author of *How to Create Your Own Unit Study*

- ♦ Phonics based
- ♦ 108 easy lessons
- ♦ 3 lessons per week
- ♦ Less than 30 minutes a day
- ♦ Fully scripted
- ♦ Christian content
- ♦ Original stories and poems

- ♦ Introduction to punctuation and capitalization
- ♦ Hands-on activities
- ♦ Writing and drawing activities
- ♦ Homeschool family tested
- ♦ 512 pages

Lesson 22

Materials: reading manual, index cards, pen, gray crayon, and black crayon.

Instructions: In today's lesson the child will review the following words from previous lessons: *nap, hat, rag, ham, dad, pan, sack, back, sail, pain, game, gave, rake, late, hay, say, day, may, way,* and *pay.* He will also review the following sight words: *is, was, to, has* and *the.*

The child will read the following sentences and complete a variety of exercises based on the sentences: *The rat is sad. The rat has a rake. The rat can rake the hay.*

Dialogue: Read the words below. Remember that the dotted letters are silent. They make no sound.

nap	hat	rag
ham	dad	pan
sack	back	sail
pain	game	gave
rake	late	hay
say	day	may
	way	pay

Read the sight words below.

is   was   to

has   the

Read the sentences below, and then I will show you a picture that goes with the sentences. (Run your finger under each word as the child reads.)

The rat is sad.

The rat has a rake.

The rat can rake the hay.

Now I will show you the picture of the rat.

What is the rat holding? That's right, he is holding a rake. What is the rat doing with the rake? Yes, he is raking the hay. Why do you think that the rat is sad? Yes, he is probably sad, because he has a lot of hay to rake.

♦ Portions of the text to be read aloud by the parent are printed in this special font.

> Read

♦ Sight words are underlined in black.

> The

♦ Short vowels are printed in gray.

> a

♦ A simple picture accompanies the story, followed by comprehension questions.

♦ Actual page size is 8 ½" x 11".

Only $45.00

♦ Long vowels are printed in bold black.

> **a**

♦ Silent letters are printed in a dotted style.

I am going to write the words from the last sentence you read on index cards. (Have the child watch as you write each word with a pen.)

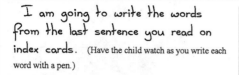

I'm going to underline the sight words with a black crayon. I am going to trace over the *aaa* sounds (as in *cat*) with a gray crayon and the bold *a* sounds (as in *cake*) with a black crayon.

I will make dotted lines over the letter *e* at the end of the word *rake* with a black crayon. I will make dotted lines over the letter *y* at the end of the word *hay* with a black crayon. Why am I dotting these letters? That's right, because these letters are silent. They make no sound.

Read the sentence. Great! Now I am going to mix the cards. I want you to put the cards in proper order to make the sentence again.

(Assist the child with putting the cards in proper order. Remind him if necessary that a sentence begins with an uppercase letter and ends with a period.)

Now read the sentence.

Copy Work: (The copy work is optional for children who have difficulty with writing.)

I will write the last sentence you just read on a piece of paper.

(Neatly write the sentence with a pen, paying close attention to letter spacing, formation, and size. Make the letters large enough for the child to easily copy. Allow space for the child to write his letters directly under yours. An alternate method is to allow the child to trace over your letters.)

Now you can copy what I wrote.

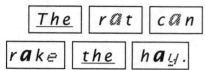

I will trace over the *aaa* sounds with a gray crayon. I will trace over the bold *a* sounds with a black crayon. I will make dotted lines over the letter *e* at the end of the word *rake* and over the letter *y* at the end of the word *hay* with a black crayon. Do you know why I am doing this? That's right, because these letters are silent. They make no sound. I will underline the sight words with a black crayon.

(Trace over the letters that you wrote. If the child wants, he can trace over his letters with the proper colors.)

I would like for you to read the sentence once more. Very good! Would you like to draw a picture to go with your sentence?

Now let's read a book together.

♦ Hands-on activities

♦ Writing Activities

♦ Introduction to capitalization and punctuation

♦ Reinforces that reading is important and enjoyable

"Reading Made Easy is a wonderful book! The lessons are short and easy to retain, which results in a contagious sense of accomplishment. Not only does *Reading Made Easy* inspire and make learning fun; it is also easy and fun for this 'mom' teacher as well. A great book with terrific plans and activities." Kathy Pelham, Tampa, Florida

"Reading Made Easy concludes with Mrs. Bendt's, twelve-chapter short story, *Gideon's Gift.* This heartfelt story emphasizes the joy of reading and writing while stressing the significance of giving God the glory in all situations and finding our God given gifts. Each chapter's suspenseful conclusion urges the child on to the next lesson. This beautifully written account exposes the child to vocabulary not normally used in today's books for children." Cathy Pierce – Children's Librarian

Visit us at www.ValerieBendt.com

Notes

Notes